ONE GOD
ONE MESSAGE

ONE GOD
ONE MESSAGE

DISCOVER THE MYSTERY
TAKE THE JOURNEY

PD Bramsen

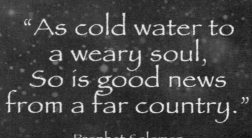

"As cold water to
a weary soul,
So is good news
from a far country."

Prophet Solomon
(Proverbs 25:25)

CONTENTS

PROLOGUE

"**F**or the good works you've done, you deserve to go to paradise, but for the message you preach, you deserve to go to hell!**"** said the village elder to my friend.

My friend and his wife had spent ten years of their lives in this man's village on the edge of the Sahara. They had established an irrigation project and a medical clinic. They had also explained the message of the prophets to any who cared to listen.

According to the village elder, what had my friend done to "deserve to go to paradise"? He had done "good works."

And what had he done to "deserve to go to hell"? He had taught "the message" of the prophets according to the Bible.

Was the village elder right in his assessment of my friend's works and message? Was he half right? Was he entirely wrong?

If you are not sure what to think, then this book is for you.

WHERE

I was born in America, but this book was born in Africa.

The site: Sahel[1] region of Senegal, West Africa.

The setting: The predawn call to prayer is ended. Pink and orange wisps of morning's first light silhouette a sandy, thorn-tree-studded horizon. The temperature is deliciously cool, but that will soon change. I sit on the porch of our village house with my laptop. A piece of clear plastic taped over the keyboard shields it from the Sahara dust suspended in the air. Except for the occasional bray of a donkey and crow of a rooster, the village is silent. The only sound I now hear is the tapping of fingers on the keyboard as thoughts become words and words become text.

WHY

I write because the One who has blessed me with life, joy, peace, and purpose has given me something to write about.

I write from a heart of respect and love for my Muslim friends, especially those in Senegal, where my wife and I have brought up our three children and spent most of our adult lives.

I write because in recent years I have received more than a thousand e-mails from Muslims around the globe. Their thought-provoking comments and questions must not be ignored.

I write out of empathy for those weary of religious leaders who offer little more than circular clichés such as, "The Bible is true because it says so!" or, "The Qur'an is true because no one can write a book like it!"

I write because I am struck by the human heart's inclination to believe anything but the consistent message of the one true God.

WHAT

ONE GOD ONE MESSAGE offers the chance of a lifetime: to take an unhurried journey through the world's all-time best seller and to discover the message of the prophets who wrote it. Those who take part in this pilgrimage will be given the opportunity to overcome countless obstacles (Part I), penetrate mysterious realms (Part II), and break out into a glorious kingdom of magnificent panoramas and satisfying truth (Part III).

WHOM

This journey is designed primarily for monotheists—those who believe in one God. Nonetheless, polytheists and pantheists, humanists and atheists[2] are equally welcome. The adventure is for anyone who estimates his or her eternity worth a dozen hours. That is about how long it takes to read this book aloud.

Whatever your background, whatever you believe or don't believe, *you* are invited to join this epic journey through the Holy Book so many claim to honor, yet so few choose to ponder.

Three thousand years ago, a prophet offered this prayer to the Creator and Owner of the universe: *"Open my eyes, that I may see wondrous things from Your law."* (Psalm 119:18)

Though we may not *like* all we see, let us not fail to *see*.

Your fellow pilgrim,
P. D. Bramsen

PART I
JOURNEY
PREPARATION

FACING THE
OBSTACLES

1

BUY THE TRUTH

"Buy the truth, and do not sell it...."
— Prophet Solomon (Proverbs 23:23[3])

I magine walking into a crowded marketplace packed with billions of people.
Yes, billions.

Stretching farther than the eye can see are ten thousand shops and booths. From every direction, zealous vendors are calling out, shouting, chanting, arguing, pleading, praying—some softly, some through loudspeakers, each claiming to offer exactly what you came to buy:

the truth!

Don't laugh. Oxford University Press has published an encyclopedia identifying *ten thousand* distinct religions worldwide. And that doesn't include the thousands of sects and denominations found within those religions.[4]

So what are we to buy? Who are we to believe?

If there is only one true God, and if He has revealed the truth about Himself and His plan for mankind, how can we possibly recognize it?

Four thousand years ago, the prophet Job raised a similar question:

"Where can wisdom be found? And where is the place of understanding? Man does not know its value... It cannot be purchased for gold, nor can silver be weighed for its price... The price of wisdom is above rubies." (Job 28:12-13,18)

Must we stumble through life confused and uncertain, or can we know the wisdom and truth of the one true God?

We are about to find out.

THE BOOK OF BOOKS

The word *Bible* comes from the Greek word *Biblia*, meaning *"book of books"* or *"library."*

After more than two millennia of communicating orally to and through men like Adam, Noah, and Abraham, God used about 40 men over more than 15 centuries to put His message in writing. These messengers were called prophets or apostles. The term *prophet* literally means "one who speaks out" and *apostle* means "messenger." Today we have what they wrote in one volume—the Bible. Terms such as *the Holy Scriptures, the Writings of the Prophets,* and *the Word of God* are also used in reference to the Bible. The *Torah, Psalms,* and *Gospels* refer to specific sections within the Bible. In Arabic, these Scriptures are called *al-Kitab-al-Muqadas,* meaning "the Holy Book."

Century after century, year after year, the Bible outsells every other book in the world. To date, in part or in whole, the Scriptures of the Bible have been translated into no less than 2,400 languages, with 1,940 languages in progress.[5] No other book comes close.

Yet despite its unparalleled popularity, the Bible is the most despised and feared book in human history. Over the centuries, world governments and leaders, secular and religious alike, have declared the all-time best seller *illegal,* persecuting and even executing citizens caught in possession of it.[6] To this day, some nations enforce this policy. Even in "Christian" countries,[7] Bible reading is banned from public classrooms and institutions.

TORTURED

When I was growing up, my father was a friend of Richard, a man who had spent fourteen years in communist prisons in Eastern Europe where he was regularly deprived of sleep, starved, hung upside down and beaten, locked in a refrigerated cell, burned with red hot pokers, and carved on with knives. With my own eyes I saw some of the deep and ugly scars on his body. Richard's wife was also arrested and sentenced to forced labor in a prison camp for the same "criminal activity" as her husband.[8]

What was their crime against the atheistic state?

They were caught teaching the Bible to others.

OSTRACIZED

My friend Ali was in big trouble. His father had arranged a family meeting of the men.

The senior uncle was present.

The younger brothers were called in.

Finally, Ali the firstborn son was set in the middle.

Ali's father gave a passionate speech, which concluded something like this, "You have shamed our family! You have betrayed our religion! You must leave the house and never come back. I must never see your face again!"

The uncle interjected, "Yes, and if you are not out by tomorrow, I'll throw your belongings into the street!"

Why the anger?

After nearly a year of reading the Bible, Ali had chosen to believe it.

THE LIVING WORD

What makes the Bible such a controversial book?

What causes governments to forbid it and parents to disown their children for believing it?

What drives millions of monotheists to share common ground with atheists in their disdain for these ancient writings?

Could the Bible's claim to be the living, active, penetrating, and judging Word of God have something to do with it?

*"For the word of God is **living** and **active**. Sharper than any double-edged sword, it **penetrates** even to dividing soul and spirit, joints and marrow; it **judges** the thoughts and attitudes of the heart."* (Hebrews 4:12 NIV)

STANDING FAST BY THE BOOK

My wife and I, and our now-grown children, have spent most of the past twenty-five years in Senegal, West Africa. Nearly all of our neighbors follow the religion of Islam. *Islam* means *surrender* or *submission,* and *Muslim* means *one who is submitted.* The book revered by Muslims is the *Qur'an* (also spelled: *Koran*). What I write flows from thousands of personal dialogues with Muslim friends and acquaintances from Senegal and around the world.

Although I have invested considerable time studying both the Bible and the Qur'an, ONE GOD ONE MESSAGE will focus on the Bible. Years ago, a Senegalese friend and I produced a 100-program chronological radio series in the Wolof language of Senegal.[9] Each broadcast features a story and a message from the prophets of the Bible. Some listeners have asked, "Why do you not also teach the Qur'an?" Here is my answer:

In this country, children begin to recite the Qur'an when they are three or four years old. Qur'anic teachers and schools can be found in every neighborhood, but who is able and willing to teach the stories and message contained in the Torah, Psalms, and Gospel? As you know, the Qur'an states that these books of the Bible have been given by God to all mankind as *"guidance and light ... and an admonition."* (Sura 5:46[10]) The Qur'an also declares: *"If thou wert in doubt as to what We have revealed unto thee, then ask those who have been reading the Book* [the Bible] *from before thee."* (Sura 10:94[11]) And to those who believe the Bible, the Qur'an says: *"O People of the Book! ye have no ground to stand upon unless ye stand fast by the Law* [Torah]*, the Gospel, and all the revelation that has come to you from your Lord."* (Sura 5:71) As one of the *People of the Book* who has been *reading the Book* and *standing fast* by it for more than three decades, it is my privilege to make known the stories and message of the prophets you seldom hear. These Scriptures, some written more than 2,000 years prior to the Qur'an, contain truth not found anywhere else.

HIS STORY

Did your parents ever counsel you, "Never trust a stranger!"? They knew that before you can safely trust another person, you need to know something of his or her history.

Think of a few people you trust.

Why do you trust them?

You trust them because, over a period of time, you have learned they are *trustworthy*. They did you good, not evil. When they told you they would do something, they did it. When they promised to give you something, they gave it. You know them to be trustworthy because you know their *history*.

The Bible provides hundreds of historical narratives of God interacting with men, women and children. Each story offers a unique opportunity to meet the Creator of heaven and earth, to hear His words and observe His works in the context of thousands of years of human history. What is He like? Yes, He is great, but in what way is He great? Is He consistent? Does He ever contradict His own laws? Does He keep His promises? Would He deceive us? Can He be trusted?

His story answers all these questions and thousands more.

The Bible is God's history book which reveals not only the big picture of *human history*; it presents **HIS story**.

THE ULTIMATE DRAMA

Everyone loves a good story.

The Bible contains hundreds of stories which together make *one story*—the most captivating story ever told. The Bible's narrative about God and man is the ultimate mystery drama—a story of love and war, good and evil, conflict and triumph. From origins to endings, it provides logical, satisfying answers to life's big questions. It has a climax and conclusion like no other.

A few years ago, after I finished telling God's story to a group of men and women in our home in Senegal, one of the ladies, with tears in her eyes, commented, "What a story! Even if people don't believe God, at least they ought to admit that He is the best screenwriter of all time!" This lady had gotten a glimpse of how each part of Scripture fits together to present the drama of the ages, in which God Himself is both the Author and Hero.

THE GREATEST MESSAGE

The Bible contains more than the most captivating story ever told. Embedded in its narratives is *a message from God*—the most compelling message ever delivered.

Over the years, I have discussed the Bible's message with thousands of Muslims. Many are personal friends, others I know only by e-mail. In both contexts, most discussions can be distilled into a single question:

What is the message of the one true God?

E-MAIL FEEDBACK

This question comes packaged in many ways.

The following e-mail came to me from the Middle East, written by a man we'll call Ahmed.[12]

Send   **Subject:**   Email Feedback

Hi. Jesus came as the Messiah and I believe in that, but he never said he was God. He was the way to God before Muhammad (pbuh[13]) came, but after that, all Christians should have become Muslims coz when Christ comes back at the end of the world, he will rule by the Koran not by your New Testament.

Christ never was crucified. If you wanna be reasonable, even if Jesus was crucified, this never means that people's sins were just deleted coz of that. This is nonsense to me. Besides if you're gonna tell me that God sacrificed his only dear unique son, then I tell you: isn't God great enough to be able to tell people what he wants and delete their sins without having to sacrifice his "dear son" and torturing him???! The whole sinners thing makes no sense to mc.

Islam is the only perfect religion that was ever sent to earth, and that's the reason why I have to think that it's true and that it's the last religion to be sent by God. It's the only religion that has a solution for every aspect of life. You are not left to guess what God's opinion will be in a certain thing.

The Koran is the greatest miracle ever sent to a prophet! Ok, create one verse that is similar, or even close to one of the Koran verses!! You will never be able to even if you were the most fluent person in high level Arabic...

Besides there are predictions in your Bible, the original one, about the coming of Muhammad...

What I believe and know is that the Bible is mostly fake right now and is corrupt since all its books were manipulated...

For your information friend, I read the New Testament, not coz of looking for the truth, but for personal interest, and not once, but twice, and I see that there's nothing in the world that comes near the greatness of Koran which is indeed the words of God, sent by his angel to Muhammad, and if you can prove the opposite, then do it. [*sic*[14]]

Peace,
"Ahmed"

Ahmed's challenge and comments must not be ignored.

Our Creator does not treat such matters lightly, and neither should we. In the ancient Scriptures of the prophets, God has provided clear answers for every issue raised by Ahmed because each issue relates to the eternally-significant question:

What *is the message of the one true God?*

The prophet Job raised a couple of similar questions:

*"**Where** can wisdom be found?"* (Job 28:12)
*"**How** can a man be righteous before God?"* (Job 9:2)

THE JOURNEY

In a confused world with thousands of conflicting responses, it is not my purpose to add my ideas or answers to the mix. Instead, I invite you to join me with mind and heart on a journey through the Book of Books to discover its embedded answers to life's ultimate questions. As we travel together, we will observe what is true according to the Scriptures and we will reflect on the prophets' responses to the challenges raised by Ahmed and others.

Following a time of orientation (Part I: chapters 1–7), our journey will officially begin where the Bible begins: at the dawn of world history. From there we will travel through time and into eternity (Parts II & III: chapters 8–30).

The journey will conclude with a visit to Paradise itself.

TRAVEL OPTIONS

ONE GOD ONE MESSAGE can be viewed as three books in one. *Part I* confronts the obstacles that prevent most people from ever exploring the Bible. *Part II* unveils the central message of the best story ever told. *Part III* goes behind the scenes for a closer look at God's awesome purposes for people.

Most travelers will find the first part extremely beneficial in preparing for the journey. Nonetheless, if you already know the Scriptures of the prophets to be trustworthy, or if you are simply anxious to hear God's story and understand His message without delay, feel free to go directly to *Part II*. Once you have completed the entire journey, you can return to *Part I*.

If you prefer to travel at an unhurried pace, you may choose to spread the book's 30 chapters over a month-long period, reflecting on one chapter per day.

If you are a Muslim, you may want to take this pilgrimage during the 30 days of Ramadan. You should be able to proceed with confidence since the Qur'an says: *"There is no compulsion in religion. The right direction is henceforth distinct from error,"* and: *"Say O Muslims: We believe in Allah and that which is revealed unto us and that which was revealed unto Abraham, and Ishmael, and Isaac, and Jacob, and the tribes, and that which Moses and Jesus received, and that which the prophets received from their Lord. We make no distinction between any of them, and unto Him we have surrendered.* " (Qur'an, Sura 2:256,136 Pickthall[15])

Whichever route you choose, here is one crucial travel tip: Once you begin, *do not skip any part of the journey.*

Each new stage builds on a previous stage. Even if you don't instantly understand all you see, keep reading and reflecting until the final page. Some parts of the journey will be strange and challenging, but there will be oases of refreshment along the way.

No matter how many obstacles you encounter, travel on.

THE TRUTH

Multitudes around the world hold the opinion that no one can know what is true or false concerning life's big questions, such as: Where did the human race originate? Why am I on earth? Where will I end up? What is right and what is wrong?

In the West today it is popular to make statements such as: "Everything is relative," or: "It is wrong to think that a person can know absolute truth!" One does not need a PhD in logic to recognize the self-contradictory nature of such declarations. If there is no absolute truth, how can those who hold such a view make assertions about "everything" or insist that anything is "wrong"?

Thankfully, the Creator of the universe, who has revealed His life-transforming truth to mankind, does not share popular opinion. To all who seek Him with an honest heart, He says:

> *"You shall **know the truth**, and the truth shall make you free."* (John 8:32)

THE RIGHT CHOICE

A couple of years ago, Musa, a 79-year-old neighbor in poor health, asked me to visit him three days a week in order to read to him from the Bible. Musa had studied the Qur'an all his life, but had never taken time to consider the Torah of Moses, the Psalms of David, and the Gospel about Jesus—books which the Qur'an sternly admonishes all Muslims to receive and believe.[16]

Musa listened intently as we explored key stories in chronological order and learned how defiled sinners can be declared righteous by their Creator and Judge. On more than one occasion Musa told me, "After each session, I don't just *think* about the things we have studied, I *meditate* on them!"

One day, after learning another important truth revealed in the Scriptures, Musa, with obvious frustration, exclaimed to his wife and daughter who were sitting nearby, "Why has no one ever taught us these things?"

Later, when Musa's neighbors learned he was "studying the Bible with a foreigner," the gossip began. The pressure became so intense that my elderly friend asked me to stop coming for a time, explaining, "I am not rejecting the truth, but the strain on my family is too much."

After waiting about six weeks (to let the gossip die down), my wife and I paid Musa and his family a visit. He welcomed us warmly and asked some well thought-out questions. Before we left, he commented, "The important thing is that I make the right choice before I die!"

Musa understood just how important it is to *"buy the truth and...not sell it."*[17] Four months later, our dear friend died.

In recalling the times we spent together, I will never forget his response to my question, "Musa, if you were to die tonight, where will you spend eternity?"

After some hesitation, he responded, "I will go to Paradise."

"How do you know?" I asked.

Grasping the Scriptures with both hands, he replied, "Because I believe this!"

THE PROMISE

I dedicate this journey of discovery to those of you who, like Musa, want to make *the right choice before you die.* May the one true God take you by the hand, help you over all the obstacles, and lead you into a clear and accurate understanding of who He is and what He has done for you.

> *"You will seek Me and find Me, when you search for Me with all your heart."* (Jeremiah 29:13)

That is God's sure promise to you.

2

OVERCOMING THE
OBSTACLES

*"Before you know it, **ignorance** will kill you."*
— Wolof proverb

Nearly three millennia ago, God declared, *"My people are destroyed for **lack of knowledge**."* (Hosea 4:6) To this day, most people, including those with college degrees, live and die ignorant of what the Biblical prophets have written.

Considering the Bible's antiquity and influence, can any one be rightly called "well-educated" apart from a basic grasp of what the Bible says?

Just as the world's population has come up with *thousands of religions*, so it has come up with *thousands of reasons* for ignoring the Scriptures. In this chapter and the next we will consider ten of those reasons. And once we begin our journey, we can expect to encounter and overcome many more obstacles.

TEN "REASONS" PEOPLE REJECT THE BIBLE:

1. "MYTHS"

In secularized Western and European nations, many declare the Bible to be little more than a collection of stirring myths and beautiful sayings invented by men. Most hold this opinion without ever having objectively investigated the Scriptures.

In Sir Arthur Conan Doyle's fictional classic, *The Celebrated Cases of Sherlock Holmes,* the detective's colleague, Dr. Watson, questions Holmes about a specific criminal case:

"What do you deduce from it?"

"I have no data yet," Holmes replies. "It is a capital mistake to theorize before one has data. Insensibly one begins to twist facts to suit theories, instead of theories to suit facts."[18]

Many people commit this "capital mistake" with the Scriptures. They draw their conclusions without sufficient data and twist facts to suit theories that won't disturb their worldview and lifestyle.

2. "TOO MANY INTERPRETATIONS"

Some people don't read the Scriptures because they hear one group proclaiming, "The Bible says this!" and another countering, "No, that is not what it means! It says this!" The assumption that the Scriptures cannot be understood is no surprise.

While the Bible allows for different points of view on certain issues of life,[19] when it comes to matters of eternal consequence it leaves no room for diverse interpretations. God's Book and message can be understood if we will observe what it says.

The legendary Sherlock Holmes also told Watson, "You see, but you do not observe. The distinction is clear. For example, you have frequently seen the steps which lead from the hall to this room."

"Frequently."

"How often?" asked Holmes.

"Well, some hundreds of times," replied Watson.

"Then how many are there?"

"How many! I don't know."

"Quite so! You have not observed! And yet you have seen. That is just my point. Now, I know that there are seventeen steps, because I have both seen and observed."[20]

Similarly, many *see* assorted statements in the Bible, but few *observe* what it actually says. Consequently, it is no surprise people come up with a variety of interpretations.

Here is a clarifying question: Do I *want* to understand God's message? Am I prepared to seek for God's truth with the same passion and scrutiny I would use to search for hidden treasure? King Solomon wrote: *"If you cry out for discernment, and lift up your voice for understanding, if you seek her as silver, and search for her as for hidden treasures;* **then you will...find the knowledge of God.**" (Proverbs 2:3-5)

3. "CHRISTIANS"

Many reject the Bible because of evil perpetrated by people who claim to follow it. "What about the Crusades in which 'infidels' were slaughtered under the banner of the cross?" they ask. "What about the Inquisition? What about injustices carried out by people today who claim to believe the Bible?" The truth is that anyone who bears the name *Christian* (meaning *Christ-like*) and fails to reflect the love and compassion of Christ, is a living contradiction to what Jesus Christ exemplified and taught. Jesus told His disciples: *"You have heard that it was said, 'Love your neighbor and hate your enemy.' But I tell you:* **Love your enemies** *and* **pray for those who persecute you.**" (Matthew 5:43-44 NIV)

Others ask, "What about Christians who lead lives characterized by dishonesty, drunkenness, and immorality?" Again, a person living in moral uncleanness is living in direct disobedience to the Scriptures which declare: *"Do you not know that the unrighteous will not inherit the kingdom of God? Do not be deceived. Neither fornicators, nor idolaters, nor adulterers, nor homosexuals, nor sodomites, nor thieves, nor covetous, nor drunkards, nor revilers, nor extortioners will inherit the kingdom of God. And such* **were** *some of you. But you were washed, but you were sanctified, but you were* **justified.**" (1 Corinthians 6:9-11) To be *"justified"* is to be *declared righteous*. Later, in our journey through the Scriptures, we will discover how sinners can be forgiven and declared righteous by God.

Still others ask, "But what about Christians who bow before statues and pray to Mary and the saints?" In brief, any who practice such things are following the traditions of their church rather than the teaching of the Word of God which declares: *"You shall not make idols for yourselves; neither a carved image nor a sacred pillar shall you rear up for yourselves; nor shall you set up an engraved stone in your land, to bow down to it; for I am the LORD your God."* (Leviticus 26:1) Bowing before statues, exalting man's authority above God's authority, praying mechanically without knowing the one true God are all forms of idolatry. Many are confused because they assume that *Christian* and *Catholic* are identical terms. They are not. Neither are *Christian* and *Protestant*. Going in and out of a church building makes a person a Christian no more than going in and out of a barn makes a person a horse.

4. "HYPOCRITES"

Another reason some give for not reading the Bible is "because of all the hypocrites." Sadly, many who claim to believe the Bible say one thing and live another. They twist the message of the Bible and use God's name for their selfish purposes. Many preachers have been exposed as self-indulgent and immoral. Some tell you that if you send them money you will be blessed with health and wealth! The Bible exposes such impostors as *"men of corrupt minds and destitute of the truth, who suppose that godliness is a means of gain. From such withdraw yourself."* (1 Timothy 6:5)

Jesus had this to say to the self-seeking, superficial religious leaders of His day:

> *"**Hypocrites**! Well did Isaiah prophesy about you, saying: 'These people draw near to Me with their **mouth**, and honor Me with their **lips**, but **their heart is far from Me**. And in vain they worship Me, teaching as doctrines the commandments of men.'"* (Matthew 15:7-9) And to His disciples, Jesus said, *"When you pray, you shall not be like the **hypocrites**. For they love to pray standing in the synagogues and on the corners of the streets, that they may be seen by men."* (Matthew 6:5)

In view of the fact that each of us has been guilty of some form of hypocrisy (pretending to be something we are not), should we let another's hypocrisy prevent us from getting to know our Creator and allowing His authentic Word to transform us into the people He intends us to be?

5. "RACISM"

Some reject the Bible because they view it as favoring certain people groups more than others. While most of us must plead guilty to some level of racism or ethnocentrism (favoring our ethnic group above others), the Bible is clear: *"God does not show favoritism."* (Acts 10:34 NIV)

For example, did you know that the prophet Moses married an Ethiopian woman?[21] Have you read the story about how God, through the prophet Elisha, cleansed the commander of the Syrian army of his leprosy after he humbled himself before God?[22] Or that God commanded the Jewish prophet Jonah to proclaim His message of repentance and salvation to the city of Nineveh (in Iraq)? Jonah hated the Ninevites and wanted God to destroy them, but God loved them and showed them mercy.[23] Are you familiar with the important role Persia (Iran) has played in God's unfolding story of providing salvation for the world?[24] Have you considered the amazing account of Jesus sharing the message of eternal life with a sinful Samaritan woman—even though the Jews avoided Samaria and considered the Samaritans "unclean"?[25]

Our world is plagued with racism, but our Creator is not. In His eyes there is only one race—the human race.

*"God, who made the world and everything in it, since He is Lord of heaven and earth, does not dwell in temples made with hands. Nor is He worshiped with men's hands, as though He needed anything, since He gives to all life, breath, and all things. And **He has made from one blood every nation** of men to dwell on all the face of the earth, and has determined their preappointed times and the boundaries of their dwellings, **so that they should seek the Lord**...though **He is not far from each one of us**; for in Him we live and move and have our being."*
(Acts 17:24-28)

This declaration that God has made all people *"from one blood"* is confirmed by modern science, which states: "The human genetic code, or genome, is 99.9 percent identical throughout the world. What's left is the DNA responsible for our individual differences—in eye color or disease risk, for example."[26]

The Creator and Owner *"of heaven and earth,"* who *"is not far from each one of us,"* cares for you and me personally and wants us to *"seek the Lord"* and understand His message. He has arranged every detail of our birth. He loves all people of every nation, language, culture and color, and invites them to call on His Name in their own heart language.

6. "THE BIBLICAL GOD SANCTIONS MURDER"

This e-mail came in from an atheist (or *secular humanist*, as he prefers to be called):

Send | **Subject:** | Email Feedback

The Bible says, "I, the Lord, am a God who is full of compassion and pity, who is not easily angered and who shows great love and faithfulness." Nice words of self-praise, but not one of them can be reconciled with his actions. God didn't seem so loving when he allowed almost a quarter of a million people to die in the December 2004 tsunami in SE Asia... In the so-called entry into Canaan, the Biblical god sanctions the murder of peaceful and innocent men, women, children and babies... Why is it that I, a mere mortal, have more compassion than my so-called "maker"? I could never allow all the conflict, hate, wars, killing, disasters, poverty, hunger, sickness, pain, grief and misery that take place on our planet if it were within my power to prevent them. I would stop it right now with a snap of my fingers!

Many ask, "If God is both good and all-powerful, *why doesn't He put a stop to evil?"* Yet, interestingly, few ask, "If God is good and all-powerful, *why doesn't He put a stop to me* when I commit evil deeds?" We want God to judge evil, but we don't want Him to judge us.

Having noted this inconsistency, we concede that our humanist friend has raised some tough challenges. While there are no simplistic answers, there are satisfying answers. Later in our journey through the Scriptures, as we come face to face with the character of God and the far-reaching consequences of sin, God's answers will become clear. Meanwhile, here are *three principles* to prevent us from judging our Creator when He allows and even orders calamities that snatch away the lives of men, women, children, and babies:

1) *Man sees only a fragment, but God sees the whole picture.*
What people classify as "unjust" tragedies in which "innocent" victims die "before their time," God sees from the perspective of eternity. He declares that a person's fleeting earthly existence is only the prelude to the main event.[27] There is more to life than meets the eye. For example, imagine a fetus in his mother's womb. If he could rationalize, based on his limited worldview, he might tell God: "What did I do to deserve being locked up in this embryonic sac? I hear kids outside laughing and playing, and here I am entombed in this dark, watery world! It isn't fair! Why is it that I, a mere fetus, have more compassion than my Maker?"

Apparently, unborn babies don't challenge their Creator in this way, but adults do. *"But who are you, O man, to talk back to God? Shall what is formed say to him who formed it, 'Why did you make me like this?'"* (Romans 9:20 NIV)

2) *What is wrong for man is not necessarily wrong for God.*
As the Source and Sustainer of life, He also has the right to terminate it. The prophet Job, who lost all his possessions and his ten children in a succession of natural disasters, declared: *"'Naked I came from my mother's womb, and naked I shall depart. The LORD gave and the LORD has taken away; may the name of the LORD be praised.' In all this, Job did not sin by charging God with wrongdoing."* (Job 1:21-22 NIV)

Our upcoming journey will provide behind-the-scenes insights into some of the strange, yet wise designs of God.[28] We will meet the Sovereign Ruler of the universe who does not force humans to love and obey Him. We will also discover why the world is in its present dire condition.

3) *In the end, God will execute perfect justice for all.*
As we struggle to make sense of past and current events, it is helpful to remember that the Creator of man has all the data about every soul; we do not. God operates, not by our moral

standards, but by His. We do not tell Him what is right and wrong; He tells us. Though God permits people to make wrong choices that adversely affect others, He is not indifferent to evil. A Day of Judgment is coming when God will judge every man, woman and child according to *His* standard of righteousness. The extremes of His love and justice are infinite.[29] *"The LORD is a God of justice; blessed are all those who wait for Him."* (Isaiah 30:18)

If you, like our e-mail correspondent, view yourself as having *"more compassion than [your] Maker,"* keep reading. God reveals His secrets to those who are humble and patient enough to hear Him out.

> *"The secret things belong to the LORD our God, but those things which are revealed belong to us and to our children forever...."* (Deuteronomy 29:29)

7. "GOD'S BOOK WOULD NOT CONTAIN..."

Some justify their dismissal of the Scriptures by saying, "If the Bible were inspired by God it wouldn't include revolting stories of people committing adultery, incest, genocide, treachery, idolatry and the like." According to their concept of inspiration and revelation, God's Book should be mostly limited to direct quotes from God.

However, since the Scriptures are intended to introduce people to their Creator within the framework of history, should it come as a surprise that the Bible records not only the words and works of God, but also the sins and shortcomings of humanity? Does God not have the right to reveal His glory, purity, justice, mercy, and faithfulness against the dark backdrop of mankind's failure? Dare we dictate to the Almighty how He should or should not reveal Himself and His message?

> *"You turn things upside down, as if the potter were thought to be like the clay! Shall what is formed say to him who formed it, 'He did not make me'? Can the pot say of the potter, 'He knows nothing'?"* (Isaiah 29:16 NIV)

The Bible records many historical events that God allowed but did not approve. The true and living God is the One who delights to transform a bad situation into something good. Perhaps you have read the gripping story of Joseph, the eleventh son of Jacob (Genesis 37-50). His ten older brothers hated and mistreated him and sold him as a slave to the Ishmaelites. Joseph was unjustly put in prison, but it was through that very adversity that Joseph ascended to the throne of Egypt and saved his brothers, the Egyptians, and the surrounding nations from starvation. Later, after his brothers had a radical change of heart, Joseph told them: *"You intended to harm me, but God intended it for good to accomplish what is now being done, the saving of many lives."* (Genesis 50:20 NIV)

8. "FULL OF CONTRADICTIONS"

Many insist that the Bible is full of contradictions, yet few take time to study it objectively. Is it fair to condemn the Scriptures based on what someone else says about them? Can any book be understood by merely reading a phrase here and there? Should a great book be read only to find a typographical error or an inconsistency in its text? Hopefully not. Yet that is how many people read the Bible.

Years ago, I received an e-mail with a long list of supposed errors and contradictions in the Bible which the correspondent copied from some website.

Here is an excerpt:

Subject: Email Feedback

Your Bible contradicts itself. For example:

* On the first day, God created light, then separated light and darkness (Genesis 1:3-5). The sun, which separates night and day, wasn't created until the fourth day. (Genesis 1:14-19)
* Adam was to die the very day that he ate the forbidden fruit (Genesis 2:17). Adam lived 930 years (Genesis 5:5).
* Jesus does not judge (John 3:17; 8:15; 12:47). Jesus does judge (John 5:22,27-30; 9:39; Acts 10:42; 2 Cor. 5:10).
* Etcetera...

> Now I would like to ask you a question: Does your religion allow me to ask questions and use my brain before accepting it or does it ask me to close my eyes and stop my brain from producing questions? Because I am asking myself if it is possible that God could have done so many errors in His Book and I naturally answer NO!? [sic]

Yes, the same God who says, *"Come now, and let us reason together"* (Isaiah 1:18), wants me "to ask questions and use my brain." God invites each of us to reflect on His Word for ourselves. Copying and pasting someone else's list of "contradictions" will not do. Solomon said, *"The simple believes every word, but the prudent considers well his steps."* (Proverbs 14:15)

The solutions to the correspondent's "contradictions" will be resolved as we think our way through the Scriptures.[30] For now, however, perhaps we can all agree on this: Life is too short and eternity too long to not do our own honest research.

If you have ever eaten a delicious, juicy mango, you know that trying to describe its flavor to someone is not enough. It must be tasted. Likewise, accepting what someone else says to you about God's Word is not good enough. You must taste it for yourself.

*"Oh, **taste and see** that the LORD is good!"* (Psalm 34:8)

It is in a person's own eternal interest to be a careful student of the Scriptures—one *"who does not need to be ashamed and who correctly handles the word of truth."* (2 Timothy 2:15 NIV) Not paying attention to the context (the entire section in which an alleged contradiction is found) is not the correct way to handle the Word of Truth.

To illustrate, there are Biblical statements commanding us *not to judge*, while others command us *to judge*.[31] Are these Scriptures *contradictory*? No, they are **complementary**. On the one hand, God's Book tells me, as a creature limited in knowledge, not to judge (condemn) another person's motives or actions from a self-righteous, fault-finding spirit. On the other hand, I am commanded to judge (discern) right from wrong and to differentiate truth from error based on what the Scriptures say.

So what about the supposed contradictions in the Bible?

I have personally found satisfying solutions for all such "contradictions." I have also discovered that until people *want* to understand the Scriptures, they will find a new "contradiction" as quickly as their old one is cleared up.[32]

Do you *want* to understand God's message? Then don't go to God's Book looking for *your* idea; go searching for *His*. Study the Bible book by book. Don't try too hard to interpret what you read. Let it interpret itself. The Scriptures, written by many prophets over many centuries, are their own best commentary.[33]

"He reveals deep and secret things; He knows what is in the darkness, and light dwells with Him." (Daniel 2:22)

9. "I DO NOT BELIEVE IN A NEW TESTAMENT"

Some time ago, I received this e-mail from a lady:

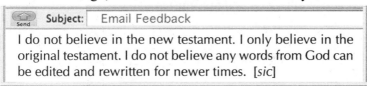

Send   Subject: Email Feedback

I do not believe in the new testament. I only believe in the original testament. I do not believe any words from God can be edited and rewritten for newer times. [*sic*]

Like so many, this correspondent had not yet understood why God's Book contains an Old and a New Testament. These two basic sections of Scripture do not mean that God's Word has been "edited and rewritten," but rather that God's plan for mankind, which was *foretold*, has been and is being *fulfilled*.

Events in history are referenced by the date they occurred. For example, the prophet Abraham's birth is dated as taking place in approximately 2000 **BC**, but the destruction of New York's Twin Towers is dated in **AD** 2001.[34] World history is divided into two parts. So is God's Book.

The Bible has an Old Testament and a New Testament. "Testament" is another word for *legal document, contract* or *covenant—an agreement between two parties*.[35] For now, let's take a cursory look at the Scripture's two parts. As we journey through the Old and New Testaments, the purpose and power of these two sections will become clear.

Part I: The Old Testament. Written in Hebrew and Aramaic, the Old Testament Scriptures contain *"the Law of Moses* [also called the Torah] *and the Prophets and the Psalms."* (Luke 24:44) These Writings, transmitted by God to some thirty prophets over more than a thousand years, provide a record of God's intervention in human history—from the creation of Adam to the time of the Persian Empire (circa 400 BC).

In a prophetic sense, the Old Testament looks down the corridor of time to the end of the world, announcing hundreds of historical events before they happen.[36]

The Old Testament describes the covenant God offered people before the birth of Jesus Christ (BC). *Christ* is the Greek word for the *Hebrew* word *Messiah* which means "The Anointed One" or "The Chosen One." By foretelling key events yet to take place, these Scriptures pointed *forward* to the Messiah who would come to rescue people from sin and its consequences. The old covenant also included this important promise:

*"Behold, the days are coming, says the LORD, when I will make a **new covenant**...."* (Jeremiah 31:31)

Part II: The New Testament. Written in Greek, the New Testament Scriptures are also called *the Gospel* (or *Injil,* Arabic for "Good News"). Written down by no less than eight men during the first century AD, the New Testament records the Messiah's initial coming to earth. It also provides a divine commentary on the Old Testament Scriptures and foretells how world history will conclude. All of its prophecies are in perfect harmony with those found in the Old Testament.

The New Testament describes God's great offer to people as a result of the Messiah's coming (AD). These Scriptures point *backward,* showing the historical fulfillment of hundreds of key events foretold by the prophets.

Like the Old Testament, the New Testament also points forward to the day when the Messiah will return to earth. It was for good reason the Messiah said, *"Do not think that I came to destroy the Law or the Prophets* [the Old Testament]. *I did not come to destroy but to **fulfill**."* (Matthew 5:17)

There is no contradiction between the Old and New Testament. Like a seed that germinates and grows into a mature tree, God's age-old plan for mankind takes root in the Old Testament and grows to maturity in the New Testament. Every section of God's Book points to the message He wants us to understand.

The lady who wrote the e-mail is correct in her belief that no *"words from God can be edited and rewritten for newer times."* What she has failed to recognize is that *"words from God"* can and will be *fulfilled*.

10. "CORRUPT"

Up to this point, we have faced nine obstacles that prevent people from reading and believing the Bible. However, the most common objection I hear from my Muslim friends has not yet been addressed. Ahmed already expressed it in his e-mail:

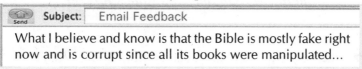

Send | **Subject:** | Email Feedback

What I believe and know is that the Bible is mostly fake right now and is corrupt since all its books were manipulated...

Is Ahmed right? Have the original Scriptures been corrupted? The next section provides the answer.

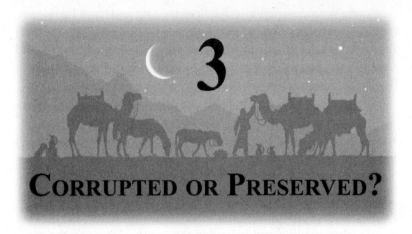

CORRUPTED OR PRESERVED?

"The grass withers, the flower fades,
But the word of our God stands forever."
— Prophet Isaiah (Isaiah 40:8)

T he following e-mail excerpts from four different parts of the world express the thinking of more than a billion people worldwide:

Subject:	Email Feedback

We believe in all divine Scriptures, but in their original form.

Subject:	Email Feedback

Don't forget you got the old testament and the new testament in which words have changed. In the holy Quran the words have been same over the years.

Subject:	Email Feedback

Your Bible is a corrupted text that has been rewritten, added to and re-edited from the very beginning to match your sick beliefs.

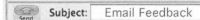

Subject:	Email Feedback

I hold that the Bible was corrupted centuries and even millennia ago, and that most if not all of the New Testament is complete hogwash created by a false Prophet named Paul. Therefore, to quote the Bible to me is a waste of typing and/or cut and pasting.

Are these allegations valid? Has the infinite God allowed finite man to corrupt and manipulate the Scriptures He revealed to His prophets so long ago?

A PERSONAL WORD TO MUSLIMS

Here I would like to speak directly to my respected Muslim reader.

As you probably know, the Qur'an clearly declares that the Biblical Scriptures—the Torah (*Tawret*), Psalms (*Zabur*) and Gospel (*Injil*)—were given by God for *"guidance and light."* (Sura 5:44-51) It also states, *"To you* [Muhammad] *We* [Allah] *sent the Scripture* [Qur'an] *in truth, confirming the Scripture* [Bible] *that came before it, and guarding it in safety."* (Sura 5:48) And, *"The Messengers We sent were but men, to whom We granted inspiration: if you do not realize this, ask of those who possess the Message* [the Bible]." (Sura 21:7) The Qur'an also warns: *"Those who reject the Book and the revelations with which We sent our messengers...in the Fire they shall be burned."* (Sura 40:70-72)

The Qur'an repeatedly[37] declares that the books of the Bible were inspired by God and that those who reject them will be sent to hell. That is what the Qur'an says.

Such Qur'anic declarations create a serious dilemma for Muslims everywhere, because the Bible and the Qur'an present two radically different messages regarding the character of God and His purpose and plan for mankind.

It is for this reason most Muslims have concluded that the Scriptures of the Bible have been corrupted. The following questions have helped many think through that conclusion.

QUESTIONS MOSTLY FOR MUSLIMS

- Do you think God is *able* to protect His own Scriptures?
- If so, do you think He is *willing* to protect them?
- If you believe that the Scriptures of the prophets have been corrupted:
  o *When* were they corrupted?
  o *Where* were they corrupted?
  o *Who* corrupted them? If you think Christians or Jews corrupted the Scriptures, why do you think they would have tampered with the sacred books for which many of them willingly died to preserve?[38]
  o *What* evidence can you present?
  o *Why* might the Almighty have allowed finite men to corrupt His written record and revelation for mankind?
- If God would allow humans to corrupt the books of prophets like Moses and David, *how* do you know that the book you trust hasn't suffered the same indignity?

The purpose here is not to overwhelm anyone with questions, but since this "corruption charge" is believed by so many and is of eternal consequence, here is one more:

- Do you think the Bible Scriptures were tampered with *before* or *after* the Qur'an was delivered?

Before you read on, take a moment to work out your response to this *before-or-after* question. You may even want to write out your answer before continuing.

BEFORE?

If your response is that the Biblical texts were corrupted *before the Qur'an* was written—then why does the Qur'an declare those Scriptures as *"guidance"* for mankind and not deception, as *"light"* and not darkness? Why does the Qur'an say, *"Let the people of the Gospel judge by what Allah has revealed therein"*? (Sura 5:46-47) And why does it declare: *"No change can there be in the words of Allah"*? (Sura 10:64)

If the Scriptures of the Bible were considered unreliable, why did the Qur'an command: *"If you are in doubt as to what We have revealed to you, ask those who read the Book before you"*? (Sura 10:94 Shakir[39]), and *"you bring the Law* [Torah] *and study it, if you be men of truth"*? (Sura 3:93)

While some were accused of *"distort[ing] the Book with their tongues"* (Sura 3:78), the Scriptures themselves were considered uncorrupted and intact.

AFTER?

On the other hand, if your response is that the Biblical texts were corrupted *after the Qur'an* was written—then it needs to be pointed out that Bibles in circulation today are translated from ancient manuscripts which predate the Qur'an by many centuries.

By the time the Qur'an was first recited, the Scriptures had already been distributed in Europe, Asia, and Africa, and had been translated into many languages such as Latin, Syriac, Coptic, Gothic, Ethiopic, and Armenian.[40]

Think about this. How could a group of men have inserted "corruption" into books of such celebrity—books translated into so many languages, copied by the hundreds of thousands, and rapidly distributed throughout the known world? Imagine endeavoring to collect all the original language copies as well as the countless translations—and then attempting to change each to create the uniformity we find in these translations today. It would be an impossible task.

The conclusion is clear:

o To claim that the Bible was corrupted *before* the Qur'an was written is to contradict dozens of Qur'anic verses.[41]

o To claim that the Bible was corrupted *after* the Qur'an was written is to contradict the historical and archaeological evidence supported by thousands of ancient manuscripts.

This conclusion raises a new set of questions.

From where did these thousands of Biblical manuscripts and translations come?

Where are the *original* writings?

ORIGINALS AND THEIR "DESCENDANTS"

Due to the fact that all things on earth, including books, fade and wear out, the Bible's *original* manuscripts (also called *autographs*) are no longer available. However, safeguarded in museums and universities around the world are thousands of early *copies* which "descended" from the originals written by the prophets.

Whether referring to the Torah, the Gospels, Aristotle the philosopher, Flavius Josephus the historian, or the much more recent Qur'an,[42] all the original documents are worn out and gone. So it is with all books of antiquity. Only the "descendants" of the originals remain.

In Senegal, most people believe that the Bible has been falsified. They do not trust it. Paradoxically, they do trust their *griots*. A griot is an *oral historian* whose main task is to memorize the genealogy and oral history of his family, clan and village, and to pass that history on to the next generation. A griot's ability to retain detailed family information and communicate it with a reasonable degree of accuracy is impressive. Yet as good as griots are at what they do, accuracy and details get lost over time. The oral method of preserving truth among men cannot match the precision of the written method.

Why are many people quick to trust the *oral testimony* of men yet slow to believe the *written testimony* of God?

Is that wise?

"If we receive the witness of men, the witness of God is greater... he who does not believe God has made Him a liar, because he has not believed the testimony that God has given." (1 John 5:9-10)

SCROLLS AND SCRIBES

The Scriptures were written long before the time of paper, printing presses and computers. The prophets wrote God's words on scrolls made from animal skins or papyrus.

These original scrolls were then hand-copied by scribes. Scribes were distinguished professional people of the ancient world who could read, write, draw up and duplicate legal documents. Some scribes also duplicated Biblical texts. Their aim was to copy them with perfect accuracy. "At the ends of some books, the scribe gave the total number of words in the book and told which word was the exact middle, so that later scribes could count both ways to be sure they had not omitted a single letter."[43]

Despite their extreme care, minor variants found their way into copies: an omitted word, phrase or paragraph, or a miscopied number.[44] However, not one foundational truth is affected by any of the variations found among ancient manuscripts.

Scholars have never had a problem with trivial copying errors in an ancient text, secular or sacred. The fact that such variants remain in these hand-copied texts strengthens the case that the Scriptures have *not* been tampered with. Unlike the Qur'an, the history of the Bible does not include anyone ever attempting to make "a perfect copy" and then burning the remaining manuscripts.[45]

God has preserved His message for us. But how can we be sure that the Scriptures of today are actually what the prophets and apostles wrote?

THE DEAD SEA SCROLLS

Until recently, the earliest known copies of the Old Testament Scriptures (written by the prophets between 1500 and 400 BC) dated back to about AD 900. Due to the great length of time between the copies and the originals, critics claimed that since these ancient texts had been copied and recopied over the centuries, it was impossible to know with certainty what the prophets had written.[46]

Then the Dead Sea Scrolls were discovered.

The year: 1947.

The place: Khirbet Qumran near the Dead Sea.

The breaking news: A Bedouin shepherd boy, in search of a lost goat, stumbles upon a cave with clay jars containing many ancient scrolls in Hebrew, Aramaic, and Greek.

Between 1947 and 1956, more than 225 Biblical manuscripts were found in eleven caves. Scholars dated these scrolls as having been penned between 250 BC and AD 68. Most of these manuscripts were more than 2,000 years old. What a find!

The scrolls had been hidden in the caves of Qumran around AD 70 (the year Rome leveled Jerusalem) by a group of Jews known as the Essenes. These men resolved that no matter what happened to them personally, these writings must be preserved for future generations. While the Jews themselves were either killed or scattered into the nations, the Scriptures were preserved. For nearly 1,900 years these papyrus parchments remained hidden in clay jars in the ideal dry climate of the Dead Sea region.

When news broke to the world about the discovery of these ancient documents, many thought they would contain significant differences from the more recent manuscripts which were one thousand years younger. Perhaps the claim that "the Bible has been changed" would be confirmed!

The skeptics were disappointed. Only insignificant differences in spelling and grammar were found. These ancient manuscripts contained the same words and message as present-day Bibles.

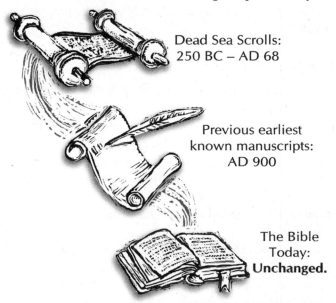

Dead Sea Scrolls:
250 BC – AD 68

Previous earliest
known manuscripts:
AD 900

The Bible
Today:
Unchanged.

What is the official verdict of Dead Sea Scroll scholars regarding the idea that these Scriptures have been tampered with or altered? *"The evidence to date suggests that such alteration did not take place."*[47]

BEST-PRESERVED BOOK IN HISTORY

As for the New Testament, there are no less than 24,000 ancient manuscripts, including 5,300 in original Greek, 230 of those dating before the 6th century. These establish the New Testament as the best-documented text in history.

By comparison, consider the writings of the Greek philosopher Aristotle, who lived between 384 and 322 BC. Aristotle is one of the most influential thinkers of all time. Yet everything we know of his philosophy and logic comes from a small number of manuscripts of which the earliest date to AD 1100—a 1,400 year gap from the time of the original writings. Still no one questions the authenticity or preservation of Aristotle's thoughts and words.

In addition to the thousands of New Testament manuscripts, scholars have found in non-Biblical texts written before AD 325 (date of the oldest complete surviving New Testament manuscript) thousands of quotes from the New Testament. These quotations are so extensive that nearly the entire New Testament could be reconstructed from these writings alone.[48]

The evidence shows the New Testament to be the best-preserved text of antiquity.

DIFFERENT BIBLES?

Perhaps you have heard someone say, "But there are so many different Bibles! Which version is correct?"

It is important to understand the difference between ancient Biblical *manuscripts* and the various *translations* of those scripts. The manuscripts were copied by scribes long ago—centuries before the Qur'an. The Bibles in print today are *translated* from these ancient texts.[49] In whole or in part, the Bible has been translated from its original languages (Hebrew, Aramaic, and Greek) into more than 2,400 *different* languages.

One of those languages is English.

The Bible is available in dozens of excellent English *translations*, called *versions*. Each English version reads somewhat differently, which is what happens whenever words are translated from one language into another. The words chosen by the translators may vary, but when honestly translated, the meaning and message remain the same.

In this book, the *New King James Version* (NKJV) is the primary translation used. It is an accurate word-for-word translation in today's English. The *New International Version* (NIV) is also used in a number of places, since it is sometimes easier to understand.

Here is an example of the same verse in these two versions:

NKJV: *"Moreover, when you fast, do not be like the hypocrites, with a sad countenance. For they disfigure their faces that they may appear to men to be fasting. Assuredly, I say to you, they have their reward."* (Matthew 6:16)

NIV: *"When you fast, do not look somber as the hypocrites do, for they disfigure their faces to show men they are fasting. I tell you the truth, they have received their reward in full."* (Matthew 6:16 NIV)

Though the wording varies slightly, the meaning is the same.

GOD IS GREATER

Ironically, perhaps the best refutation of the allegation that men have falsified God's written Word is announced throughout the day from mosques around the world.

I heard it this morning.

"Alla-hu Akbar! Allaaaaa-hu Akbar!"
(God is greater! God is greater!)

Yes, *God is greater*—greater than man and the eons of time. For the blessing of all nations and for the sake of His own reputation, the true and living God has safeguarded His message for every generation.

God is not only the Creator and Sustainer of His world; He is the Author and Guardian of His Word.

"Forever, O LORD, Your word is settled in heaven."
(Psalm 119:89)

ENDLESS OBSTACLES

At this point it would be nice to think that everyone preparing for the journey has overcome the obstacles that keep them from listening to God's Word. Yet experience shows otherwise. For many, there will always be another barricade on truth's pathway, and another, and another.[50] Recently I received this e-mail:

Subject: Email Feedback

Thanks for your answers. I remember somewhere that God said: 'We will make man in OUR image.' I've always wondered who the 'our' referred to. Aren't there different versions of the Bible? Which is the correct one? Aren't there too many religions? Would the twin towers still exist if there were no religions? Isn't Christianity responsible for many deaths? And why are you sure of what you believe? **Why, why, why, why?** We can go on forever questioning a myth and invent answers as so many preachers do to keep the money coming in. And who created God? I've forgotten. Thank you.

While God's Book does provide satisfying answers to this man's questions, at some point, those who want to discover eternal truth this side of the grave must stop focusing on *man's **whys*** and start reflecting on *God's **words***.

REAL REASONS PEOPLE IGNORE THE BIBLE

The Bible reveals the real reasons people reject God's truth.
Here are three:

1. CORRUPTED HEARTS

Some people never reflect on the Scriptures simply because they *do not want* to know their Creator-Owner.

In assessing the human heart (not the cardiovascular pump, but the inner control center—the soul) the Scripture declares: *"They are corrupt. ... The LORD looks down from heaven upon the children of men, to see if there are any who understand, who seek God. They have all turned aside...."* (Psalm 14:1-3)

Man's rejection of the Bible has nothing to do with corrupted Scriptures; it has everything to do with corrupted hearts.

King Solomon wrote: *"God made man upright, but they have sought out **many schemes**."* (Ecclesiastes 7:29) If left to our natural inclinations, we will choose to go our own way, come up with our own schemes, and live and die in the religion of our parents. We will actually search for reasons *not* to seek to know God. Shortly after we begin our journey through the Scriptures, we'll discover why we are like that. For now, know that it is with good reason God's Book repeatedly warns: *"He who has ears to hear, let him hear!"* (Matthew 13:9)[51]

2. WORRIES AND WEALTH

Some people never study God's Book because their *total focus* is on the here and now. *"The worries of this life and the deceitfulness of wealth choke it."* (Matthew 13:22 NIV)

Jesus of Nazareth told the story of a rich man who had ignored the Scriptures of the prophets during his entire life. Perhaps this man had tried to ease his conscience by claiming the Scriptures were unreliable. Whatever the case, the man eventually died and found himself in hell. To provide the living with clear warning, God allowed this man to communicate briefly with the prophet Abraham in Paradise. The rich man asked for a drop of water to cool his tongue, but received none. Once this man comprehended that he was forever without hope, he begged Abraham to send someone back from the dead to warn his five surviving brothers, *"lest they also come to this place of torment!"*

Abraham's response was clear.

*"Abraham said to him, 'They have [the Scriptures of] Moses and the prophets; **let them hear them**.'*

And he said, 'No, father Abraham; but if one goes to them from the dead, they will repent.'

But he said to him, 'If they do not hear Moses and the prophets, neither will they be persuaded though one rise from the dead.'" (Luke 16:27-31)

God has declared His written Word to be a more convincing confirmation of His truth than miraculous signs and wonders. God has provided *and preserved* the Scriptures of His prophets for us and He expects us to *"hear them."*

3. FEAR OF MAN

Some people never study the Bible because they are *afraid* of how others will react.

A neighbor once told me, "If it wasn't for my family, I would read the Bible!" Meanwhile, the Bible tells me: *"The fear of man brings a snare, but whoever trusts in the LORD shall be safe."* (Proverbs 29:25)

How about you? Do you fear what family and friends might think, say, or do if they catch you reading the writings of the very prophets they claim to honor?

Fear not. *"Whoever trusts in the LORD shall be safe."*

From God's perspective, there is no legitimate reason to ignore His message.

SCIENCE AND THE BIBLE

*"He hangs the earth on **nothing**."*
— Prophet Job (Job 26:7)

S everal years ago, my wife and I toured a cavern deep in the earth. As our guide pointed out impressive rock formations, stalactites and stalagmites, she said something like: "It all began with a drop of water. A shallow inland sea covered this area 330 million years ago, depositing layers of sediment that eventually hardened into limestone...."

It sounded so scientific, as if man had been there as an observer in the beginning. As she talked, God's words to the prophet Job echoed in my mind: *"Where were you when I laid the foundations of the earth? Tell Me, if you have understanding!"* (Job 38:4) At the end of the excursion, I thanked our guide for the tour and then asked her how geologists know the cavern is so many millions of years old. She admitted they do not really know this and added, "I just told you what I have been trained to say."

GENUINE SCIENCE

The word *science* comes from the Latin word *scientia*, meaning *to know*.[52] *To know* means *to regard as true beyond any doubt*. While a scientist may choose to label a hypothesis or theory as "science," that does not make it science.

In the mid-1970s, the French Doctor Maurice Bucaille, King Faisal's personal physician, wrote a book called *The Bible, the Qur'an and Science*. This book—prominently displayed in bookstores and mosques across the Muslim world—asserts that the Bible contradicts modern science. Bucaille suggests that the creation narrative recorded in the Bible's first chapter is "probablement la traduction d'un mythe" (probably translated from a myth), because it does not line up with man's changing theories about the origin of the universe.[53] Like so many, Bucaille mistakenly equates evolutionary *theory*[54] with genuine *science*.

It is important to understand that the Scriptures were not given to teach *physical science*, but to reveal *spiritual science*. God gave us His Book to show us *who He is, what He is like,* and *what He has done for us*. He also gave it to teach us *where we came from, why we are on earth* and *where we will end up*. Such information cannot be discovered or verified in a research laboratory. Nevertheless, since the Bible deals with every aspect of life, it should not come as a surprise that it also includes data about the natural world which was unknown to man at the time the Scriptures were written.

GOD SAID IT FIRST

Let's consider **seven examples** where God's Book recorded scientific data long before modern-day scientists discovered it. Later, as we think our way through the Scriptures, we will encounter other striking examples of science in the Bible.

1. ROUND EARTH Most modern history books teach that the Greeks, in 500 BC, "were the first to theorize that the Earth was round... Greek philosophers also concluded that the Earth could only be a sphere because, in their opinion, that was the 'most perfect' shape."[55] Yet more than a millennium earlier, the prophet Job had already declared that the God who *"hangs the earth on nothing... drew a **circular horizon** on the face of the waters, at the boundary of light and darkness."* (Job 26:7,10) And 400 years before the Greeks, the prophet Solomon stated that God *"drew a **circle** on the face of the deep."* (Proverbs 8:27) And in 700 BC, still 200 years before Greek philosophers came along, Isaiah announced: *"It is He who sits above the **circle** of the earth."* (Isaiah 40:22) The word for *circle* in Hebrew can also be translated *sphere* or *roundness*. So who was first to speak of the earth's round shape—the Greeks or God? Yes, it was God, Earth's Architect.

2. WATER CYCLE   The book of Job also describes the hydrologic cycle: *"**He draws up drops of water, which distill as rain from the mist,** which the clouds drop down and pour abundantly on man. Indeed, can anyone understand the spreading of clouds, the thunder from His canopy?"* (Job 36:27-29) Thus, the Bible describes the rain cycle which first becomes vapor, condensing into tiny liquid water droplets in the clouds, and then combining into drops large enough to overcome the updrafts that suspend them in the air. Job also refers to the incredible amount of water that can be held as condensation in the clouds: *"He binds up the water in His thick clouds, yet the clouds are not broken under it."* (Job 26:8)[56]

3. COMMON ANCESTRY   Thirty-five hundred years ago, the prophet Moses wrote: *"Adam called his wife's name Eve, because **she was the mother of all living."*** (Genesis 3:20). According to the Bible, all humans descend from one common mother. Evolutionary scientists were unconvinced of this fact until 1987. After extensive analysis of mitochondrial DNA (section of human genetic code passed down intact from mother to child) taken from placentas around the world, the research concluded that all humans today come from *"a common ancestral female."*[57] Several years later, studies also concluded that all humans descend from one common male parent.[58] Little did these researchers realize that all their effort and expense would confirm the accuracy of the Bible!

4. *LIFE BLOOD* Moses also stated: *"the life of the flesh is in the blood."* (Leviticus 17:11) This fact was understood only fairly recently by the medical community, which practiced the potentially fatal technique of "blood letting" until the 19th century.[59]

5. *EARTH WINDING DOWN* Three thousand years ago, the prophet David wrote that the earth will one day *"perish"* and *"grow old."* (Psalm 102:25-26) Modern science concurs that the universe is winding down, the earth's magnetic field is decaying, and its protective ozone layer is thinning.

6. *OCEANOGRAPHY* David also wrote about *"the paths of the seas."* (Psalm 8:8) It was this little phrase that inspired Admiral Matthew Fontaine Maury (1806-1873) to dedicate his life to discover and document these ocean currents. He figured if God spoke of *"paths"* in the seas, then he should be able to map them. Maury did just that and became known as "the father of oceanography."[60]

7. *ASTRONOMY* Nearly 2,000 years ago, the apostle Paul wrote: *"There is one glory of the sun, another glory of the moon and another glory of the stars; for **one star differs from another star** in glory."* (1 Corinthians 15:41) To the naked eye, all stars look much alike. Yet today, by means of powerful telescopes and light spectra analysis, astronomers affirm that "stars *differ* greatly in color and brightness. Some stars look yellow, like the sun. Others glow blue or red."[61] "Each individual star is *unique*."[62] How could Paul have known this in the first century AD?

BLIND FAITH?

Though many more cases of "science in the Bible" could be listed, the point to be gleaned from these seven examples is this: Although the Bible is not a science textbook, whenever it does speak on science, it is accurate and true.

Some label belief in the Bible as "blind faith." Is it? Or is it *intelligent faith* rooted in incontrovertible evidence? Since the data consistently lines up with what is written in the Bible, are we being foolish or wise to accept these Writings as true—even when they teach things we cannot fully explain or prove?

God does not ask us to commit intellectual suicide. He has provided us with *"many infallible proofs"* (Acts 1:3) which affirm the trustworthiness of His Book.

HISTORY, GEOGRAPHY, ARCHAEOLOGY

In the last chapter, we examined some of the evidence that shows the Old and New Testaments to be the best preserved books of antiquity. But what about the actual information contained in these Scriptures? Can it be trusted?

The Bible provides scholars and skeptics with thousands of opportunities to check up on its accuracy since almost every page names a historical person, place or event.

What do history, geography and archaeology reveal?

For centuries, many men have sought to discredit the historical accuracy of the Bible. One such skeptic was Sir Walter Ramsay (1851–1939), one of the all-time great archaeologists and the Nobel Prize winner for chemistry in 1904. As a young man, Ramsay was convinced that the Bible could not be trusted. But his discoveries changed his thinking and compelled him to write, "Luke is a historian of the first rank; not merely are his statements of fact trustworthy... this author should be placed along with the very greatest of historians."[63]

Luke was a doctor, a historian, a follower of Jesus, and the writer of both the *Gospel according to Luke* and the *Acts of the Apostles*. These two Biblical books refer to 95 geographical locations (32 countries, 54 cities, and 9 islands), as well as numerous historical personalities and events. Critics have worked hard to find an incongruity between what Luke recorded and what archaeology, geography, and extra-Biblical history reveal. They have been disappointed. Luke's writings have been proven accurate on every count.

To illustrate, let's look at one sentence in Luke's Gospel. It is a phrase designed to establish the historical setting for the earthly ministry of Jesus of Nazareth.

*"Now in the fifteenth year of the reign of **Tiberius Caesar**, **Pontius Pilate** being governor of Judea, Herod being*

*tetrarch of Galilee, his brother Philip tetrarch of Iturea
and the region of Trachonitis, and **Lysanias** tetrarch of
Abilene, while Annas and **Caiaphas** were high priests, the
word of God came to John the son of Zacharias in the
wilderness. "* (Luke 3:1-2)

WAS LUKE RIGHT?

The many names and details naturally make us ask, "Was
Luke accurate?" As a test, let's check up on four of the people
mentioned—the names highlighted in the previous quotation.

First, Luke mentions *the Roman emperor Tiberius Caesar*
and *provincial governor Pontius Pilate.* Were they historical
figures? Did they rule at the same time? In 1961, in the area of
Herod's restored theater in Caesarea (also mentioned by Luke
[Acts 12:19-24]), a one-meter high stone was discovered that bears
an inscription confirming that Pontius Pilate was indeed governor
while Tiberius Caesar was Emperor. The non-Biblical historian
Josephus (AD 37–101) also wrote of these same people, places
and events.[64]

Luke was right.

Luke also mentions *Lysanias* as the tetrarch (joint governor) of
Abilene, a province in Syria. For years scholars used this "factual
error to prove Luke was wrong" because the only Lysanias known
to historians was the ruler of Chalcis, Greece, who was killed
about 60 years before the time period of which Luke writes (circa
AD 27). Historians knew nothing of *Lysanias tetrarch of Abilene,*
Syria, until an inscription, dated between AD 14 and 29, was found
near Damascus. It bears the name: "Lysanias the Tetrarch."[65] So
there were two people named Lysanias.

Luke was right.

Luke also wrote of *Caiaphas,* a co-high priest in the
Jewish temple when Jesus was on earth. In December of 1990,
Caiaphas' family tomb was accidentally discovered by workers
constructing a road just south of Old Jerusalem. Archaeologists
were called to the scene. The tomb contained twelve ossuaries
(limestone bone boxes). The most beautifully decorated of the
ossuaries was inscribed with the name "Joseph son of Caiaphas."

That was the full name of the high priest who arrested Jesus.[66] Inside the box were the remains of a 60-year-old male, almost certainly those of the Caiaphas of the New Testament.[67]

Luke was right.

Renowned archaeologist Nelson Glueck observed: "It may be clearly stated categorically that no archaeological discovery has ever controverted a single Biblical reference. Scores of archaeological findings have been made which confirm in clear outline or exact detail historical statements in the Bible."[68] This cannot be said of other books revered by the world's religions. For example, archaeological finds have shown the Book of Mormon to be inconsistent with history and geography.[69]

Archaeologist Joseph Free, chairman of the department of archaeology at Wheaton College, concludes his book *Archaeology and Bible History* with these words: "I thumbed through the book of Genesis and mentally noted that each of the 50 chapters was either illuminated or confirmed by some archaeological discovery—the same would be true for most of the remaining chapters of the Bible, both the Old and New Testaments."[70]

WHAT SCIENCE CANNOT PROVE

While genuine archaeological data consistently affirms the Bible's reliability as an accurate historical document, archaeology cannot *prove* divine inspiration. And while impressive scientific statements are found in the Bible, science cannot *prove* any book to be the true Word of God. This needs to be said since some people try to convince others that their sacred book is inspired by God since it contains some scientific sounding statements.

Spiritual truth cannot be proven by *scientific* discovery, nor can scientific facts in a book prove it to be from God. Satan, who has been around a long time, knows a lot about science too. Early on in our journey through the Scriptures, we will meet this former heavenly angel—now called *Satan* and *the devil*—who has become God's adversary. For now, just keep in mind that Satan is incredibly intelligent and is capable of inspiring humans to write impressive things.

The prophet Daniel was a wise man whom God used to write one of the most profound books in Scripture, yet when it comes to natural capacities, Satan, the spirit who opposes God's truth, is even *"wiser than Daniel."* (Ezekiel 28:3) The devil is the mastermind behind false religion. He is proficient in the art of deception. The very term *devil* means "accuser" or "slanderer."

An Arab proverb summarizes the danger: *"Beware! Some liars tell the truth."*

WHAT POETRY CANNOT PROVE

Some religions claim that their book is proven to be from God because it is written in a style of writing that no mere human could produce.[71] As Ahmed wrote in his e-mail:

> **Subject:** Email Feedback
>
> The Koran is the greatest miracle ever sent to a prophet! Ok, create one verse that is similar, or even close to one of the Koran verses!! You will never be able to even if you were the most fluent person in high level Arabic. ...there's nothing in the world that comes near the greatness of Koran... and if you can prove the opposite, then do it.

Ahmed's challenge is based on a verse from the second chapter (sura) of the Qur'an which says: *"If ye are in doubt as to what We have revealed from time to time to Our servant, **then produce a Sura like thereunto....**"* (Sura 2:23)

The difficulty with this claim is that it cannot be proved or disproved.

To illustrate, suppose I organize an art contest, enter my own painting, act as the judge, declare myself the winner and then challenge the other contestants, "No one can paint like me. If you doubt that I am the world's greatest artist then produce a painting like mine!"

Would that prove my painting is the best? Would that prove I am the greatest artist? No. Yet neither would anyone be able to prove me wrong! Why not? Beauty is in the eye of the beholder.

So it is with rhythmic, literary beauty. It is subjective.

The Bible is rich in amazing Hebrew poetry and mind-boggling numerical patterns.[72] Yet it is not because of such literary eloquence that God expects us to believe His Word.

Just as science cannot *prove* divine inspiration, neither can beautiful-sounding prose prove a book to be from God.

It is wise to keep in mind that Satan, the great imitator, can also inspire mesmerizing poetry and *"great swelling words."* (Jude 16) The Scriptures warn us not to be deceived *"by smooth words and flattering speech [that] deceive the hearts of the simple"* (Romans 16:18), especially when those words contradict the plan and message the Creator made known from the beginning of time.

Neither science, nor archaeology, nor poetry can prove any book to be the true Word of God. Such proof of divine inspiration must be based on a higher court of judgment—on stronger, indisputable evidence.

It is that evidence we will now consider.

GOD'S SIGNATURE

"Let all the nations...hear and say, 'It is truth.'"
— God (Isaiah 43:9)

Most legal documents require an official signature. The Old and New Testament Scriptures, which claim to be God's authorized record and covenant, are signed, not with a pen, but with an utterly distinctive signature called *fulfilled prophecy.*

"This is what the LORD says... 'I am the first and I am the last, apart from me there is no God. Who then is like me? Let him proclaim it. **Let him declare** *and lay out before me* **what has happened** *since I established my ancient people,* **and what is yet to come—yes, let him foretell what will come.** *...Who foretold this long ago, who declared it from the distant past? Was it not I, the LORD?'"* (Isaiah 44:6-7; 45:21 NIV)

Let us not fail to grasp God's logic.

It is because the Bible is full of detailed prophecies which have been accurately fulfilled that we know we can trust what it declares about the past, present, and future.

POSITIVE PROOF

Only the One who exists outside of time can announce and record history before it happens.

Mortal men and women have, at times, made educated guesses about what might occur in the future, but only God sees the future as though it has already happened. Only God knows what will take place a thousand years from now. Apart from divine revelation, neither humans, nor angels, nor Satan, nor demons can authoritatively foretell a future event.

Some would say, "But what about mediums, witchdoctors and fortune tellers? They predict the future!"

First, it is important to understand that Satan is able to give extra-terrestrial knowledge and power to those who have *"been taken captive by him to do his will."* (2 Timothy 2:26)

Second, Satan—the master imitator and psychologist who has been observing human history for thousands of years—has become quite proficient at forging God's "signature."

Third, while the devil is relatively good at forecasting the way certain events may turn out, he does not *know* the future. His "prophecies" are often proven wrong. Furthermore, they are vague. For example, a fortune teller may tell a young lady, "Within the next several years you will get married and find true love." You and I know the odds are quite good that such a "prophecy" will come true to some extent. When speaking of *fulfilled Biblical prophecies*, we are not talking about those kinds of ambiguous predictions.

Let's consider **three examples of Biblical prophecies**— about a place, a people, and a person.

PROPHECIES ABOUT A PLACE

Around 600 BC, the prophet Ezekiel prophesied against the ancient Phoenician city of Tyre. Located on the coast of Lebanon, Tyre was a world capital for over two thousand years. It was known as *the queen of the seas*. Yet while it was at the peak of its power, God told Ezekiel to proclaim and write down a detailed prophecy about the destruction to come upon Tyre as a result of its wickedness and arrogance before God.

The prophet Ezekiel predicted:

1. *Many nations would come up against Tyre.*
   (Ezekiel 26:3)
2. *Babylon under King Nebuchadnezzar* would be the
   first to attack it. (v. 7)
3. *Tyre's walls and towers would be broken down.* (vv.4,9)
4. The people of Tyre would be *slain by the sword.* (v.11)
5. The *rubble and soil of the city would be cast into the
   sea.* (v. 12)
6. It would be scraped bare *"like the top of a rock."* (v. 4)
7. It would become a fisherman's workplace *"for
   spreading nets."* (vv. 5,14)
8. The great city of Tyre would *"never be rebuilt, for I
   the LORD have spoken."* (v.14)

Secular history records that all eight predictions came true:

1. *Many nations did come up against Tyre.*
2. The first was *Babylon led by King Nebuchadnezzar.*
3. After a 13-year siege (585–572 BC), Nebuchadnezzar
   broke down mainland Tyre's walls and towers,
   fulfilling the first of Ezekiel's prophecies.
4. Nebuchadnezzar *massacred the inhabitants* who were
   unable to escape to Tyre's island fortress, located
   about a kilometer out in the Mediterranean Sea.
5. Secular history documents that in 332 BC, "Alexander
   the Great became the first to conquer the island portion
   of Tyre. He achieved this by destroying the mainland
   portion of the city and using the rubble to build a road
   to the island."[73] Thus, he unwittingly fulfilled another
   portion of the prophecy by *casting the rubble from
   the destroyed city into the sea.* Alexander's conquest
   brought a permanent end to the Phoenician Empire.[74]
6. The city was scraped bare *"like the top of a rock."*
7. It became *"a place for spreading nets."*
8. In succeeding years many efforts were made to
   rebuild Tyre, only to have it destroyed repeatedly.

Today in Lebanon there is a modern city named Tyre, but the ancient Phoenician city against which Ezekiel prophesied never recovered. Below a photo of stone pavement, National Geographic magazine has this caption: "Today the Phoenicians' Tyre lies buried beneath these paving stones and columns of a Roman metropolis. Only a small dig reaches down to the lost world of the Phoenicians."[75]

What would have been the chance of the man Ezekiel, in his own wisdom, looking at the city of Tyre in his day and making these eight predictions?

Since only God sees history before it happens, only God could have given Ezekiel this information.

PROPHECIES ABOUT A PEOPLE

The Bible contains hundreds of precise prophecies about numerous people and nations: Egypt, Ethiopia, Arabia, Persia, Russia, Israel, and many more.

Before we proceed with this next example of fulfilled prophecy, let us remember that our purpose is not to make these prophecies say what we want to hear, nor to push a political or religious agenda. Our job is to learn what the Scriptures declare.

Here is an easy-to-interpret yet hard-for-many-to-accept case of fulfilled prophecy about one particular nation.

Around 1920 BC, God promised Abraham, *"To your descendants I will give this land."* (Genesis 12:7)

Later God repeated the same promise to Isaac and Jacob.[76]

The descendants of Abraham, Isaac and Jacob were first called *Hebrews*, later *Israelites*, and still later *Jews*.

Hundreds of years afterward, God informed Moses what would happen to them if they failed to trust and obey their God:

"I will scatter you among the nations and draw out a sword after you; your land shall be desolate and your cities waste." (Leviticus 26:33)

"You will become a thing of horror and an object of scorn and ridicule to all the nations where the LORD will drive you. ...Among those nations you will find no repose, no resting place for the sole of your foot. There the LORD will give you an anxious mind, eyes weary with longing, and a despairing heart." (Deuteronomy 28:37,65 NIV)

The Old Testament contains scores of similar prophecies.

Around AD 30, affirming the words of the prophets, Jesus of Nazareth foretold the destruction of Jerusalem: *"Now as [Jesus] drew near, He saw [Jerusalem] and wept over it, saying, '...days will come upon you when your enemies will build an embankment around you, surround you and close you in on every side, and level you, and your children within you, to the ground...because you did not know the time of your visitation.'"* (Luke 19:41-44) In speaking of the temple itself, Jesus foretold: *"The days will come in which not one stone shall be left upon another that shall not be thrown down."* (Luke 21:6)

Forty years later, these events took place.

The historian Flavius Josephus, born in AD 37, recorded his eye-witness account. In AD 70, the Roman army *surrounded* Jerusalem, *built an embankment* around the city, and, after three years of siege, the army *leveled* Jerusalem. Though Caesar himself had ordered his troops to spare the great temple, the enraged Roman soldiers set it on fire, killing the Jews hiding inside. The temple's gold and silver melted and ran between the stones. The temple was pulled down, exactly as Jesus had foretold. *"Not one stone [was] left upon another."*[77] And just as Moses and the prophets had predicted, the Jews were *scattered* worldwide. Over the next two millennia, history would witness the fulfillment of these prophecies, as the wandering Jew became *"an object of scorn and ridicule to all the nations"* with *"no resting place."*

Whatever our personal feelings, there is another side to this Biblical prophecy none can deny. God also told His prophets that, against all odds, the Jews would be preserved among the nations as a distinct people and would one day return to the land God had given to Abraham, Isaac and Jacob.

Moses prophesied to the children of Israel: *"God will... gather you again from all the nations where the LORD your God has scattered you."* (Deuteronomy 30:3) The prophet Amos added: *"I will bring back the captives of My people Israel; they shall build the waste cities and inhabit them... I will plant them in their land, and no longer shall they be pulled up from the land...."* (Amos 9:14-15)

News networks around the world report the fulfillment of these events.

What has happened with the Hebrew nation is unique in world history. For one thing, it goes directly against *the law of assimilation*. This law demonstrates that whenever a nation is conquered by another nation, within a few generations the dispersed survivors will be assimilated by the nations in which they have settled. They intermarry, adopt the new language and culture—and lose their national identity. This did not happen with the Jews. Though millions desperately tried to blend in and be absorbed, they could not.[78]

Understandably, many find these words painful to accept. Recently, a friend in Lebanon wrote: *"As concerns the fulfillment of prophecy* [concerning God's pledge to bring the Jewish people back to the land], *I cannot overlook the implications of accepting such a belief. Accepting it would be detrimental to my cause."*

Let us be clear. Recognizing the survival and reestablishment of the Jews as a people and nation does not mean that we must endorse Israeli government policies. I understand and sympathize with my Lebanese friend. His mother's family and neighbors were driven from their homes in 1948 along with many others. His country has suffered terribly. Nevertheless, the point to be grasped is this: the words of the Biblical prophets are taking place before our eyes.

The fact that most Jews today reject the message of the very prophets they claim to honor is also a fulfillment of Scripture. As a nation they are spiritually blind. *"Even to this day, when Moses* [their own Torah!] *is read, a veil lies on their heart."* (2 Corinthians 3:15) As a nation they will not enter into God's true blessings until a coming day when they repent (have a radical change of mind and heart) and believe God's age-old message.[79]

Near the end of our journey through the Scriptures, we will observe how these events fit into God's program for the end times. We'll also hear some prophecies about the blessings God has in store for the Middle East and the entire world.

> *"I know the thoughts that I think toward you, says the LORD, thoughts of peace and not of evil, **to give you a future and a hope.**"* (Jeremiah 29:11)

PROPHECIES ABOUT A PERSON

Scattered throughout the Old Testament are hundreds of prophecies about a Messiah-Deliverer whom God promised to send into the world. The Dead Sea Scrolls affirm that these Scriptures were written hundreds of years before Messiah's birth. Here is a sampling of those predictions.

- *Prophecy to Abraham, 1900 BC:* **The Messiah would enter the world through the family line of Abraham and Isaac.** (Genesis 12:2-3; 22:1-18. *Fulfilled: Matthew 1*)
- *Prophecy by Isaiah, 700 BC:* **He would be born of a virgin, having no earthly biological father.** (Isaiah 7:14; 9:6. *Fulfilled: Luke 1:26-28; Matthew 1:18-25*)
- *Prophecy by Micah, 700 BC:* **He would be born in Bethlehem.** (Micah 5:2. *Fulfilled: Luke 2:1-20; Matthew 2:1-12*)
- *Prophecy by Hosea, 700 BC:* **He would be called out of Egypt.** (Hosea 11:1. *Fulfilled: Matthew 2:13-15*)
- *Prophecy by Malachi, 400 BC:* **The Messiah would be preceded by a forerunner.** (Malachi 3:1; Isaiah 40:3-11. *Fulfilled: Luke 1:11-17; Matthew 3:1-12*)
- *Prophecy by Isaiah, 700 BC:* **He would cause blind to see, deaf to hear, lame to walk, and preach good news to the poor.** (Isaiah 35:5-6; 61:1. *Fulfilled: Luke 7:22; Matthew 9; etc.*)
- *Prophecy by Isaiah, 700 BC:* **He would be rejected by His own people.** (Isaiah 53:2-3; 49:5-7; also: Psalm 118:21-22. *Fulfilled: John 1:11; Mark 6:3; Matthew 21:42-46; etc.*)
- *Prophecy by Zechariah, 500 BC:* **He would be betrayed for 30 pieces of silver, which would be used to buy a field.** (Zechariah 11:12-13. *Fulfilled: Matthew 26:14-16; 27:3-10*)

- *Prophecy by Isaiah, 700 BC:* **The Messiah would be rejected, falsely accused, tried and executed by the Jews and Gentiles.** (Isaiah 50:6; 53:1-12; also: Psalm 2 & 22; Zechariah 12:10. *Fulfilled: John 1:11; 11:45-57; Mark 10:32-34; Matthew 26 & 27*)
- *Prophecy by David, 1000 BC:* **His hands and feet would be pierced, He would be mocked by onlookers and lots would be cast for His garments, etc.** (Psalm 22:16,8,18. *Fulfilled: Luke 23:33; 24:39*) (Keep in mind that this prediction was made long before crucifixion had been invented as a form of capital punishment.)
- *Prophecy by Isaiah, 700 BC:* **Though killed like the worst criminal, He would be buried in the tomb of a rich man.** (Isaiah 53:8. *Fulfilled: Matthew 27:57-60*)
- *Prophecy by David, 1000 BC:* **The Messiah's body would not decay in the tomb, He would overcome death.** (Psalm 16:9-11 [See also: Matthew 16:21-23; 17:22-23; 20:17-19; etc.]. *Fulfilled: Luke 24; Acts 1 & 2*)

The laws of probability reveal the "impossibility" of any one person fulfilling such specific, verifiable prophecies.

Yet that is exactly what happened.

Later, you may want to come back to this list, pick up a Bible, and read each Old Testament prophecy and the fulfillment recorded in the New Testament.

PROPHETICAL SYMBOLS AND PATTERNS

In addition to hundreds of *prophecies*, scattered throughout the Old Testament Scriptures are hundreds of *symbols* and *patterns* (also referred to as *types, pictures, prefigurations, and illustrations*). God designed each of these visual aids to teach the world about Himself and His plan for mankind.

In our journey though the Scriptures, many symbols and patterns will be encountered. For example, one prominent *symbol* is that of a *sacrificed lamb*, which is clearly explained in chapters 19 to 26 of this book.

In chapter 21, we will learn about a special tent called *the tabernacle* which God commanded His people to construct as *a pattern.* The tabernacle and all that went with it is a powerful visual aid to help people understand what God is like and how sinners can be forgiven and qualified to live with Him forever.

A comparative study between the life of Joseph son of Jacob and Jesus of Nazareth provides a striking example of the kind of *prefigurations* found in Scripture. There are more than a hundred parallels between the life of Joseph and the life of Jesus. God used the life of Joseph to paint a picture of Jesus who would come into the world 1700 years later.[80]

There is only one reasonable explanation for such patterns and prophecies...

God.

THE PURPOSE OF PROPHECY

While on earth, the Messiah said:

*"I am telling you now **before it happens**, so that **when it does happen** you will **believe** that I am He."*
(John 13:19 NIV)

The prediction of future events, followed by their realization in history, is one way God has validated His messengers and His message. To strengthen our faith in His Word, the true and living God has *"declare[d] **the end from the beginning**, and from ancient times **things that are not yet done**, saying, 'My counsel shall stand....'"* (Isaiah 46:10)

Our upcoming journey through the Scriptures will begin in the Bible's first book—*Genesis*—which reports how the world began. Our journey will conclude in the Bible's final book—*Revelation*— which foretells the closing events of world history.

How can we be certain that Biblical statements about the unverifiable past and the unforeseeable future are true? We can be certain by applying the same logic by which we are confident the sun will rise tomorrow. For thousands of years, our solar system has a perfect record. The earth has never failed to rotate. The sun consistently rises and sets. So it is with Biblical prophecy. In all that can be verified, God's Book has a perfect record.

GOD'S CHALLENGE

Some religious people claim that their holy book also contains prophecies which have been fulfilled. If you hear someone make this claim, respectfully ask them to provide you with a short list of three or four of their holy book's most convincing prophecies. It is unlikely they will comply, but if they do, first verify that the prophecies were written down *before* the events they foretold, and then compare them with secular history to confirm their fulfillment. From my experience, any such predictions are, at best, few and ambiguous.

It is for good reason the true and living God presents the following challenge to all religions and imagined deities:

> *"'Present your case,' says the LORD. 'Set forth your arguments... Bring in your idols to **tell us what is going to happen**. Tell us what the **former things were**, so that we may consider them and **know their final outcome**. Or declare to us **the things to come**, tell us **what the future holds**, so we may know that you are gods. Do something, whether good or bad, so that we will be dismayed and filled with fear. But you are less than nothing and your works are utterly worthless; he who chooses you is detestable.'"*
> (Isaiah 41:21-24 NIV)

When it comes to multiple, detailed prophecies which have been precisely fulfilled, the Bible stands alone.

The true and living God has authenticated His message to mankind by writing history before it happens.

Fulfilled prophecy is *His signature.*

6

CONSISTENT WITNESS

<blockquote>
*"If you want to know
what the water is like,
don't ask the fish."*
— Chinese proverb
</blockquote>

Imagine this.

One hot day, as you are walking alongside a river, you consider going for a swim. However, you wonder if the water is to your liking. Is the current too swift? Is the temperature too cold? Or are the conditions right?

The Chinese proverb counsels, *"Don't ask the fish."*

Why are the fish that live in that very river unqualified to tell you *"what the water is like"* (besides the fact that they don't speak your language!)? The fish are unable to provide such information for the simple reason that they have no reference point outside the confines of their watery existence. That limited, murky world is all they know.

Likewise, if we are ever to understand this world in which we live and why we are here, such information must come from outside man's limited and self-focused worldview.

The good news is that the God of heaven has provided that information for all who want it.

*"All Scripture is **God-breathed** and is useful for teaching, rebuking, correcting and training in righteousness...."*
(2 Timothy 3:16 NIV)

How can we know that the Biblical Scriptures are *"God-breathed,"* that is, inspired by God? In the previous chapter, we observed that the Creator has put His stamp of authenticity on the Bible by embedding in its pages hundreds of prophecies which have been fulfilled.

Only God can repeatedly predict the distant future with 100% accuracy.

Another way God has established the trustworthiness of His revelation is by revealing it to many prophets over many centuries.

ONE WITNESS IS NOT ENOUGH

God told Moses, *"**One witness is not enough** to convict a man accused of any crime or offense he may have committed. **A matter must be established by the testimony of two or three witnesses.**"*
(Deuteronomy 19:15 NIV)

This principle is recognized around the world. More than one witness is required in a court of law to establish truth. Before a statement can be accepted as factual, it must be substantiated by several reliable sources.

In revealing His truth, God did not set aside His own law which states: *"One witness is not enough."* The Scriptures declare that *"the living God, who made the heaven, the earth, the sea, and all things that are in them, [has]... allowed all nations to walk in their own ways. Nevertheless, **He did not leave Himself without witness**...."* (Acts 14:15-17)

Even the most isolated tribes on earth have the *outward witness of creation* (seeing the things their Creator has made) and the *inward witness of conscience* (an inbred sense of right, wrong, and eternity). Every person on earth has been given some light—some truth. Thus, God declares mankind to be *"without excuse."*[81] Nonetheless, He promises to give further light to all who diligently seek to find and know their Creator.

CONTINUOUS WITNESS

God has never left Himself without witness.

During the first thousand years of human history, God either spoke directly with people or He made His truth known through the *oral testimony* of the first humans. Adam, the first man, lived to be 930 years old. People living in the first millennium of human history were without excuse for not knowing the truth about their Creator-Owner since they could have interviewed *the original witnesses*, Adam and Eve.[82] The longevity of the first humans was about eleven times longer than the average life-span today, which the Creator later reset at *"seventy years—or eighty, if we have the strength."* (Psalm 90:10 NIV)

Around 1920 BC, God singled out an aged man to whom He gave the name Abraham. God promised to make of Abraham a *nation* through which He would teach the nations of the world important lessons about Himself and His plan for mankind. It would also be through that chosen nation that God would provide the *prophets* and the *Scriptures,* and send the *Messiah* into the world. Around 1490 BC, God called on a man from within that nation to be His spokesman. His name was *Moses.*

WRITTEN WITNESS

God inspired Moses to write the first section of Holy Scripture, *the Torah*. The Creator of heaven and earth purposed to make His truth available in *written form* for future generations until the end of time. He put into Moses' mind the words to be written. God authenticated His Word to the nations with mighty *miracles* by the hand of Moses. God also revealed *future events* which Moses announced to the Egyptians and Israelites. Everything happened exactly as Moses predicted. God left no room for reasonable doubt. Even the toughest skeptics had to admit that the God who spoke through Moses was the true and living God.[83]

Moses was the first in a long line of prophets who recorded God's Word over more than fifteen centuries.[84] The prophets came from a variety of backgrounds. Some had no formal education. And though they lived in different generations, what they wrote presents a perfectly unified message from start to finish.

God chose men like Moses, David, Solomon, and about thirty others to write the Old Testament Scriptures. He authenticated His Word with fulfilled promises and prophecies, and with miraculous signs and wonders.

In the New Testament, the origin, life, words, works, death, and resurrection of the Messiah are recorded by four men: Matthew, Mark, Luke and John. These four men wrote the Gospel record (called the *Injil* in Arabic), thus providing the world with four separate testimonies. God also inspired Peter (a fisherman), James and Jude (Jesus' half brothers), and Paul (a scholar and former terrorist) to explain in glorious detail God's present and ultimate purposes for His people. The apostle John wrote the final book of the Bible which graphically foretells how world history, as we know it, will conclude.

CONSISTENT WITNESS

In all, God used about forty men over more than fifteen centuries to record His revelation for mankind. Even though most of these witnesses never knew each other, all they wrote fits together to form the ultimate story and message.

Who, but the One unfettered by the span of a lifetime, could have transmitted such a consistent narrative?

*"Prophecy never had its origin in the will of man, but **men spoke from God as they were carried along by the Holy Spirit**. "* (2 Peter 1:21 NIV)

Over the centuries, many have tried to discredit the New Testament writers and their message. The writings of the apostle Paul are especially attacked. Some even refer to those of us who believe the Bible as "Paulines," since we believe the entire volume of Scripture, including what God revealed to Paul.

The apostle Peter exhorts us to take Paul's writings seriously: *"Paul also wrote you with the wisdom that God gave him. ... His letters contain some things that are hard to understand, which ignorant and unstable people distort, as they do **the other Scriptures**, to their own destruction. "* (2 Peter 3:15-16 NIV)

All the apostle Paul wrote is in perfect harmony with what the prophets wrote. As Paul himself testified, *"Having obtained help from God, to this day I stand, witnessing both to small and great,* **saying no other things than those which the prophets and Moses said would come... Do you believe the prophets?"** (Acts 26:22,27)

CONSISTENT OR INCONSISTENT?

The trustworthiness of a witness is tested, not by the amount of truth contained in the person's testimony, but by the absence of any inconsistency. This is illustrated by the following anecdote:

One sunny day, four high school boys couldn't resist the temptation to skip classes. The next morning they explained to their teacher that they had missed her class because their car had a flat tire. To their relief, she smiled and said, "Well, you missed a quiz yesterday." But then she added, "Take your seats and get out a pencil and paper. The first question is: Which tire was flat?"[85]

The boys' conflicting answers on this one point exposed their fabricated story.

In contrast to the contradictory testimony of these four boys, God's testimony is consistent. Using dozens of witnesses and writers over countless generations, our Creator has revealed Himself and His plan with flawless consistency.

In the midst of the turbulent ocean of man's contradictory religions and philosophies, God has provided and preserved for us an immovable rock upon which we can rest our souls.

That rock is *His Word.*

"We have **the prophetic word confirmed,** *which you do well to heed as a light that shines in a dark place... But there were also* **false prophets among the people,** *even as there will be* **false teachers among you...** *And many will follow their* **destructive ways,** *because of whom the way of truth will be blasphemed.* **By covetousness they will exploit you with deceptive words.** *"* (2 Peter 1:19-2:3)

FALSE PROPHETS

Thus, the Word of God warns against covetous, self-seeking prophets and teachers who *"will exploit you with deceptive words."*[86] The Bible includes numerous stories about men who claimed to speak for God, but their message was, in fact, inspired by *"a lying spirit."* (1 Kings 22:22)

The Scriptures describe a time in Israel's history when there were 850 false prophets and only one true prophet, Elijah. While 7,000 Israelites remained faithful to the one true God, millions of others chose to believe the self-serving, false witnesses.[87]

Micah, one of God's faithful prophets, wrote:

*"Thus says the LORD concerning **the prophets who lead My people astray**... They cry, 'Peace,' but against him who puts nothing in their mouths, they declare holy war."*
(Micah 3:5 NAS)

That is the pattern of history, which is why Jesus warned:

*"**Wide** is the gate and **broad** is the way that leads to **destruction**, and there are **many** who go in by it. Because narrow is the gate and difficult is the way which leads to life, and there are few who find it. **Beware of false prophets**, who come to you in **sheep's clothing**, but inwardly they are **ravenous wolves**. You will know them by their fruits. Do men gather grapes from thornbushes or figs from thistles? Even so, every good tree bears good fruit, but a bad tree bears **bad fruit**."* (Matthew 7:13-17)

Over the centuries, countless bad prophets and teachers have come and gone. Some have influenced hundreds and thousands, while others have led millions and even billions of souls down *"the way that leads to destruction."*

If you want to avoid becoming one of the *"many"* who blindly follow a false prophet to *"destruction,"* then filter that person's teaching through this grid:

The message of a true prophet always harmonizes with the confirmed prophetic Scriptures that preceded him.

Consider the following **three case studies** of men who claimed to be prophets of God. Were they true or false prophets?

CASE #1: A BURIED "MESSIAH"

History catalogues dozens of self-proclaimed prophets and messiahs who lived after the time of Christ.[88] One was Abu Isa.

Abu Isa of Persia lived in the latter part of the 7th century. His followers believed him to be the Messiah because he said he would lead them to victory, and, although he was illiterate, he reportedly wrote books. But his message contradicted the Scriptures.

Abu Isa taught his followers to pray seven times a day and to follow him into battle, promising them divine protection. However, after Abu died in battle, was buried, and failed to come back to life, his followers had to admit that he was not the Messiah.

Long before Abu's time, Jesus had warned His listeners:

"False christs [messiahs] *and false prophets will rise and show great signs and wonders to deceive, if possible, even the elect. **See, I have told you beforehand.**"* (Matthew 24:24-25)

CASE #2: A SUICIDE "PROPHET"

Jim Jones founded a cult called *the People's Temple*. In the early 1970s, Jim was a popular preacher in San Francisco, California. He was known for his ability to mobilize multitudes to participate in politics and projects to help the poor. Jim called himself "the Prophet" and claimed to have power to heal cancer patients and raise the dead.

Eventually, Jim Jones convinced more than a thousand of his followers to follow him to "Jonestown" in Guyana, South America. In this new community, "the prophet Jim" promised his adherents a life of peace and happiness. But it was a huge lie.

Jim was nothing more than a ravenous wolf in sheep's clothing. As reported by the *San Francisco Chronicle*, "November 18 [1978]: Jones orders his flock to kill themselves by taking cyanide. Those who refuse are forced to take the poison. Children are killed with injections. Eventually, 914 bodies are found in Jonestown, including that of Jones himself."[89]

CASE #3: UN UNCONFIRMED "HOLY BOOK"

Joseph Smith was born in North America in 1805. Reared in poverty and superstition, as a young man, he began to tell people that he was God's prophet. He claimed that God had spoken to him in a series of visions through an angel of light named Moroni.

Joseph wrote: "I was seized upon by some power which entirely overcame me, and had such an astonishing influence over me as to bind my tongue so that I could not speak. Thick darkness gathered around me, and it seemed to me for a time that I was doomed to sudden destruction." Next Smith tells how a "pillar of light" appeared over his head "above the brightness of the sun, which descended gradually until it fell upon" him.[90] Joseph proclaimed that God had revealed to him a new holy book—the *Book of Mormon*. He told his followers that the Bible came from God, but that his new book was God's latest revelation. Joseph taught people to recite prayers, fast, give alms, do good works, and accept him as a prophet. Meanwhile, he himself practiced and legitimized a self-seeking and sensuous lifestyle.

Although Joseph Smith's "revelations" were unconfirmed by any other witnesses (though he claimed to have three), and despite the fact that his book contradicts the Bible, history and archaeology,[91] today millions of people adhere to the religion of *Mormonism*. The affluent Mormon Church sends its missionaries all over the world, and every day hundreds of people become *Mormons* (also called *Latter-day Saints*). Most Mormons are sincere, nice people, but if you compare the message of "the prophet Joseph" with what the prophets of the Bible proclaimed and wrote, you will discover two radically different messages.

To stake our eternal destiny on the conflicting, unconfirmed message of a self-proclaimed prophet—no matter how articulate or intelligent he may be—is unwise. *"For Satan himself transforms himself into an angel of light."* (2 Corinthians 11:14)

A CONFIRMED MESSAGE

In a confused world where multitudes have *"exchanged the truth of God for the lie"* (Romans 1:25), the one true God has clearly distinguished His truth from the multitude of counter-voices.

One way God has confirmed His message is by revealing it progressively with perfect consistency to many prophets over many generations. Only the Author who exists outside of time could have inspired such a revelation.

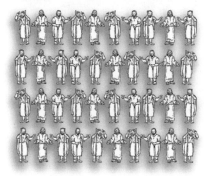

The *40 men* in this illustration represent the messengers who, over 15 centuries, recorded God's consistent, confirmed message in the Scriptures.

The *solitary man* represents any messenger who came along later with a clashing, unconfirmed message.

In the past few chapters, we have encountered many proofs that show the Bible to be God's Word. Yet as convincing as these and other evidences are, the most compelling certification of God's message is found simply in hearing it, understanding it, and embracing it.

The unfolding drama of God's Book reveals the One who is infinitely above and beyond our imaginative powers. It displays our Creator's glorious and perfectly balanced nature. It delivers people from the fear of death and provides them with the sure hope of everlasting life. It transforms their character and conduct. It leads them to the one true God.

No devil or man could have come up with such a message.

But don't take my word for it.

*"**Test all things**; hold fast what is good."*
(1 Thessalonians 5:21)

THE FOUNDATION

"A wise man...
built his house on the rock."
(Matthew 7:24)

I n His *Sermon on the Mount,*
Jesus of Nazareth concluded with these words:

*"Therefore whoever hears these sayings of Mine, and does them, I will liken him to **a wise man who built his house on the rock**: and the rain descended, the floods came, and the winds blew and beat on that house; and **it did not fall**, for it was founded on the rock. But everyone who hears these sayings of Mine, and does not do them, will be like **a foolish man who built his house on the sand**: and the rain descended, the floods came, and the winds blew and beat on that house; and it fell. And **great was its fall**."* (Matthew 7:24-27)

What was the difference between the house that withstood the storm and the house that was destroyed?

The foundation.

The wise man built his house on solid rock; the foolish man built his house on shifting sand.

In the Scriptures, God has laid a rock-solid foundation for the message He wants everyone to understand and believe. That foundation is *the Torah* (also known as *the Law of Moses*, *Pentateuch*, or *Tawret*).

THE BOOK OF BEGINNINGS

The Torah of Moses contains the first five books of Scripture. The opening book is called **Genesis**, meaning *"origin."* Genesis is *the Book of Beginnings* in which God makes known the origins of earth, life, humans, marriage, families, societies, nations, and languages. Genesis provides the answers to life's greatest mysteries. What is God like? Where did man come from? Why are we here? What is the source of evil? Why do people suffer? How can imperfect people be accepted by a perfect God?

While the answers to these and other vital questions are developed later in the Scriptures, it is in Genesis that the Creator has laid the groundwork for His answers. The first book of the Bible is the foundation for all that follows.

GOD'S STORY

The Bible contains hundreds of stories which took place over thousands of years. Together these stories form *one story*—the best story ever told. It is in that story God has embedded *one main message*—the best news ever announced.

God's dramatic story includes many climaxes. As we make our way through the Scriptures, one high peak will be encountered in *the Gospel* records. Another stunning climax will burst upon us in the Bible's closing book, entitled *the Revelation*, which means "the Unveiling."

Despite the fact that God has unveiled His plan, His design for people remains a mystery for most.

FIRST THINGS FIRST

The book of Genesis contains 50 of the Bible's 1,189 chapters.[92] To read through the entire Bible non-stop would take about three days and three nights.

In our upcoming journey, while we must pass by most stories contained in the Scriptures, we plan to visit many classic, key stories which make known "the big picture" of God's amazing plan for mankind. A significant part of our travel time will be spent in *the first four chapters* of the Bible since these opening pages unlock the great truths found elsewhere in God's Word.

The importance of the Bible's first few chapters cannot be overemphasized.

When we tell or read a story to a child, where do we begin? Do we start in the middle of the story and then jump to the end, reading a line or two? No, we start at the beginning. Yet when it comes to the Scriptures, most readers only skip around. Could it be that God's story remains a mystery to them because they have neglected the first pages of God's Book? Is it any wonder most people concur with Ahmed who wrote in his e-mail: *"The whole sinners thing makes no sense to me"*? (Chapter 1)

If we are unacquainted with the beginning of God's story, we will have a hard time appreciating the rest. However, once we understand the first few chapters, the rest will make amazing sense.[93]

A SEED PLOT

Picture a single grain of wheat. It might not seem to be much, but concealed in that simple-looking seed is the complex code and latent power required to produce a mature plant loaded with grain. The Scripture describes the process:

> *"The earth yields crops… first the blade, then the head, after that the full grain in the head."* (Mark 4:28)

God did not design grains, fruits, and vegetables to ripen immediately, nor did He design His story and message to be revealed all at once. Just as God chose to provide food for man's body by means of plants that grow progressively, so He has chosen to provide spiritual food for man's soul by means of *truth revealed progressively.*

*"Precept must be **upon** precept, precept **upon** precept, line **upon** line, line **upon** line, here a little, there a little."*
(Isaiah 28:10)

The book of Genesis is like a fertile plot of land in which God has neatly planted His "seeds" of truth. From those truths His message sprouts and matures in the remaining books of Scripture, offering life and refreshment to the world.

AN EMBRYO

Thanks to modern technology, things once shrouded in mystery can now be seen. For example, today we can view clear images of a developing human embryo. Phenomenal! Within eight weeks, the fertilized egg in the mother's womb develops into a peanut-sized baby, complete with eyes, ears, nose, mouth, arms, hands, legs, and feet. It even has its own fingerprints. Though not fully formed, it contains all the parts.

Similarly, today we know that every essential truth revealed by our Creator about Himself and His plan for mankind can be found in embryonic form in the book of Genesis. However, it is in the rest of the completed Scriptures that *"the mystery of God"* (Revelation 10:7) grows to maturity.

To this day, God's personality and purposes remain a mystery to most, but unnecessarily so, since *"**the mystery** which has been hidden from ages and from generations ... **now has been revealed**."* (Colossians 1:26)

God invites us to understand His mystery, but we must *want* to understand it.

BITS AND PIECES

The Bible is somewhat like a jigsaw puzzle.

The way some pieces fit together is obvious, while others are not so obvious. Patience and perseverance are required. Similarly, it is only by taking time to reflect on the Word of God that confusion will evaporate and God's harmonious plan will emerge.

In recent times, I have had the privilege of corresponding with an aspiring journalist in Lebanon. Though we have not yet met, we have become friends. In his first e-mail to me he wrote:

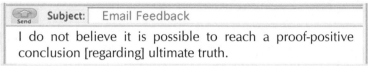

Subject: Email Feedback

I do not believe it is possible to reach a proof-positive conclusion [regarding] ultimate truth.

I encouraged him to lay aside all preconceived ideas and read the Bible for himself, allowing it to speak for itself. This he has been doing, as evidenced by this e-mail:

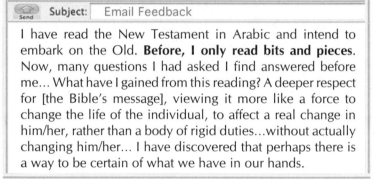

Subject: Email Feedback

I have read the New Testament in Arabic and intend to embark on the Old. **Before, I only read bits and pieces.** Now, many questions I had asked I find answered before me... What have I gained from this reading? A deeper respect for [the Bible's message], viewing it more like a force to change the life of the individual, to affect a real change in him/her, rather than a body of rigid duties...without actually changing him/her... I have discovered that perhaps there is a way to be certain of what we have in our hands.

Recently, he observed:

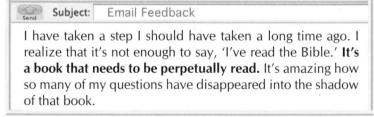

Subject: Email Feedback

I have taken a step I should have taken a long time ago. I realize that it's not enough to say, 'I've read the Bible.' **It's a book that needs to be perpetually read.** It's amazing how so many of my questions have disappeared into the shadow of that book.

For this man, God's message is beginning to emerge.

Our upcoming journey through the Scriptures will assemble the most important pieces of history's great puzzle, and God's amazing story and message will become clear.

It is as we *"perpetually read"* the Scriptures for ourselves, that we will discover where other *"bits and pieces"* fit.

LOVE LETTERS

The tale is told of a soldier who loved a young lady. While his affection for her was deep, how she felt about him was unclear. In due time, the soldier was sent to a distant land. He faithfully wrote letters to the lady, although she never sent any to him.

Finally, the day came for his return. Upon arrival, his first stop was to visit the one he loved. He found her at home. While she acted pleased to see him, a dusty box in the corner of the room exposed her heart's true condition.

It was full of unopened letters—his.

FROM HEAVEN TO EARTH

The Scriptures are like a series of letters from God to you. In His writings, the Creator-Owner of heaven and earth is introducing Himself to you, expressing His love, and telling you how you can live with Him in the glory and joy of His eternal home.

Here is part of a "letter" He sent to earth 2,700 years ago:

"Everyone who thirsts, come to the waters;
And you who have no money, come buy and eat...
Why do you spend money for what is not bread,
And your wages for what does not satisfy?
Listen diligently to Me, and eat what is good,
And let your soul delight itself in abundance.
Incline your ear, and come to Me.
Hear, and your soul shall live;
And I will make an everlasting covenant with you...
For as the heavens are higher than the earth,
So are My ways higher than your ways,
And My thoughts than your thoughts." (Isaiah 55:1-3,9)

Love,
Your Creator

Have you opened His letters to you?
Have you read them?
Have you responded to Him?
Let the journey begin.

PART II
THE JOURNEY

DISCOVERING
THE MYSTERY

8

WHAT GOD IS LIKE

The journey begins where God's
Book begins—with one of the
greatest declarations of all time:

*"In the beginning God created the
heavens and the earth."* (Genesis 1:1)

No attempt is made to prove God's
existence. It is self-evident.

If you are walking along a deserted beach and come upon a
set of fresh footprints in the sand, you instinctively conclude that
you are not alone. You know those evenly spaced tracks didn't
create themselves. You know the wind and water did not form
them. Those footprints were caused by someone.

You know that.

Yet many people contend that they do *not* know that the
sand in which the footprints were formed, and the human being
who caused the footprints, were also caused by Someone. In an
attempt to explain creation apart from a Creator, man has come up
with many elaborate theories, some imagining a string of causes
stretching back billions of years. But once they arrive at what they
call "the beginning," they are no closer to answering the original
question: *What caused it?*

The Scripture says: *"What may be known about God is plain to them, because God has made it plain to them. For since the creation of the world God's invisible qualities—his eternal power and divine nature—have been clearly seen, **being understood from what has been made**, so that men are without excuse."* (Romans 1:18-20 NIV)

The rationale is elementary: design necessitates a designer.

Just as this is true with man-made things like footprints, cars, and computers, so it is true with mechanisms like feet, cells, and constellations. Whether observed with the naked eye, or through a microscope or telescope, the irreducible complexity and intricate order of the universe necessitates a Creator and a Sustainer.

Just as a footprint requires a footprint-maker, so a universe requires a Universe-Maker.

> *"The heavens declare the glory of God; the skies proclaim the work of his hands."* (Psalm 19:1 NIV)

So who is this Universe-Maker? How can we know what He is like? We can *know* because He has made Himself *known*.[94]

ETERNAL

Earlier we read an e-mail from a correspondent who asked sarcastically, "Who created God? I've forgotten." Here's the answer: *No one.* God is eternal. *"In the beginning **GOD**"* teaches us that our Creator is like no one and nothing else.

> *"Before the mountains were brought forth, or ever You had formed the earth and the world, even **from everlasting to everlasting, You are God**."* (Psalm 90:2)

Past, present, and future are as nothing to God. He is the *"Lord God Almighty, Who **was** and **is** and **is to come!**"* (Revelation 4:8)

He is timeless and incomprehensible.

No created being will ever know everything about God. He is *"the High and Lofty One who **inhabits eternity**."* (Isaiah 57:15)

He never changes. *"You are **the same**, and Your years will have **no end**."* (Psalm 102:27)

GREATER

God is greater than anything we can imagine.

Just as the eternal One makes no attempt to *prove* His existence, because it is self-evident, so He makes no attempt to *explain* His existence, because our finite minds are incapable of grasping that which exists apart from time, space, and matter.

As a little boy, I remember looking up into the sky and thinking that if I could travel high enough and far enough, I would eventually come to a ceiling and the end of the universe. What I failed to consider was the endless space on the opposite side of my imaginary ceiling!

Some things can only be understood by believing what the Creator has revealed.

Faith in the consistent and proven Word of God is the key to the highest level of wisdom and knowledge.

> *"Without faith it is impossible to please God, because anyone who comes to him must believe that he exists and that he rewards those who earnestly seek him. ... **By faith we understand** that the universe was formed at God's command, so that what is seen was not made out of what was visible."* (Hebrews 11:6,3 NIV)

Modern science affirms that *"what is seen was not made out of what was visible."* Physicists tell us that matter is made of invisible atoms which are made of electrons which whirl around a nucleus made of protons and neutrons which are made of quarks which are made of...? Mankind has discovered so much, yet we know so little! Those who are wise recognize the limitations of human intellect.

What science will never be able to prove or disprove is *"that the universe was formed at God's command."* We can only *know* this through our God-given sixth-sense: *faith.*

It is *"by faith **we understand**"* life's greatest themes and questions. The reason for this is obvious:

> *"God is **greater** than man."* (Job 33:12)

So what else has this great One revealed about Himself?

LIMITLESS

He is all-powerful. *"Ah, Sovereign LORD, you have made the heavens and the earth by your great power and outstretched arm. Nothing is too hard for you."* (Jeremiah 32:17 NIV) The Creator transcends His creation. He is above and beyond anything we can imagine.

He is all-knowing. *"You know when I sit and when I rise; You perceive my thoughts...."* (Psalm 139:2 NIV) The Creator knows everything—past, present and future. He does not grow wiser over time. *"His understanding is **infinite**."* (Psalm 147:5)

He is everywhere present. *"Where can I go from Your Spirit? Or where can I flee from Your presence?"* (Psalm 139:7) The infinite One can be with you at the same time He is with me. At the same moment He is speaking with the angels in heaven, He can be speaking with men on earth.

He is limitless.

SPIRIT

Here is another significant piece of information about this limitless One:

*"God is **Spirit**."* (John 4:24)

God is the invisible, infinite, and personal Spirit who is present in all places at one and the same time. Although He needs no body, He is able and free to manifest Himself as He chooses. The Scriptures report several occasions when God appeared to men and women in unique, visible ways—*"face to face, as a man speaks to his friend."* (Exodus 33:11)

God the Supreme Spirit wants to be known, trusted, and worshiped by the spiritual beings He has created for that purpose.

"The Father is seeking such to worship Him. God is Spirit, and those who worship Him must worship in spirit and truth." (John 4:23-24)

THE FATHER OF SPIRITS

One of God's titles is *"the Father of spirits."* (Hebrews 12:9)

Before God created the earth,[95] He created countless millions of powerful, magnificent *spirit beings* called *angels* to live with Him in His heavenly home. *Angel* means *"messenger"* or *"servant."* God, who purposed to have a kingdom of loving subjects with whom He could share eternity, created these spirits to know, worship, obey, serve, and enjoy Him forever.

> *"I heard the voice of **many angels** around the throne… and the number of them was ten thousand times ten thousand, and thousands of thousands…."* (Revelation 5:11)

From the start, God created as many angels as He wanted, since they were not designed to reproduce. These angels were in no way equal to God, although they shared certain likenesses with their Creator. God gave them a high level of intelligence. He also gave them emotions, a will, and the capacity to communicate with Him. Like their Maker, angels are invisible to man unless they are sent on a mission in which they must become visible.[96]

In His kingdom of created spiritual beings, God is the uncreated, infinite, all-powerful, all-knowing, limitless Spirit.

ABOVE ALL

> *"There is… one Spirit… one Lord… one God and Father of all, who is **above all**…."* (Ephesians 4:4-6)

Although the One who *"is above all"* is not confined to time and space, there is an actual place in the universe where He dwells and rules. *"The LORD has established His throne in heaven, and His kingdom rules over all."* (Psalm 103:19) In meditating on the greatness and the nearness of God, King Solomon prayed these words to His Creator:

> *"Will God indeed dwell on the earth? Behold, heaven and **the heaven of heavens** cannot contain You."* (1 Kings 8:27)

The Bible speaks of three different *heavens*. Two are visible to man; one is not.

There is the *atmospheric heaven*—the blue sky over our heads.

There is the *interstellar heaven*—the black space in which God placed the planets and stars.

And there is the *heaven of heavens*—the brilliant sphere where God dwells. This heavenly home of our Creator and realm of angels is also called *the highest heaven, the third heaven, the Father's house, His dwelling, Paradise*, and simply, *Heaven.*[97]

> *"The LORD looks from **heaven**; He sees all the sons of men. From the place of **His dwelling** He looks on all the inhabitants of the earth; He fashions their hearts individually; He considers all their works."* (Psalm 33:13-15)

GOD IS ONE

The first verse of the Bible affirms that there is only one God: *"In the beginning **God**."*

Both the Old and New Testament Scriptures declare: *"The LORD our God, **the LORD is one**."* (Deuteronomy 6:4) *"There is **only one God**."* (Romans 3:30)

God is ONE.

He has no competition. He has no equal.

In theological terms this is called *monotheism*: belief in only one God. Monotheism stands in stark contrast to *polytheism* (belief in many gods and goddesses) and *pantheism* (belief that God is everything and everything is God). Polytheists and pantheists blur the distinction between the Creator and His creation. As a result, they deny that God is a personality with character traits.

COMPLEX

*"In the beginning **God**"* is an elementary truth, but it is *not a simple truth.*

The Infinite One is not simple. He is complex. His oneness is a multi-dimensional oneness.

The Hebrew word used for *"God"* is the masculine plural

noun *Elohim*. Hebrew grammar has singular (one), dual (two only) and plural (three or more) noun forms. *Elohim* is grammatically plural, but has a singular meaning.

The one true God is complex and unlimited in His capacities. The first three sentences of Scripture declare:

> *"In the beginning* **GOD** *[plural noun]* **created** *[singular verb conjugation] the heavens and the earth. The earth was without form, and void; and darkness was on the face of the deep. And the* **SPIRIT OF GOD** *was hovering over the face of the waters. Then* **GOD SAID**, *'Let there be light'; and there was light."* (Genesis 1:1-3)

Thus, the opening statement of God's Book tells us *how* He carried out His work of creation. He accomplished it by *His Spirit* and *His Word*.

First, *God's own Spirit* was sent down from heaven to carry out His commands. Like a dove hovering over her nest, *"the Spirit of God was hovering over"* the newborn world. The Hebrew word used for "Spirit" is *ruach*, denoting *spirit, breath,* or *energy*. This *"Spirit of God"* is the energy-giving presence of God Himself.

> *"You send forth* **Your Spirit** *[ruach], they are created."*
> (Psalm 104:30)

Next, *God spoke*. Ten times the first chapter of Genesis states: *"God said...."* When God spoke, what He commanded happened.

> *"By* **the word of the LORD** *the heavens were made, and all the host of them by* **the breath** *[ruach] of His mouth."*
> (Psalm 33:6)

God created the world by His Word and by His Spirit.

THE COMMUNICATOR

The fact that God created all things *by speaking* teaches us something else about God:

He communicates.

Before there was creation there was communication.

> *"In the beginning was **the Word**, and **the Word** was with*
> *God, and **the Word** was God. **He was in the beginning***
> ***with God.** "* (John 1:1-2)

This term, *"the Word,"* comes from the Greek word *Logos,*
meaning: *the expression of thought.* [98] In the Scriptures, *Logos* is
one of God's personal titles. *The Word* is entirely one with God.

All things were created by *the Word.*

God could have just *thought* the world into existence and in
an instant all would have been in place and functioning. But that
is not what He did. He *expressed* His thoughts. He *spoke.*

The Word spoke the world into existence in six orderly days.

Did the Almighty *need* six days to accomplish the task?

No, the timeless One did not need any amount of time.
However, by creating our world in this way, God not only
established the seven-day week,[99] He also provided us with
insights into His personality and character. This is important since
an unknown God can neither be trusted, obeyed, nor worshiped.

Let us now look, listen, and learn from the creation account,
as reported by the Creator Himself.

DAY 1: LIGHT AND TIME – GOD IS HOLY

> *"Then God said, 'Let there be light'; and there was light.*
> *And God saw the light, that it was good; and God divided*
> *the light from the darkness. God called the light Day,*
> *and the darkness He called Night. So the evening and the*
> *morning were the first day."* (Genesis 1:3-5)

On day one, God brought light to the creation scene. He also
established time, causing the earth to begin its 24-hour rotation:
the astronomical clock that regulates day and night. Yet God would
not create the sun, moon, and stars until day four.

There was a time when scientists argued that the existence of
light before the existence of *the sun* was scientifically inaccurate.
This is no longer the case. Today even scientists who don't believe

the creation record assert that light existed before and independent of earth's sun.[100]

By providing *light* (Day 1) before creating earth's *light-bearers* (Day 4), the Creator was demonstrating that He is the uncreated Source of light—physical and spiritual. Apart from Him, there is only darkness.

As we make our way through the Scriptures, we will continually encounter the Source of Light, culminating with a peek into Paradise itself where God's people *"will not need the light of a lamp or the light of the sun, for the Lord God will give them light."* (Revelation 22:5 NIV)

Light remains a mystery even to the best minds. Physicists know a good bit about what it *does*, but understand little about what it *is*. In science, light is an *absolute*. It travels at 300,000 kilometers (186,000 miles) per second. In physics, when Albert Einstein discovered $E = mc^2$ (energy equals mass multiplied by the speed of light squared), the awesome and terrifying atomic-nuclear age began. Light is unaffected by its environment. It can shine on a stinking garbage dump, but the light itself remains pure. Light cannot coexist with darkness. It dispels it.

God, the Source of light, is *the ultimate absolute.* His splendor is awesome and terrifying to any living being unequipped to live in His presence.

God is pure and holy.

The word *holy* means: *divided, set apart,* or *that which is other.* God is *other.* There is none like Him. The angels surrounding His radiant throne in Heaven continually cry out, *"Holy, holy, holy is the LORD!"* (Isaiah 6:3) Holiness is the only characteristic of God that is repeated in groups of three in Scripture—for emphasis. He is holy, *"dwelling in unapproachable light."* (1 Timothy 6:16)

God cannot coexist with evil. He separates light from darkness. Only pure and righteous beings can dwell with Him.

> *"**God is light** and in Him is no darkness at all. If we say that we have fellowship with Him, and walk in darkness, we lie and do not practice the truth."* (1 John 1:5-6)

The first day of creation proclaims that God is **holy**.

DAY 2: AIR AND WATER – GOD IS ALMIGHTY

"Then God said, 'Let there be a firmament in the midst of the waters, and let it divide the waters from the waters.' ... and it was so. And God called the firmament Heaven. So the evening and the morning were the second day."
(Genesis 1:6-8)

The second day of creation focuses on two elements upon which all living organisms would depend: air and water.

The Hebrew word *firmament* refers to the great arch of expanse over our heads, in which are placed the atmosphere and clouds, and in which the stars can be seen. Think of the atmosphere's perfectly balanced composition of gases such as oxygen and nitrogen, water vapor and carbon dioxide, ozone and more. Change the mix and we're dead. God knew what He was doing.

Think of the trillions of tons of water vapor suspended in the atmosphere above us. What kind of wisdom and power was required to create and maintain that precise mixture of air and water—just by speaking?

*"**He spoke, and it was done**; He commanded, and it stood fast."* (Psalm 33:9)

Like every other day of creation, the second day reminds us that our Creator is **almighty.**

DAY 3: LAND AND PLANTS – GOD IS GOOD

"Then God said, 'Let the waters under the heavens be gathered together into one place, and let the dry land appear'; and it was so. ... And God saw that it was good. Then God said, 'Let the earth bring forth grass, the herb that yields seed, and the fruit tree that yields fruit according to its kind, whose seed is in itself... And God saw that it was good." (Genesis 1:9-12)

On day three God divided the land from the sea and spoke into existence all vegetation. *"And God saw that it was good."* He put just the right amount of liquid water on our planet. He has never needed to add any since that day.[101]

God designed each plant and tree to yield seed and to produce vegetables or fruit *"according to its kind."* Why did God make all this food? He made it because He *"formed the earth...to be inhabited."* (Isaiah 45:18) The earth is unique in our solar system. It is the only planet designed to sustain and enrich life.

Think, for example, of some benefits we reap from plants: vital oxygen, nourishing vegetables, delicious fruits, refreshing shade, useful woods, necessary medicines, colorful and fragrant flowers, beautiful landscapes, and much more.

When it comes to food, God could have made just a few things for us to eat—like bananas, beans, and rice. We could live on that. But that is not what God did. Scientists estimate that our earth has two million varieties of plants used for food and forage.

In Genesis chapter one, God declares seven times that His creation was *"good."* Throughout the Scriptures, the number seven denotes perfection. Everything God made was perfectly good.

That's because He is perfectly good.

"God...gives us richly all things to enjoy." (1 Timothy 6:17)

Day three teaches us God is **good**.

DAY 4: CELESTIAL LIGHTS – GOD IS FAITHFUL

"Then God said, 'Let there be lights in the firmament of the heavens to divide the day from the night; and let them be for signs and seasons, and for days and years...' Then God made two great lights: the greater light to rule the day, and the lesser light to rule the night. He made the stars also." (Genesis 1:14-16)

Day four reveals a God of order. He is the One *"who appoints the sun to shine by day, who decrees the moon and stars to shine by night."* (Jeremiah 31:35 NIV) By night, the fixed order of the stars provides a reliable map for travelers on land and sea. By day, the sun dependably clicks off days and years. The moon regulates the months and tides.

Like the sun and stars, earth's moon bears constant witness to the dependability of the One who made it. God calls the moon *"the faithful witness in the sky."* (Psalm 89:37) From every location on earth, the lunar planet constantly faces the earth, never revealing its backside.[102] With clockwork precision it waxes and wanes. The moon is faithful because the One who made it is faithful.

Because God is faithful, there is something He *cannot* do. He cannot contradict His own nature, nor can He ignore His own laws. *"He remains faithful; He cannot deny Himself. ...It is impossible for God to lie."* (2 Timothy 2:13; Hebrews 6:18) Many people think God is so "great" that He can do that which is contrary to His own character, or go back on His word. That is not God's definition of "great."

Fickleness is not a part of His character—*faithfulness* is. Like the fixed order of the planets and constellations, our Creator-Sustainer is dependable.

You can trust Him.

> *"Every good gift and every perfect gift is from above, and comes down from **the Father of lights**, with whom there is **no variation** or shadow of turning."* (James 1:17)

The fourth day of creation bears witness that God is **faithful**.

DAY 5: FISH AND FOWL – GOD IS LIFE

On day five, in His infinite wisdom and power, God created creatures of every kind to inhabit the sea and the sky, equipping them to move efficiently in their unique environments—the fish in the water with their gills and fins, and the birds in the air with their light bones and feathers.

> *"God said, 'Let the water teem with living creatures, and let birds fly above the earth across the expanse of the sky.' So God created the great creatures of the sea and every living and moving thing with which the water teems, according to their kinds, and every winged bird according to its kind. And God saw that it was good."* (Genesis 1:20-21 NIV)

Notice the wording, *"Let the water teem with living creatures."* *Teem* means *"to be crammed, packed with."* Microbiologists tell us that a single drop of pond water can contain millions of living microorganisms and that many are as complex as some larger animals! The largest of the ocean's incredible array of creatures, the blue whale, feeds entirely on plankton—minuscule plants and animals that float in the sea.

The ocean is one huge collection of God's living miracles.

The same could be said of the amazing assortment of birds that fly across the sky.

Notice also the words, *"according to their kinds."* This phrase is repeated ten times in Genesis chapter one, declaring the stability of each kind of living organism. The Author of Life decreed that each plant and creature should reproduce *"according to its kind."* Man's hypothesis of evolution goes against this invariable natural law. While there can be variations, mutations and adaptations within each kind of living creature, none can "evolve" beyond the distinct limits set by the Creator. The fossil record is witness.

God alone is the Source and Sustainer of that unique energy called *life*. Apart from Him there is only death.

> *"All things were made through Him, and without Him nothing was made that was made. In Him was life."* (John 1:3)

The abundant living creatures created on day five teach us that God is **life**.

DAY 6: ANIMALS AND MAN – GOD IS LOVE

At the start of the sixth day, the Creator made tens of thousands of fascinating mammals, reptiles, and insects.

> *"God made the beast of the earth according to its kind, cattle according to its kind, and everything that creeps on the earth according to its kind. And God saw that it was good."* (Genesis 1:25)

God made them all, some big and some small, giving to each the intuitive knowledge required to live and contribute to the natural world, each producing offspring in its own likeness, each caring for its young.

When God created the animal kingdom everything *"was good."* No evil or bloodshed had yet entered the scene. Animals were designed to live on a vegetarian diet. God said, *"To every beast of the earth, to every bird of the air, and to everything that creeps on the earth, in which there is life, I have given every green herb for food."* (Genesis 1:30) There was no creature-eat-creature food chain. Hostility and fear were unknown. God's kindness was reflected in everything. A lion would graze next to a lamb, and a cat and bird would enjoy one another's company. The world was a perfectly peaceful place.

Once God finished creating the animals, it was time to form His masterpiece: *man and woman.* God had a plan whereby humans would become His devoted subjects in a glorious, joyful, everlasting kingdom of love.

For our Creator, love is more than something He does. Love is what He *is.*

*"God **is** love."* (1 John 4:8)

God's creative acts on day six declare that He is **love**.

"LET US"

It is because God is love that He created a beautiful world for the people who were to become the objects and recipients of His love. And so still on the sixth day:

"Then God said, 'Let Us make man in Our image, according to Our likeness…'" (Genesis 1:26)

Wait! Wait!! What was that? Did God really say, *"Let **Us** make man in **Our** image"*?
Since God is ONE, who is the *"US"* and *"OUR"*?
To whom was He speaking?

9

NONE LIKE HIM

"God is God... the great God, mighty and awesome...."
— Prophet Moses (Deuteronomy 10:17)

WARNING: This next stage of the journey will take travelers outside their comfort zone. Minds will be stretched and hearts will be tested. Nonetheless, all who make it through this section will be well-equipped to face the remaining challenges that lie ahead.

GOD IS GOD

Most of us share the belief that God is greater than what we would naturally conceive Him to be.

The sincerity of our belief is about to be tested.

On the sixth day of creation, after God finished creating the animal kingdom, He said: *"Let Us make man in Our image, according to Our likeness."* (Genesis 1:26)

In the next chapter, we will muse on some of the ways the original man and woman were made to reflect God's nature and likeness, but first another question must be answered.

Since God is *One*, why did He say, *"Let Us make..."*? Why did He not declare, "**I** will make man in **My** image, according to **My** likeness"? Why does God sometimes refer to Himself as *Us, Our*, and *We?*[103]

Some contend that God's use of *"Us"* and *"We"* is the "plural of majesty," such as a king who speaks of himself as "we." While God is incomparably majestic in power and glory, Hebrew grammar provides no solid basis for this "plural of majesty" explanation.

Others believe God was speaking to the angels when He said, *"Let Us make man in Our image,"* even though angels are not mentioned in the text, nor was man made in the image of angels.

What is clear from a plain reading of the Scriptures and from a scrutiny of the grammar, is that our Creator chose to describe Himself in a plural yet singular fashion.

PLURAL: *"God said, 'Let Us make man in Our image.'"*
SINGULAR: *"So God created man in His own image."*
(Genesis 1:26-27)

God's description of Himself as both plural and singular is consistent with who He is and who He has always been.

The complexity and magnitude of God's oneness goes far beyond many people's superficial definition of "one." The Infinite One will not fit into man's self-conceived mold.

God is God.

"From everlasting to everlasting, You are God."
(Psalm 90:2)

GOD'S COMPLEX ONENESS

God's Book opens with these words:

"In the beginning GOD [Elohim – masculine plural noun] created [singular verb conjugation]... And the Spirit of God was hovering over the face of the waters. Then God said, 'Let there be light'; and there was light."[104]
GOD created all things by His Word and His Spirit.

"By the word of the LORD the heavens were made, and all the host of them by the breath of His mouth."
(Psalm 33:6)

HIS WORD

For all who want to learn about their complex Creator, the Scriptures provide ample information. For example, the Gospel according to John opens with these words:

> *"In the beginning was **the Word**,*
> *and the Word was **with God**,*
> *and the Word was **God**.*
> ***He** was in the beginning with God.*
> *All things were made through **Him**...."* (John 1:1-3)

As we considered in the previous chapter, *"the Word"* is *the outward expression of God's inward thoughts*. Even as you are one with your thoughts and words, so God is One with His Word. *"The Word"* is declared to be both *"with God"* (distinct from Him) and *"God"* (one with Him).

It is also helpful to observe that the personal pronouns *"He"* and *"Him"* are used when referring to *"the Word."*

HIS SPIRIT

Just as the LORD God describes *His Word* in a distinctive, personal way, so He describes *His Spirit* in a distinctive, personal kind of way.

> *"You send forth **Your Spirit**, they are created;*
> *and **You** renew the face of the earth."* (Psalm 104:30)

> *"**By His Spirit He adorned** the heavens."* (Job 26:13)

> *"Where can I go from **Your Spirit**?*
> *Or where can I flee from **Your presence**?"* (Psalm 139:7)

> *"**The Holy Spirit**... **He** will teach you all things."* (John 14:26)

Like *the Word* (who spoke forth creation), *the Holy Spirit* (who carried out the commands of *the Word*) is perfectly One with God.

GOD IS GREAT

Most monotheists have no problem agreeing with the following excerpt from one of King David's many recorded prayers: *"You are great, O LORD GOD. For there is none like You, nor is there any God besides You,* according to all that we have heard with our ears."* (2 Samuel 7:22)

Yet many who are quick to affirm, "God is great! God is God, there is none like Him!" are equally quick to reject God's own revelation of His plural yet singular nature.

Since "there is none like Him," should we be surprised if the Almighty reveals Himself to be greater and more complex than we would naturally imagine? God urges us to think correct thoughts about Him.

> *"You thought that I was altogether like you; but I will rebuke you!"* (Psalm 50:21)

GOD IS ONE

Orthodox Jews regularly repeat a prayer known in Hebrew as the *Shema*, which states: *"Adonai Eloheynu, Adonai echad,"* meaning, *"The Lord our God, the Lord is one."* This prayer is from the Torah: *"Hear [Shema], O Israel: The LORD [YHWH] our God, the LORD is one [echad]!"* (Deuteronomy 6:4)

The Hebrew word used to describe God's oneness is *echad*. This word is often used to describe *a multiple unity*, such as *a cluster* of grapes. Elsewhere in Scripture, *echad* is translated *"a unit"* in referring to a captain and his soldiers.[105] In the next chapter, this word will pop up again as the first man and his wife become *echad*, that is, *"one flesh."* (Genesis 2:24) By looking at other verses in which this same Hebrew word is used it becomes clear that the term by which God describes His oneness can include more than one entity.

The Old Testament contains scores of verses alluding to and affirming God's plural oneness.[106] Here is one example:

> *"From the beginning... I was there. And now the Lord GOD and His Spirit have sent Me."* (Isaiah 48:16)

Who is *"the Lord GOD"?*
Who is *"His Spirit"?*
Who is the *"I"* and the *"Me"* sent by *"the Lord GOD and His Spirit"?*
These questions will be answered with clarity as we think our way through the Scriptures.

TRI-UNITIES WE AGREE ON

Our English word "unity" comes from the Latin *unus*, meaning "one." While most people reject the concept of God as an eternal tri-unity, few dare deny the three-in-one unities that fill our everyday lives.

For example, **time** forms a kind of tri-unity with its *past, present,* and *future.*

Space is another, consisting of *height, length,* and *width.*

A human is composed of *spirit, soul,* and *body.*

One man can be a *father,* a *son,* and a *husband.*

The sun is also a tri-unity. Even though earth has only one sun, yet we call

the *celestial body* **the sun,**

its *light* **the sun,**

and its *heat* **the sun.**

Does that make three suns? No. The sun is not three, but one. There is no contradiction between the sun being one and a tri-unity. So it is with God. As the light and the heat of the sun proceed from the sun, so *the Word of God* and *the Spirit of* God proceed from God. Yet they are ONE, even as the sun is one.

Of course, all earthly illustrations fall short of adequately explaining the complexity of the one true God. Unlike the sun, He is a personal, loving, and knowable Being. Nonetheless, such illustrations should lead us to common ground since all agree that tri-unities exist in creation and most agree that the Creator transcends His creation.

"He who built the house has more honor than the house. For every house is built by someone, but He who built all things is God." (Hebrews 3:3-4)

If God's creation is filled with complex unities, should it surprise us if God Himself is a complex unity? If, with all our scientific knowledge, we cannot fully explain the world in which we live, how much less can we explain the One who created it? God is God.

> *"Can you fathom the mysteries of God? Can you probe the limits of the Almighty? They are higher than the heavens—what can you do? They are deeper than the depths of the grave—what can you know? Their measure is longer than the earth and wider than the sea."*
> (Job 11:7-9 NIV)

It is as we probe *"the mysteries of God,"* that we will be privileged to discover and experience one of the most wonderful attributes of His eternal nature:

> *"God is **love.**"* (1 John 4:8)

WHOM DID GOD LOVE?

The love of God is an incomprehensibly deep affection that flows from His Father-heart and expresses itself in practical ways.[107] Since God *is* love, His love is not contingent on the loveliness of the recipient.

> *"How great is **the love the Father has lavished** on us, that we should be called children of God!"* (1 John 3:1 NIV)

Here is something to think about. Love requires a recipient. I don't just say, "I love," but I can say, "I love my wife, I love my children, I love my neighbors," and so on.

Love calls for an object.

So whom did God love before He created special living beings as objects of His love? Did He *need* to create angels and people? No, our Creator is *self-sufficient.* He created spirit beings and human beings not because He *needed* them, but because He *wanted* them. The difference is significant.

As we already learned: ***God speaks.***

Speech can only exist in a meaningful way in the context of a relationship. ***With whom did He speak*** *before He created angels and humans?* Did He *need* to create other beings to have someone to understand His words? No, all God "needs" is within Himself. He needs nothing. God is self-sufficient and self-satisfied. Yet it is part of His nature to want to speak and be spoken to, to love and be loved.

This leads us to another truth: ***God is relational.***

Love and speech can only exist in a meaningful way in the context of a relationship. ***With whom did God enjoy a relationship*** *before He created other beings?* The answer is embedded in God's complex unity.

In eternity, before He created angels or man, our relational God enjoyed a satisfying and intimate relationship of love and communication within Himself—with His personal Word and personal Spirit.

PEELING BACK THE LAYERS

In response to such deep thoughts about the plural, interpersonal nature of God, one e-mail correspondent wrote:

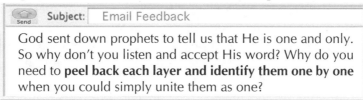

Send Subject: Email Feedback

God sent down prophets to tell us that He is one and only. So why don't you listen and accept His word? Why do you need to **peel back each layer and identify them one by one** when you could simply unite them as one?

While it is true that we will never be able to understand all there is to know about our infinite Creator, nonetheless, since God has revealed so many great truths about Himself in the writings of His prophets, shouldn't we seek to understand those truths? If we are to think of God at all, we must think about Him accurately.

Most of us agree that God is ONE, but what has this ONE GOD revealed about Himself? What can we discover about Him in the Scriptures as we "peel back each layer"?

We encounter a personal, knowable, and trustworthy *God* who is ONE with His *Word* and *Spirit*.

In His infinite greatness, God has identified Himself as *the Father*, His Word as *the Son*, and His Spirit as *the Holy Spirit*. These are the three personal distinctions within the one true God. Let's look at a few Scriptures that "peel back" this truth.

THE SON OF GOD

The Scripture makes it clear that the same *Word* who was with God in the beginning is also called *God's one and only Son.*

> *"In the beginning was the Word, and the Word was **with God**, and the Word **was God**. ... No one has ever seen God, but **God the One and Only, who is at the Father's side**, has made him known. ... Whoever believes in him is not condemned, but whoever does not believe stands condemned already because he has not believed in the name of **God's one and only Son**."* (John 1:1,18; 3:18 NIV)

In Senegal, people sometimes react to the term *"Son of God"* by muttering, *"Astaghferullah!"* This Arabic formula carries the idea: *"May God forgive you for uttering such blasphemy!"* (Blasphemy can be defined as *"mockery of God."*) On occasion, I have responded to their rebuke by quoting one of their own proverbs: *"Before you slap the shepherd on the mouth, you should find out what he is whistling about."* They laugh and then I tell them, "Before you reject the expression *'Son of God,'* you should find out what God has said about it."

The Scriptures contain more than a hundred verses that directly refer to God's *"Son,"* yet none of these verses imply "more than one God," nor do they suggest that God "took a wife and had a son," as some choose to interpret the term. Such thinking is not only blasphemous, it also reveals a shallow grasp of the Scriptures.[108]

God invites us to think His thoughts.

> *"As the heavens are **higher** than the earth, so are My ways **higher** than your ways, and My thoughts than your thoughts."* (Isaiah 55:9)

Many years ago a well-known Senegalese businessman was killed in an automobile accident. Senegal's national newspaper reported that this man's two thousand employees were "like his own children," and eulogized him as "a great son of Senegal."[109] Did these words imply that the country of Senegal had relations with a woman and engendered a son? Of course not! The Senegalese people have no problem honoring a well-loved citizen with this title. They understand what the expression "son of Senegal" means. They also know what it does *not* mean.

The term "son" is used in a number of ways. When the Qur'an and Arabs refer to a *wayfaring traveler* as a "son of the road," (*ibn al-sabil* [Sura 2:177,215]) we know what they mean. When Almighty God refers to *His Word* as *His Son*, we should know what He means too.

Let us not mock the titles and terms our Creator magnifies.

*"**God**, who at various times and in various ways spoke in time past to the fathers by the prophets, has in these last days **spoken to us by His Son**, whom He has appointed heir of all things, through whom also He made the worlds; who being the brightness of His glory and the express image of His person, and upholding all things by **the word** of His power...."* (Hebrews 1:1-3)

God wants us to know that He has *"spoken to us by **His Son**."* He also wants us to understand that *His Son* is *the Word* by which all things in heaven and earth were created and are sustained. In Arabic translations of the Bible, the Son's title as *"the Word of God"* is translated *"Kalimat Allah,"* a title both the Bible and Qur'an ascribe to the Messiah. Later in our journey, we'll take a closer look at this.

THE SPIRIT OF GOD

Even as God is One with *His Word-Son*, so He is One with *His Holy Spirit*.

The Holy Spirit of God was involved both in creating the world and in inspiring God's written Word. The second sentence of the Bible declares that, when God created the world, *"the Spirit of God was hovering over the face of the waters."* And later the Scripture states: *"Prophecy never had its origin in the will of man, but men spoke from God as they were carried along by* **the Holy Spirit.** *"* (2 Peter 1:21 NIV)

Some people teach that the Holy Spirit is the angel Gabriel. Others have convinced themselves that the Spirit of God is a prophet. Such conclusions do not come from the Scriptures of the prophets. Angels and men are created beings. The Holy Spirit is the uncreated, *"eternal Spirit."* (Hebrews 9:14)[110]

The Holy Spirit is *"the Spirit of truth"* (John 14:17), by whom God carries out His purposes in the world. He is *"the Helper"* (John 14:16) who reveals God in a close and experiential way to all who believe God's message. Many people on earth today know *about* God without *knowing God*. Such knowledge does not satisfy God or man. It is the Holy Spirit who makes it possible for people to enjoy a personal relationship with God. Later, we will learn more about God's wonderful Holy Spirit.[111]

How goes the journey? A bit overwhelming? These are not easy-to-grasp thoughts. Some people claim their religion and definition of God must be true "because it is so simple." Their definition of God may be simple, but God is not simple.

> *"'My thoughts are not your thoughts, nor are your ways My ways,' says the LORD."* (Isaiah 55:8)

FOREVER ONE

The Scriptures are clear. There has never been a time in all eternity when the Father, Son, and Holy Spirit did not exist.[112] They have always been ONE. In the context of human history, the Scriptures reveal the *Father* as the One who speaks from *heaven*, the *Son* as the One who spoke on *earth* and the *Holy Spirit* as the One who speaks to the *heart*.[113] Each is distinct in His role, yet they are ONE.

It is as people grow in the knowledge of God's revelation of Himself that they begin to delight in the richness of the ONE who is love and who shows His infinite love in practical ways.

Love can only exist in a meaningful way in the context of a relationship. The Father, the Son, and the Holy Spirit have always enjoyed an interactive relationship of perfect love and unity. Elsewhere in Scripture, we hear the Son saying, *"I love the Father"* and *"the Father loves the Son."* The Scripture also declares that *"the fruit of the Spirit is love."* (John 5:20; 14:31; Galatians 5:22)

The best of human relationships—such as the oneness between a man and his wife, or the bond between father, mother, and child—flow out of *who God is*. Such earthly relationships, at their very best, are but faint reflections of God's awe-inspiring oneness and love. Our Creator is the original source, pattern, and purpose of all that is good.

> *"God is love."* (1 John 4:8)

The best part about *"God is love"* is that He invites you and me to enjoy a close relationship with Him forever! He simply wants our trust, even though He cannot be fully explained.

GOD IS TRUSTWORTHY

Think back over what we observed about God from the six days of creation. As a mathematical equation, it looks like this:

$$
\begin{aligned}
& \text{Day 1: God is } \textit{holy} \\
&+\ \text{Day 2: God is } \textit{almighty} \\
&+\ \text{Day 3: God is } \textit{good} \\
&+\ \text{Day 4: God is } \textit{faithful} \\
&+\ \text{Day 5: God is } \textit{life} \\
&\underline{+\ \text{Day 6: God is } \textit{love}} \\
&=\ \textit{TRUSTWORTHY GOD}
\end{aligned}
$$

Isn't it strange that we are quick to trust people who fall short in these qualities, yet we are reluctant to trust the One who possesses these attributes in perfection?

When I drop a letter in the mailbox, I trust the postal service to deliver that letter. How much more should I be able to trust the Creator-Sustainer-Owner of the universe to keep His promises!

*"If we receive the witness of men, **the witness of God is greater**... he who does not believe God has made Him a liar, because he has not believed the testimony that God has given of His Son."* (1 John 5:9-10)

GOD'S PERSONAL NAME

God wants us to know Him, trust Him, and call on His name.

*"Those who **know Your name** will put their **trust in You;** for You, **LORD**, have not forsaken those who seek You."*
(Psalm 9:10)

Many people think that God's name is simply *"God"*—or *Elohim* (Hebrew) or *Allah* (Arabic[114]) or *Alaha* (Aramaic) or *Dieu* (French) or *Dios* (Spanish) or *Gott* (German), or whatever generic term is used in the language they speak.

Indeed, God is God (the Supreme Being), but is "God" His *name*? Would that not be like me saying my name is "Human"? I am a human, but I also have a personal name. God is God, but He also has names by which He has revealed Himself and by which He invites us to address Him as a Person.

Many imagine God to be some kind of unknowable source of energy like gravity and wind, or like "the Force" portrayed in a popular series of science fiction films. This is not the Biblical concept of God.

God is the Ultimate Personality who wants you to know Him in a personal way.

Not only is the concept of God as a personality Biblical, it is logical. Just as humans are not mere balls of cosmic energy, neither is the One who made all things. He is a Personal Being with a name.

God's primary personal name is first revealed in the second chapter of Genesis.

*"This is the history of the heavens and the earth when they were created, in the day that **the LORD** God made the earth and the heavens."* (Genesis 2:4)

Did you notice the name by which God refers to Himself? His name is *"the LORD."* At least that is how it has been translated into English. Thankfully, God is fluent in all languages and does not require us to address Him in any one particular language. He invites us to speak to Him in our mother tongue, at any time, in any place, facing any direction, in our heart language.

I AM

In Hebrew, God's primary personal name, *"the LORD,"* is written with four consonants: **YHWH**. When vowels are added, it is pronounced as *YaHWeH* or *YeHoWaH*. The name is derived from the Hebrew verb *"to be"* and literally means *"I AM"* or *"HE IS."* This teaches us that God is *the Self-Existent Eternal One.* This personal name of God is used more than 6,500 times in the Old Testament, more than any other name of God.

Listen to what God declared, when Moses, who had been raised in polytheistic Egypt, asked God to tell him His name.

> *"God said to Moses, 'I AM WHO I AM.' And He said, 'Thus you shall say to the children of Israel, 'I AM has sent me to you.'"* (Exodus 3:14)

Only a personal being can say "I am." God wants us to understand that He is the Ultimate Person.

He is *the One who IS.*

Past, present, and future are nothing to Him. His existence transcends time and space.

He is self-sufficient.

You and I need air, water, food, sleep, housing, and other elements to live, but He needs nothing. He is the One who reasons and exists by His own power. He is the Great *I AM*—the LORD. (Note: In the English Bible, whenever the name *LORD* appears in capital letters, the original Hebrew word for *LORD* is *YHWH*, meaning *the Self-Existing Eternal One.*)

God has not left it up to man to define Him.

He is the self-defining One.

HUNDREDS OF NAMES

In His eternal existence as Father, Son and Holy Spirit, the LORD bears hundreds of names and titles. God's names reflect His character. Each title is intended to help us better understand who God is and what He is like. For example, He is called:

The Creator of Heaven and Earth, the Author of Life, the Most High, the True Light, the Holy One, the Righteous Judge, the LORD who Provides, the LORD who Heals, the LORD our Righteousness, the LORD our Peace, the LORD my Shepherd, the God of Love and Peace, the God of All Grace, the Author of Eternal Salvation, the God who is Near at Hand...

Whatever our present understanding of our Creator, each of us should humbly admit that *He is God and **there is none like Him***. Even though He cannot be fully explained or understood, He wants us to know His name and to trust Him, love Him, and live forever with Him. It was with this purpose in mind that God said:

"Let Us make man in Our image, according to Our likeness." (Genesis 1:26)

What did He mean? How could visible man bear the image of the invisible God?

10

A SPECIAL CREATION

T wo chapters ago, we reflected on one of the greatest declarations of all time: *"In the beginning God created the heavens and the earth."* (Genesis 1:1) Here is another:

"God created man in His own image." (Genesis 1:27)

God designed humans to be the crown of His creation.

IN THE IMAGE OF GOD

*"Then God said, 'Let Us make man in **Our image**, according to **Our likeness**; let them have **dominion** over the fish of the sea, over the birds of the air, and over the cattle, over all the earth and over every creeping thing that creeps on the earth.' **So God created man in His own image; in the image of God He created him; male and female He created them**."* (Genesis 1:26-27)

God creating man *"in His own image"* does *not* mean the first humans were like God in every way. God has no equal.

*"God created man **in His own image**"* means that humans would *share in God's nature.* Man was designed to reflect God's character. God gave the first man and woman characteristics that would allow them to enjoy a meaningful relationship with Him.

God blessed humans with an *intellect*, giving them the ability to ask big questions, reason logically, and grasp deep truths about their Creator.

God made them with *emotions* so they could experience feelings such as joy and empathy.

He also gave them a *will*, which included both the freedom and the responsibility to make choices of eternal consequence.

Further, He endowed them with the ability to communicate—to speak, gesture, and sing. He also enabled them to make long-term plans and to carry out those plans with amazing creativity. Most importantly, He entrusted them with *an eternal soul and spirit* so they might worship and enjoy their Creator-Owner forever.

Such capacities set mankind apart from the animal kingdom.

God created humans *for Himself.* The God who *"is love"* (1 John 4:8) created man and woman, not because He *needed* them, but because He *wanted* them. People would become the recipients and reflectors of His love.

THE HUMAN BODY

While chapter 1 of Genesis presents a concise history of how God created the world, chapter 2 fills in the details, particularly with regard to the creation of humans.

"The LORD God formed man of the dust of the ground and breathed into his nostrils the breath of life; and man became a living being." (Genesis 2:7)

Although the LORD created the heavens and the earth from nothing, He chose to create the first man from *dust*. Present day biologists affirm this fact: "In a way, the body seems almost unimpressive. The twenty-odd commonplace elements that compose it are all present in the earth's dry *dust*."[115]

While the human body is composed of such lowly elements, it is a miraculous piece of craftsmanship put together with approximately seventy-five trillion (75,000,000,000,000) living cells—each with its specific role to play.

The cell is the basic unit of life. A cell is so small that it can only be seen under a powerful microscope, yet it is packed with millions of working parts. Each cell contains a two-meter-long (six foot) microscopic twisted strand of DNA, the genetic code for a person's basic features.

Bill Gates, the famous computer software guru, stated, "Human DNA is like a computer program but far, far more advanced than any software ever created."[116] There are at least 200 different types of cells in the human body. Some make liquids such as blood, others create soft tissues and organs, while still others unite to make hard bones. Some cells bind body parts together, while others organize the body's functions, such as the digestive and reproductive systems.[117]

Think of your body's structure and working parts: the skeleton with its 206 bones bound and garnished with ligaments, tendons, muscles, skin and hair; or the circulatory system with veins, arteries and blood, transporting the ingredients of life itself. Then there is the stomach, intestines, kidneys and liver. There is also the intricately-wired nervous system connected to your brain. And don't forget the faithful pump called the heart, or that God has provided you with eyes, ears, a nose, mouth and tongue, along with vocal cords, taste buds and teeth! Those feet and hands are rather useful too! And have you ever thanked God for giving you thumbs? Try to use a broom or hammer without one! Those fingernails come in pretty handy too...

No wonder the prophet David wrote,

"I will praise You, for I am fearfully and wonderfully made; Marvelous are Your works, and that my soul knows very well!" (Psalm 139:14)

SOUL AND SPIRIT

As marvelous as the human body is, it is not the body that makes humans so special. Animals, birds, and fish have amazing bodies too. Man's uniqueness is found in his *human soul* and *eternal spirit*. It is the soul and spirit that set apart the first man and woman as special beings made *"in the image of God."*

Thus, once God finished forming man's body from dust, He *"breathed into his nostrils the breath of life; and man became a living being."* (Genesis 2:7) The body God made for Adam was merely the housing, or tent, into which God placed Adam's eternal spirit and soul.

God gave man a body so that he could be aware of the world around him, a soul so that man could be aware of his inner self, and a spirit so that man could be aware of God.

The *body* was to be governed by the soul,
the *soul* was to be governed by the spirit,
and the *spirit* was to be governed by God Himself. [118]

> *"**God is Spirit**, and those who worship Him must worship in **spirit and truth**."* (John 4:24)

CREATED FOR A PURPOSE

The Master Craftsman created man to be a kind of tri-unity, linking *"spirit, soul, and body"* (1 Thessalonians 5:23) and making it possible for humans to enjoy close friendship with their Creator. God had given life to man and now it would be man's exalted privilege to live for the pleasure and praise of his Creator-Owner.

> *"**Everyone who is called by My name, whom I have created for My glory**... This people I have formed for **Myself**; they shall declare **My praise**."* (Isaiah 43:7,21)

Humans were created for God's glory.

The earth was made for mankind, but mankind was made for God. The Creator's intent was that the first humans might know Him, enjoy Him, and love Him forever. That is also His intent for you and me.

> *"You shall **love the LORD your God** with all your **heart**, with all your **soul**, with all your **mind**, and with all your **strength**."* (Mark 12:30)

A PERFECT ENVIRONMENT

After God created Adam, He planned and planted a luxuriant garden called *Eden.*

"The LORD God planted a garden eastward in Eden, and there He put the man whom He had formed. And out of the ground the LORD God made every tree grow that is pleasant to the sight and good for food. The tree of life was also in the midst of the garden, and the tree of the knowledge of good and evil. Now a river went out of Eden to water the garden, and from there it parted and became four riverheads." (Genesis 2:8-10)

Eden, probably located in the land known today as Iraq[119], was a vast garden of endless delights, filled with wonderful sights, sounds, and smells. The garden was watered by a sparkling river. Luscious fruit trees lined its banks. There were untold varieties of fruits to be tasted, sweet-smelling flowers to be appreciated, towering trees and lush meadows to be gazed on, beasts, birds and bugs to be studied, mysterious woods to be explored, gold and precious stones to be discovered. Indeed, God had provided for Adam *"richly all things to enjoy."* (1 Timothy 6:17)

God also planted two special trees in the middle of the garden: the tree of life and the tree of the knowledge of good and evil.

Eden means *pleasure.* God had created this wonderful home for man's enjoyment, but the greatest of all pleasures would be for man to enjoy fellowship with his Creator.

Nothing is more wonderful than knowing God personally and being with Him. *"**In Your presence** is fullness of joy; **at Your right hand** are pleasures forevermore."* (Psalm 16:11)

A SATISFYING TASK

Once the garden was ready, the LORD put man in it. God didn't ask Adam if he wanted to live there. God was man's Maker and therefore man's Owner. The LORD knows what is best for mankind and doesn't have to answer to anyone for what He does.

"Then the LORD God took the man and put him in the garden of Eden to tend and keep it." (Genesis 2:15)

God gave Adam two responsibilities in his new home.

First, he was *"to tend"* the garden, but without sweat, toil and tiredness. It would be a thoroughly enjoyable task, since everything was good. There were no thorns to get pricked on and no weeds to pull.

Second, Adam was given the responsibility to *"keep it."* Could this last phrase hint of some malevolent, dangerous element lurking in the universe?

That question will be answered soon enough.

A SIMPLE RULE

Since man was a person and not a puppet, God also gave Adam one straightforward rule to obey.

> *"The LORD God commanded the man, saying, 'Of every tree of the garden **you may freely eat**; but of the tree of the knowledge of good and evil **you shall not eat**, for in the day that you eat of it you shall surely die.'"*
> (Genesis 2:16-17)

God gave the man this command before He created the woman. God had appointed Adam to be the head of the human race and God held Adam responsible to uphold this one rule.

THE FIRST WOMAN

Next, God created the woman. And what a special creation she was!

> *"The LORD God said, 'It is not good for the man to be alone. I will make a helper suitable for him.' ...So the LORD God caused the man to fall into a deep sleep; and while he was sleeping, he took one of the man's ribs and closed up the place with flesh. Then the LORD God made a woman from the rib he had taken out of the man, and*

he brought her to the man. The man said, 'This is now bone of my bones and flesh of my flesh; she shall be called 'woman,' for she was taken out of man.' For this reason a man will leave his father and mother and be united to his wife, and they will become one flesh. The man and his wife were both naked, and they felt no shame."
(Genesis 2:18,21-25 NIV)

Thus, God performed the first operation, fashioning from Adam's side a beautiful and lovely wife and then personally presenting her to Adam.

How Adam rejoiced in the close and loving companion and *"helper"* God had provided for him! The late Biblical scholar Matthew Henry wrote, "The woman was made... out of the side of Adam; not made out of his head to rule over him, nor out of his feet to be trampled upon by him, but out of his side to be equal with him, under his arm to be protected, and near his heart to be beloved."[120]

Like the man, the woman was made *in the image and likeness of God*—created to reflect the LORD's character and enjoy spiritual oneness with Him forever. While the Creator established definite order and distinctive roles for the man and the woman, He declared them equal in value and importance.

Today, contrary to God's intention, many societies treat their women like a piece of property. I have seen people celebrate when a male child is born and express disappointment when a female is born. Some men show more care and concern for their livestock than for their wife. Some societies have gone to another extreme, choosing to ignore the distinct male-female roles and responsibilities God has assigned to each. Both extremes degrade women.

THE FIRST WEDDING

Notice who officiated the first marriage ceremony.

It was *the LORD*. The Scripture says, *"He brought her to the man."* From the start, the Creator was directly involved in the lives of the people He had created for Himself. He is the One who declared that *"a man will leave his father and mother and be united to his wife, and they will become one flesh."* The Hebrew word used for *"one"* is *echad*, denoting oneness and unity. God designed the first couple to enjoy and serve one another, *and* to enjoy and serve HIM, forever in perfect harmony. He wanted the man and woman to make their Creator-Owner the nucleus of their lives—individually and corporately.

Tragically, in our present world, most people ignore God's original blueprint for marriage and are clueless as to how increasingly wonderful the relationship between one man and one woman can be as the years go by. As a result, they fail to reflect the loving, faithful, unselfish, and cherished relationship that the LORD, from the beginning, intended for a man and his wife.

The Creator's authorship of marriage between man and wife is a reflection of God's immeasurable heart of love. God intends for the bond of marriage to illustrate the even closer, more wonderful, growing, *spiritual* relationship He invites people to enjoy with Him now and throughout eternity.

Did you notice how the Author of marriage defines marriage? *"For this reason a man will leave his father and mother and be **united** to his wife, and they will **become one flesh."** And the Scripture adds: *"The man and his wife were both naked, and they felt **no shame**."*

God's plan for marriage is for a couple to be united in purpose and in body, free from shame. On an even higher plane, God's plan was for people to shamelessly enjoy *spiritual* oneness with HIM throughout eternity.

MANKIND GIVEN DOMINION

After God presented the woman to the man, He spoke to them directly and personally. It seems that God appeared to them in a visible kind of way, since the Scripture speaks of *"the LORD God **walking** in the garden."* (Genesis 3:8)

Now imagine the Lord leading the man and his wife up a high mountain from where they could gaze over their Creator's glorious, pristine creation...

"Then God blessed them, and God said to them, 'Be fruitful and multiply; fill the earth and subdue it; have dominion over the fish of the sea, over the birds of the air, and over every living thing that moves on the earth.' And God said, 'See, I have given you every herb that yields seed which is on the face of all the earth, and every tree whose fruit yields seed; to you it shall be for food.'"
(Genesis 1:28-29)

God put Adam and Eve[121] and their descendants in charge of His creation. He gave them the privilege and responsibility of being the "starter couple" of the human race. He granted them *"dominion"* over all creation. *Dominion* means *"authority"* and *control.* Adam and Eve and their offspring were to enjoy, care for, and wisely rule the earth. They were to use it but not abuse it.

The Creator designed creation to be in harmony with mankind. In the beginning, the earth cooperated with whatever man wanted or needed. Adam and Eve never had to wonder about where their next meal would come from. All they had to do was reach up and pick a delicious piece of fruit from any of the countless varieties of fruit trees. Hard soil, weeds and thorns, sickness and death were non-existent. Every corner of creation was submitted to Adam and Eve. Man had dominion.

Creation would be in submission to man as long as man was in submission to his Creator.

GOD AND MAN TOGETHER

From the beginning, the LORD God intended for humans to live in close, sweet fellowship with Himself. That is why He gave Adam and Eve *minds* and *hearts* (intellect and emotions) with which to understand and love Him, and freedom of *choice* (a will) with which to decide whether or not to trust Him and obey Him. The element of choice was absolutely necessary since true love and loyalty cannot be coerced. The Sovereign Lord would hold Adam and Eve responsible for their choices.

Make no mistake about it: though the Creator and Owner of the universe needs nothing and no one, He is deeply relational.

Just as we want to be known and loved, so God wants to be known and loved by the people He made for Himself. It is part of His eternal nature to desire a heart-level friendship with those He created *"in His image."*

I hear people say, "I am God's slave and nothing more!" Admittedly, it is an immense honor to serve God as a willing servant works for his master, but the Scriptures are clear: God's design was never that man should be *"a slave, but a **son**."* (Galatians 4:7) *"A **slave** does not abide in the house forever, but a **son** abides forever."* (John 8:35) God, expressing His heart's desire anthropomorphically (in human terms), tells us what He has planned for all who trust Him:

> *"**I will be a Father to you,** and **you shall be My sons and daughters,** says the LORD Almighty."* (2 Corinthians 6:18)

What's more, God does not stop at likening His love for us to the love parents have for their children. Our Creator takes the imagery to another level, comparing the bond and depth of His love for people with the love a man has for his beloved bride.

> *"'It shall be, in that day,' says the LORD, 'that you will call Me '**My Husband,**' and no longer call Me 'My Master,' ... **I will betroth you to Me forever;** Yes, I will betroth you to Me in righteousness and justice, in lovingkindness and mercy; I will betroth you to Me in faithfulness, **And you shall know the LORD.**'"* (Hosea 2:16,19-20)

Imagine the most satisfying relationship possible between two individuals on earth, and then reflect on this: The relationship God invites us to experience with Him is infinitely more wonderful than the best possible human relationship on earth.

Apart from entering into a personal relationship with your Creator, your life will be incomplete and unsatisfying. No amount of earthly possessions, pleasure, prestige, people, or prayers can fill the void in your soul. Only the LORD can occupy the empty room in your heart that He designed for Himself.

*"**He satisfies** the longing **soul**, and fills the hungry **soul** with goodness."* (Psalm 107:9)

Here is a point not to be missed: The one true God does not delight in the *rituals of religion*, but in a *genuine relationship* with those who trust Him.

At varying levels, God has enjoyed and will forever enjoy fellowship with:

- HIMSELF. For all eternity, love and fellowship has flowed between the Eternal Father, the Eternal Son, and the Eternal Holy Spirit. For example, the Scriptures record the Son saying to the Father, *"Father... You loved Me before the foundation of the world."* (John 17:24)
- ANGELS. He created angelic beings to know Him and love Him, and appreciate His awesome glory forever. *"Let all the angels of God worship Him."* (Hebrews 1:6)
- PEOPLE. God created humans to one day have a closer relationship with their Creator than even the angels enjoy. King David wrote: *"When I consider Your heavens, the work of Your fingers, the moon and the stars, which You have ordained, what is man that You are mindful of him, and the son of man that You visit him? For You have made him a little lower than the angels, and You have crowned him with glory and honor."* (Psalm 8:3-5) God wanted to be with His people. However, man must first be tested.

DAY 7: CREATION FINISHED

The creation narrative concludes with an important piece of information:

*"Then God saw everything that He had made, and indeed it was **very good**. So the evening and the morning were the sixth day. Thus the heavens and the earth, and all the host of them, were **finished**. And on the seventh day God ended His work which He had **done**, and He rested on the seventh day from all His work which He had **done**."* (Genesis 1:31; 2:1-2)

God's creative work was *done*. It was time to rejoice in all He had made. The LORD did not rest on the seventh day because IIe was tired. The self-existing One whose name means *"I AM"* is never tired. God rested—ceased working—because His creative work was *finished*.

The LORD God was satisfied.

Everything was perfect.

Imagine a perfect world inhabited by two perfect people who had been privileged to enjoy a growing friendship with their perfect Creator. That was the state of our planet in the beginning.

Alas, today this old earth is far from perfect. Evil and immorality, grief and pain, poverty and hunger, hatred and violence, and disease and death abound.

What happened to God's perfect world?

That is the next part of the story.

11

EVIL'S ENTRANCE

*"Praise the LORD, O my soul, and forget not all **his benefits**...*
*Praise the LORD, you **his angels**...who obey **his word**.*
*Praise the LORD, all **his heavenly hosts**...who do **his will**.*
*Praise the LORD, all **his works** everywhere in **his dominion**...!"*
— King David (Psalm 103:2,20-22 NIV)

B efore God made humans, He created an innumerable host of spirit beings called *angels*. God made them for His pleasure and praise. They were *"all **HIS** heavenly hosts,"* purposefully designed to know, enjoy, serve, and exalt their Creator-Owner forever. God did not create angels to be like animals, which operate mainly on instinct. As with mankind, God gave angels the moral obligation to choose for themselves whether or not they would obey His word, do His will, and praise Him.

THE SHINING ONE

The most powerful and privileged spirit-being was named *Lucifer,* meaning, *the shining one.*[122] This brilliant angel is described as *"the seal of perfection, full of wisdom and perfect in beauty."* (Ezekiel 28:12)

While God has not revealed all the details, we know that it was through this magnificent angelic being that evil and imperfection first entered the universe.

God says of Lucifer,

"You were perfect from the day you were created, till
iniquity was found in you! ...Your heart was lifted up
because of your beauty. ... For you have said in your heart:
    'I will ascend into heaven,
        I will exalt my throne above the stars of God;
        I will also sit on... the farthest sides of the north;
        I will ascend above the heights of the clouds,
        I will be like the Most High.'"
                              (Ezekiel 28:14,17; Isaiah 14:13-14)

Instead of praising and obeying God, five times Lucifer said,
"I will!" He wanted to *"be like the Most High."*

Blinded by his own beauty and intelligence, and forgetting
WHO had given him everything he had, this angelic being deceived
himself into thinking he was wiser than God. He wanted the host
of angels to praise *him* instead of the Creator, who alone is worthy
of worship and praise.

Lucifer also persuaded a third of the angels of heaven to join
forces with him in his revolt.[123]

Thus, *the shining one* schemed to topple God's dominion and
to sit on the throne of heaven.

Sin had entered God's universe.

WHAT IS SIN?

The Scriptures define sin for us.

* *"Sin is **lawlessness**."* (1 John 3:4)
* *"All **unrighteousness** is sin."* (1 John 5:17)
* Sin is to *"know...to do good and...**not do it**."* (James 4:17)
* Sin produces *"all manner of **evil desire**."* (Romans 7:8)
* Sin is to *"**fall short** of the glory of God."* (Romans 3:23)

"The glory of God" refers to God's absolute purity and
flawless perfection. To *"fall short"* means to miss "the bull's eye"
on the target of perfect righteousness.

Sin is failure to live in complete conformity to the holy nature
and will of God.

In its distilled form, *sin* is whenever an eternal being, whether angelic or human, chooses to exalt self and *turn "to his own way"* (Isaiah 53:6), instead of exalting and following God's way.

To think or act independently of God is *sin*.

That was the path chosen by Lucifer and the angels who sympathized with him. Instead of depending on their Creator, they became proud in heart and turned to their own way.

*"Everyone **proud in heart** is an **abomination** to the LORD; though they join forces, none will go unpunished."*
(Proverbs 16:5)

Abomination is a strong word, meaning *"an object of disgust, a detestable act, a pollution, or idolatry."* God hates self-centered pride. It is sin.

Allowing sin to reside in His presence is more nauseating to God than a rotting pig carcass in your house would be to you. A single sin is as unacceptable to God as a single drop of poison in my tea would be to me. Why are we unable to tolerate a putrid carcass in our house or a drop of poison in our tea?

Such things go against our nature.

Sin goes against God's nature.

"Are You not from everlasting, O LORD my God, my Holy One? ...You are of purer eyes than to behold evil, and cannot look on wickedness." (Habakkuk 1:11,13)

SATAN, DEMONS, AND HELL

Because Lucifer wanted to steal God's glory and usurp His authority, God expelled him from his place in the highest heaven, along with the angels who chose to side with him. Lucifer's name was changed to *Satan*, meaning ***"adversary."*** He is also called *the devil*, meaning ***"accuser."*** The fallen angels became known as evil spirits or *demons*, meaning ***"knowing ones."***

The devil and his demons know who God is and tremble before Him, nevertheless they are doing all they can to defeat Him.

But they will not win.

The Scripture foretells that, on a pre-appointed day, Satan and his demons will be cast into *"the eternal fire prepared for the devil and his angels."* (Matthew 25:41) This *"eternal fire"* is a real place where God will forever quarantine all that is not conformed to His holy nature.

One of the words in the Greek New Testament used to describe the place of punishment for those who join forces with Satan is *gehenna*, often translated *"hell."*[124] This word literally means *"a burning garbage dump."*

Not far from where my wife and I raised our children in Senegal was a dumping ground where people would throw their trash and refuse. The dump was often smoldering as those living nearby would attempt to burn the foul-smelling garbage. Anything considered worthless was tossed into the fire.

Hell is God's "garbage dump" where the departed dead who die in their sins are presently being held. One day, Satan, his demons, and all the inhabitants of hell will be tossed into a final place of judgment called *the lake of fire and brimstone.*[125]

Sin will not pollute God's universe forever.

SATAN'S OBJECTIVE

As for the devil and his demons, they are not yet in the lake of fire. Rather, they are at work in our world. The Scriptures identify Satan as *"the prince of the power of the air, the spirit that now works in the sons of disobedience."* (Ephesians 2:2)

It is important to understand that though Satan is powerful, he is not *all*-powerful. He is a created being and a fallen one at that. The devil is no match for the LORD. Satan is called *"the god of this age."* His goal is to prevent people from knowing the one true God and from embracing the purpose for which they were created.

> *"If our gospel* [God's good news of salvation] *is veiled, it is veiled to those who are perishing, **whose minds the god of this age has blinded**, who do not believe, lest the light of the gospel...should shine on them."* (2 Corinthians 4:3-4)

What is Satan's objective? He seeks to blind minds and keep people from hearing and believing God's message. He is at war with God. It is a war which Satan cannot win, but he is doing all he can to take down with him as many as possible. And he hopes that will include you.

Knowing Adam and Eve had been created for God's glory and pleasure, Satan plotted to spoil the friendship that existed between God and man. Of course, the LORD God, who *"knows the secrets of the heart"* (Psalm 44:21), knew everything the devil planned to do and all that was about to happen.

God had a plan of His own.

ONE RULE

God gave man freedom to choose whether or not to love, praise, and obey his Creator. True love cannot be forced or preprogrammed. Love involves a person's mind, heart, and will. While it is true that God is the Sovereign King over His universe, it is also true that He holds man responsible for making choices of eternal impact.

Even before God created the woman, God gave the man a command. Since Adam would be the head of the human race, God put the test before him.

> *"The LORD God commanded the man, saying, 'Of every tree of the garden you may freely eat; but of the tree of the knowledge of good and evil you shall not eat, for in the day that you eat of it you shall surely die.'"* (Genesis 2:16-17)

Notice God's simple instructions. Adam could freely partake of all the delicious fruits from the abundant trees in the garden, *except one*. God told Adam what would happen if he disobeyed. *"In the day that you eat of it **you shall surely die.**"*

To cross over that line would be to *trespass*, another term for *sin*. As in Lucifer's case, rebellion against the Lord of the universe would result in solemn consequences.

Although the first man was perfect, he was not perfectly mature. With this one rule, man was given the chance to grow in his relationship with his Creator. God wanted Adam to choose to obey Him from a heart of gratitude and love. That should have been easy enough, considering all God had done for him.

Think of it! God had given Adam a body, soul, and spirit. He blessed him with the privilege of reflecting his Creator's holy and loving nature. He placed him in a glorious garden and provided every benefit imaginable to make his life one of pure joy and satisfaction. God also gave him the freedom and capacity to make responsible choices. He gave Adam a lovely wife and committed to them the oversight and care of the created world. Best of all, the LORD Himself would come into the garden to walk and talk with Adam and Eve. God gave them the opportunity to get to know their Creator-Owner. It was a perfect world.

Then one day the serpent showed up.

"HAS GOD INDEED SAID?"

It is in Genesis chapter three that the most tragic and far-reaching event in human history is recorded.

One day as Eve and Adam were near the forbidden tree, Satan appeared to them in the subtle form of a serpent. We know it was Satan because later the Scripture identifies him as *"that serpent of old, called the Devil and Satan, who deceives the whole world."* (Revelation 12:9)

Just as God had a plan for mankind, so did Satan.

> *"Now the serpent was more cunning than any beast of the field which the LORD God had made. And he said to the woman, 'Has God indeed said, 'You shall not eat of every tree of the garden'?'"* (Genesis 3:1-2)

Satan chose to speak with the woman rather than the man. Did you hear the first thing he said to Eve?

"Has God indeed said...?"

Satan wanted Eve to *not* believe **God's word**. He wanted her to question God's wisdom and authority. He dared Eve to challenge her Creator, just as he, Lucifer, had done. To this day, the devil fights against the truth, because it discredits and disarms him. As light dispels darkness, so God's Word dispels Satan's deceit.

Satan also attacked God's character by encouraging Eve to doubt *God's goodness*.

> *"Has God indeed said, 'You shall not eat of every tree of the garden'?"*

Satan distorted God's word, as if their generous Maker, who had given them life and the right to freely eat from all trees but one, wanted to keep them from ultimate good.

"YOU WILL NOT SURELY DIE!"

> *"The woman said to the serpent, 'We may eat the fruit of the trees of the garden; but of the fruit of the tree which is in the midst of the garden, God has said, 'You shall not eat it, nor shall you touch it, lest you die.'*
>
> *Then the serpent said to the woman, 'You will not surely die. For God knows that in the day you eat of it your eyes will be opened, and you will be like God, knowing good and evil.'"* (Genesis 3:3-5)

Not only did the devil want Eve to doubt God's word and goodness, he also wanted her to doubt *God's righteousness*, as though God would not actually impose the death penalty if she tasted the forbidden fruit.

God had made it clear:

> *"In the day you eat of it you will surely die!"* (Genesis 2:17)

Satan denied it, saying, "You will *not* surely die!"

Satan's basic method has not changed. He continues to *distort* and *deny* God's message. He wants us to *doubt God's Word, goodness, and righteousness*.

Satan wants us to believe that God cannot be trusted, that He is not really who He claims to be.

THE VERY RELIGIOUS DEVIL

The devil is extremely fond of religion. It is for that reason there are more than ten thousand religions in the world today. Notice how Satan pretended to speak for God by telling Eve, *"**God** knows that in the day you eat of it your eyes will be opened."*

Satan likes to impersonate the Almighty. He is an expert at taking God's truth and mixing it with his own lies. He is the great syncretist, imitator, and counterfeiter. Even the most bizarre belief systems in the world contain hints of truth. That is what makes them believable. Again, the Arab proverb states it well: *"Beware: some liars tell the truth!"*

In his first effort to start a counterfeit religion, Satan told Eve, *"You will be like God, knowing good and evil."* When Satan told Eve, *"You will be like God,"* he spoke a *lie*, because the one who sins is not like God but like Satan who wants to usurp God's authority. However, when Satan said, *"You will know good and evil,"* he spoke *truth*, but he did not tell them about the bitterness, suffering, and death that would accompany such knowledge.

Notice that Satan, in speaking of the LORD, only used the generic term *God*. Satan is quite happy if you believe in one God, as long as you perceive that God to be distant and unknowable.

"You believe that there is one God. You do well. Even the demons believe—and tremble!" (James 2:19)

The devil and his demons are all monotheists who tremble before Almighty God. This will be revealed with shocking clarity several chapters from now. Satan and his fallen angels know that there is only one true God, but oh, how they hate Him!

They do not want *you* to know, love, worship, and obey your Creator-Owner.

THE CHOICE

The moment had arrived for Adam and Eve to choose between the word of their loving Lord and the word of their archenemy.

The formula for victory was obvious: *Trust the wisdom of the Creator.* How simple! All Adam and Eve had to do was quote God's inspired, inerrant Word, saying, "The LORD God commanded us: *'Of the tree of the knowledge of good and evil you shall not eat.'* We will not eat from it! Period."

Had Adam and Eve stood firm on God's unchanging word, the tempter would have fled. But that is not what they did.

> *"So when the woman saw that the tree was good for food, that it was pleasant to the eyes, and a tree desirable to make one wise, she took of its fruit and ate. She also gave to her husband with her, and he ate."* (Genesis 3:6)

She ate it. He ate it.

Instead of submitting to the word and will of their holy and loving Creator, they submitted to God's enemy. They trespassed into the forbidden realm.

Once Adam tasted the unlawful fruit, the consequences were immediate.

> *"Then the eyes of both of them were opened, and they knew that they were naked; and they sewed fig leaves together and made themselves coverings. And they heard the sound of the LORD God walking in the garden in the cool of the day, and Adam and his wife hid themselves from the presence of the LORD God among the trees of the garden."* (Genesis 3:7-8)

Notice the change. Instead of rejoicing when the Lord came to visit them, they were now filled with fear and shame.

What caused these intimately relational beings to want to run from their loving Lord? What made them imagine they could hide from their all-seeing Creator? Why did our first parents feel the need to cover their bodies with leaves?

They had sinned.

12

THE LAW OF
SIN AND DEATH

*"Whoever commits sin is **a slave of sin.**"*
— Jesus of Nazareth (John 8:34)

Adam and Eve had disobeyed their Creator-Owner. Like Satan, they lost their connection with God and became slaves of sin. Like children who have disobeyed their father's clear command, Adam and Eve no longer wanted to be with the One who loved and cared for them. Feelings of delight and confidence had been displaced by feelings of fear, defilement, and shame.

> *"They heard the sound of the LORD God walking in the garden in the cool of the day, and Adam and his wife hid themselves from the presence of the LORD God among the trees of the garden."* (Genesis 3:8)

Adam and Eve were now contaminated by sin, causing them to want to hide from their Maker and Master. Their newly-acquired conscience gave them a sense of good and evil, instinctively teaching them that only holy people can live in the presence of a holy God. Adam and Eve were no longer pure before God and they knew it. The close bond between God and man was broken.
The relationship was dead.

A BROKEN BRANCH

One day, as I was chatting with some men under a tree near a mosque, the conversation turned to the subject of sin and death.

I broke a branch off the tree and asked them, "Is this branch dead or alive?"

One of the men answered, "It's dying."

Another said, "It is dead."

I chided him, "How can you say it's dead? Look how green it is!"

"It looks alive, but it's dead because it is separated from its source of life," he answered.

"Exactly," I replied. "You have just given an accurate definition of DEATH according to the Scriptures. DEATH is not annihilation, but *SEPARATION* from the Source of Life. That is why, when a loved one dies, even before the body is buried, we say, 'He's gone.' We say that because we know the person's spirit has left his body. *Death* means *separation*."

Next, I reviewed for the men the command God had given to Adam. Then I asked them, "What did God say would happen to Adam if he sinned against God? Did He tell Adam that if he ate of the forbidden fruit, he must start doing religious rituals, praying, fasting, giving alms, and attending a mosque or church?"

"No," they replied, "God said Adam would die."

"Right. God made it clear: the punishment for sin would be DEATH. But, tell me, after Adam and Eve disobeyed God and ate the forbidden fruit, did they fall over dead that same day?"

"No!" they answered.

"Well, then, what did God mean when He told Adam, 'In the day you eat of this fruit, you will surely die!'?"

From there I went on to tell the men about God's definition of death: a three-dimensional separation brought on by man's choice to disobey his Creator.

THE THREE-FOLD SEPARATION CAUSED BY SIN:

1.   Spiritual death: *SEPARATION of a person's spirit and soul from God.*

On the day Adam and Eve first sinned against God *they died spiritually*. Like a branch broken from the tree, Adam and Eve's close relationship with the LORD God had died. And the news gets worse. All of Adam and Eve's descendants are a part of that same spiritually dead "branch."

"In Adam all die...." (1 Corinthians 15:22)

Despite the clear teaching of the Scriptures, many people who concede that the human race descended from Adam also insist that newborn babies are born with a pure, sinless nature.

Consider again the severed branch. What part of it is "dead" as a result of being separated from the tree? The entire branch is dead, including the little twigs at its tip. If those twigs and leaves could talk, perhaps they would say something like, "Now wait a minute! It's not our fault the branch got broken from the tree! We are not affected by what someone else did!" But they are affected. Similarly, God's Word declares the entire human race to be *"in Adam."* Each of us are a part of the same separated, fallen "branch," and we suffer the consequences. Like it or not, when Adam sinned, he contaminated himself *and* the entire human family yet to come from him.

The village from which I write gets its water from the Senegal River located several kilometers away. Our village has a well, but no one drinks its water. Why not? The well is contaminated. Its water is saline. Every bucket of water drawn from this well is contaminated with salt. Not a drop is pure, no, not one.

In a similar way, every person born of Adam is contaminated with sin. That is why even little children sin—naturally. Sin is part of their nature. Being good and kind requires a conscious effort and struggle, whereas being selfish and hurtful involves no special effort. The prophet David explains why we sin instinctively:

"I was brought forth in iniquity, and in sin my mother conceived me." (Psalm 51:5) *"The wicked are estranged from the womb; they go astray as soon as they are born, speaking lies."* (Psalm 58:3) *"They have all turned aside, they have together become corrupt; there is none who does good, no, not one."* (Psalm 14:3)

The Wolof people of Senegal have several great proverbs which have helped some understand this truth. For example, they say, *"A rat does not beget offspring which do not dig."* Likewise, sin-tainted Adam could not beget offspring which do not sin.

Another proverb says, *"An epidemic does not confine itself to the one who caused it."* Tragic but true. Like an inherited birth defect or an infectious disease, Adam's sin nature has spread to us and our children.

*"**Through one man** sin entered the world, and death through sin, and thus **death spread to all** men, because **all sinned**."* (Romans 5:12)

Notice the first phrase: *"Through one man sin entered,"* and the last phrase: *"all sinned."* Each of us is a sinner by birth **and** by practice. We cannot blame Adam for sins we commit. The Scripture says:

*"**Your** iniquities have separated **you** from **your** God; and **your** sins have hidden His face from **you**."* (Isaiah 59:2)

Once a person is old enough to know right from wrong, God holds him or her responsible.[126] The entire human branch is separated from its Creator. Man is spiritually *"**dead in trespasses and sin**."* (Ephesians 2:1)

2. **Physical death:** *SEPARATION of a person's spirit and soul from his or her body.*

When Adam and Eve sinned, they not only died *spiritually*, they also began to die *physically*. Even as the leaves on a broken branch do not dry up instantly, so Adam and Eve's bodies did not drop dead the day they sinned. Nonetheless, their flesh had been invaded by death—an enemy from which they could not escape.

For Adam and Eve and their descendants, it was only a matter of time until physical death would catch up with them. *"Death rides a fast camel,"* says the Arab proverb. No one can escape Death. God's Word puts it like this:

> *"It is appointed for men to die once, but after this the judgment."* (Hebrews 9:27)

3. **Eternal death:** *SEPARATION of a person's spirit, soul, and body from God forever.*

A living branch is designed to bear leaves, flowers, and fruit. Dead branches are gathered and burned. When Adam sinned against God, he forfeited the privilege for which he was designed: to glorify God and live with Him throughout eternity. Man, created to exist forever, had disobeyed his infinite Creator-Owner. The penalty was *eternal* separation from God.

Unless the LORD in His mercy provided a remedy for Adam and Eve's sin, once their bodies died, they faced the horror of being forever quarantined in the "garbage dump" prepared for the devil and his demons. The Bible calls this *"the second death"* because it occurs after physical death. It is also called *"everlasting punishment."*[127] The notion of a temporary purgatory from which people will one day escape is the invention of man.

If *"everlasting punishment"* seems unfair or unreasonable, perhaps it is due to our failure to understand the nature of God, the gravity of sin, and the concept of eternity.

Later, we will reflect on God's purity and sin's defilement.

As for the concept of eternity, we might as well admit it: the very word *eternity* overloads our mental capacities, since our frame of reference is *time*.

Eternity is *timeless*.

If we imagine someone spending billions of years in hell, our thinking is wrong. Eternity is not composed of years. It is *an eternal now*. Once people enter that inescapable realm, they will comprehend its solemn logic. Do you remember the account of the rich man who ended up in hell (chapter 3)? He is still there.

God is clear about His entrance requirements for Paradise:

"There shall by no means enter it anything that defiles, or causes an abomination or a lie." (Revelation 21:27)

On this point, there will be no compromise. Just as God's natural laws cause a severed branch to die and wither, so God's spiritual laws require sin to be punished with *spiritual, physical, and eternal separation*.

SIN AND SHAME

It is time to return to Adam and Eve where we last saw them—attempting to hide from God among the trees of the garden.

Before they sinned, Adam and Eve had been surrounded by God's glory and perfection. They were totally comfortable in the presence of their Creator. However, the moment they broke God's law, they viewed themselves differently. Now they were uncomfortable—not just because of their physical nakedness, but also because of their *spiritual* nakedness.

Before they transgressed, Adam and Eve were God-conscious and *"felt no shame."* (Genesis 2:25 NIV) Now they had become unnaturally self-conscious and felt unclean before their holy God. Adam and Eve had become the opposite of their Creator. They were now *unholy*. They no longer wanted to be in the purity and brightness of God's presence. Like cockroaches scurrying for cover when a light is flicked on, they now *"loved darkness rather than light, because their deeds were evil. For everyone practicing evil hates the light and does not come to the light, lest his deeds should be exposed."* (John 3:19-20)

Adam and Eve were exposed and embarrassed. They felt out of place in the perfect garden. The sound of God's voice filled them with terror. They no longer wanted to be with their holy, loving Creator. Nonetheless, He came into the garden to seek them out.

It is a part of God's nature *"to seek and to save what was lost."* (Luke 19:10 NIV)

GOD SEEKING MAN

"Then the LORD God called to Adam and said to him, 'Where are you?'

So he said, 'I heard Your voice in the garden, and I was afraid because I was naked; and I hid myself.'

And He said, 'Who told you that you were naked? Have you eaten from the tree of which I commanded you that you should not eat?'" (Genesis 3:9-11)

Notice God's first recorded question to man.

"Where are you?"

With this loving, penetrating query, God wanted Adam to recognize what sin had done to him and his wife. He wanted them to admit that they had transgressed. He wanted them to understand that their sin had come between them and their holy Lord.

Their sin was the cause of their predicament. Their sin was what caused them to feel ashamed and try to hide behind trees and fig leaves. But Adam and Eve could not hide from God, nor could they escape His righteous, all-knowing judgment.

SIN EARNS DEATH

God was not joking when He informed Adam: *"In the day that you eat of it you shall surely **die**."* (Genesis 2:17) Deep down in our hearts, we know that those who rebel against their Creator deserve to be separated from Him.

Most of us have watched movies where the "bad guys" are killed and the "good guys" are victorious. Do we feel sorry for the "bad guys"? No, we figure they got what they deserved. The solemn reality is that in God's eyes, all of Adam's offspring are "bad guys."

*"They have **all** turned aside, they have **together** become corrupt; there is **none** who does good, **no, not one**."* (Psalm 14:3)

According to the Creator's standard of justice, we *all* deserve the death penalty. God's Book refers to this as:

*"**The law of sin and death**."* (Romans 8:2)

The law of sin and death demands that every act of disobedience against God must be punished with separation from God. No exceptions. Sin brings death.

It is because of God's holy and faithful nature that He upholds this law. By one act of sin our original ancestors separated themselves from God's kingdom of righteousness and life, and joined Satan's kingdom of sin and death.

Instantly, they died *spiritually*—like a branch severed from a tree. Their relationship with God was dead.

Also, they began to die *physically*—like a withering branch. It was only a matter of time until their bodies returned to the ground.

Worst of all, unless the LORD provided a remedy for their sin and shame, they faced the horrific prospect of dying *eternally*— forever separated from God in the everlasting fire prepared for the devil and his demons.

The Scriptures are clear:

*"The soul who **sins** shall **die**."* (Ezekiel 18:20)
*"For the wages of **sin** is **death**...."* (Romans 6:23)
*"**Sin**, when it is full-grown, brings forth **death**."* (James 1:15)

It is for good reason God calls this solemn reality *the law of sin and death*. It is *the LAW*.

Sin's penalty must be carried out.

It will be carried out.

13

MERCY AND JUSTICE

W**hat can man do that God cannot do?**
God's Book answers this riddle.

*"God is not a man, that He should **lie**, nor a son of man, that He should **repent**. Has He said, and will He **not do**? Or has He spoken, and will He not make it good?"*
(Numbers 23:19)

Every day men lie, change their minds, and break their promises. God cannot do these things. The Infinitely Perfect One cannot act contrary to His own character.

"He cannot deny Himself." (2 Timothy 2:13)

Some time ago, I received this e-mail:

Send	**Subject:**	Email Feedback

You say Allah cannot forgive arbitrarily. You say that Allah's hands are tied by His own laws. You wrote: "God can do everything except deny Himself and ignore His own laws." Why would our most merciful Creator prevent Himself from having the capacity to forgive his servants who ask for forgiveness? Why would He place such a constraint on His mercy? ...Can you not see that this makes no sense?

> Even if He were to make such a law, He could break it immediately as He is all powerful! It is illogical to argue that Allah with ultimate power is limited in any way. If He wished, He could hurl us all into the fire of hell, but He is the most merciful one and is always looking to forgive his servants so they can succeed when they are judged. May Allah grant us all his forgiveness and have mercy on us on the day when we are all gathered together and must stand to be judged alone!

In light of what we considered in the last chapter, is there a problem with this man's reasoning? Is our Creator free to ignore His own established laws and contradict His own holy character?

MERCY WITHOUT JUSTICE

Imagine this courtroom scene:

The judge is seated at the bench. Standing before him is a man found guilty of bank robbery and cold-blooded murder. The court is filled with witnesses. The wife and family of the murder victim are present along with employees from the robbed bank. News crews are on hand to record the moment.

What sentence will this murderer receive? The death penalty? Life in prison without parole?

All in the courtroom are told to rise.

Looking directly at the guilty man, the judge says, "I have observed that you are faithful in giving alms and regular in your prayers. The way you finger those prayer beads is impressive. And I hear that you are a hospitable man, always ready to share your meal with a stranger. It's a close call, but your good works have outweighed your bad works. I grant you mercy. You are pardoned and free to go."

The judge strikes the gavel.

Shocked gasps and angry murmurs fill the room...

Such a courtroom scenario is unheard of. Scales may be used to symbolize weighing the evidence against a criminal, but once he or she is found guilty of a crime, an appropriate sentence must be passed. Whether or not the criminal has done "good works" is irrelevant. We all know that.

Now if the "good-works-outweighing-bad-works" system is never used in man's earthly courtrooms, would such an unfair system be used in God's heavenly courtroom?

THE RIGHTEOUS JUDGE

God is not like the judge in our imaginary story. One of His titles is *"the Righteous Judge."* (2 Timothy 4:8) Four thousand years ago, the prophet Abraham asked, *"Shall not the Judge of all the earth do right?"* (Genesis 18:25)

God never sets aside justice to show mercy. To do so would erode the foundation of His righteous throne and mar the reputation of His holy name.

> *"**Righteousness and justice** are the foundation of Your throne; **Mercy and truth** go before Your face."*
> (Psalm 89:14)

To suggest, as our e-mail correspondent, that God can use His "ultimate power" to disregard His own laws is to imply that *"the Judge of all the earth"* is less righteous than the sinners He will judge.

How strange that we humans should have a profound, innate sense of justice, yet resist the obvious truth that our Creator has that same sense of justice! Deep in our hearts we all know that there is nothing "great" about a judge who fails to punish evil.

The prophet Jeremiah wrote:

> *"**Great** is Your **faithfulness**! 'The LORD is my portion,' says my soul, 'Therefore I hope in Him.'"*
> (Lamentations 3:23-24)

Notice the prophet did not say, "Great is Your unpredictability!" or "Great is Your fickleness!" What kind of hope could we have in a whimsical god like that? God is great in *faithfulness*. Many who habitually address God as *"the Merciful and Compassionate"* forget that He is also the God who is *"faithful and just."* (I John 1:9)

A one-sided perspective leads to a distorted view of God.

GOD'S BALANCED NATURE

For a bird to be able to fly, which wing is essential—the left or the right?

Obviously, the bird needs both wings to fly! Anyone who thinks a bird can fly with one wing is ignoring the nature of birds and the laws of gravity and aerodynamics.

Likewise, anyone who suggests that God can show mercy apart from upholding justice is ignoring the nature of God and the law of sin and death.

God's *mercy* and *justice* are always in perfect balance. King David wrote:

> *"I will sing of **mercy** and **justice**; to You, O LORD, I will sing praises."* (Psalm 101:1)

David, who had committed some heinous sins, knew that he did not deserve God's mercy. By definition, mercy is *undeserved.*

Justice *is receiving the punishment we deserve.*
Mercy *is not receiving the punishment we deserve.*

The reason David could sing praises to God was that he knew the LORD had devised a way to show mercy to undeserving sinners without setting aside justice. That is why David sang *"of mercy **and** justice."*

Forgiveness of sin is not a simple matter for our holy God. He never pardons a sinner apart from the satisfaction that the sinner's transgressions have been sufficiently judged and punished. As human beings, if someone wrongs us, we may say to him or her, "It's OK. Just forget it. It's no big deal." We may graciously choose to forgive a person like that, but the infinitely holy Judge cannot.

God's mercy never negates God's justice. He never says, "I love you, so I won't judge your sin." Nor does He say, "Since you have sinned, I don't love you." God loves sinners, but must quarantine and punish their sin.

If this is what God is like, how can He possibly extend mercy to guilty sinners?

MERCY WITH JUSTICE

Think back to Adam and Eve's situation.

Because **God is *loving and merciful***, He did not want Adam and Eve to be separated from Him. He wanted them to live with Him forever and not end up in the everlasting fire.

"The Lord...is not willing that any should perish."

(2 Peter 3:9)

However, since **God is *righteous and just***, He could not ignore Adam and Eve's sin. He had to punish it.

"You are of purer eyes than to behold evil, and cannot look on wickedness." (Habakkuk 1:13)

So what would God do? Was there a way to punish sin without punishing the sinner? How could sin's contamination be removed and perfect purity be restored? Is there a satisfying answer to the prophet Job's question, *"How can **a man** be **righteous** before God?"* (Job 9:2) Thank God, there is.

The Scripture reveals what the Righteous Judge has done to be both *"just **and** the justifier"* of condemned sinners like Adam and Eve, and like you and me (Romans 3:26). Do you know what He has done to offer you mercy while upholding justice?

The answer is up ahead. Journey on.

NOT MY FAULT

For now, let's listen to the conversation that took place between our defiled ancestors and their Creator who had become their Judge.

"Then the LORD God called to Adam and said to him, 'Where are you?'

So he said, 'I heard Your voice in the garden, and I was afraid because I was naked; and I hid myself.'

And He said, 'Who told you that you were naked? Have you eaten from the tree of which I commanded you that you should not eat?'

> *Then the man said, 'The woman whom You gave to be*
> *with me, she gave me of the tree, and I ate.'*
> *And the LORD God said to the woman, 'What is this*
> *you have done?'*
> *The woman said, 'The serpent deceived me, and I ate.'"*
> (Genesis 3:9-13)

Why did the LORD question Adam and Eve?

He questioned them for the same reason a parent questions a disobedient child, even when the parent knows what the child has done. God wanted Adam and Eve to recognize their sin and guilt. However, instead of admitting their sin, each tried to blame another.

Adam accused God and Eve: *It's not my fault! The woman You gave me—it's her fault!*

Eve held the snake liable: *The serpent tricked me!*

Because they were humans and not programmed robots, God held each of them accountable for the choices they had made. They had no one to blame but themselves.

> *"Let no one say when he is tempted, 'I am tempted by*
> *God'; for God cannot be tempted by evil, nor does He*
> *Himself tempt anyone. But each one is tempted when he is*
> *drawn away by his **own desires** and enticed. Then, when*
> *desire has conceived, it gives birth to sin; and **sin**, when it*
> *is full-grown, brings forth **death**."* (James 1:13-15)

Instead of following their Creator's plan, Adam and Eve followed their *"own desires"* which led them down the path of *sin* and *death.*

Eve was enticed and *deceived* by Satan. As for Adam, to whom the Lord had given the command not to eat of the tree of the knowledge of good and evil, he *deliberately* chose to disobey his Creator.

> *"Adam was **not** deceived, but the woman being **deceived**,*
> *fell into transgression."* (1 Timothy 2:14)

Deliberate or deceived, both were guilty, but it was only after Adam ate the forbidden fruit that the Scripture declares, *"Then the eyes of **both** of them were opened."* (Genesis 3:7)

God held Adam, not Eve, responsible for leading humankind out of the kingdom of righteousness and life, and into the dominion of sin and death. God had privileged Adam to be the head of the entire human race, but with great privilege came great responsibility.

Adam's sin has contaminated us all, but we cannot blame him for the choices we make.

> *"**Each of us** shall give account of himself to God."*
> (Romans 14:12)

14

THE CURSE

The time for cover-ups and excuses was over. Adam had chosen his own path, but he would not choose the consequences of that path. All creation would keep silent as the Righteous Judge pronounced a series of curses and consequences brought on by man's sin.

THE SERPENT

The Lord began by pronouncing the doom of *"the serpent."*

*"So the LORD God said to the serpent: 'Because you have done this, **you are cursed** more than all cattle, and more than every beast of the field; on your belly you shall go, and you shall eat dust all the days of your life. And I will put enmity between you and the woman, and between your seed and her Seed; He shall bruise your head, and you shall bruise His heel.'"* (Genesis 3:14-15)

Who was this *serpent* to whom God was talking? Was the Creator angry with a reptile?

God's words in Scripture sometimes include a two-level message, especially in parables and prophecies. There is the obvious *surface meaning* and then there is a less-obvious *deeper meaning*. That is the case with this pronouncement.

The curse that came upon the serpent has **two levels**.

LEVEL 1: AN ENDURING ILLUSTRATION

First, by cursing (pronouncing judgment on) the serpent, the LORD was putting before mankind an enduring object lesson. The reptile that Satan had used to tempt man to sin would henceforth slither on the ground. All serpents would have this same trait. Before Adam and Eve sinned, apparently snakes had legs like other reptiles. To this day certain snake species, such as pythons and boa constrictors, have remnants of upper-leg bones.[128]

Sin produces far-reaching ramifications for guilty and guiltless alike. It is because of sin that *"the whole creation groans."* (Romans 8:22) Even the innocent animal world has been affected.

It is for good reason man's choice to sin is called *the Fall*.

LEVEL 2: SATAN'S IMPENDING DOOM

The Bible says, *"No prophecy of Scripture is of any private interpretation."* (2 Peter 1:20) Scripture interprets Scripture. What God announced in the second half of His curse on *"the serpent"* forces us to dig deeper into the Scriptures.

> *"And I will put enmity between you and the woman, and between your seed and her Seed; He shall bruise your head, and you shall bruise His heel."* (Genesis 3:15)

Who is *the serpent* to whom God was speaking? The Scriptures identify him as the proud angel who was *"cut down to the ground."* (Isaiah 14:12) He is *"that **serpent of old**, called **the Devil** and **Satan**, who deceives the whole world."* (Revelation 12:9)[129]

The serpent was none other than *Satan*.

Using language fit for a serpent, the LORD was pronouncing the doom of the devil and all who follow him. There would be *"enmity,"* (irreconcilable hostility) between Satan's *"seed"* (offspring) and the woman's *"Seed"* (Offspring). In the end, the serpent's *"head"* would be crushed by *"her Seed."*

All this would be fulfilled according to God's timetable.

THE TWO "SEEDS"

What are these two *seeds* all about? To whom do *the seed of the serpent* and *the Seed of the woman* refer?

The seed of the serpent refers to those who rebel against God even as Satan did. Those who follow Satan's lies are, in a spiritual sense, *the children of the devil.*

> *"You belong to your father, the devil, and you want to carry out your father's desire. He was a murderer from the beginning, not holding to the truth, for there is no truth in him. When he lies, he speaks his native language, for he is a liar and the father of lies."* (John 8:44 NIV)

Who then is **the Seed of the woman**?

This is a unique concept. Throughout Biblical history, a person's posterity was attributed to the man rather than the woman. Yet on the day sin entered the world, God spoke of *the posterity of a woman.* Why?

This declaration by God was the first prophecy pointing to the Messiah who would be born of a woman, but not of a man. *Messiah* literally means *the Anointed One,* or *the Chosen One.* Throughout the Bible, whenever a man was chosen by God to be a leader of the people, an authorized person, such as a prophet, would anoint him (pour oil on his head) to show that he was chosen by God for a specific task.[130]

However, the Messiah would be different from all others. He would be *The* Anointed One. At just the right moment in history, God's Chosen One would enter the world to *"destroy him who had the power of death, that is, the devil, and release those who through fear of death were all their lifetime subject to bondage."* (Hebrews 2:15)

While God did not reveal His full plan on the day sin entered the human race, this embryonic prophecy gave Adam and Eve and their posterity a glimmer of hope. This initial promise contains numerous foundational truths which God's prophets would later develop in detail.[131]

THE CURSE

Following His carefully worded prophecy about *the Seed of a woman* who would crush the head of the serpent, the LORD informed Adam and Eve of some of the practical consequences of their sin. These consequences are known as *the Curse*.

> *"To the woman He said: 'I will greatly multiply your sorrow and your conception; in pain you shall bring forth children; your desire shall be for your husband, and he shall rule over you.'*
>
> *Then to Adam He said, 'Because you have heeded the voice of your wife, and have eaten from the tree of which I commanded you, saying, 'You shall not eat of it': Cursed is the ground for your sake; in toil you shall eat of it all the days of your life. Both thorns and thistles it shall bring forth for you, and you shall eat the herb of the field. In the sweat of your face you shall eat bread till you return to the ground, for out of it you were taken; for dust you are, and **to dust you shall return.** '"* (Genesis 3:16-19)

Adam and Eve's choice to rebel against their Creator came with a horrific price tag.

The joys of having a family would now be accompanied by trouble and pain. Instead of naturally producing grains, fruits and vegetables, earth's cursed soil would naturally produce weeds, thorns and thistles. Rest and enjoyment would be displaced by struggle and toil. Worse, man's fleeting life would be overshadowed by a tyrant named *Death*.

Man had lost dominion. Sin had brought a curse.

IS DEATH NORMAL?

Those who disregard the Scriptures tend to view hardship, suffering, loss, broken relationships, disease, old age and death as *normal*. Understanding the truth about sin's curse is one of the keys to understanding why things are the way they are on our groaning planet. Many intelligent people point to humankind's pitiful condition as evidence for the non-existence of God. They reason this way because they do not recognize the entrance and effects of sin.[132]

In Senegal, people sometimes say (mainly at funerals), "God created death before He created life." Many draw comfort from that philosophy. Such thinking contradicts both logic and the Scriptures which depict death as *"the last enemy that will be destroyed."* (1 Corinthians 15:26)

Evil, grief, hardship, suffering and death may seem normal, but such invasive elements are no more natural to this world than cancer cells are natural to a healthy person's body.

The thorns on a sweet-smelling rosebush, the struggle required to harvest a crop, the stubbornness seen in adorable little children, the way a husband mistreats his lovely wife, the pain that accompanies the wonder of childbirth, the diseases that ravage a body's immune system, the cruelty of old-age, the harsh reality of death and of our bodies returning to dust—these are not a part of God's original plan. God did not design creation to fight against itself.

Before sin entered, man had dominion over creation. All things were in perfect submission to Adam and his wife. Righteousness and peace filled the earth. Then our first ancestor went down the path of sin and death, and with him went the whole defiled and dying human race.

ALL CREATION AFFECTED

"But that isn't fair!" says someone, "Why should anyone have to suffer because of another man's sin?"

Each of us makes our own choices and it is for those choices God holds us responsible, but it is also true that we live in a cursed world. The reality behind the Wolof proverb is self-evident: *"An epidemic does not confine itself to the one who caused it."*

That's the nature of sin. Life is no longer fair. As a result of Adam's one sin *"the whole creation has been groaning as in the pains of childbirth right up to the present time."* (Romans 8:22 NIV) All are affected by sin's curse.

The good news is that, from the beginning, our Creator had a bold rescue plan. Much like a watchmaker builds into a watch a mechanism by which it can be adjusted to deal with the forces that cause it to get off time, so the Maker of the universe built into His world a "mechanism" by which He would offset the destructive forces of Satan, sin and death. From the beginning, God had a *purpose* in allowing sin to enter as well as a *plan* to reverse sin's curse and display His grace to all who trust Him.

Grief, pain, and death were not around at the beginning of God's story, nor will they be around at the end. One day sin and its curse will be abolished. *"God will **wipe away every tear** from their eyes; there shall be **no more death, nor sorrow, nor crying**. There shall be **no more pain**, for the former things have passed away... And there shall be **no more curse**."* (Revelation 21:4; 22:3) We'll learn more of this glorious future near the end of our journey.

GOD'S GRACE

Do you remember what Adam and Eve did after they ate from the tree of the knowledge of good and evil?

They made fig leaf coverings for themselves. It was man's first attempt to cover up his sin and shame. God did not accept Adam and Eve's self-efforts. Instead, God did something for them.

"For Adam and his wife the LORD God made tunics of skin, and clothed them." (Genesis 3:21)

God provided for Adam and Eve clothing made of animal skins. To do this, blood was shed.

Imagine the LORD selecting a couple of sheep or other appropriate animals, sacrificing them, and then making *"tunics of skin"* for Adam and Eve. God was teaching them vital lessons about the high cost of sin, about His holy nature, and about how shamefully unfit sinners can be made acceptable to Him.

By providing this special clothing for Adam and Eve, their Creator was showing His grace to those who had just revolted against Him. They did not deserve God's kindness, but that's what grace is: **undeserved** *kindness.*

Justice is receiving *what we deserve* (= eternal punishment).
Mercy is *not* receiving what we deserve (= no punishment).
Grace is receiving *what we don't deserve* (= eternal life).

GOD'S RIGHTEOUSNESS

By killing animals for Adam and Eve, God wanted them to understand that He is not only *"the gracious God"* (Psalm 86:15 NIV), but also *"the righteous God."* (Psalm 7:9) Sin must be punished with death. Imagine Adam and Eve's thoughts as they saw the blood pulsate from these beautiful, innocent creatures. God had put before them a vivid illustration: the penalty for their sin was *death.*

God Himself performed the first blood sacrifice. Millions more would follow.

Notice also that it was the LORD who *"clothed them"* with the animal skins He had provided. Adam and Eve had tried to cover their sin and shame, but their efforts did not satisfy God. He alone had the remedy for their sin problem. God wanted them to understand this. He wants us to understand this too.

SINNERS SHUT OUT

Chapter 3 of Genesis concludes like this:

"Then the LORD God said, 'Behold, the man has become like one of Us, to know good and evil. And now, lest he put out his hand and take also of the tree of life, and eat, and live forever'—therefore the LORD God sent him out of the garden of Eden to till the ground from which he was taken. So He drove out the man; and He placed cherubim [special angels that surround God's heavenly throne] *at the east of the garden of Eden, and a flaming sword which turned every way, to guard the way to the tree of life."*
(Genesis 3:22-24)

Just as Lucifer and the angels that sinned were expelled from the heavenly Paradise after they exerted their will against God's will, so the man and his wife were expelled from the earthly paradise when they acted against God's will.

Thus, man was banned from God's holy presence and from *the tree of life* (not to be confused with *the tree of the knowledge of good and evil*). Near the conclusion of our journey through the Scriptures we will get another glimpse of this special tree in the heavenly Paradise. The tree of life symbolizes the gift of eternal life God gives to all who trust in Him and His plan.

By eating from the tree of the knowledge of good and evil, Adam and Eve rejected the way of everlasting life and chose the way of everlasting death. The delightful connection between heaven and earth was broken by sin.

Adam and Eve had a serious problem. So do we.

15

DOUBLE TROUBLE

Escaped Convict Recaptured After 38 Years On the Run, announced a May 2006 news headline.

The report told of a certain Mr. Smith who had escaped from a California prison in 1968 while serving time for robbery.

For 38 years, using his mother's maiden name, he had moved from place to place, finally living in a trailer in a heavily wooded area in mid-America. It was there the authorities found him.

"He looked at the ground a little bit, then he looked up and said, 'Yeah, that's me,'" Creek County Sheriff's Detective said. "He didn't dream people would be looking for him for so long."[133]

Even as Mr. Smith was unable to evade the persistent arm of the law, so no breaker of God's laws will escape the limitless reach of the Righteous Law-Giver and Judge.

And just who are these lawbreakers?

"Everyone who sins breaks the law; in fact, sin is lawlessness." (1 John 3:4 NIV)

Anyone who disobeys God's good and perfect laws is a lawbreaker. That is what Lucifer did. That is what Adam and Eve did. That's what we have done too.

All sin is against God. Many people view their sin as a small thing, but in God's sight, all unrepentant, unpardoned sinners—no matter how "good" or religious—are criminal outlaws.

OPTIMISTIC MIRAGE CHASERS

Some time ago a neighbor told me, "I'm an optimist; I think I'll make it into paradise."

Can his optimism and self-efforts save him from eternal punishment when it comes time to be judged?

Once while traveling through California's Death Valley (one of the hottest deserts on earth), I saw in the distance what appeared to be a shimmering lake, but as I got closer, the "lake" disappeared. Looking ahead I saw another such "lake." It also vanished.

It was a mirage.

A mirage is caused by light rays being refracted through layers of air of different temperatures and densities. The lakes looked real, but they were not real. Similarly, a sinner may feel optimistic about his or her chance of making it into paradise, but the Scriptures expose the truth. Adam's descendants are *"without strength"* to save themselves from judgment (Romans 5:6).

Like a man lost in a parched desert who has spilled his only water supply, mankind is helpless to regain the everlasting life lost because of sin.

"We will surely die and become like water spilled on the ground, which cannot be gathered up again...."
(2 Samuel 14:14)

The lost man may see what he sincerely believes to be a life-saving oasis, but the "oasis" turns out to be only more blistering heat waves. The desperate, dehydrated man plods from mirage to mirage until at last, he dies.

So it is with a sinner's optimism, sincerity, and religions of self-effort.

*"There is a way that **seems right** to a man, but its end is the way of **death**."* (Proverbs 14:12)

In an effort to deal with their defiled condition, billions of people around the world today follow ways that *seem right* to them. They perform religious rituals, ceremoniously wash their bodies, recite mechanical prayers, refrain from certain foods, give money, burn candles, finger beads, repeat formulas, and do what they believe to be "good deeds." Others focus on submitting to their spiritual leaders, while still others hope to gain access to paradise by dying as martyrs for a cause they deem holy and just.

Is it possible they are chasing a mirage?

AN ACCURATE VIEW OF SELF

"Truth is a hot pepper," says a Wolof proverb.

Even if it makes us uncomfortable, God tells us the grim truth about ourselves. He invites us to be honest with Him about our sin. Apart from such honesty, we are like a seriously ill neighbor lady my wife and I knew. She refused to recognize her need for a proper doctor, insisting that she would be fine. She died a few weeks later.

While on earth, the Messiah told a group of self-righteous religious leaders:

"Those who are well have no need of a physician, but those who are sick. I did not come to call the righteous [those who think they are good enough], *but sinners, to repentance."* (Mark 2:17)

Despite the clarity of Scripture, many churches, mosques and synagogues today only tell people how good they are, or that they just need to try a little harder. They don't teach people about the pristine righteousness of God and the solemn consequences of sin.

A mosque in Canada has this message posted over its entrance:

WE ACCEPT EVERYONE
AND TELL NO ONE HE IS A SINNER

God has posted a different message over the entrance to Paradise:

"THERE SHALL BY NO MEANS ENTER...
ANYTHING THAT DEFILES"
(Revelation 21:27)

The Scripture says: *"All have sinned and fall short of the glory of God."* (Romans 3:23) God accepts *no one* based on his or her own merits and tells *everyone* they are sinners.

Only those who are cleansed in a way that satisfies God's perfect standard of justice and purity will enter Paradise.

AN ACCURATE VIEW OF GOD

One day the prophet Isaiah was given a vision of the LORD's absolute purity and awesome glory. Isaiah wrote:

> *"In the year that King Uzziah died, I saw the Lord sitting on a throne, high and lifted up, and the train of His robe filled the temple. Above it stood seraphim* [special angels connected with God's throne]*; each one had six wings: with two he covered his face, with two he covered his feet, and with two he flew. And one cried to another and said:* **'Holy, holy, holy is the LORD of hosts;** *the whole earth is full of His glory!' And the posts of the door were shaken by the voice of him who cried out, and the house was filled with smoke. So I said:* **'Woe is me, for I am undone! Because I am a man of unclean lips, and I dwell in the midst of a people of unclean lips; for my eyes have seen the King, the LORD of hosts.'"** (Isaiah 6:1-5)

The burning splendor surrounding God's throne in heaven is so great that even the perfectly pure angels cover their faces and feet. These angels are so awe-struck by God's holiness and glory that they cannot sit in His presence. Instead, they fly around His throne, crying out, *"Holy, holy, holy is the LORD of hosts; the whole earth is full of His glory!"*

Why do most people fail to see sin for what it is?

Perhaps it is because they have never seen God for Who He is. They have never contemplated His blazing purity. Isaiah was a godly prophet, yet his vision of the holy splendor of the Lord made him conscious of his own defilement and filthiness. *"Woe is me! I am a man of unclean lips!"* said he. Compared to the Lord, Isaiah knew he and the entire nation of Israel were in desperate shape!

Later, Isaiah wrote: *"**All** we like sheep have gone astray; we have turned **everyone** to his **own way**... We are **all** like **an unclean thing**, and **all** our righteousnesses are like **filthy rags**."* (Isaiah 53:6; 64:6) Isaiah knew that no amount of ritual washings or self-effort could make him pure before the LORD.[134] In the estimation of our holy Creator, *"we are all like **an unclean thing**."*

The prophet Job showed an understanding of man's defiled condition when he asked, *"**How can a man be righteous before God?** ...If I wash myself with snow water, and cleanse my hands with soap, yet You will plunge me into the pit, and my own clothes will abhor me."* (Job 9:2,30-31) And the prophet Jeremiah wrote down these words of God: *"'Although you wash yourself with soda and use an abundance of soap, the stain of your guilt is still before me,' declares the Sovereign LORD."* (Jeremiah 2:22 NIV)

An accurate view of God leads to an accurate view of self. Inadequate thoughts of our Creator leave us with inflated thoughts of ourselves.

A man dressed in filthy, disease-infested rags may imagine himself to be clean and acceptable, but that doesn't make him so. Likewise, a sinner may imagine himself to be righteous, but that does not make him so.

When compared with God's glory and righteousness, our best efforts are *"like filthy rags."*

A LESSON FOR ALL

One of God's purposes in forming the nation of Israel was to teach *all* nations some vital lessons. Though the LORD was constantly faithful to Israel, the Israelites consistently failed the LORD. God wants *us* to learn from them. *"Now these things became **our examples**, to the intent that we should not lust after evil things as they also lusted."* (1 Corinthians 10:6)

In Exodus, the second book of the Torah, Moses records how the Israelites failed to see sin as God sees it. With a strong arm, God had delivered them from centuries of slavery in Egypt. Yet there was much they still did not understand about the LORD and His character. They imagined they could somehow be obedient enough to escape God's judgment.

The people of Israel were so self-confident that they told Moses,

"All that the LORD has spoken we will do." (Exodus 19:8)

They did not see themselves as helpless sinners, nor did they comprehend God's requirement of flawless righteousness. They had forgotten that it only took one sin to separate Adam and Eve from their Creator. To help the Israelites see their sin and feel their shame, God gave them an examination with ten points.

The Scripture describes how the LORD descended on Mount Sinai in power and glory. *"There was **thunder** and **lightning**, with a **thick cloud** over the mountain, and a **very loud trumpet blast**. Everyone in the camp **trembled**."* (Exodus 19:16 NIV) Then the Voice of God boomed out ten rules:

THE TEN COMMANDMENTS

1. *"You shall have no other gods before Me."* To worship anyone but the LORD is sin. To fail to love God, every moment of every day, with all our heart, mind and strength, is sin. (Exodus 20)[135]

2. *"You shall not make for yourself a carved image... you shall not bow down to them nor serve them."* This is not limited to bowing down before an image or venerating an object. Anything that takes God's place is a transgression of this law.
3. *"You shall not take the name of the LORD your God in vain."* If you claim to be submitted to the one true God, but are not seeking to know Him and obey His Word, then you are taking His holy name in vain.
4. *"Remember the Sabbath day, to keep it holy... In it you shall do no work."* God required the Israelites to cease from work every seventh day to honor Him.

5. *"Honor your father and your mother."* Anything less than perfect obedience is sin. For a child to disrespect or even have a bad attitude toward his or her parents is a violation of this command.

6. *"You shall not murder."* God also says, *"Whoever hates his brother is a murderer."* (1 John 3:15) Hatred equals murder. God looks at the heart and requires selfless love at all times.

7. *"You shall not commit adultery."* This law not only refers to immoral use of the body, but also to impure desires in the mind and heart. *"Whoever looks at a woman to lust for her has already committed adultery with her in his heart."* (Matthew 5:28)

8. *"You shall not steal."* Taking more than is rightfully yours, cheating on taxes or an exam, or not working faithfully for your employer are all forms of stealing.

9. *"You shall not bear false witness against your neighbor."* To make a statement about someone or something that is less than perfectly true is sin.

10. *"You shall not covet...anything that is your neighbor's."* To crave anything that belongs to another is sin. We are to be content with what we have.

GUILTY!

After the LORD had announced these ten rules, the Scripture narrates, *"Now all the people witnessed the thunderings, the lightning flashes, the sound of the trumpet, and the mountain smoking; and when the people saw it, **they trembled and stood afar off.**"* (Exodus 20:18)

No longer were they boasting that they could do *"all that the LORD has spoken!"*

They had failed the exam.

How about you? How did you do?

If you scored less than 100% on all ten commands, (that means flawless obedience 24 hours a day, 7 days a week, from the time you were born up to this very minute) then you, like the children of Israel, and like me, have failed the exam.

"Whoever shall keep the whole law, and yet stumble in **one point,** *he is* **guilty of all."** (James 2:10)

In the first chapter of this book, we noted that the Bible is not only the world's most sold book; it is also the world's most shunned book. One reason it is so unpopular is because it exposes our sin and strips away our pride. It tells us: *"You say, 'I am rich; I have acquired wealth and do not need a thing.' But you do not realize that* **you are wretched, pitiful, poor, blind and naked,"** and: *"There is* **not a just man on earth** *who does good and does not sin."* (Revelation 3:17 NIV; Ecclesiastes 7:20)

God's Law does not make us feel good about ourselves.

WHY THE TEN COMMANDMENTS?

So what is the purpose of these commandments? If no one can measure up to God's standard, then why did He bother to make it known?!

One obvious reason is that God gave these commandments to provide mankind with a clear moral standard for maintaining order in society. Any civilization lacking a consensus of what is right and what is wrong will be controlled by anarchy or tyranny. God knows mankind needs the rule of law in society. Yet God had some even more critical reasons for giving the Ten Commandments.

The LORD gave His Law so *"that every mouth may be stopped, and all the world may become guilty before God. Therefore by the deeds of the law no flesh will be justified in His sight, for* **by the law is the knowledge of sin."** (Romans 3:19-20)

THREE FUNCTIONS OF THE TEN COMMANDMENTS:

1. God's Law shuts up self-righteous people. *"That every mouth may be stopped, and all the world may become* **guilty** *before God."* The Ten Commandments tell us, "No matter how good you think you are, you will never satisfy God's standard of perfect righteousness. You are a guilty law-breaker. Stop boasting!"[136]

2. God's Law exposes our sin. *"For by the law is the* **knowledge** *of sin."* The Law is like an X-ray. Radiography can reveal a broken bone, but it cannot repair it. Likewise, *"by the* *deeds of the law no flesh will be justified* [declared good enough] *in His sight."* The Ten Commandments are to a sinner what a mirror is to someone with a dirty face. The mirror can show the filth, but it cannot remove it. God's Law reveals our sin and defilement, but it cannot remove it.

A few years ago, I explained the purpose of God's Law to a Roman Catholic middle-school math teacher in Senegal. It was for him a shocking revelation. With frustration in his voice, he commented, "OK, so the Ten Commandments teach us that we are helpless sinners before God who is holy and must judge sin, and that we cannot save ourselves by our good works or by praying and fasting. So how CAN we be made acceptable to God? What IS the solution?"

3. God's Law points us to God's solution. Just as the X-ray technician in a hospital points the man with a broken leg to a qualified physician who can set the broken bone, so the Law and the Prophets point us to the only "Physician" who can *"redeem us from the curse of the law."* (Galatians 3:13) We shall hear more about Him shortly.[137]

HELP!

If you were about to drown and there was someone nearby who could save you from drowning, would you be too proud to cry for help?

Recognizing your powerlessness to save yourself from sin's deadly penalty is not a defeat; it is the first step to victory. Man needs help—help that only God can provide.

Perhaps you've heard the saying: "God helps those who help themselves." While that adage applies to some areas of life, when it comes to our sinful and spiritually-dead condition, the exact opposite is true: God helps those who know that they *cannot* help themselves.

God helps those who admit they need a Savior.

A popular African proverb says, *"Even if a log soaks a long time in water, it will never become a crocodile."*

Neither can man change his defiled nature and make himself righteous.

CONTAMINATED

Think back to Adam. God had given him one rule: *Do not eat from the tree of the knowledge of good and evil.*

If Adam and Eve had obeyed their Creator, they could have lived forever, growing in a wonderful relationship with Him. But that is not what happened.

Our ancestors transgressed and their relationship with God was broken. As sinners, they now tried to hide from God. They felt ashamed and attempted to cover their nakedness with fig leaves. But God sought them out, gave them a glimpse of His mercy and justice, and then put them out from His presence. Unless He provided a way back, they would be banished forever. They stood contaminated and condemned before their holy Creator and Judge.

Here is an important question. How many sins did Adam and Eve have to commit before God expelled them from the perfect Garden of Eden?

One sin is all it took.

No amount of previous "good" or subsequent self-effort on their part could undo the consequences of the one sin.

"Good" is God's *normal* standard. When Adam sinned, he was no longer "good" in God's estimation. He had become like a glass of pure water into which one puts a drop of cyanide. If you have a glass of poisoned water, will adding more pure water remove the poison? No. Neither can any amount of good works undo our sin-problem. And, even if good works could remove sin, the reality is we have no "pure water," that is, no truly righteous works, to add to our sinful nature.

In God's estimation, our best efforts are polluted.

Adam's soul was contaminated by sin, as was Eve's. And so is ours. We all come from the same contaminated source. The prophet David gives us God's verdict:

*"The LORD looks down from heaven upon the children of men... They have **all** turned aside, they have **together** become corrupt; There is **none** who does good, **no, not one**."* (Psalm 14:2-3)

OUR DOUBLE TROUBLE

A century-old story is told of a man in a British jail who was condemned to die. One day the cell door swung open and in walked the jailer.

"Cheer up!" said the jailer, "the Queen has pardoned you."

To the jailer's surprise, the man showed no emotion.

"Man, I tell you, cheer up!" shouted the jailer, holding up a document, "Here is the pardon. The Queen has pardoned you!"

At this, the man lifted his shirt, and pointing to an awful-looking tumor he said, "I have a cancer that will kill me in a few days or weeks. Unless the Queen can remove this also, the pardon is useless to me."

The man knew he needed more than *pardon* for his crimes; he needed *new life*.

Every member of Adam's race is like this condemned man. As sinners by choice and sinners by birth, we have a double dilemma: We need pardon for our crimes against God *and* we need the righteous, eternal life from God that will qualify us to live in His holy presence.

Here is our double trouble:

* **SIN**: We are *guilty sinners*. God alone can *cleanse us* from sin and rescue us from everlasting punishment.

  We need *God's **pardon***.

* **SHAME**: We are *spiritually naked*. God alone can *clothe us* with His righteousness and give us His eternal life.

  We need *God's **perfection***.

Our sin and shame require a double cure that we cannot produce.

The good news is that God has provided it for us.

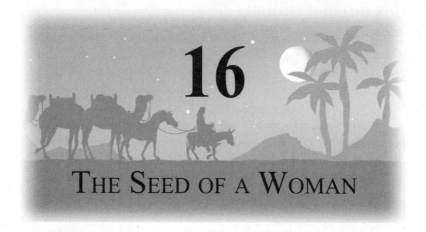

16

THE SEED OF A WOMAN

O ne cold, foggy night two small children fell into a deep, slippery pit. Both were injured, frightened, and helpless. Neither could save the other since they were both in the same predicament. Death would soon claim them unless rescue came from outside the pit. Later three men found them. With a rope, one of the men was lowered into the dark, slimy hole. The children were pulled out.

Their deliverance came from above.

The day Adam and Eve first sinned, they became like those two children. They were helpless to save themselves from the pit of sin into which they had fallen. If they were to be delivered from eternal death, rescue must come from outside the fallen human race; from above.

Make no mistake about it. The human condition is serious, with no self-remedy.

Down through the centuries, without exception, all of Adam's descendants—born of man and woman—have inherited a sin-bent nature. All are born under the curse of sin.

To deliver sinners from sin's curse and consequences, God planned to bring into the world a sinless Man who would provide deliverance for all who want to be rescued from the pit of sin.

How would God do this? How could anyone be born into the human family without inheriting Adam's sin nature? God gave the first clue on the day sin infected the human race.

The LORD forewarned "the Serpent," that is, Satan:

*"I will put enmity between you and the woman, and between your seed and **her Seed**; He shall bruise your head, and you shall bruise His heel."* (Genesis 3:15)

In speaking of *"her Seed,"* the LORD was foretelling that it would be through a male child, born of a woman, that He would rescue sinners and ultimately crush Satan and put away evil. This was only the first of hundreds of prophecies to follow, each pointing with increasing clarity to a moment in history when this Savior-Messiah would visit the world.

WHY "HER SEED"?

Why would the Messiah enter the human race as *"her Seed"*? Why must He be *"born of **a woman**,"* but *not born of a man*? (Galatians 4:4)

Here is the answer. While the Savior of sinners would visit Adam's sinful race as a human, He must come from outside the pit of sin. He would descend from above.

Long after God announced this initial prophecy about *the Seed of a woman,* the prophet Isaiah wrote:

*"The Lord Himself will give you a sign: **Behold, the virgin shall conceive and bear a Son**, and shall call His name Immanuel* [which means 'God with us']. *"* (Isaiah 7:14)

The Savior would enter the human family through the womb of a young lady who never had physical relations with a man. This would be the Messiah's way of visiting Adam's fallen race without inheriting Adam's sinful nature.

"But wait a minute," someone says, "Women are also sinners. Even if the Messiah was born uniquely of a woman, would He not be contaminated by His mother's sin nature?"

A couple pages from now, we will hear how the Holy Spirit of God Himself brought about the miraculous conception of this holy Child. However, let us first reflect on a few less obvious elements in God's design to bring His sinless Son into the world via a virgin's womb. How could the Messiah be born unspoiled by the sin that had spread to all of Adam's offspring?

UNTAINTED BY SIN

As we already learned in chapter 13, God held *Adam* responsible for leading the human race into Satan's kingdom of sin and death. Eve was deceived, Adam was not. While females are born with sinful natures just like males, the Scripture makes it clear that it is our connection with Adam that causes us to be born with a sin nature.[138]

In Hebrew, *Adam* (*Adamah*) literally means "red earth." God formed his body from the earth's soil. After Adam sinned, God told him, *"Dust you are, and **to dust you shall return**."* (Genesis 3:19)

Contrastingly, *Eve* means "life," *"because she was the mother of all living."* (Genesis 3:20) On the day sin entered the world, God announced His plan to deal with our sin-problem and provide eternal life for the world through *"her Seed."* (Genesis 3:15)

Even though the Messiah would take on a body of flesh and blood, He would not originate from Adam's sin-infected blood line. He would be untainted by sin.

Incidentally, from a purely biological standpoint, today it is known that the gender of a child is determined by its father's "seed" (sperm), not its mother's "seed" (egg). It is also known that from conception, a baby in the womb has a circulatory system distinct from its mother's. Medical science tells us: "The placenta forms a unique barrier that keeps the mother's blood separate while allowing food and oxygen to pass through to the embryo."[139]

Even before God created the first human, He had planned every detail of the Messiah's coming to earth.

Remember the illustration of the broken branch. Like that separated, dead branch, the human family is spiritually dead, cut off from the Source of Life. Although the Savior of sinners would live among Adam's spiritually dead and sin-defiled family,

He would not originate from it. He Himself would be *"the true vine"* (John 15:1), the Source of Life.

He would be *perfect.*

"Perfect" does not mean that He would never have a pimple, bruise, or scratch on His body. It means that He would be perfect in character. He would possess a sinless nature. He would never violate God's Law. He would be *"holy, blameless, pure, set apart from sinners, exalted above the heavens."* (Hebrews 7:26 NIV)

Is it any surprise the sinless Messiah is called *"the second Man"* and *"the last Adam"*?

THE SECOND MAN

*"It is written, 'The **first man Adam** became a living being.' The **last Adam** became a life-giving spirit. However, the spiritual is not first, but the natural, and afterward the spiritual. The **first man** was of the earth, made of dust; the **second Man** is the Lord from heaven."* (1 Corinthians 15:45-47)

Even as *"the first man"* led the entire human population into Satan's dark kingdom of defilement and death, so *"the second Man"* would lead many people out of Satan's kingdom and into God's glorious kingdom of righteousness and life. That is why, on the same day sin contaminated the human race, the LORD served notice to Satan that the Seed of a woman would one day come to earth to bruise and ultimately crush him.

The prophet Micah wrote this about the promised Savior:

*"**Bethlehem** Ephrathah, though you are little among the thousands of Judah, yet out of you shall come forth to Me the One to be Ruler in Israel, **Whose goings forth are from of old, from everlasting**...He shall be great to the ends of the earth; And this One shall be peace."* (Micah 5:2,4-5)

Micah not only foretold that the Messiah would be born in the town of *"Bethlehem"*[140], but he also declared the Savior's pre-existence as being *"from of old, from everlasting."*

The Everlasting One would step out of eternity and into time.

FORETOLD BY THE PROPHETS

The prophets, who foretold that the Messiah would be conceived of a virgin and born in Bethlehem, also prophesied that He would be preceded by a forerunner who would announce His arrival. They wrote that God's Chosen One would bear the titles *Son of God* and *Son of Man*. They foretold that He would make the blind see, the deaf hear and the lame walk. He would enter Jerusalem on a donkey and be rejected by His own people. He would be mocked, spit upon, flogged and crucified. He would have no sin of His own, but would die for the sins of others. He would be buried in the tomb of a rich man, but His dead body would not decompose. Instead, He would conquer death, show Himself alive and return to heaven from where He had come.[141]

What person in history filled this profile penned by the prophets?

It is the same Person who split the world's calendar in two.

His name is *Jesus*.

GOD KEEPS HIS PROMISE

Down through the centuries, God promised to send the Savior into the world through the family of Abraham, Isaac, Jacob, Judah, David and Solomon. Thus, the Gospel (Arabic: *Injil*) of Matthew, the first book in the New Testament, begins with these words:

"The book of the genealogy of Jesus Christ, the Son of David, the Son of Abraham: Abraham begot Isaac, Isaac begot Jacob, and Jacob begot Judah..."

What follows is a long list of genealogies which includes *"David the king begot Solomon,"* and closes with *"Joseph the husband of Mary, of whom was born Jesus who is called Christ."* (Matthew 1:1-2,16) *Christ* is the Greek word for the *Hebrew* word *Messiah* which means *"the Anointed* [Chosen] *One."*[142] Such genealogies document Jesus' legal right to the throne of King David and show that Jesus was a direct descendant of Abraham, Isaac and Jacob through whom God had promised to offer His blessings to all people on earth.

The time had come for God to put into action His rescue plan, the plan *"which He promised before through His prophets in the Holy Scriptures, concerning His Son...."* (Romans 1:2)

THE SON OF THE HIGHEST

Luke chapter one records the captivating story of the visit of the angel Gabriel to Zacharias, whose job was to offer up sacrifices at the temple in Jerusalem. Even though Zacharias and his wife Elizabeth were too old to have children, Gabriel informed him that his wife would have a son, whom they would name John. This John would become the Messiah's forerunner.

The drama then continues with Gabriel's visit to a godly young woman named Mary.

> *"The angel Gabriel was sent by God to a city of Galilee named Nazareth, to a virgin betrothed to a man whose name was Joseph, of the house of David. The virgin's name was Mary.*
>
> *And having come in, the angel said to her, 'Rejoice, highly favored one, the Lord is with you; blessed are you among women!' But when she saw him, she was troubled at his saying, and considered what manner of greeting this was.*
>
> *Then the angel said to her, 'Do not be afraid, Mary, for you have found favor with God. And behold, **you will conceive in your womb and bring forth a Son, and shall call His name JESUS**. He will be great, and will be called **the Son of the Highest**; and the Lord God will give Him the throne of His father David... and of His kingdom there will be no end.'*
>
> *Then Mary said to the angel, '**How can this be, since I do not know a man?**'*
>
> *And the angel answered and said to her, '**The Holy Spirit will come upon you, and the power of the Highest will overshadow you; therefore, also, that Holy One who is to be born will be called the Son of God....For with God nothing will be impossible.**'"* (Luke 1:26-38)

SAVIOR OF SINNERS

Some months later, Joseph learned that Mary, his betrothed wife, was pregnant. He mistakenly assumed the obvious: that Mary had been unfaithful. Joseph decided to annul their approaching marriage.

> *"Then Joseph...being a just man, and not wanting to make [Mary] a public example, was minded to put her away secretly.*
>
> *But while he thought about these things, behold, an angel of the Lord appeared to him in a dream, saying, 'Joseph, son of David, do not be afraid to take to you Mary your wife, for that which is conceived in her is of the Holy Spirit. And she will bring forth a Son, and you shall call His name JESUS, for He will save His people from their sins.'"* (Matthew 1:19-21)

As revealed in the first chapter of Genesis, the *Holy Spirit* is God Himself.[143] *God* is the One who had supernaturally placed His eternal *Word* in Mary's womb.

The name *JESUS* is the English transliteration from the Greek word *IESOUS*, which comes from the Hebrew word *YEHOSHUA*, or its shortened form, *YESHUA*.

This name means, *"the LORD saves."*

> *"So all this was done **that it might be fulfilled** which was spoken by the Lord through the prophet, saying: 'Behold, the virgin shall be with child, and bear a Son, and they shall call His name Immanuel,' which is translated, '**God with us.'**
>
> *Then Joseph, being aroused from sleep, did as the angel of the Lord commanded him and took to him his wife, and did not know her till she had brought forth her firstborn Son.*[144]
>
> *And he called His name JESUS."* (Matthew 1:21-25)

THE WORD OF GOD FULFILLED

God was implementing the plan He began to reveal the day sin entered the world. *"Her Seed"* was about to be born!

A few pages ago we read Micah's prophecy about where the Messiah would be born. The LORD foretold that He would be born in *Bethlehem*—King David's home town.

But there was a problem.

Mary and Joseph lived in Nazareth, several days' journey from Bethlehem.

How would Micah's prediction be fulfilled?

No problem.

God would mobilize the Roman Empire to help fulfill this prophecy.

> *"And it came to pass in those days that a decree went out from Caesar Augustus that all the world should be registered. This census first took place when Quirinius was governing Syria. So all went to be registered, everyone to his own city.*
>
> *Joseph also went up from Galilee, out of the city of Nazareth, into Judea, to the city of David, which is called Bethlehem, because he was of the house and lineage of David, to be registered with Mary, his betrothed wife, who was with child.*
>
> *So it was, that while they were there, the days were completed for her to be delivered. And **she brought forth her firstborn Son**, and wrapped Him in swaddling cloths, and laid Him in a manger, because there was no room for them in the inn."* (Luke 2:1-7)

The promised Messiah was not born in a comfortable and pompous palace. Rather, He was born in a lowly shed and laid in a manger, a feeding trough for livestock. He came into the world in such a way that even the poorest and most common people might come to Him and not be afraid.

THE ANGEL'S PROCLAMATION

*"Now there were in the same country shepherds living
out in the fields, keeping watch over their flock by night.
And behold, an angel of the Lord stood before them, and
the glory of the Lord shone around them, and they were
greatly afraid.*

*Then the angel said to them, '**Do not be afraid, for
behold, I bring you good tidings of great joy which will
be to all people. For there is born to you this day in the
city of David a Savior, who is Christ the Lord.** And this
will be the sign to you: You will find a Babe wrapped in
swaddling cloths, lying in a manger.'*

*And suddenly there was with the angel a multitude
of the heavenly host praising God and saying: '**Glory to
God in the highest, and on earth peace, goodwill toward
men!**'"* (Luke 2:8-14)

It was a momentous night in world history.
The long wait was over.

*"And she brought forth **her** firstborn Son...."* (Luke 2:7)

The Seed of the woman had arrived

Everything was happening just as the prophets had foretold it,
in God's way and at God's time.[145]

Not only did God send angels to announce and celebrate Jesus'
birth, He also honored this joyous event by positioning a special
star in the night sky. A group of astronomers and wealthy wise
men from the East observed and followed that star. They knew
that it marked the promised Messiah's arrival. After completing
a grueling journey from far-away Persia, these distinguished men
went to King Herod in Jerusalem. They had one question:

*"**Where is He** who has been born King of the Jews?
For we have seen **His star** in the East and have come to
worship Him."* (Matthew 2:2)[146]

THE PERSON IN THE BABY

So who was this baby boy who was born in a shed, laid in a feeding trough, foretold by prophets, heralded by angels, visited by shepherds, honored with a star, and worshiped by wise men?

Let's listen again to what the angel told the shepherds:

"Do not be afraid, for behold, I bring you good tidings of great joy which will be to all people. For there is born to you this day in the city of David a Savior, who is **Christ the Lord.***"*

(Luke 2:10-11)

The Person in that tiny body was **the Lord**.

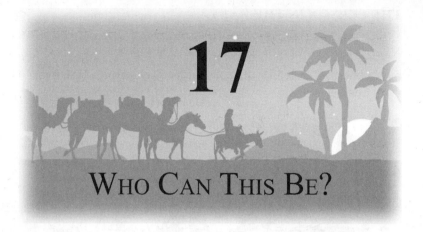

17

WHO CAN THIS BE?

*"Bounding gazelles do **not** beget burrowing offspring."*
— Wolof Proverb

Just as gazelles produce offspring with gazelle-like characteristics, so sinners produce offspring with sinful characteristics. Left to himself, man has no way to break out of this sin cycle. And it shows.

THE SINFUL ONES

Consider the motion picture industry in America. Each year, Hollywood produces and exports blockbuster movies featuring heroes and heroines who exhibit selfishness, immorality, perversion, filthy language, violence, revenge and deceit. Why do screenwriters intentionally include sinful characteristics in the "good guys" portrayed in their films? Why not make movies that portray the "hero" as righteous, kind, selfless, forgiving and honest? It is because the human race is infected by sin. Even man's best imaginary characters are contaminated. And such contamination is not limited to Hollywood.

Man's sin-bent nature reveals itself in countless subtle ways. For instance, if you are from the Arab world, you are probably familiar with a centuries-old literary figure named Juha. The folk tales of Juha and his donkey make us smile. Hundreds of anecdotes have been written about this clever character whose words and ways are characterized by wit and humor— and, more often than not, by self-centeredness, an insulting spirit, impure thoughts, revenge, deceit and broken promises. Think of it! Even our favorite invented characters are contaminated! Here is one simple example from a short anecdote of Juha:

> A friend came to him.
> "You promised," the friend said, "to lend me some money. I've come to take you up on it."
> Juha told him, "My friend, I don't lend my money to anyone, but I'll give you my promises to your heart's content!"[147]

We can relate to the fictional Juha because we too have made promises we never intended to keep. In our fallen human nature, we are just like *Juha.*

There is, however, one Person in history[148] who kept all His promises. He always spoke the truth. He never deceived, insulted, threatened or sought revenge.

His name is ***Jesus.***

> *"He committed **no sin**, and **no deceit** was found in his mouth. When they hurled their insults at him, **he did not retaliate**; when he suffered, he made **no threats**."*
> (1 Peter 2:22-23 NIV)

THE SINLESS ONE

The life of Jesus stands in powerful contrast to the sin-dominated cultures of the world. He was the only sinless person ever to be born. He was *"in all points tempted as we are, yet **without sin.** "* (Hebrews 4:15) No impure thought ever crossed His mind. No unkind word ever formed on His lips. As Jesus grew up with His half-brothers and sisters in a lowly home in Nazareth,[149] He *naturally* obeyed the Ten Commandments and every other law of God—outwardly and inwardly. Though Jesus had a physical body like ours, He did not have our sin-bent nature.

*"He was manifested to take away our sins, and in Him
there is no sin."* (1 John 3:5)

At age thirty, Jesus began his official work on earth.[150] The
war between God and Satan was about to escalate. Satan knew
that the Son of God had come to crush him, but he did not know
how Jesus planned to do it.

Just as Satan had tempted the first perfect man to disobey
God's Law, so now he would try to tempt the second Perfect Man
to act contrary to God's Laws.

*"Then Jesus...was led by the Spirit into the wilderness,
being **tempted for forty days by the devil**. And in those
days He ate nothing, and afterward, when they had ended,
He was hungry.*

*And the devil said to Him, '**If You are the Son of God**,
command this stone to become bread.'*

*But Jesus answered him, saying, '**It is written, 'Man
shall not live by bread alone, but by every word of God.'**'"*

(Luke 4:1-4)

Notice that Satan was not trying to get Jesus to do anything
"evil." The devil merely wanted this sinless Man (who had
invaded "his" territory!) to act independently of God the Father in
heaven, since, as we observed back in chapter 11, *to think or act
independently of God is **sin**.*

The point is this: If the Messiah had committed a single sin He
could not have fulfilled His mission to rescue Adam's cursed race
from the law of sin and death.

Just as a man who is deep in debt is not qualified to pay the
debt of another, neither is a sinner able to pay for the sins of
another sinner. However, *the Son of God*, who had become *the Son
of Man*,[151] had no sin-debt of His own. He could have by-passed
death altogether since He was free from sin, but, as we shall soon
discover, that was not God's plan.

Meanwhile, Satan repeatedly attempted to entice Jesus to sin
by acting independently of God's perfect plan. Each time Jesus
answered the devil by quoting the Scriptures.[152]

> *"Then the devil, taking Him up on a high mountain, showed Him all the kingdoms of the world in a moment of time. And the devil said to Him, 'All this authority I will give You, and their glory; for this has been delivered to me, and I give it to whomever I wish. Therefore, if You will worship before me, all will be Yours.'*
> *And Jesus answered and said to him, 'Get behind Me, Satan!* **For it is written, 'You shall worship the LORD your God, and Him only you shall serve.'"** (Luke 4:5-8)

Just as God had given Adam dominion over creation, so now Satan was offering to Jesus "the dominion" which Satan had usurped when Adam chose to follow him.[153]

In contrast to Adam, Jesus did **not** obey Satan.

The Word of God had become flesh.

JESUS' FOLLOWERS

Shortly after Jesus began His official mission, He chose twelve men to accompany Him wherever He went. Many women also followed Jesus. These men and women became eyewitnesses of all that Jesus said and did.

> *"He went through every city and village, preaching and bringing the glad tidings of the kingdom of God. And **the twelve** were with Him, and **certain women** who had been healed of evil spirits and infirmities...and many others who provided for Him from their substance."* (Luke 8:1-3)

Jesus showed equal respect to men, women and children. The Gospel Scriptures abound with narratives in which we read of Jesus treating women with a dignity and kindness that transcended the Jewish and Roman culture of that day.

Jesus viewed every person on earth as infinitely valuable, but He never coerced anyone to listen to Him, believe Him, or follow Him. He loved spending time with people whose minds and hearts were inclined to hear and embrace the truth, no matter how much it cost them.

A KEY QUESTION

While many of the common people followed Jesus, the Jewish religious leaders did not.

One day Jesus asked them a crucial question:

> *"What do you think about the Christ? Whose Son is He?"* (Matthew 22:42)

They responded by saying that the Messiah would be a descendant of King David. Jesus reminded them that David had prophesied that the promised Savior would be both *the earthly son of David* and *the heavenly Son of God.*[154]

Earlier, Jesus had asked His disciples a similar question:

> *"'Who do men say that I, the Son of Man, am?'*
> *So they said, 'Some say...one of the prophets.'*
> *He said to them, 'But who do you say that I am?'*
> *Simon Peter answered and said, 'You are the Christ, the Son of the living God.'*
> *Jesus answered and said to him, 'Blessed are you, Simon... for flesh and blood has not revealed this to you, but My Father who is in heaven.'"* (Matthew 16:13-17)

Sooner or later, we must all answer this same question: What do you think about Jesus? Whose Son is He?

WHAT SOME SAY

For many Westerners, *Jesus* is no more than a familiar curse word.

Others say He was a great moral teacher, but nothing more.

Orthodox Jews avoid even pronouncing Jesus' name, referring to him only as "that man."

Hindus view Jesus as one of many divine self-embodiments among their multitude of gods and goddesses.

My Muslim neighbors tell me: "We honor Jesus as a great prophet, but he is not the Son of God." An e-mail correspondent put it like this:

> **Subject:** Email Feedback
>
> I live in Saudi Arabia...We believe that Jesus was simply a prophet and not God's son. Jesus was not killed. He will come back and everyone will see which side he joins. I hope this happens in your lifetime so you can join our beautiful religion and see the true light.

And a Malaysian correspondent wrote:

> **Subject:** Email Feedback
>
> I believe that God is One and has never been or looked like a human... If there is any person that thinks of God as existing in human form, then he/she is a great blasphemer.

These viewpoints flow from what the Qur'an (or *Koran*) declares about Jesus.

WHAT THE QUR'AN SAYS

The Qur'an repeatedly states that Jesus was *"no more than a prophet."* (Sura 4:171-173; 5:75; 2:136) Nevertheless, the book revered by Muslims also declares Jesus to be unique among the prophets in that He had no biological father, calling Him *Isa ibn Maryam*, *"Jesus the Son of Mary."* (Sura 19:34) The Qur'an refers to the sins of the prophets, but never attributes sin to Jesus. He is called the *"holy Son."*[155] The Qur'an also presents Jesus as the only prophet with the power to create life, open the eyes of the blind, cleanse the lepers, and raise the dead.[156] And it is to Jesus alone the Qur'an attributes the lofty titles of *Al Masih* (the Messiah), *Ruh Allah* (Soul/Spirit of God) and *Kalimat Allah* (the Word of God).[157]

Having noted these Qur'anic affirmations of Jesus' uniqueness, it must also be pointed out that the Qur'anic portrayal of *"the Messiah, Jesus Son of Mary"* is radically different from the Bible. For example, the same Qur'anic verse that ascribes to Jesus the above-mentioned titles, states: *"The Messiah, Jesus son of Mary, was **only a messenger of Allah**, and **His word** which He conveyed unto Mary, and **a spirit from Him**. So believe in Allah and His messengers, **and say not 'Three.' Cease!** it is better for you!*

*Allah is only One Allah. **Far is it removed from His Transcendent Majesty that He should have a son.*** (Sura 4:171 Pickthall)

In Senegal, children and adults alike are not only quick to say: "Jesus is *not* the Son of God! God has *no* son!" but with equal conviction declare: "Jesus was *not* crucified!"

Where did they get the idea that Jesus was not crucified?

This idea also comes from the Qur'an, which declares: *"[The Jews] uttered against Mary a grave false charge; that they said in boast, 'We killed Christ Jesus the son of Mary, the Messenger of Allah'; **but they killed him not, nor crucified him**, but so it was made to appear to them, and those who differ therein are full of doubts, with no certain knowledge, but only conjecture to follow, **for of a surety they killed him not**. Nay, Allah raised him up unto Himself; and Allah is Exalted in Power, Wise."* (Sura 4:156-158)

WHAT THE BIBLE SAYS

Centuries before the Qur'an was written, the forty prophets and apostles who wrote the Old and New Testament Scriptures painted a different portrait of the Messiah and His mission.

Concerning Jesus' title as "the Son of God," John, who walked and talked with Jesus for more than three years, testified of Him:

> *"Jesus did many other miraculous signs in the presence of his disciples, which are not recorded in this book. But these are written that you may believe that **Jesus is the Christ, the Son of God,** and that by believing you may have **life in his name.**"* (John 20:30-31 NIV)

The apostle John also wrote:

> *"In the beginning was **the Word**, and **the Word was with God**, and **the Word was God**. He was with God in the beginning. Through him all things were made; without him nothing was made that has been made... **The Word became flesh and made His dwelling among us**. We have seen his glory, the glory of **the One and Only, who came from the Father**, full of grace and truth."* (John 1:1-3,14 NIV)

Years ago, a Muslim friend confided to me, "The Qur'an gives Jesus the title of *Kalimat Allah* (Word of God) and *Ruh* Allah (Soul of God). If Jesus is *God's Word* and *Soul*, then He is God!"

Later, some accused my friend of blasphemy and *shirk* (Arabic: *associating partners with God*[158]). At least he was in good company! In Jesus' day, the Jewish religious leaders accused Jesus in a similar fashion.

Jesus said:

"'I and My Father are one.'
Then the Jews took up stones again to stone Him.
Jesus answered them, 'Many good works I have shown you from My Father. For which of those works do you stone Me?'
The Jews answered Him, saying, 'For a good work we do not stone You, but for blasphemy, and because You, being a Man, make Yourself God.'" (John 10:30-33)

The Jews accused Jesus of doing the same thing Lucifer had tried to do: usurp the unique, exalted position that belongs to God alone. They accused Jesus of *making Himself God*.

But they had it backwards.

INCARNATION, NOT DEIFICATION

Neither Jesus nor the prophets taught that *a man would become God*, rather, the Scriptures made it clear that *God would become man*.

For example, 700 years before the Messiah was born, the prophet Isaiah wrote:

"The people who walked in darkness have seen a great light; those who dwelt in the land of the shadow of death, upon them a light has shined. ...For unto us a Child is born, unto us a Son is given, and the government will be upon His shoulder. And His name will be called Wonderful, Counselor, Mighty God, Everlasting Father, Prince of Peace." (Isaiah 9:2,6)[159]

Isaiah also wrote these words about the coming Messiah:

"You who bring good tidings, lift up your voice with strength, lift it up, be not afraid; say to the cities of Judah, 'Behold your God!'" (Isaiah 40:9)

From the beginning, God's plan included *incarnation* (God taking on human flesh), not *deification* (a human making himself into a god). To suggest that a man became God is blasphemy, but to recognize that *the eternal Word became man* is to embrace God's age-old plan.

ON PAPER *AND* IN PERSON

If you want to know someone well, which method is best?
* Limit your communication to written letters.
* Or, after exchanging letters for a certain period of time, meet the person face to face and spend time together.

As wonderful as the Scriptures are, God, who once walked and talked with Adam and Eve and planned for their descendants to know Him personally, never intended to limit His communication to *paper*. From the beginning, He planned to communicate with us in *person*. The LORD, who for centuries had His prophets record His Word on papyrus scrolls and *animal skins*, promised to reveal Himself to mankind in *human skin*. God not only planned to provide us with His words in *a book*, He would also provide His Word in *a body*.

*"When **He** came into the world, He said: '… **A body** You have prepared for Me.'"* (Hebrews 10:5)[160]

*"Beyond all question, the mystery of godliness is great: **He** appeared in **a body**."* (1 Timothy 3:16 NIV)

BENEATH HIS MAJESTY?

Despite God's repetitive declarations about His plan to dwell with man, I hear people say: "Far be it from God's transcendent majesty that He should become man!"

While the concept of the incarnation is mind-boggling, is it really below God's majesty? Or is it an integral part of God's nature and plan to establish a close relationship with the people He created for Himself?

In life, we often feel closest to those who have experienced what we have experienced. The ones most qualified to comfort and help are those who have gone through similar struggles and sorrows. Our Creator is the Ultimate Comforter.

> *"**Inasmuch then as the children have partaken of flesh and blood, He Himself likewise shared in the same**...For in that He Himself has suffered, being tempted, He is able to aid those who are tempted. ...For we do not have a High Priest who cannot sympathize with our weaknesses, but was **in all points tempted as we are, yet without sin**."*
> (Hebrews 2:14,18; 4:15)

From the beginning, it was God's plan to take on the limitations and discomforts of a body of flesh, get dirt under His fingernails, hunger, hurt, and experience what we experience. Those who teach otherwise are not only rejecting God's prophets and plan; they are rejecting God's nature and attributes. Instead of accepting God's revelation of Himself as the faithful and loving Creator who wants people to know Him in a personal way, they are declaring Him to be unpredictable and unknowable.

There is nothing "majestic" about being unwilling to come down to another's level to serve them and bless them. Never in history has our Creator despised the thought of coming down to our level. It was His design and His delight to do so.[161]

> *"Though **He was rich**, yet for your sakes **He became poor**, that you through His poverty might become rich."*
> (2 Corinthians 8:9)

It is for your sake and mine that the Eternal Word visited our planet—in person. The Creator of the universe who *"was rich"* in glory and honor, *"became poor,"* taking the place of a servant, so that we might become rich, not with money and material possessions, but with all spiritual blessings such as forgiveness, righteousness, eternal life, and a heart filled with His love, joy, peace, and holy desires.

GREATNESS DEFINED

Many think God is *too great* to come to earth in a body of flesh and blood. Could it be they think this way because their definition of *great* differs from God's definition of *great*?

Jesus defined true greatness when He told his disciples:

> *"You know that those who are regarded as rulers of the Gentiles lord it over them, and their high officials exercise authority over them. Not so with you. Instead, whoever wants to become **great** among you must be your **servant**, and whoever wants to be **first** must be **slave of all**. For even the **Son of Man did not come to be served, but to serve, and to give his life as a ransom for many**."* (Mark 10:42-45 NIV)

The greatest person is the one who humbles himself the most and serves others the best.[162]

That is what our Creator did for us.

MASTER OF WIND AND WAVES

One day Jesus was with His disciples in their fishing boat on the Sea of Galilee.

> *"Suddenly **a great tempest** arose on the sea, so that the boat was covered with the waves. But [Jesus] was asleep.*
>
> *Then His disciples came to Him and awoke Him, saying, 'Lord, save us! We are perishing!'*
>
> *But He said to them, 'Why are you fearful, O you of little faith?' Then He arose and rebuked the winds and the sea, and there was **a great calm**.*

> *So the men marveled, saying, 'Who can this be, that even the winds and the sea obey Him?'"* (Matthew 8:24-27)

How would *you* answer the disciples' question?

"WHO CAN THIS BE?"

Clearly, Jesus was a man. He was asleep in the boat; He knew what it was to be tired, hungry and thirsty. But then He stood up and rebuked the storm. Instantly the violent wind ceased and the raging sea became calm.

No wonder the disciples asked:

"Who can this be?"

A millennium earlier, the Psalmist had written:

> *"Who is mighty like You O LORD? ... You rule the raging of the sea; when its waves rise, You still them."* (Psalm 89:8-9)

"Who can this be?" The Gospel also tells of Jesus walking on the sea.[163] Once again, Jesus' disciples *"were greatly amazed in themselves beyond measure, and marveled."* (Mark 6:51) But Jesus didn't tread on the waves of the sea to make men marvel; He did it to help them understand who He is.

Two millennia earlier, the prophet Job said this about God:

> *"He alone spreads out the heavens, and treads on the waves of the sea."* (Job 9:8)

"Who can this be?" God invites us to connect the dots and understand who Jesus was and is.

Tragically, most never do.

> *"He was in the world, and though the world was made through him, the world did not recognize him."* (John 1:10 NIV)

"Who can this be?" Jesus Himself answered this question one day as He was speaking with a hostile religious crowd.

"I AM"

"Jesus spoke to them again, saying, 'I am the light of the world. He who follows Me shall not walk in darkness, but have the light of life... Most assuredly, I say to you, if anyone keeps My word he shall never see death.'

Then the Jews said to Him, '...You have a demon! Abraham is dead, and the prophets; and You say, 'If anyone keeps My word he shall never taste death.' Are You greater than our father Abraham, who is dead? And the prophets are dead. Whom do You make Yourself out to be?'

Jesus answered, '...Your father Abraham rejoiced to see My day, and he saw it and was glad.'

Then the Jews said to Him, 'You are not yet fifty years old, and have You seen Abraham?'

Jesus said to them, 'Most assuredly, I say to you, before Abraham was, I AM.'

Then they took up stones to throw at Him; but Jesus hid Himself and went out of the temple, going through the midst of them, and so passed by." (John 8:12,52-53,56-59)

Why did the Jews attempt to stone Jesus? Because He said: *"If anyone keeps My word he shall never see death,"* and: *"Before Abraham was, I AM."* Not only had Jesus asserted His authority over death and His seniority over Abraham (who had died 1900 years earlier), He also used God's personal name, *"I AM."*[164]

Jesus' hearers understood what He meant. That is why they accused Him of blasphemy and picked up stones to throw at Him.

WORSHIP GOD ALONE

Jesus consistently taught that God alone is worthy to be the Object of our worship. That is why Jesus said, *"You shall worship the LORD your God, and Him only you shall serve."* (Matthew 4:10) Yet the Gospel records no less than ten occasions when people bowed down before Jesus and worshiped Him.

One day, *"a leper came and worshiped Him,*[165] *saying, 'Lord, if You are willing, You can make me clean.' Then Jesus put out*

His hand and touched him, saying, 'I am willing; be cleansed.' *Immediately his leprosy was cleansed."* (Matthew 8:2-3) Did Jesus scold the leper for worshiping Him?

No, He simply touched him and cured him.

After Jesus rose from the dead, a disciple named Thomas fell down before Jesus and said, *"My Lord and my God!"* Did Jesus rebuke him for blasphemy?

No, Jesus simply said, *"Thomas, because you have seen Me, you have believed. Blessed are those who have not seen and yet have believed."* (John 20:28-29)

What does this teach us about who Jesus is?

YOU DECIDE

What each of us decides to believe about Jesus is our personal choice, but let none embrace a self-contradictory estimation of Him. If Jesus was "a great prophet," as my neighbors tell me, then He was also who He claimed to be: *the eternal Word and Son of God.* To declare Jesus to be "no more than a prophet," is to deny both the testimony of Jesus and the message of the prophets.[166]

C.S. Lewis, a former skeptic and one of the great intellectuals of the twentieth century, wrote this about Jesus:

"I am trying here to prevent anyone saying the really foolish thing that people often say about Him: 'I'm ready to accept Jesus as a great moral teacher, but I don't accept His claim to be God.' That is the one thing we must not say. A man who was merely a man and said the sort of things Jesus said would not be a great moral teacher. He would either be a lunatic or else he would be the Devil of Hell. You must make your choice. Either this man was, and is, the Son of God: or else a madman or something worse. You can shut Him up for a fool, you can spit at Him and kill Him as a demon; or you can fall at His feet and call Him Lord and God. But let us not come with any patronizing nonsense about His being a great human teacher. He has not left that open to us. He did not intend to."[167]

"TELL US PLAINLY"

Every so often, someone says to me: "Show me in the Bible where Jesus said, 'I am God'!" The religious leaders of Jesus' day tried to coerce Him to make similar statements.

> *Jesus said, "'I am* **the door**. *If anyone enters by* **Me**, *he will be saved'...the Jews surrounded Him and said to Him, 'How long do You keep us in doubt? If You are the Christ,* **tell us plainly**.*'*
> *Jesus answered them, 'I told you, and you do not believe. The works that I do in My Father's name, they bear witness of Me....I and My Father are one.'*
> **Then the Jews took up stones again to stone Him**.
> *Jesus answered them, 'Many good works I have shown you from My Father. For which of those works do you stone Me?'*
> *The Jews answered Him, saying,* **'For a good work we do not stone You, but for blasphemy, and because You, being a Man, make Yourself God.'"** (John 10:9,24-25,30-33)

Why did the religious crowd want to stone Him?

It was because Jesus had said, *"I and my Father are one."* In their thinking, Jesus' claim of oneness with God was blasphemy. Nonetheless, these same Jews regularly declared their faith in God by saying, *"Adonai Eloheynu Adonai* **echad**,*"* meaning: *"The Lord our God, the Lord is* **one** [a plural oneness].*"* Jesus was declaring Himself to be the Son of God who has always been one with God.[168] That is why the Jews accused Him of blasphemy.

Jesus never flaunted His eternal existence as the Word and Son of God. He did not go around saying, "I am God! I am God!" Instead, He lived on earth as He intends for all of mankind to live—in perfect humility and willing submission to God.

Jesus is the only Person who could say: *"I have come down from heaven,* **not to do My own will**, *but* **the will of Him** *who sent Me."* (John 6:38) The glory of Jesus' life was that He, the exalted *Son of* **God**, had humbled Himself to become the *Son of* **Man**.

The Lord Jesus chose to communicate who He was in humble yet powerful ways.

Once, a wealthy young man came to Jesus and addressed Him with the title *"Good Teacher."* So Jesus asked the man, *"Why do you call Me good? No one is good but One, that is, God."* (Luke 18:19)[169] This rich man did not believe Jesus was God, but Jesus—the personification of divine goodness—was inviting him to put the pieces of the puzzle together and understand who He is.

He wants us to understand too.[170]

BACKING WORDS WITH WORKS

The countless mighty miracles Jesus performed displayed His authority and power over every element of a fallen, sin-cursed creation. He knew the thoughts of men, forgave sin, multiplied bread and fish for thousands, calmed storms, and commanded evil spirits to depart. With a word or a touch, He healed the sick and made the lame to walk, the blind to see, the deaf to hear, and the dead to be raised to life. Just as the prophets had foretold, the Messiah was *"the Arm of the LORD"* on earth.[171]

Jesus' transcendent majesty shone through every part of His Being for those who had eyes to see it. His works authenticated His words. For example, as we just read, Jesus claimed to be *"the Life."* And how did He authenticate this claim? He proved it by commanding the dead to live again.

On one occasion, the Lord Jesus was at the graveside of Lazarus, a man who had died four days earlier. Lazarus' corpse had been buried in a cave-tomb. Jesus told the weeping sister of the deceased not to cry; that her brother would live again.

The sister told Jesus, *"I know that he will rise again in the resurrection at the last day."*

Jesus replied, *"I am the resurrection and the life. He who believes in Me, though he may die, he shall live."* (John 11:24-25)

Then to authenticate His claim, Jesus *"cried with a loud voice, 'Lazarus, come forth!' And he who had died came out bound hand and foot with grave clothes, and his face was wrapped with a cloth.*

Jesus said to them, 'Loose him, and let him go.'
Then many of the Jews who had...seen the things Jesus did,
believed in Him. But some of them went away to the Pharisees
and told them the things Jesus did. ... Then, ***from that day on,***
they plotted to put Him to death... *The chief priests plotted to*
put Lazarus to death also, *because on account of him many of the*
Jews...believed in Jesus." (John 11:43-46,53; 12:10-11)[172]
How hard the human heart!

HARD HEARTS

In light of Jesus' claims and growing popularity, the envious
religious and political leaders of the Jews became united by a
growing passion: Jesus must be silenced! They were desperate to
find a reason, any reason, to accuse Him so they might have Him
put to death. But how do you accuse the only perfect man ever to
be born?

One Sabbath, as Jesus was teaching in the synagogue...

"A man was there who had a withered hand. So [the
religious leaders] watched [Jesus] closely, whether He
would heal him on the Sabbath, so that they might accuse
Him. And He said to the man who had the withered hand,
'Step forward.' Then He said to them, 'Is it lawful on the
Sabbath to do good or to do evil, to save life or to kill?'
But they kept silent.
And when He had looked around at them with anger,
being grieved by the hardness of their hearts, *He said to*
the man, 'Stretch out your hand.'
And he stretched it out, and his hand was restored as
whole as the other.
Then the Pharisees *[religious party]* ***went out and***
immediately plotted with the Herodians *[political party]*
against Him, how they might destroy Him.
But Jesus withdrew with His disciples to the sea.
And a great multitude...came to Him. ...He healed many,
so that as many as had afflictions pressed about Him to
touch Him.

> *And the unclean spirits, whenever they saw Him, fell down before Him and cried out, saying, 'You are the Son of God!'"* (Mark 3:1-11)

DEMONIC INSIGHT

The demons (literally, *"knowing ones"*) knew who this Healer was, which is why they addressed Him by His proper title, yelling out, *"You are the Son of God!"*

These fallen angels were all too familiar with Jesus' previous history.

Millennia earlier, they had witnessed His awesome power and unfathomable wisdom as He spoke the heavens and earth into existence. They shuddered as they recalled the day when He, in His righteous wrath, had cast them out of heaven after they chose to follow Satan in his rebellion.[173] And now here He was on earth living among men!

The writing was on the wall.

Their master's authority was crumbling.

The curse of sin was beginning to be reversed.

The Eternal Son Himself, as the Seed of a woman, had invaded their domain. Thus, the demons *"fell down before Him and cried out, saying, 'You are the Son of God!'"* Meanwhile, the religious leaders *"plotted...against Him, how they might destroy Him."*

Once, after I told this story to some guests, one of the men commented, "Incredible! The demons had more respect for Jesus than did the religious leaders!"

Incredible, but true.

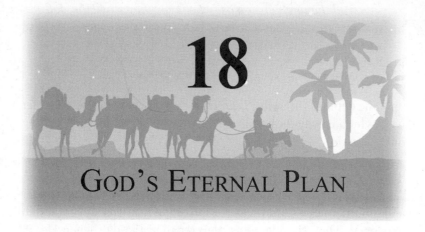

GOD'S ETERNAL PLAN

*"Known to God **from eternity** are all His works."*
(Acts 15:19)

Before time began, God had a clear plan in mind for people. The same day sin contaminated the human family, the LORD began to announce that plan, but in an encoded kind of way. The Scripture refers to this plan as *"the **mystery** of God."* (Revelation 10:7)

To this day, God's plan and purpose for humanity remains a mystery to most people, but needlessly so, since *"the **mystery** which has been hidden from ages and from generations ... **now has been revealed**."* (Colossians 1:26)

MORE PRIVILEGED THAN THE PROPHETS

Here is an amazing thought. When it comes to understanding God's story and message, you and I are more privileged than the prophets who wrote the Scriptures.

We have God's full revelation; they did not.

We can read the end of God's Book; they could not.

"Concerning this salvation, the prophets, who spoke of the grace that was to come to you, searched intently

and with the greatest care, trying to find out the time and circumstances to which the Spirit of Christ in them was pointing when he predicted the sufferings of Christ and the glories that would follow. ***It was revealed to them that they were not serving themselves but you, when they spoke of the things that have now been told you*** *by those who have preached the gospel to you by the Holy Spirit sent from heaven.* ***Even angels long to look into these things.***" (1 Peter 1:10-12 NIV)

WHY GOD ENCODED HIS PLAN

Some have asked, "Why didn't God immediately tell fallen mankind exactly what He planned to do? Why did He enshroud His message in mystery?"

Despite the fact that the Sovereign God of the universe owes us no explanation, in His kindness, He has given us some insights as to why He encoded His plan for man. Here are **three reasons** God chose to unfold His program progressively and prudently.

First, as explained in chapters five and six, by gradually revealing His plan, God provided humanity with countless *confirming prophecies and symbols,* as well as multiple *confirming witnesses,* so that later generations could know with certainty the message of the one true God.

Second, God revealed His truth in such a way that only those who care enough to *search it out diligently* will discover it. *"It is the glory of God to conceal a matter, but the glory of kings is to* ***search out*** *a matter."* (Proverbs 25:2) Many people can't find truth for the same reason a thief can't find a police officer; they don't want to.[174]

Third, God encoded His plan in order to ***conceal it*** from Satan and his followers.

*"We speak **the wisdom of God in a mystery, the hidden wisdom** which God ordained before the ages for our glory, **which none of the rulers of this age knew; for had they known, they would not have crucified the Lord of glory.**"* (1 Corinthians 2:7-8)

If Satan and those who sided with him had understood God's integral plan to defeat them, they would not have done what they did. God designed His plan in such a way that the very ones who plotted to thwart it would fulfill it!

And just what was that plan?

REDEMPTION!

God promised to send a sinless Savior into the world—as *the Seed of a woman*—to deliver Adam's wayward, law-breaking descendents from eternal damnation. At the right moment in human history, God fulfilled His promise.

> *"When the fullness of the time had come, God sent forth His Son, born of a woman, born under the law, **to redeem** those who were under the law."* (Galatians 4:4-5)

To redeem means *to buy back* by paying the required price.

As a boy growing up in California, I had a small dog. I would feed her, care for her and play with her. She would follow me around and get excited when I returned home from school. But she had a fault. Sometimes she would wander into the neighborhood, though she always came back. Until one day.

I came home from school, but my dog wasn't there to greet me. At bedtime, she was still nowhere to be found. The next day, my father suggested I call the local animal shelter, a place that holds stray cats and dogs for a limited time. Unclaimed animals are euthanized (put to death).

I called the shelter. Yes, they had a small dog that met my description. She had been picked up by "the dog catcher." My dog was helpless to save herself. If someone didn't come to her rescue, she would pay for her going astray with her life.

I went to the shelter. I was about to get my dog back! But the official at the front desk told me that if I wanted her back I must pay a penalty. It was against the law for a dog to be running loose on the street. I paid the required ransom and my dog was released. How glad she was to be out of that awful cage and back with the one who cared for her! She had been *redeemed*.

My boyhood experience in buying back my wayward dog gives us a faint idea of our own situation. As rebellious, condemned sinners, we have no way to rescue ourselves. God sent His Son into the world to redeem us by paying the necessary ransom price. It was more than any of us could pay.

> *"None of them can by any means* **redeem** *his brother, nor give to God a* **ransom** *for him—* **For the redemption of their souls is costly**... *But God will* **redeem** *my soul from the power of the grave...."* (Psalm 49:7,15)

So just what was the price of our redemption?

THE PROPHETS ANNOUNCED IT

In Genesis chapter 3, we encountered God's encoded, embryonic prophecy about His plan to redeem sinners from Satan's grasp. Let's listen again to what God said to Satan.

> *"I will put enmity between you and the woman, and between your seed and her Seed; He shall bruise your head, and you shall bruise His heel."* (Genesis 3:15)

With these words, God set forth a mysterious and methodical outline of His plan to deal with Satan and sin in a way consistent with His holy nature. The LORD was announcing that He would provide mankind with a Redeemer-Messiah who would defeat Satan by bruising his *"head."* The prophecy also foretold that Satan would bruise the Messiah's *"heel."*

> *"He* [Messiah] *shall bruise your* [Satan's] **head**, *and you* [Satan] *shall bruise His* [Messiah's] **heel**.*"

How would the Seed of the woman *"bruise"* Satan's head? The Hebrew word translated "bruise" means "to bruise, break, wound, or crush." According to this initial prophecy, both Satan and the Messiah would be "crushed," but only one of the wounds would be irreversibly fatal. A crushed head is fatal; a crushed heel is not.

God was foretelling that, despite the fact that the promised Redeemer would be "wounded" by Satan and his followers, He would ultimately be victorious over Satan.

Later, God inspired the prophet David to write these words of the Messiah:

"They pierced My hands and My feet." (Psalm 22:16)

David also predicted that, though the Messiah would be killed, His corpse would not decay in the grave.

"You will not...allow Your Holy One to see corruption."
(Psalm 16:10)

The promised Deliverer would overcome death.

The prophet Isaiah declared the purpose of the Messiah's sufferings, death, and resurrection:

*"He was **wounded for our transgressions**, He was **bruised for our iniquities**... Yet it pleased the LORD to bruise Him; He has put Him to grief. When **You make His soul an offering for sin**, He shall see **His seed**, He shall prolong His days, and the pleasure of the LORD shall prosper in His hand."* (Isaiah 53:5,10)[175]

Though Satan would persuade people to torture and murder the Messiah sent by God, all would take place according to the plan announced by the prophets. The final outcome would be total triumph for the LORD and *His Anointed.*

WORDS OF WISDOM AND WARNING

A thousand years before Christ was born, David wrote:

*"**Why do the nations rage, and the people plot a vain thing?** The kings of the earth set themselves, and the rulers take counsel together, **against the LORD and against His Anointed** [Messiah]...He who sits in the heavens shall laugh...Then He shall speak to them in His wrath, and*

*distress them in His deep displeasure. Yet I have set **My** **King** on My holy hill... Now therefore, be wise, O kings; be instructed, you judges of the earth. Serve the LORD with fear, and rejoice with trembling. **Kiss** [honor] **the** **Son**, lest He be angry, and you perish in the way, when His wrath is kindled but a little. **Blessed are all those who put their trust in Him**.* (Psalm 2:1-2, 4-6,10-12)

In Senegal, where wrestling is the national traditional sport, the people have this proverb:

"An egg should not wrestle with a rock."

Why shouldn't an egg fight with a rock? Because the egg has no chance of winning the contest! Likewise, all who *"set themselves against the LORD and against His Anointed"* will not succeed. To resist God's plan is to *"plot a vain thing."*[176]
The Senegalese also have this proverb:

"A woodcutter doesn't intentionally cut down the meeting-place tree."

In this arid region of the world, most villages have a large, centrally located shade tree. This "meeting-place tree" provides a place of refuge from the intense midday heat; a place where people can relax, talk and sip tea. How would the villagers react if a woodcutter started chopping at the "meeting-place tree"? With displays of great indignation, they would put a stop to his chopping—immediately!
All who set themselves against God's plan of redemption are like a woodcutter who chops at the villagers' favorite tree.
They will not succeed.

"Be wise O kings... Kiss the Son, lest He be angry, and you perish in the way, when His wrath is kindled but a little. Blessed are all those who put their trust in Him."
(Psalm 2:10,12)

BLIND TO GOD'S PLAN

In the final weeks of His ministry on earth, Jesus began to inform His disciples that, instead of receiving Him as their King, the political and spiritual leaders would demand that He be executed. What those who plotted Jesus' death did not realize was that they would actually be taking part in fulfilling what the prophets had foretold: that the Messiah's hands and feet would be pierced as part of God's plan to redeem Adam's wayward, helpless descendants from Satan's grasp.

> *"From that time on Jesus began to explain to his disciples that He **must** go to Jerusalem and suffer many things at the hands of the elders, chief priests and teachers of the law, and that He **must** be killed and on the third day be raised to life.*
>
> *Peter took Him aside and began to rebuke Him. 'Never, Lord!' he said. 'This shall never happen to you!'*
>
> *Jesus turned and said to Peter, '**Get behind Me, Satan! You are a stumbling block to Me; you do not have in mind the things of God, but the things of men.**'"*
> (Matthew 16:21-23)

Peter's thinking was similar to that of a celebrated debater I heard declare, "A crucified Messiah is like a married bachelor!"

Like the debater, Peter had not yet understood God's plan. He thought that the Messiah should immediately establish His promised worldwide government; not submit to the horror and humiliation of being nailed to a cross!

Peter was right in thinking that God planned to install Jesus as the Sovereign Ruler over all the earth, but he was wrong in thinking that the Messiah could bypass the suffering and shame of the cross. Later Peter would understand God's plan and proclaim with boldness: *"The prophets… predicted the sufferings of Christ and the glories that would follow!"* (1 Peter 1:11 NIV)[177]

The Messiah's crucifixion would not be an accident. God anticipated and planned it *"from eternity."* The prophets foretold it. *The Seed of the woman* came to fulfill it.

Some time ago this e-mail came to my box:

Send **Subject:** | Email Feedback

You are **so blind** that you believe that **God can't even save his own son from being crucified.** This is to say God has a limitation and he is so weak that he let his son be humiliated and killed by humans. Anything that has limitation is weak and should not be called God. **God has the ultimate power.** He is the one and only and nothing is equal to him.
Allahuakbar.

Like Peter at the first, this e-mail correspondent had not yet understood why the Messiah *"must be killed and on the third day be raised to life."*

Why was such a dreadful plan necessary? Since, as our e-mail correspondent rightly stated, *"God has the ultimate power,"* why did God not simply cast Satan into hell and declare Adam's sinful descendants forgiven? The LORD created the world by just speaking, so why didn't He redeem the world by just speaking?

Why was it necessary that the Creator-Word become man? Why did God's plan include a suffering, bleeding, dying Messiah?

The next stage of our journey provides the answer.

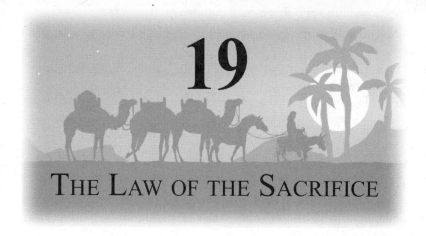

THE LAW OF THE SACRIFICE

*"It is the blood that makes **atonement** for the soul."*
— The LORD (Leviticus 17:11)

T he first family's history is recorded in Genesis, chapter four. It is here we first learn that when Adam and Eve were put out of the idyllic Garden of Eden, the entire human race was put out. All their descendants would be born and raised in a cursed world under enemy control.

FIRSTBORN SINNER

*"Now Adam knew Eve his wife, and she conceived and bore **Cain**, and said, 'I have acquired a man from the LORD.'"* (Genesis 4:1)

Cain means *acquire*. In the midst of the pain and wonder of the first childbirth, Eve exclaimed, *"I have acquired a man from the LORD!"* Perhaps she thought Cain was the promised Deliverer sent by God to rescue them from sin's deadly consequences.

Eve was right in believing that the promised Savior would come *"from the LORD."* She was also right in believing that the Messiah would be *born of a woman,* but if she thought her husband's offspring was the promised Deliverer, she was wrong.

Any such misconceptions were cleared up all too quickly.

Adam and Eve soon discovered that their darling little firstborn son had an inbred sin nature. Cain sinned *naturally*. He exhibited pride and self-will—just as Satan had done and just as his parents had done. Cain was not the promised Redeemer. He was just another helpless sinner in need of redemption.

By the time Adam and Eve's second son came along, they had a more realistic perspective of man's condition.

*"Then she bore again, this time his brother **Abel**."*
(Genesis 4:2)

ʼ Adam and Eve named their second son *Abel*, meaning *vanity* or *nothing*. There was no way they could produce a righteous child. The promised Savior of sinners could not come from Adam's sinful line. Together, Adam and Eve could only procreate another sinner like themselves. If there was to be a righteous Man to save them from sin's penalty, He must come from the LORD.

As we learned in Genesis chapter one, the first man and woman were created *in the image and likeness of God*. This amazing privilege included the solemn responsibility of making right choices. God's will for Adam and Eve and their descendants was that they reflect their Creator's holy and loving nature. However, when Adam and Eve chose to disobey their Creator-Owner, they ceased reflecting His image. Instantly, they fell from being *God*-centered to being *self*-centered. And they gave birth to children like themselves.

*"Adam...had sons and daughters... **in his own likeness, after his image**."* (Genesis 5:3)

As goes the Wolof proverb: *"Bounding gazelles do not beget burrowing offspring."* Neither do sinful parents beget righteous offspring. The Scripture says,

*"**Through one man** sin entered the world, and death through sin, and thus death **spread to all men**, because all sinned."* (Romans 5:12)

SINNERS WORSHIP

*"Now **Abel** was a keeper of sheep, but **Cain** was a tiller of the ground. In the process of time it came to pass that Cain brought an offering of the fruit of the ground to the LORD. Abel also brought of the firstborn of his flock and of their fat."* (Genesis 4:2-4)

Cain became a farmer and Abel a shepherd. Although sin's effects were around them and in them, they were still surrounded by the glory of God's creation and sustained by His loving care. Though Cain and Abel were both sinners, God loved them and wanted them to know Him and approach Him in worship. However, for this to happen, they needed a remedy for their sin-problem. God is holy and *"those who worship Him must worship in spirit and truth."* (John 4:24)

Clearly, these boys were well-taught by their parents who had once enjoyed close friendship with their Creator. Both Cain and Abel understood that sin was an offense to God. Like their parents, they were shut out from God's presence. If they were to have a relationship with Him, it must be on His terms.

The good news was that God had opened a way by which Cain and Abel could have their sins covered if they would trust Him and approach Him in the way He had established.

Let's listen again to the narrative:

*"In the process of time it came to pass that **Cain brought an offering of the fruit of the ground to the LORD. Abel also brought of the firstborn of his flock and of their fat.** And the LORD respected Abel and his offering, but He did not respect Cain and his offering."* (Genesis 4:3-5)

As with any well-told story, not all the details are immediately given. The narrative simply tells *what* Cain and Abel did. *Why* they did what they did is explained elsewhere in Scripture. Both young men wanted to worship the one true God. Each *"brought an offering...to the LORD."*

Cain came with an impressive selection of fruits and vegetables which he had diligently cultivated.

Abel brought an innocent, unblemished lamb, killed it and burned its body on a simple altar made of stone or earth.[178]

By outward appearances, Abel's bloody offering was brutal and appalling, while Cain's agricultural offering was beautiful and appealing. Yet the Scripture says:

> *"The LORD respected Abel and his offering, but He did not respect Cain and his offering. And Cain was very angry, and his countenance fell."* (Genesis 4:4-5)

Why did God accept Abel's offering and reject Cain's?

Abel trusted God's plan.

Cain did not.

ABEL'S FAITH AND LAMB

The Scriptures tell us Abel came to God *"by faith,"* indicating that God had revealed to Cain and Abel what He required.

> *"By faith Abel* [who believed God's plan] *offered to God a more excellent sacrifice than Cain* [who did not believe God's plan], *through which [Abel] obtained witness that he was righteous... But without faith it is impossible to please Him."* (Hebrews 11:4,6)

The faith that pleases God is faith that believes and submits to His plan.

When Adam and Eve first sinned, God rejected their self-efforts to fix their sin-problem. Instead, God performed the first animal sacrifice and provided Adam and Eve with a covering for their sin and shame. By putting to death some innocent animals, God was teaching them that *"the wages of sin is death, but the gift of God is eternal life...."* (Romans 6:23)

Later, Cain and Abel were taught the same lesson, but only one believed it.

Abel approached God *by faith,* humbly
and obediently presenting to the LORD
a healthy firstborn lamb.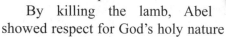
Visualize Abel laying his hand on the
lamb's head and quietly thanking
the LORD that though he, Abel,
deserved the death penalty,
God would accept the lamb's
blood as a temporary payment
for sin. Next, Abel takes
the knife and slits the gentle
creature's throat and watches
as its life-blood pulsates out.
By killing the lamb, Abel
showed respect for God's holy nature
and for the law of sin and death. It was because Abel trusted God's
plan that God forgave Abel of his sins and declared him righteous.
Abel was set free from the penalty of sin because that penalty had
been carried out against the lamb. Abel's sacrifice symbolized and
pointed to the perfect Sacrifice God promised to provide one day
to take away the sin of the world.

That is why *"the LORD respected Abel and his offering."*

CAIN'S WORKS AND RELIGION

Then there was Cain. What a religious young man he was! He
set before God an admirable array of fruits and vegetables he had
worked hard to produce. But God rejected Cain and his offering.

Cain's error was not the worship of a false god, but false
worship of the one true God.

Instead of approaching his Creator by faith, Cain came with
his own ideas and efforts. God had not accepted his parents' self-
conceived covering of fig leaves and neither would He accept
Cain's self-conceived offering of vegetables.

Some argue, "But Cain brought what he had!"

God didn't want what Cain had. He wanted Cain to trust Him
and worship Him on the basis of a death payment—the blood of
a lamb. If Cain didn't have a lamb, he could have traded some

vegetables for one of Abel's lambs or he could have humbly approached the LORD at Abel's altar where the blood of the lamb had been shed. But Cain was too proud for that. He chose to "worship" God with the works of his own hands.

That is why God *"did not respect Cain and his offering."*

THE SIN-DEBT

Why was the LORD so categorical? Why did He accept Abel's slain lamb, but not Cain's fresh vegetables?

God refused Cain's offering for the simple reason that the penalty for sin is *death*, not self-effort. *The law of sin and death* which God first made known to Adam had not changed. All who break God's laws owe a debt that can only be paid with *DEATH*. The Righteous Judge of the universe will not permit an infraction of His laws to be penalized with anything less.

No amount of sincerity, self-effort, or good works can cancel the debt of sin.

To illustrate, imagine that a major bank lends me several million dollars. Instead of investing this enormous sum of money wisely, I squander it and default on the loan. The police come to my house and arrest me. In court, I tell the judge, "Never in my lifetime will I be able to pay back the millions of dollars I owe, but I have a plan to erase my financial debt. Here is what I will do: Instead of paying back the debt with money, I will pay it back with good works! Every day I will bring to the president of the bank a bowl of cooked rice. One day each week I will skip a meal and give that food to feed the poor. I will also take a ceremonial bath several times a day to wash away the shame of my debt. This I will do until my debt is paid off."

Would the judge accept such an irrational arrangement as payment for a financial debt? Never! Neither will the Judge of all the earth accept praying, fasting, and good works as payment for a sin-debt. There is only one way to pay for sin. It must be paid for with *DEATH—eternal separation from God.*

Is there a way for helpless sinners to be delivered from this unbending *law of sin and death*?

Thank God, there is.

THE LAW OF THE SACRIFICE

I don't play cards, but I do know some cards "trump" others. Due to a card's assigned value, it wins over cards of lesser value.

The Old Testament books of Daniel and Esther tell of ancient kings making laws that could *"not be changed, according to the law of the Medes and Persians, which [do] not alter."* (Daniel 6:8) If a king wanted to overcome a certain law, instead of abolishing it, he established a stronger law that would "trump" the previous one.[179]

Similarly, from the beginning, God's righteous way of overcoming *"the law of sin and death,"* was to bring in a stronger law, namely, *"The law of the sin offering,"* (Leviticus 6:25) or, as it is also called: *"The law of the sacrifice."* (Leviticus 7:11)

God, who upholds all His laws, established the *law of the sacrifice* to trump the still legally binding *law of sin and death.*

The law of the sacrifice offered *mercy* to guilty sinners while, at the same time, carrying out *justice* against sin. (For a review as to why God must maintain *mercy and justice* in perfect balance, see chapter 13.) The law of the blood sacrifice provided a way for God to punish sin without punishing the sinner. Here is God's explanation of how that could happen:

> *"The life of the flesh is in the **blood**, and I have given it to you upon the altar to make atonement for your souls; for it is the blood that makes **atonement** for the soul."*
> (Leviticus 17:11)

This law contained two basic principles:

1. BLOOD PROVIDES LIFE — God said: **"The life of the flesh is in the blood."** Modern science affirms what the Scriptures have declared for thousands of years: *a creature's life is in its blood.* Healthy blood transports all the elements necessary to sustain life and to cleanse away impurities. The blood is precious; without it, humans and animals alike die.

2. SIN REQUIRES DEATH — God also said: **"It is the blood that makes atonement for the soul."** The word *atonement* comes from the Hebrew word *kaphar* which means to *"cover, cancel, cleanse, forgive, and reconcile."*[180] It was only through the poured-out blood that sinners could be cleansed and reconciled to their righteous Creator. Since the penalty for sin is death, God was saying He would accept the blood (forfeited life) of an acceptable sacrifice as *a payment and covering for man's sin.*

A SUBSTITUTE

The underlying principle of *the law of the sacrifice* can be summed up in a word: **substitution**. An innocent animal would die as the condemned sinner's substitute.

In the generations prior to the coming of the Messiah, the LORD made it known to Adam's descendants that He would temporarily accept the shed blood of a suitable animal, such as a lamb, sheep, goat, or bull. Even pigeons and doves could be offered.[181] No matter how rich or poor, good or bad a person was, all were to approach God recognizing their sinfulness and believing that God would grant them forgiveness based on the shed blood.

The condemned creature had to be *"without blemish."*[182] It could not have any sickness, broken bones, cuts, or scratches. It had to be symbolically perfect. The sinner offering the sacrifice was to *"lay his hand on the head of the [animal], and kill it ... It is a sin offering."* The fat of the animal would then be burned on the altar.

And what did God say such an offering would accomplish?

"His sin... shall be forgiven him." (Leviticus 4:23-26)

The person placing his or her hand on the head of a sacrifice symbolized the transfer of sin to the flawless creature. The sin-bearer then perished *in the place of* the sinner.

On the basis of this principle of *substitution*, sin was punished and the sinner was pardoned. The death penalty for sin fell on the "perfect," innocent animal instead of on the guilty man or woman.

The law of the sin offering taught sinners that God is holy and that *"without the shedding of blood* [a death payment] *there is no forgiveness* [removal of sin's penalty]. *"* (Hebrews 9:22 NIV)

By means of the animal sacrifice, God was carrying out His justice against sin and showing His mercy to sinners who trusted in Him. God promised to bless all who came to Him in this way. On the same day God gave His ancient people the Ten Commandments, God told them that the only way they could be accepted by Him was to approach Him on the basis of a blood sacrifice presented on an altar.

*"An altar of earth you shall make **for Me**, and **you shall sacrifice on it** your burnt offerings and your peace offerings, your sheep and your oxen. **In every place where I record My name I will come to you, and I will bless you.** "* (Exodus 20:24)

The main intent of this blood-for-sin provision was to demonstrate God's righteous wrath against sin until such time as the promised Savior arrived.

The Messiah's purpose would be to fulfill *the true meaning* of the law of the sacrifice.

In God's estimation, the life of one human is worth more than all the animals in the entire world. Animals were not created in the image of God. Animals do not have eternal souls. Consequently, animal blood could *only symbolize* what was necessary to cancel man's debt of sin.

Abel's slain lamb is only the first recorded story among scores of Old Testament narratives in which we see believers coming to God in worship with the poured-out blood of innocent, flawless animals. Among these numerous animal-sacrifice stories, one stands above the rest.

It's the one remembered each year by Muslims around the world.

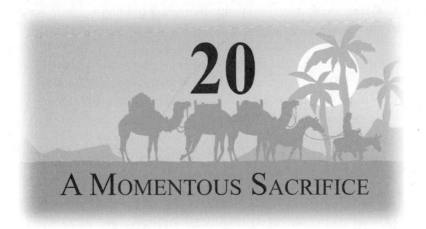

A MOMENTOUS SACRIFICE

T he family is gathered around.
The subdued creature is held to the ground.
Old and young alike lay their hand on the sheep or on the father bearing the knife.
The cut is swift and onto the sand pulsates the animal's life.
The sacrifice is over—until next year.

On *Eid al-Adha*, "the Feast of the Sacrifice," Muslims point back to a four thousand year-old Biblical event when God provided a ram to die instead of Abraham's son.[183] The Qur'an concludes its brief account of this classic story with these words: *"And We ransomed him with a momentous sacrifice."* (Sura 37:107)

To understand the full significance of this dramatic story, let us return to the book of Genesis.

ABRAHAM

Abraham[184] was born around 2000 BC in the land of Ur, modern-day Iraq. Like all descendants of Adam, he was born with a sin nature. Although Abraham grew up among pagan idol worshipers, he became a believer in the one true God. Abraham did not share the opinion of many people today who think they must be loyal to the religion of their parents no matter what.

Like Abel, Abraham approached the LORD God in worship with the shed blood of sacrificed animals.

When Abraham was seventy-five years old and his wife was
sixty-five, the LORD appeared to him and said:

*"Leave your country, your people and your father's
household and go to the land I will show you.* **I will make
you into a great nation and I will bless you;** *I will make
your name great, and you will be a blessing. I will bless
those who bless you, and whoever curses you I will curse;*
and all peoples on earth will be blessed through you.*"*
(Genesis 12:1-3 NIV)

God promised to make of Abraham a *"great nation"* through
which He would provide salvation for all people groups on earth.
This nation would be *"great,"* not in *size*, but in *significance*. To
make this new nation a reality, Abraham and his childless wife
Sarah were commanded by God to move to a land He promised to
give to their descendants—though they still had none.

How did Abraham react to God's seemingly impossible
promises? He trusted God and obeyed, leaving his father's
household and heading to the land of Canaan, which today is
known as Israel and Palestine.

ABRAHAM'S FAITH

Once Abraham arrived in Canaan, the LORD said to him,
*"'To your descendants I will give this land.' And there he built an
altar to the LORD, who had appeared to him."* (Genesis 12:6-7)

God's promise was nothing short of amazing. The land of
Canaan was populated with many different people groups. How
could Abraham and his descendants possess it? He and his wife
had no descendants.

Imagine an elderly couple coming from a far away land to
visit your country. When they arrive, you tell them, "One day
you and your descendants will possess this whole country!" The
old man laughs and says, "Very funny! I don't even have any
descendants! I am an old man; I have no children and my wife is
unable to conceive and you tell me that my descendants are going
to multiply and possess this country? Are you ill?"

This is the kind of staggering promise God made to Abraham. And how did Abraham react? The Scripture says he *"believed in the LORD, and He accounted it to him for righteousness."* (Genesis 15:6) Because of Abraham's childlike faith in God's promise, God declared him righteous. After he died, Abraham would live forever with the LORD in Paradise.

The word in the original Hebrew text for *"believed"* is *aman*, from which comes the expression, *"Amen!"* which means: "So be it!" or "It is trustworthy and true!"

Don't miss this. To *believe in the LORD* is to hear what He has declared and to respond with a heart-felt "Amen!" It is such childlike faith that connects with God. Whether or not we have accepted God's Word as true will be demonstrated by our actions. Abraham's faith was authenticated by the fact that he chose the hard path, turning his back on his father's religion in order to follow the LORD.

> *"'Abraham believed God, and it was accounted to him for righteousness.' And he was called the friend of God."*
> (James 2:23)

Abraham was God's friend because He believed God's Word. However, this does not mean that Abraham always trusted God in every area of life. Judicially, God had declared him perfectly righteous, but in his everyday living, Abraham was less than perfect. The Scriptures do not hide the sins and shortcomings of the prophets.

ISHMAEL

Abraham and Sarah lived in the land of Canaan as nomads, dwelling in tents, moving from place to place. In time, Abraham grew extremely wealthy in livestock.

More than ten years had passed since God promised to make of Abraham a great nation. He was now eighty-six years old and his wife was seventy-six, and they still had no children. How could Abraham become a great nation if he had no offspring? Abraham and his wife decided to "help" God fulfill His promise.

Instead of waiting for the LORD to work out His plan in His time, they followed their own common sense and local culture. Sarah gave her Egyptian house girl Hagar to Abraham so he could sleep with her and have a child by her. Hagar bore Abraham a son whom they named *Ishmael.*

Thirteen years later, when Abraham was ninety-nine years old, Almighty God appeared to him and told him that Sarah his wife would have a son.

*"Then Abraham fell on his face and laughed, and said in his heart, 'Shall a child be born to a man who is one hundred years old? And shall Sarah, who is ninety years old, bear a child?' And Abraham said to God, 'Oh, that Ishmael might live before You!' Then God said: 'No, Sarah your wife shall bear you a son, and you shall call his name Isaac; I will establish My covenant with him for an everlasting covenant, and with his descendants after him. **And as for Ishmael, I have heard you. Behold, I have blessed him, and will make him fruitful, and will multiply him exceedingly. He shall beget twelve princes, and I will make him a great nation. But My covenant I will establish with Isaac**, whom Sarah shall bear to you at this set time next year.'"* (Genesis 17:17-21)

ISAAC

God kept His promise. Sarah, in her old age, bore to Abraham a son named *Isaac.*

"So the child grew and was weaned. And Abraham made a great feast on the same day that Isaac was weaned. And Sarah saw the son of Hagar the Egyptian, whom she had borne to Abraham, scoffing." (Genesis 21:8-9)

Ishmael did not appreciate God's plan to use Isaac to raise up a nation through which the LORD would communicate His truth and provide salvation for the world. Instead, Ishmael ridiculed his half-brother. Tensions increased to the point where Abraham had to send Ishmael and Hagar away. This was an agonizing experience for Abraham who loved his son Ishmael.

> *"But God said to Abraham, 'Do not let it be displeasing in your sight because of the lad* [Ishmael] *or because of your bondwoman* [Hagar]*... for in Isaac your seed shall be called. ... So God was with the lad* [Ishmael]*; and he grew and dwelt in the wilderness, and became an archer. He dwelt in the Wilderness of Paran; and his mother took a wife for him from the land of Egypt."*
> (Genesis 21:12,20-21)

As the LORD promised, Ishmael became the father of a great people which God has blessed in many ways. Yet the LORD made it clear to Abraham that it would be *"in Isaac"* that He would fulfill His covenant to provide salvation for the world.

ISRAEL

Later, Isaac would marry and have twin sons, Esau and Jacob. God eventually gave Jacob a new name, telling him, *"Israel shall be your name."* (Genesis 35:10) Jacob had twelve sons, the forefathers of the twelve tribes of Israel, which in the time of Moses, God organized into a nation. The LORD called these descendants of Abraham, Isaac and Jacob *His chosen people.*[185]

Why did He choose *them*? Were they better than the other nations? No, in fact God told the Israelites that they were *"the least of all peoples."* (Deuteronomy 7:7) The LORD chose these weak, despised Hebrew people so that no man could take the credit and praise for what God planned to accomplish.

This is how God delights to work.

> *"God has chosen **the weak things** of the world to put to shame the things which are mighty; and **the base things** of the world and **the things which are despised** God has chosen, and **the things which are not**, to bring to nothing the things that are, **that no flesh should glory in His presence.**"* (1 Corinthians 1:28-29)

A COMMUNICATION CHANNEL

God raised up this new nation as a channel through which He would communicate His message to the ends of the earth. God created this "channel of communication" long before the time of radio and television, but it would be no less effective. The mighty acts of the one true God in the midst of this nation would be heard throughout the world. For example, the Scripture records this testimony of a Canaanite woman: *"We have heard how the LORD dried up the water of the Red Sea for you when you came out of Egypt... The LORD your God, He is God in heaven above and on earth beneath."* (Joshua 2:10-11)

Furthermore, it would be from this nation that God would select *the prophets* who would write *the Scriptures*.

Most importantly, it would be through this nation that God would provide *a Descendant*, who would Himself be the channel of blessing to the world. As we already observed (in chapter 16), this Descendant was none other than *the promised Seed of the woman* who came down from heaven to be born of a poor, Jewish maiden who was a virgin.

Whether we approve or not, this ancient nation was the communication channel established *by God* to transmit His truth and eternal blessings to every nation on earth. And it all began with the LORD telling Abraham to leave his father's house and go to the land of Canaan.

God's great covenant to Abraham had two major parts:

1) *"I will make you into a **great nation** and I will bless you..."*
2) *"And **all peoples on earth** will be blessed through you."*

God's love is not limited to one special group. He didn't just want to bless Abraham or Israel. His heart of compassion yearns after *"all peoples on earth."* The Old Testament abounds with stories of God using the small and stubborn nation of Israel to offer His grace to all nations and language groups on earth.[186] God's purpose to bless all nations through this despised nation must be kept in mind whenever the Bible tells of the LORD protecting the Israelites from those who attempted to eradicate them. God was defending them, *not because they were better* than other nations, but *because they were the channel* through which He determined to display His power and glory and provide salvation for the world. By protecting the descendants of Abraham, Isaac and Jacob, God was protecting His blessings for *"all peoples on earth."*

What's more, the LORD God's reputation was at stake. He had sworn by His own great name to bless all nations through this weak and despised nation.[187]

God would do precisely what He promised—for the honor of His name. Would we not do the same if our reputation, or the honor of our family, was at stake?

GOD TESTS ABRAHAM

Let us now return to the classic story of Abraham's momentous sacrifice.

Here is the setting: Abraham was very old. Ishmael had been sent away many years earlier. Only Abraham's son Isaac remained at home.

God was about to test Abraham's faith to the extreme. The LORD God was also about to set before the world some patterns and prophecies about what He Himself planned to do to redeem the children of Adam from sin's death sentence.

> *"Now it came to pass after these things that God tested Abraham, and said to him, 'Abraham!'*
> *And he said, 'Here I am.'*
> *'Take now your son, your only son Isaac, whom you love, and go to the land of Moriah, and offer him there as a burnt offering on one of the mountains of which I shall tell you.'"* (Genesis 22:1-2)

God directed Abraham to travel to a specific mountain ridge and there to kill and burn his beloved son on an altar! What a dreadful request! This is something God had never before and would never again ask a man to do. Yet, because Isaac—like all descendants of Adam—had a sin-debt, the sentence upon him was a just verdict: death.

"So Abraham rose early in the morning and saddled his donkey, and took two of his young men with him, and Isaac his son; and he split the wood for the burnt offering, and arose and went to the place of which God had told him." (Genesis 22:3)

Abraham trusted God, but it was not easy. For three agonizing days Abraham, his son, and two servants journeyed, each step bringing them closer to the site of execution.

"Then on the third day Abraham lifted his eyes and saw the place afar off. And Abraham said to his young men, 'Stay here with the donkey; the lad and I will go yonder and worship, and we will come back to you.'" (Genesis 22:4-5)

Abraham told the servants, *"We will come back to you."*
How could both Abraham and his son *"come back"* if Isaac was to be killed and burned on an altar? Elsewhere the Scripture provides the answer. Since God had promised to make of Isaac a great nation, Abraham believed that once he had offered up his son, God would raise him back to life.[188] Abraham had learned that the LORD God always keeps His promises!

GOD PROVIDES A SUBSTITUTE

"So Abraham took the wood of the burnt offering and laid it on Isaac his son; and he took the fire in his hand, and a knife, and the two of them went together." (Genesis 22:6)

As father and son walked up the mountain, Isaac said,

"'My father!'
'Here I am, my son.'
*Then he said, 'Look, the fire and the wood, but **where is the lamb** for a burnt offering?'*
*And Abraham said, 'My son, **God will provide for Himself the lamb for a burnt offering**.'*

Then they came to the place of which God had told him. And Abraham built an altar there and placed the wood in order; and he bound Isaac his son and laid him on the altar, upon the wood. And Abraham stretched out his hand and took the knife to slay his son.

But the Angel of the LORD called to him from heaven and said, 'Abraham, Abraham!'

So he said, 'Here I am.'

And He said, 'Do not lay your hand on the lad, or do anything to him; for now I know that you fear God, since you have not withheld your son, your only son, from Me.'

Then Abraham lifted his eyes and looked, and there behind him was a ram caught in a thicket by its horns."
(Genesis 22:7-13a)

The LORD intervened. Abraham's son would be spared the death penalty!

Abraham turned around, and in the distance, on the same mountain ridge, he spotted movement in the undergrowth. What was it…? Could it be…? Yes! Praise God! An unblemished *"ram caught in a thicket by its horns!"*

In keeping with His own *"law of the sacrifice"* God had provided a substitute.

*"So Abraham went and took the ram, and offered it up for a burnt offering **instead of his son**."* (Genesis 22:13b)

Why did Abraham's son escape the death sentence that hung over him? The ram had died *"instead of his son."*
God had provided a substitute.

THE LORD *WILL* PROVIDE

*"And Abraham called the name of the place, **The–LORD– Will–Provide**; as it is said to this day, '**In the Mount of The LORD it shall be provided.**'"* (Genesis 22:14)

Why, after Abraham had killed the ram in place of his son, did he name the site, *"The–LORD–**Will**–Provide"*? Why did Abraham **not** name it, *The–LORD–**Has**–Provided*?

In saying, *"the LORD **will** provide,"* the prophet Abraham was announcing a future event that would take place nearly two thousand years later. For it would be on this same mountain ridge (where Jerusalem was later built) that the LORD would provide another sacrifice—not to deliver just one man from death, but to provide a full and final ransom for the whole world.

Do you recall what Abraham said to his son Isaac as they were plodding up the mountain where the sacrifice was to be offered? He told him,

"My son, God will provide for Himself the lamb for a burnt offering."

What was Abraham talking about? Had God provided a *lamb* to die in the place of Abraham's son? No, He did not provide a lamb. God had provided a *ram*. So what did the prophet Abraham mean when he spoke of God providing *"for Himself the lamb"*?

The amazing answer will soon emerge, but first a few more stories must be told.

MORE SHED BLOOD

L et's be honest.
   When it comes to spiritual truth, we are slow learners.
   God knows that.

> *"In fact, though by this time you ought to be teachers, you need someone to teach you* **the elementary truths** *of God's word all over again. You need milk, not solid food!"*
> (Hebrews 5:12 NIV)

Ouch!

Mercifully, God is the most patient of teachers, repeating and restating elementary truths we should have learned long ago. To help us out, He has included in His Book hundreds of stories which graphically illustrate one of the most important truths:

> *"Without the shedding of blood there is no forgiveness."*
> (Hebrews 9:22 NIV)

Forgiveness of sin has never been a simple matter for our perfectly holy Creator. From the day sin entered the world, God began to teach sinners that only the blood of a suitable sacrifice could atone for (cover) sin. That is how God, the Righteous Judge, would punish sin without punishing the sinner.

The LORD rejected Adam and Eve's self-efforts to cover their sin. Apart from a death payment, God could not pardon sin. Cain and Abel's story taught us the same lesson. So did Abraham and Isaac's.

The Old Testament books which follow Genesis, such as Exodus and Leviticus, abound with stories of men and women who submitted to this law of the sacrifice.[189]

"I WILL PASS OVER"

The book of Exodus relates the captivating story about God organizing Abraham's descendants into a nation, just as He had promised.

Through a divinely arranged series of events which God foretold to Abraham,[190] the descendants of Israel became slaves under the Egyptian Pharaohs. In His appointed time, God promised to redeem them from their slavery and in the process, transmit to the world "pictures" of His plan to redeem the children of Adam from their slavery to sin.

This is the story of the Passover.

Around 1490 BC, the LORD brought upon the land of Egypt ten awesome plagues by the word of Moses. The first nine of these miraculous signs—in which the LORD challenged and defeated the false gods of polytheistic Egypt—did not cause Pharaoh to submit to the word of God and let the Israelites go.[191] Thus, God told Moses to inform the people that the firstborn in each family, Egyptian and Israelite, was condemned to die. At midnight on the appointed date, the angel of death would pass through the land and slay the firstborn in each home.

That was the bad news.

The good news was that God provided a way of deliverance from this death plague. The LORD told Moses to tell each family to select a *"lamb... without blemish, a male of the first year...from the sheep or from the goats."* (Exodus 12:5) Then, at the appointed time, the lamb was to be killed, and its blood applied to the top and sides of the door-frame of each house. All who put the blood of a lamb on the doorposts and remained in that house when the plague of death passed through the land would be saved.

The LORD promised:

"When I see the blood, I will pass over you; and the plague shall *not* be on you to destroy you." (Exodus 12:13)

Everything happened as God had said. That night, God preserved all firstborn who were *under the blood*; all others perished. But every household witnessed a death.

Yes, *every* household.

Either *a lamb* had died or *the firstborn* died.

That night, those who had applied the blood to their doorposts walked away from a life of oppression and slavery. They went out a free, redeemed people.

What was the ransom price of their deliverance?

The blood of a lamb.

Once again, *the law of the sacrifice* had trumped *the law of sin and death*. In succeeding years, the Jews would celebrate *the Passover*, an annual feast in which they were to remember the great deliverance God had provided through the blood of a lamb.

GOD LEADING HIS PEOPLE

On the night of the original *Passover*, God led the Israelites away from four hundred years of bondage in Egypt and out into the desert. God planned to bring them back to the land He had promised to Abraham, Isaac and Jacob and their descendants. As they journeyed, God Himself accompanied them in a visible, comforting kind of way.

"The LORD went before them by day in a pillar of cloud to lead the way, and by night in a pillar of fire to give them light, so as to go by day and night." (Exodus 13:21)

Not only did the LORD lead His people through the desert and give them light, but by His mighty Arm, He opened a path through the Red Sea, and delivered them from Pharaoh's pursuing army. And then, just as He had promised to Moses, He brought them to Mount Sinai.[192]

There, at the base of that mountain, this new nation of more than two million people set up camp for a whole year. How could they possibly survive in that arid desert? God, in His goodness and grace, provided bread from heaven and water from a rock.[193] Though the Israelites consistently failed to thank, trust, and obey the One who had redeemed them from slavery, the LORD was always faithful to them. He judged them when they sinned against Him and blessed them when they believed Him. The LORD worked with His chosen nation in this way so that the surrounding nations might see, observe, and know His way of redemption. God also wanted people to understand that He can be known in a personal way.

After giving Israel the Ten Commandments and other laws, the LORD commanded His people to construct a unique sanctuary called *the Tabernacle*, or *Tent of Meeting*.

THE TABERNACLE

> *"Let them make **Me** a sanctuary, **that I may dwell among them**. According to **all that I show you**, that is, **the pattern of the tabernacle** and **the pattern** of all its furnishings, just so you shall make it."* (Exodus 25:8-9)

For what purpose were God's ancient people to construct this special tent? And why was it so important that it be made exactly *"according to...the pattern"* given to them by God?

God planned to use this tabernacle to teach them, in a very visual way, what He is like and how He must be approached.

The Bible contains fifty chapters about the tabernacle and what accompanied it, so it can't all be explained here. We can only point out some of the most basic elements.

ONE WAY

God designed the tabernacle to teach the world that even though He is perfectly holy, He still wants to dwell with people. However, there is a major barrier between God and man.

That barrier is SIN.

The special tent that symbolized God's presence among humans was enclosed within a huge, rectangular courtyard. The *fence* of this courtyard was constructed of bronze pillars and fine linen material. It was two and a half meters in height—high enough so no man could see over it. God wanted people to understand that they are shut out from His presence. That was the bad news.

The good news was that God provided a way for sinners to come near to Him. The wall had a door which was made of blue, purple, and scarlet thread. The only way sinners could approach God was to enter through that *one door*[194] with a lamb or other suitable blood sacrifice.

The LORD told the Israelites to construct a large *altar* of acacia wood and overlay it with bronze. This altar was to be placed between the door and God's special tent. Those bringing a sin-offering would place their hands on the innocent creature's head and confess their condition as helpless sinners. Then the animal would be killed and its body burned upon the altar. Once again, God was telling people that *the law of sin and death* could only be overcome by *the law of the sacrifice.*[195]

God's rule was clear: Without the shedding of blood, there could be no covering for sin. Without a covering for sin, there could be no reconciliation (right relationship) with God.

God also told Moses to construct a unique wooden chest overlaid with gold. This piece of furniture was called *the Ark of the Covenant*. It symbolized God's throne in heaven. The stone tablets on which God had etched the Ten Commandments were placed inside this golden chest. The solid gold cover of the box, called *the Mercy Seat*, was overshadowed by figures of two cherubim made of gold. Cherubim are the magnificent angels that surround God's throne in heaven. God told Moses to place the Ark of the Covenant in the innermost room of the tabernacle.

THE HOLIEST PLACE

The tabernacle was divided into two rooms. The front room was called *the Holy Place* and the innermost room was called *the Holiest Place* or *the Holy of Holies*. This inner sanctuary *"was only a copy of the true one... **heaven itself.**"* (Hebrews 9:24 NIV)

The Holiest Place symbolized Paradise, God's dwelling place. This special room was shaped like a cube—its length, width, and height were equal. Near the end of our journey through the Scriptures, we will see that the heavenly city, which will one day be home to all believers, is also in the shape of a cube.

Many people today talk about a cathedral, church building, mosque, synagogue, or shrine as being holy, even though these places are often filled with people who reject God's way of redemption. True holiness is found not in a place, but in receiving God's provision of forgiveness and righteousness.

THE VEIL

The tabernacle's exterior was simple: a large tent made of animal hides. It was unimpressive on the *outside*, but stunningly beautiful on the *inside*.[196]

The tabernacle's two rooms were divided by a thick curtain called *the veil*.

> *"You shall make **a veil** woven of **blue**, **purple**, and **scarlet** thread, and fine woven **linen**. It shall be woven with an artistic design of cherubim."* (Exodus 26:31)

The veil shut man out from *the Holiest Place* which housed the glory and light of God's Presence. To one and all, the veil declared: ***KEEP OUT or DIE!***

This special curtain symbolized God's standard of righteousness. God had informed mankind of that standard by giving Moses the Ten Commandments. Nonetheless, those ten rules only provided a limited view of what God demands. God's ultimate plan was to send to earth His Son who would demonstrate what God requires: PERFECTION.

The Messiah would be God's Standard. God designed the veil to make us think of ***Him***.

This beautiful curtain was made of pure linen material, picturing the Messiah's purity. He would be holy; without sin.

Woven into the pure cloth were three brilliant colors—blue, purple, and scarlet (red).

Blue = color of the heavens. The Messiah would be the Lord from heaven.

Red = color of earth, man, and blood.[197] The Messiah would take on a body of flesh and blood in order to suffer and die in the place of sinners.

Purple = blend of blue and red. The Messiah would be the God-Man. Purple is the color of royalty: the Messiah would establish His spiritual kingdom in the hearts of all who trust in Him. Later, He would establish His physical kingdom on earth.

Just as purple is the intermediary color between blue and red, so the Messiah would come to mediate between God and man.

> *"For there is one God and **one Mediator between God and men**, the Man Christ Jesus, who gave Himself a ransom for all, to be testified in due time...."* (1 Timothy 2:5-6)

THE GLORY CLOUD

Once the tabernacle was constructed and everything was in place according to God's plan, He sent down from heaven's throne the glory of His Presence—contained in a majestic cloud.

> *"Then the cloud covered the tabernacle of meeting, and **the glory of the LORD filled the tabernacle**. And Moses was not able to enter the tabernacle of meeting, because the cloud rested above it, and the glory of the LORD filled the tabernacle."*
> (Exodus 40:34-35)

The LORD placed the dazzling light of His Presence in the Holiest Place between the two cherubim on the Mercy Seat of the Ark of the Covenant.

God had come in a visible kind of way to be with His people.

"The LORD reigns; let the peoples tremble! **He dwells** *between the cherubim; Let the earth be moved!"*
(Psalm 99:1)

By placing His glory in the Holiest Place and His cloud above the tabernacle, the Creator was teaching the nations of the world, and generations yet to be born, an all-important lesson: the one true God invites sinners to have a relationship with Himself, but only under certain conditions.

VISUAL ILLUSTRATIONS

The tabernacle provided countless visual aids for those who wanted to know about God and His plan for people.

Picture the scene.

In accordance with God's precise instructions, this redeemed nation of slaves—the twelve tribes of Israel—had pitched their tents at the foot of Mount Sinai in an orderly fashion in the form of a cross. The tabernacle was at the center, with three tribes pitching their tents to the south, three tribes to the north, three tribes to the west, and three tribes to the east.[198] With the radiant glory cloud hovering overhead, none could deny that the one true God was in their midst.

Other visual lessons could be learned from the fact that the tabernacle-tent was surrounded by a high, white linen wall with only one door. Inside the door was an altar. Sinners were shut out from the glory of God, unless they approached Him on the basis of the shed blood of a symbolically perfect sacrifice.

"The life of the flesh is in the blood, and I have given it to you **upon the altar to make atonement for your souls;** *for* **it is the blood that makes atonement for the soul.**"
(Leviticus 17:11)

Apart from a death payment there could be no forgiveness of sin. And since it was impossible for people to bring a sacrifice to the tabernacle each time they sinned, God commanded that a lamb be killed and burned on the altar every day of the year: every morning and every evening. All who trusted in the LORD and His plan could enjoy the benefits of these daily offerings, a restored relationship with their Creator.

> *"This is what you shall offer on the altar: two lambs of the first year,* ***day by day continually***. *One* ***lamb*** *you shall offer in the morning, and the other* ***lamb*** *you shall offer at twilight ... This shall be a* ***continual burnt offering*** *throughout your generations at the door of the tabernacle of meeting before the LORD,* ***where I will meet you to speak with you.***" (Exodus 29:38-39,42)

THE DAY OF ATONEMENT

To illustrate His truth further, God told His people there was only one manner by which man could enter the Holiest Place— that special room that symbolized heaven itself. One day a year, a specially-chosen man, called the high priest, would be allowed to enter that inner sanctuary. On this *Day of Atonement*,[199] the high priest would go past the veil. He would take with him the blood of a sacrificed goat and sprinkle it seven times on the Mercy Seat, that is, on the lid of the Ark of the Covenant. If the high priest entered the presence of God in any other way, he would be struck dead.

It was on the basis of that sprinkled blood God promised to forgive the sins of the Israelites for another year—if they would simply trust in Him and His provision.

All the details of the tabernacle, its furniture, and activities, were designed to transmit vivid pictures to the world about how condemned sinners could have their sins covered and their broken relationship restored with their perfectly holy Creator. It all pointed to the promised Messiah and His mission.

Thus, down through the centuries, using the channel of His chosen nation, the LORD broadcast hundreds of pictures and communicated many wonderful promises to a world lost in sin.

THE TEMPLE AND ITS SACRIFICES

Five hundred years after Moses and the children of Israel built this special tent to house the Presence of the LORD, God directed King Solomon to replace the *portable tabernacle* with a more *permanent temple.* The layout of this new structure in Jerusalem was similar to the tabernacle, but it was much larger and even more beautiful. Solomon's Temple became one of the architectural wonders of the ancient world.

Just as the glory of God had descended from heaven to fill the Holiest Place in the tabernacle on the day of its inauguration, so the glorious, uncreated light of God's Presence came down and filled the temple.

*"When Solomon had finished praying, fire came down from heaven and consumed the burnt offering and the sacrifices; and **the glory of the LORD filled the temple.** And the priests could not enter the house of the LORD, because the glory of the LORD had filled the LORD's house. "* (2 Chronicles 7:1-2)

The temple was built on the same mountain ridge where, a thousand years earlier, Abraham had sacrificed a ram in place of his son.[200] To dedicate this special temple to God, King Solomon ordered that 120,000 sheep and 22,000 bulls be sacrificed.[201] This extravagance symbolized the incalculable worth of the precious blood to be shed a millennium later on a nearby hill.

Thus, from the time of Adam, Abel, Abraham, and onward, millions of symbolic blood sacrifices were offered on altars to cover sin—year after wearying year...

Then the Messiah came.

THE LAMB

*"God is **love**."* (1 John 4:8)

*"God is **great**."* (Job 36:26)

The God who is *love* desires a close relationship with His people. The theme of God's social-relational nature is revealed in the first chapter of His Book.

God created Adam and Eve *"in His own image"* so that He might enjoy fellowship with them (Genesis 1:27). This same *"God with us"* theme[202] carries through to the last chapter of God's Book, when His redeemed people *"shall see His face"* and be with Him forever (Revelation 22:4). Anyone who fails to see this has missed the central theme of God's Book.

The God who is *great* can do anything He wants to do.

"Behold, I am the LORD, the God of all flesh. Is there anything too hard for Me?" (Jeremiah 32:27)

No genuine monotheist can claim that God cannot become man if He wanted to. If there were something the Almighty could not do (apart from contradicting Himself), then He would be less than God.

The question is not: *Can* God become man?

The question is: Did God *choose to* become man?

GOD'S TRUE TABERNACLE

One thousand five hundred years after God commanded the Israelites to construct a unique tabernacle-tent so that He might *"dwell among them"* (Exodus 25:8), the Scriptures declare:

> *"In the beginning was the Word, and the Word was with God, and the Word was God...The Word became flesh and **made his dwelling among us**. We have seen **his glory**, the glory of the One and Only, who came from the Father, full of grace and truth."* (John 1:1,14 NIV)

The phrase translated *"made his dwelling"* comes from a Greek word meaning *to set up a tent or tabernacle*. It can be translated literally: *"He set up His tent among us."* The Scriptures describe a person's body as the *"tent"* or *"temple"* in which his or her soul and spirit dwell.[203] As we learned in chapter 16, the eternal Son of God was born as a baby boy. His human body was *the tent* in which He chose to dwell.

In Moses' day, the tabernacle structure in which God placed the glorious, uncreated light of His Presence was covered with *animal skins*. But in the Person of Jesus, God's glorious, uncreated light and Presence had come to dwell in *human skin*. Thus, His disciples could say, *"We have seen His glory, the glory of the One and Only who came from the Father!"*

The Scripture declares that Jesus was *"**the true tabernacle** which the Lord erected, and not man."* (Hebrews 8:2)

In Old Testament times, the tabernacle, and later the temple, was a place where sinners could present animal sacrifices to cover their sin. When Jesus was a boy and as He grew into manhood, He visited the temple in Jerusalem on many occasions, but we never read of Him offering a sacrifice for sin. Why not? He had no sin. Jesus had *"appeared to put away sin by the sacrifice of **Himself**."* (Hebrews 9:26) He would become the offering and a Roman cross would become the altar.

Jesus was the reality behind the symbols.

*"**God** was manifested **in the flesh**."* (1 Timothy 3:16)

On one occasion, Jesus was standing near the great temple in Jerusalem and told a group of men:

*"'Destroy **this temple**, and in three days I will raise it up.'*

Then the Jews said, 'It has taken forty-six years to build this temple, and will You raise it up in three days?'

But He was speaking of the temple of His body. *Therefore, when He had risen from the dead, His disciples remembered that He had said this to them; and they believed the Scripture and the word which Jesus had said."* (John 2:19-22)

The Jews didn't understand that *"the temple"* of which Jesus spoke was His body. They thought He was talking about the magnificent temple in Jerusalem. But the light and glory of God's Presence was no longer in the Holiest Place of that man-made temple.

It was now in the *"temple"* of Jesus' body.

Near the end of His earthly ministry, Jesus allowed three of His disciples to witness this glorious outshining of God.

"Jesus took Peter, James, and John his brother, led them up on a high mountain by themselves; and He was transfigured before them. ***His face shone like the sun, and His clothes became as white as the light.***

And behold... ***a bright cloud overshadowed them;*** *and suddenly a voice came out of the cloud, saying,*

'This is My beloved Son,
in whom I am well pleased.
Hear Him!'" (Matthew 17:1-5)

The blazing, dazzling, pure light of God that causes angels in heaven to cover their faces was *in Jesus*. The same glorious Presence that had resided in the Holiest Place of the tabernacle and temple was dwelling *in Jesus*.

The brilliant cloud that had once overshadowed the tabernacle now overshadowed the place where Jesus stood.

Jesus was God's visible Presence on earth.

This radiant outshining of the glory of the Son of God was accompanied by the Father speaking from heaven:

> *"This is **My beloved Son**, in whom I am well pleased. **Hear Him!**"*

God is serious about this.

A thousand years before the Son of God became the Son of Man, the prophet David wrote, *"**Kiss the Son**, lest He be angry, and you perish in the way, when His wrath is kindled but a little. Blessed are all those who put their trust in Him!"* (Psalm 2:12)

"Kiss the Son," means **honor the Son**.

From time to time, I see people kissing the heads and hands of religious leaders—men who are helpless sinners like themselves. I see those same people making pilgrimages to honor men whose flesh has returned to dust. Meanwhile, God has announced to the world *"that **all should honor the Son just as they honor the Father**. He who does not honor the Son does not honor the Father who sent Him... for **the Father loves the Son**."* (John 5:23,20)

THE FORERUNNER

Isaiah was one of two prophets who wrote about a specially chosen herald who would *"prepare the way of the LORD."* (Isaiah 40:3) That forerunner was the prophet John, son of Zacharias.[204] While previous prophets proclaimed, "God *will send* the Messiah into the world," the prophet John had the distinct honor to announce, "The promised Messiah, the LORD Himself, *is here!*"

> *"In those days John the Baptist came preaching in the wilderness of Judea, and saying, 'Repent, for the kingdom of heaven is at hand!' For this is he who was spoken of by the prophet Isaiah, saying: 'The voice of one crying in the wilderness: 'Prepare the way of the LORD; Make His paths straight.'''* (Matthew 3:1-3)

REPENTANCE

To prepare people for the LORD's arrival, John's message to the people was simple.

"Repent!"

The word *repent* comes from the Greek word *metanoeo*. It has two parts: *meta* and *noeo*. The first part means *"movement"* or *"change."* The second part refers to the *thoughts of the mind.* Therefore the basic meaning of *repent* is to have *a change of mind; to replace your wrong thinking with right thinking.*

To put the term "repent" into an everyday context, suppose I want to travel by bus from one city to another—let's say from Beirut to Amman. I climb on what I believe to be the correct bus and settle into my seat for a nap. Some time later, as the bus is speeding along the highway, I discover that it is not heading south to Amman, but north to Istanbul! What should I do?

I have two choices:

Being too proud to admit my error, I can *remain* on that bus and end up at the wrong destination.

Or, I can humble myself and *repent*, that is, have a change of mind, admitting that I chose the wrong bus. The sincerity of my repentance becomes evident when I get off at the next stop and get on the proper bus.

True repentance leads a person to *turn from falsehood* and *trust the truth.*

Repentance can be compared to the two sides of a coin.

One side says: **REPENT!**

The other side says: **BELIEVE!**

The two sides are part of the same truth:

*"...**repentance** toward God and **faith** toward our Lord Jesus Christ."* (Acts 20:21)

Repentance means to have a change of mind about what you are trusting for salvation. *Faith* means to trust in God's provision of salvation.

There is no true faith apart from repentance.

Accordingly, the prophet John's message went something like this: "Repent of your wrong thinking! Admit that you cannot save yourselves and welcome the promised Messiah-King from Heaven! He has come to deliver you from your worst enemies—if you will stop trusting in yourselves and start trusting in Him!"

Those who admitted their sinful condition before God were baptized by John in the river. That is why John became known as *John the Baptizer*. Being baptized in water could not and cannot wash away sin. Being immersed in the river was a way for people to express *outwardly* that they had embraced *inwardly* God's message about the Messiah who was coming to cleanse repentant, believing sinners from their defiled condition.

THE CHOSEN ONE

At the start of His earthly ministry, Jesus came to John to be baptized in the Jordan River. The sinless Messiah did not need to repent of anything, but by being baptized He identified Himself with the human race He had come to deliver.

What followed Jesus' baptism is a scene never to be forgotten. It gives us another glimpse of the one true God in His complex oneness and majesty.

*"When He had been baptized, **Jesus** came up immediately from the water, and behold, the heavens were opened to Him, and He saw **the Spirit of God** descending like a dove and alighting upon Him. And suddenly **a voice came from heaven**, saying, 'This is **My beloved Son, in whom I am well pleased.**'"* (Matthew 3:16-17)

As on the first day of creation, this narrative reveals the Presence of the Father, the Son, and the Holy Spirit. However, at this key moment in history, God was revealing His plural oneness with greater clarity. In our journey through the Scriptures, this is one of those spots where each traveler needs to stop, take some pictures, and reflect.

Here is the scene. Under a dramatic and radiant sky, *the Son of God* (*the Word* by whom heaven and earth were created) walks up out of the river. At the same moment, *the Spirit of God* (*the Spirit* who was hovering over the face of the waters on the first day of creation) descends from heaven, hovering over and settling on Jesus in the form of a dove. And, finally, the voice of *God the Father* resounds from heaven: *"This is My beloved Son, in whom I am well pleased."*

Throughout the previous thirty years, Jesus had lived behind the scenes in a poor family in the modest town of Nazareth. Though He was out of the public eye, the Father in Heaven had his eye on His beloved Son all those years. And now we hear God's verdict on Jesus' life: *"I am well pleased."*

God could not say this of any other human being ever born. Only Jesus pleased Him in every detail—inwardly and outwardly. As the Son from Heaven, He was holy, undefiled, and qualified to do what He came to do. He was the Messiah—*the Anointed One*—God's Chosen One. God anointed Him, not with oil (as was done for priest and kings[205]), but with the Holy Spirit Himself.

*"**God anointed Jesus** of Nazareth **with the Holy Spirit** and with power...."* (Acts 10:38)

Jesus was the One about whom all the prophets had written.

THE LAMB OF GOD

*"The next day John saw Jesus coming toward him, and said,
'Behold! The Lamb of God who takes away the sin of
the world!'"* (John 1:29)

The prophet John's announcement is loaded with meaning.

- **"Behold! The Lamb of God..."**
  John's audience understood to some extent the meaning of
  the lamb. Ever since sin's entrance, people had been bringing
  lambs as burnt offerings. Over fifteen long centuries, lambs
  had been sacrificed morning and evening on the brazen
  altar. And now *God's own Lamb* was on the scene! Two
  millennia earlier, Abraham had told Isaac, *"God will provide
  for Himself the lamb for a burnt offering."* (Genesis 22:8)
  God did indeed provide a substitute to die instead of
  Abraham's son, but it was not *"the lamb."* It was *"a ram."*
  (Genesis 22:13) *"The lamb"* in Abraham's prophecy was the
  Messiah Himself. Abraham was pointing forward to Jesus.
  That is why Jesus said, *"Abraham rejoiced to see My day,
  and he saw it and was glad."* (John 8:56)

- **"...who takes away the sin..."**
  Since the time of Adam, innocent animal blood had
  symbolically *covered* the sin of those who trusted in God
  and His plan, but what Jesus came to do would be different.
  He would *take away sin*—completely and forever.

- **"...of the world!"**
  In the past, blood sacrifices for sin had been offered on
  behalf of a *person, a family,* or *a nation.* But the blood of
  Jesus would make available a full and final payment for
  the past, present, and future sin-debt of the *entire world.*

Does the Lamb of God taking away the sin of the world mean
that every person ever born is automatically forgiven by God? No.
From the day sin entered the human race God has always required
personal faith in Him and His provision.[206]

*"He came to His own, and His own did not receive Him.
But **as many as received Him**, to them He gave the right
to become children of God, **to those who believe** in
His name."* (John 1:11-12)

SHADOWS AND SYMBOLS

In bygone years, each innocent, spotless
lamb sacrificed for sin was *"a shadow of the
good things to come."* (Hebrews 10:1)

A shadow is not to be confused with the object
that creates the shadow. If you are looking down at the ground as
a friend walks in your direction, you may see his shadow before
you see him, but once he is standing before you, will you not look
at your friend and speak with him instead of his shadow?

Old Testament sacrifices were God-designed *shadows* that
outlined and announced the coming Messiah.

Jesus the Lamb of God cast those shadows.

*"It is **not possible** that the blood of bulls and goats could
take away sins. Therefore, when **He** [Messiah] came into
the world, He said: 'Sacrifice and offering You did not
desire, **but a body You have prepared for Me**. In burnt
offerings and sacrifices for sin You had no pleasure. Then
I* [Messiah] *said, 'Behold, **I have come**—in the volume of
the book it is written of Me—to do Your will, O God.'...
He takes away the first* [animal sacrifices] *that He may
establish the second* [His own sacrifice]. *By that will we
have been sanctified* [made holy] *through the offering of
the body of Jesus Christ **once for all**."* (Hebrew 10:4-7,9-10)

Animal-blood sacrifices were mere *symbols* of what God
would ultimately require. Animals were not created in God's
image. The value of a lamb is not equal to the value of a man. Just
as you can't take a toy model car to a car dealer and offer it as
payment for a real car, so the blood of a lamb could not pay man's
sin-debt. A sacrifice of equal or greater value was required.

Jesus came to provide that Sacrifice.

A POOR PLANNER?

A couple of years ago, I corresponded with a doctor of philosophy. In response to the declaration that Jesus came to *"take away the sin of the world,"* he wrote:

📧 **Subject:** Email Feedback
What happens to the people who were born and died before God decided to concoct this charade only 2000 years ago? It seems that the Christian God is a poor planner and a late thinker because it took him thousands if not millions of years to find a way of forgiving 'the sins' of mankind.

It seems that this man, who has since passed away, failed to recognize the meaning behind millions of sacrificed lambs and hundreds of prophecies, all which pointed to the day when the Messiah would endure the penalty for the sins of mankind—past, present and future. From the beginning, God's rescue plan included paying for *"the sins that were **previously** committed, to demonstrate at the present time His righteousness."* (Romans 3:25-26)

God forgave sinners before the time of Christ on the same basis He forgives sinners today—by faith in the promises and provision of God.

Of course, there was a difference.

Believers who lived before the time of Jesus Christ had their sins *covered*. It would be only after Jesus had shed His blood and overcome death that a sinner's debt could be forever *canceled* from the record books.

Before *Jesus the Lamb of God* came to earth, a man offering an animal sacrifice on an altar was somewhat like a struggling businessman who takes out a loan at the bank.

A wealthy friend agrees to cosign the loan, promising to repay the debt if the businessman fails to repay the borrowed money. With each passing year, the businessman fails to pay back the loan, going deeper and deeper in debt. And each year his rich friend signs another note at the bank to cover the struggling man's debt. What keeps the failing businessman from going bankrupt and to jail? Only the notes of guarantee from his wealthy, trustworthy friend cover for him.

Old Testament animal sacrifices were a sinner's "notes of guarantee," temporarily accepted by God. The Record Keeper of the universe, who has a flawless history of upholding His covenants and balancing His books, promised to accept the blood of blemish-free animals as a *covering* for sin. But animal blood could not *cancel* man's accumulated sin-debt. It only served as *"a reminder of sins every year. For it is not possible that the blood of bulls and goats could take away sins."* (Hebrews 10:3-4)

Sin is a serious problem that only the shedding of the blood of God's eternal Son could resolve. Jesus, the Lamb of God, came to pay off the sin-debt of mankind.

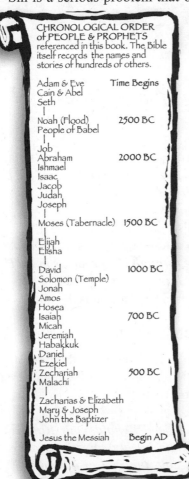

CHRONOLOGICAL ORDER
of PEOPLE & PROPHETS
referenced in this book. The Bible
itself records the names and
stories of hundreds of others.

Adam & Eve	Time Begins
Cain & Abel	
Seth	
Noah (Flood)	2500 BC
People of Babel	
Job	
Abraham	2000 BC
Ishmael	
Isaac	
Jacob	
Judah	
Joseph	
Moses (Tabernacle)	1500 BC
Elijah	
Elisha	
David	1000 BC
Solomon (Temple)	
Jonah	
Amos	
Hosea	
Isaiah	700 BC
Micah	
Jeremiah	
Habakkuk	
Daniel	
Ezekiel	
Zechariah	500 BC
Malachi	
Zacharias & Elizabeth	
Mary & Joseph	
John the Baptizer	
Jesus the Messiah	Begin AD

What do *you* think?

Is God "a poor planner and a late thinker"? Or did the prophet John and his followers have good reason for identifying Jesus of Nazareth as *"the Messiah... of whom Moses in the law, and also the prophets wrote,"* and as *"the Lamb of God who takes away the sin of the world"*? (John 1)

God, the Best of Planners, never had any other plan for dealing with sin. From His timeless perspective, His beloved Son always was, is, and shall evermore be:

"...the Lamb slain
from the foundation
of the world."
(Revelation 13:8)

FULFILLING SCRIPTURE

*"A **promise** is a cloud, **fulfillment** is rain."*
— Arab proverb

For thousands of years the prophets announced God's plan to send the Savior to earth, *"but when the fullness of the time had come, God sent forth His Son."* (Galatians 4:4) God's prophets provided *clouds of promise.*
Jesus of Nazareth was God's *rain of fulfillment.*
The Creator's plan was no afterthought. It is *"the gospel of God, which **He promised before through His prophets** in the Holy Scriptures, concerning His Son Jesus Christ...."* (Romans 1:2-3)
The Scriptures are the clouds. The Messiah is the rain.

ENTERING JERUSALEM ON A DONKEY

The Messiah knew His mission. Five hundred years earlier, the prophet Zechariah had written about one of the many events that would lead to His crucifixion.

*"Shout, O daughter of Jerusalem! **Behold, your King is coming to you; He is just and having salvation, lowly and riding on a donkey, a colt, the foal of a donkey."***
(Zechariah 9:9)

Jesus fulfilled this prophecy. All four Gospel records report this event. Matthew, an eyewitness and disciple of Jesus, wrote:

> *"Now when they drew near Jerusalem... Jesus sent two disciples, saying to them, 'Go into the village opposite you, and immediately you will find **a donkey tied, and a colt with her**. Loose them and bring them to Me. And if anyone says anything to you, you shall say, 'The Lord has need of them,' and immediately he will send them.' All this was done **that it might be fulfilled** which was spoken by the prophet, saying: '**Behold, your King is coming to you, lowly, and sitting on a donkey, a colt, the foal of a donkey.**'"* (Matthew 21:1-5)

Thus, Jesus offered Himself to the nation as their King—only to be rejected, just as the prophets had foretold.[207]

The Gospels record in detail what happened after Jesus entered Jerusalem on a donkey. He went into the temple and drove out all who were using it to make money. Then Jesus said to the startled sellers, *"'It is written, 'My house shall be called a house of prayer,' but you have made it a 'den of thieves!' Then the blind and the lame came to Him in the temple, and He healed them."* (Matthew 21:13-14)

Over the next few days, Jesus sat in the temple and taught the people the true sayings of God. The religious leaders tried to trick Him into saying something whereby they could accuse Him and have Him put to death. They failed.

Jesus handled their questions with heavenly wisdom, so that everyone marveled.[208]

Then it was time.

THE HOUR HAD COME

Jesus is the only Person who knew precisely:
   when He would die,
      where He would die,
         how He would die,
            and *why* He would die.

*"Now it came to pass, when Jesus had finished all these sayings, that **He said to His disciples, 'You know that after two days is the Passover, and the Son of Man will be delivered up to be crucified.'***

Then the chief priests, the scribes, and the elders of the people assembled at the palace of the high priest, who was called Caiaphas, and plotted to take Jesus by trickery and kill Him. But they said, 'Not during the feast, lest there be an uproar among the people.'" (Matthew 26:1-5)

The self-serving religious leaders were desperate. On several occasions they had *"sought to take Him; but no one laid a hand on Him, because **His hour had not yet come.**"* (John 7:30)

Then they got the break they wanted.

Judas, a disciple of Jesus outwardly but not inwardly, went to the temple priests and offered to betray Jesus into their hands. The priests agreed to pay Judas thirty silver coins. This act of treachery fulfilled several more Old Testament prophecies.[209]

Thus, the day arrived when Jesus told His disciples, *"**The hour has come.**"* (John 12:23)

It was time for God's Lamb to die.

PASSOVER WEEK

Jerusalem's narrow streets were teeming with locals and foreigners. The bleating of sheep and bellowing of bullocks filled the air. Buyers haggled with merchants over the price of a proper lamb. It was Passover week.

Passover was part of a week-long celebration established by God fifteen centuries earlier. It was an occasion *to look back* and remember how He had delivered His "nation of communication" from slavery and death on that fateful night when their ancestors had applied lamb's blood to the doorposts of their homes. From God's perspective, it was also an occasion *to look forward* to the day when the Messiah would fulfill the deeper meaning of the Passover.

However, few, if any, understood that Jesus of Nazareth was about to shed His blood as the final Passover Lamb and fulfill the symbolism of all the lambs that had been sacrificed annually since the time of Moses. In contrast to Moses' mission of delivering people from the *physical tyranny* of human taskmasters, the Messiah's mission was to deliver people from the *spiritual tyranny* of Satan, sin, and death.

Interestingly, the religious leaders determined to kill Jesus, but *"not during the feast lest there be an uproar among the people."* (Matthew 26:5) Yet it was during that very feast that Jesus planned to die! The Lamb of God must be slain during the Passover feast.[210] Everything would happen just as God planned it.

Ironically, the very ones who rejected God's plan would play a major role in fulfilling it! Little did Satan realize—that by inciting the religious leaders to kill Jesus—he was arranging his own doom! The Scriptures call this twist of events *"the hidden wisdom which God ordained before the ages...which none of the rulers of this age knew; for had they known, they would not have crucified the Lord of glory."* (1 Corinthians 2:7-8)

THE BREAD AND THE CUP

On the appointed evening, Jesus and His disciples gathered in a private, upstairs room for the Passover. After sharing a meal of lamb and bitter herbs, the Lord took some bread, gave thanks, broke it, passed it out, and told them to eat it, saying, *"Do this in remembrance of Me."* (Luke 22:19) *The broken bread* symbolized His body about to be bruised and punished for them.

Next, He passed around a cup containing the wine of crushed grapes. *"This cup,"* He told His disciples, is the *"blood of the covenant, which is poured out for many for the forgiveness of sins."* (Matthew 26:28)

The cup represented the blood Jesus was about to shed to inaugurate the promised new covenant.

These two simple symbols point to the central message of God's prophets: that our Creator would take on human flesh in order to suffer and shed His blood for Adam's sinful race.

After comforting His disciples with many incomparably wonderful promises and truths,[211] Jesus led them to a nearby garden called Gethsemane. Prostrating Himself on the ground, in profuse sweat and intense agony of soul, He prayed, *"O My Father, if it is possible, let this cup pass from Me; nevertheless, not as I will, but as You will."* (Matthew 26:39)

What was *"this cup"* that Jesus dreaded so? It was the cup of suffering for sin—the unprecedented separation from His Father that He was about to endure, and the concentrated horror of hell He would suffer for you and for me.

After voicing this same prayer three times, the Son willingly submitted to His Father's will. As the prophet David had predicted, the Messiah would restore that which He did not take. *"Though I have stolen nothing, I still must restore it."* (Psalm 69:4)

Jesus would become the full and final Sacrifice for sin.

THE ARREST

Just as Jesus finished speaking with His Father, into the garden marched a detachment of soldiers sent by the chief priests, scribes and elders. With their torches, clubs and swords, they had come to arrest the One who had calmed storms, cast out demons, and raised the dead back to life.

> *"**Jesus therefore, knowing all things that would come upon Him**, went forward and said to them, 'Whom are you seeking?'*
>
> *They answered Him, 'Jesus of Nazareth.'*
>
> *Jesus said to them, '**I am** He.' ...Now when He said to them, '**I am** He,' they drew back and fell to the ground. Then He asked them again, 'Whom are you seeking?'*
>
> *And they said, 'Jesus of Nazareth.'*
>
> *Jesus answered, 'I have told you that **I am** He.'"*
> (John 18:4-8)

To those who came to arrest Him, Jesus identified Himself with God's own name, *"I AM."* [212] Clearly, if Jesus was to go with them, it would be because He chose to do so.

As the soldiers closed in, the disciple Peter drew his sword, but only managed to cut off the ear of the chief priest's servant. Jesus graciously healed the man's ear and then said to Peter,

> *"Put your sword in its place, for all who take the sword will perish by the sword. Or do you think that I cannot now pray to My Father, and He will provide Me with more than twelve legions of angels?* **How then could the Scriptures be fulfilled, that it must happen thus?"**
> (Matthew 26:52-54)

What a refreshing contrast Jesus provides to all who use violence in the name of religion. Though Jesus knew that these men intended to mock, torture, and kill Him, He showed them patience and kindness rather than hatred and revenge.

THE PROPHETS FORETOLD IT

Then, to those who had come to arrest Him, Jesus said, *"Have you come out, as against a robber, with swords and clubs to take Me? I sat daily with you, teaching in the temple, and you did not seize Me."* And the Scripture adds this commentary:

> *"But all this was done* **that the Scriptures of the prophets might be fulfilled.**
> *Then all the disciples forsook Him and fled.*
> *And those who had laid hold of Him* **led Him away** *to Caiaphas the high priest, where the scribes and the elders were assembled."* (Matthew 26:55-57)

Why did the One who controlled the wind and the waves allow Himself to be arrested, bound, and led away?

He did it out of love and obedience to His Father.

He did it to save you and me from everlasting judgment.

He did it *"that the Scriptures of the prophets might be fulfilled."*

Hundreds of years earlier, the prophet Isaiah had written, *"He was* **led as a lamb** *to the slaughter."* (Isaiah 53:7)

The prophet Abraham had declared, *"God will provide for Himself the lamb for a burnt offering."* (Genesis 22:8)

And the prophet Moses had written, *"The priest shall take one male lamb and offer it... Then he shall kill the lamb in the place where he kills the sin offering."* (Leviticus 14:12-13)

Don't miss the irony.

The priests, responsible for killing and burning lambs on the brazen altar of the temple, were the very ones who had arrested Jesus in order to have Him killed. Yet they had no clue they were about to sacrifice *the Lamb* of whom all the prophets had written.

CONDEMNED BY RELIGIOUS LEADERS

"And they led Jesus away to the high priest; and with him were assembled all the chief priests, the elders, and the scribes." (Mark 14:53)

The religious leaders of the Jews had organized an illegal nighttime trial.

"Now the chief priests and all the council sought testimony against Jesus to put Him to death, but found none. For many bore false witness against Him, but their testimonies did not agree...

And the high priest stood up in the midst and asked Jesus, saying, 'Do You answer nothing? What is it these men testify against You?'

But He kept silent and answered nothing.

Again the high priest asked Him, saying to Him, 'Are You the Christ, the Son of the Blessed?'

Jesus said, 'I am. And you will see the Son of Man sitting at the right hand of the Power, and coming with the clouds of heaven.'

Then the high priest tore his clothes and said, 'What further need do we have of witnesses? You have heard the blasphemy!'" (Mark 14:55-56,60-63)

Why did the high priest become enraged, tear his clothes, and accuse Jesus of blasphemy? He did so because Jesus declared Himself to be the Son of God and the Son of Man—the Messiah of whom all the prophets had written. Jesus had also called Himself by God's own personal name, *"I AM!"* And by speaking of *"the Son of Man sitting at the right hand of Power, and coming with the clouds of heaven,"* Jesus was quoting from the Scriptures of the prophets and declaring Himself to be the Judge of all the earth.[213] That is why *"the high priest tore his clothes and said,*

> *'What further need do we have of witnesses? You have heard the blasphemy! What do you think?'*
> *And they all condemned Him to be deserving of death.*
> *Then some began to **spit** on Him, and to blindfold Him, and to **beat** Him, and to **say** to Him, 'Prophesy!' And the officers **struck** Him with the palms of their hands."*
> (Mark 14:63-65)

Seven hundred years earlier, the prophet Isaiah foretold the Messiah's willing sufferings: *"**I gave** My back to those who **struck** Me, and My cheeks to those who **plucked out** the beard; **I did not hide** My face from **shame** and **spitting**."* (Isaiah 50:6)

CONDEMNED BY POLITICAL LEADERS

At daybreak, the priests and religious leaders led Jesus to Pontius Pilate, the Roman governor of Judea. The religious leaders demanded that Pilate sentence Jesus to death by crucifixion. At that time in history, the Jews were under the rule of Rome's Empire and did not have authority to sentence a criminal to death.

During "the trial," three times Pilate declared, *"I find no fault in Him,"* but the mob, incited by the priests who were incited by the devil, only cried out the louder, *"**Away with Him, away with Him! Crucify Him! Crucify Him!**"*[214]

Pilate gave in to the pressures of the religious leaders and sentenced Jesus to the extreme penalty of Roman law: a brutal, bone-exposing flogging, followed by crucifixion.

*"And when he had **scourged** Jesus, he delivered Him to be crucified.*

*Then the soldiers of the governor took Jesus into the Praetorium and gathered **the whole garrison around Him**. And they **stripped Him** and **put a scarlet robe on Him**. When they had **twisted a crown of thorns, they put it on His head**, and a reed in His right hand. And they bowed the knee before Him and **mocked Him**, saying, 'Hail, King of the Jews!'*

*Then they **spat on Him**, and took the reed and **struck Him on the head**. And when they had **mocked Him**, they took the robe off Him, put His own clothes on Him, and **led Him away to be crucified**."* (Matthew 27:26-31)

THE MOUNT OF THE LORD

Thus, the Lord of glory—His holy body now a bloody mass of shredded flesh, His head bearing a crown of twisted thorns, and on His back a heavy wooden cross—was led outside the city and up the same mountain ridge where, nearly two thousand years earlier, Abraham had prophesied:

*"**God will provide for Himself the lamb for a burnt offering**.... **In the Mount of The LORD it shall be provided**."* (Genesis 22:8,14)

All the elements had converged—the people, the proceedings, the Person, the place. Everything was happening just as the prophets had foretold.

It was time for the transaction of the ages.

24

PAID IN FULL

Crucifixion is the cruelest state-sponsored method of execution ever devised. The Roman Empire reserved it for the most treacherous criminals.

Execution by crucifixion is what we, the human race, chose for our Creator when He came to visit us.[215]

> *"There were also two others, criminals, led with Him to be put to death. And when they had come to **the place called Calvary**,[216] **there they crucified Him**, and the criminals, one on the right hand and the other on the left."*
> (Luke 23:32-33)

CRUCIFIED!

Crucifixion was designed to inflict upon a victim the most excruciating agony and the greatest possible indignity. I have never seen, nor would I want to see, an artist's painting or a movie which adequately portrays the shame and pain Jesus endured while hanging on the cross. For instance, artists and screenwriters always put a piece of clothing on Him, but the historical reality is that the Roman soldiers would strip condemned criminals naked before sadistically slamming them against a tree or a cross and driving spikes through their wrists and heels.

Death by crucifixion was shameful, painful, and slow.

Jesus willingly endured this penalty—the shame and the pain—for you, for me, and for Adam's entire race. The intense torment that was heaped on Jesus is meant to help us understand the severe penalty our sin deserves.

Centuries before the Romans even invented crucifixion, the prophet David described the Messiah's sufferings on the cross:

*"The congregation of the wicked has enclosed Me. **They pierced My hands and My feet;** I can count all My bones. They look and stare at Me. They divide My garments among them, and for My clothing they cast lots. ...They shake the head, saying, 'He trusted in the LORD, let Him rescue Him; Let Him deliver Him, since He delights in Him!'"* (Psalm 22:16-18,8) And the prophet Isaiah foretold: *"He poured out His soul unto death, and He was numbered with the transgressors, and He bore the sin of many, and made intercession for the transgressors."* (Isaiah 53:12)

In the following excerpt from the gospel, see how many fulfillments you can identify based on the prophecies we just read.

"They crucified Him, and the criminals, one on the right hand and the other on the left. Then Jesus said, 'Father, forgive them, for they do not know what they do.' And they divided His garments and cast lots. And the people stood looking on. But even the rulers with them sneered, saying, 'He saved others; let Him save Himself if He is the Christ, the chosen of God.' The soldiers also mocked Him.

Then one of the criminals who were hanged blasphemed Him, saying, 'If You are the Christ, save Yourself and us.'

But the other, answering, rebuked him, saying, 'Do you not even fear God, seeing you are under the same condemnation? And we indeed justly, for we receive the due reward of our deeds; but this Man has done nothing wrong.' Then he said to Jesus, 'Lord, remember me when You come into Your kingdom.'

And Jesus said to him, 'Assuredly, I say to you, today you will be with Me in Paradise.'

Now it was about the sixth hour, and there was darkness over all the earth until the ninth hour. Then the sun was darkened....." (Luke 23:33-36,39-45)

THE TRANSACTION

Over the centuries, countless victims have endured the agonies of crucifixion. Before the fall of Jerusalem in AD 70, the Roman soldiers were crucifying five hundred Jews a day.[217] Some victims languished on the cross for days before expiring. Jesus suffered on the cross for a relatively shorter period of six hours before He died. What made His sufferings unique?

One significant difference is that the prophets foretold Jesus' sufferings and death. Another distinction is that—while many have shed their blood while impaled on a cross—only the Lord Jesus shed *perfect* blood. And the narrative we just read reveals another utterly unique dimension of Jesus' death.

*"Now it was about the sixth hour, and **there was darkness over all the earth** until the ninth hour."* (Luke 23:44)[218]

Jesus was nailed to the cross at nine o'clock in the morning. From noon until three o'clock, the whole earth was covered in darkness. Why? During those three hours, hidden from the view of the world, the most significant transaction of all time was taking place. God was dealing with our sin in time so that we might not have to deal with it in eternity.

During those hours of supernatural darkness, God in heaven dumped on His beloved, righteous Son the concentrated, everlasting punishment our sins require. It was for that purpose the Son of God had taken on a body of flesh and blood.

"He Himself is the propitiation [sufficient sin-offering that absorbed God's wrath] *for our sins, and not for ours only, but also for the whole world."* (1 John 2:2)

Seven centuries earlier, the prophet Isaiah had already described this transaction of the ages:

*"He was wounded for our transgressions, He was bruised for our iniquities; the chastisement for our peace was upon Him, and by His stripes we are healed... **the LORD has laid on Him the iniquity of us all**. ...He was led as a lamb to the slaughter... **it pleased the LORD to bruise Him**; He has put Him to grief. When You make **His soul an offering for sin**... He shall see the labor of His soul, and be satisfied. By His knowledge **My righteous Servant shall justify many, for He shall bear their iniquities**."* (Isaiah 53:5-7,10-11)

During those hours on the cross, as the planet was enveloped with darkness, the LORD laid on His willing, sinless Son the contamination and condemnation of our sins. What actually transpired between the Father and Son we may never comprehend, but one thing is sure: It was the greatest transaction of all time.

ALONE!

As the thick darkness covered the earth, *"Jesus cried out with a loud voice, saying, 'Eli, Eli, lama sabachthani?' that is, '**My God, My God, why have You forsaken Me?**'"* (Matthew 27:46)

Why did Jesus utter this gut-wrenching cry from the cross? He cried out thus because God had left Him to pay sin's penalty...

alone.

On the behalf of all, Jesus suffered the **three levels of separation** caused by sin:

- He experienced *spiritual death*. God in heaven turned away His holy face from His Son on earth—on whom He had loaded the sins of the human race.
- He went through *physical death*. The moment Jesus willingly died, His spirit and soul left His body.
- He also tasted *the second death*. He suffered the agony of hell—for you and for me.

Hell is a God-forsaken place of darkness and isolation; a place devoid of all that is good; a place of separation from the presence and love of the heavenly Father. While on the cross, for the first and last time in eternity, the eternal Son was separated from His eternal Father. Jesus endured that horrific separation, so that we might never experience it.

The holy Lamb of God became our Sin-Bearer: *our Substitute.* He bore the full weight of sin's curse, accepting the shame, the pain, the thorns, and the nails. On the altar of the cross, Jesus became the full and final *"burnt offering"* for sin.[219]

HELL IN A FEW HOURS?

Jesus took our hell.

How could one Man pay the penalty for the entire human race? How could Jesus suffer an eternity of punishment in a few hours of time?

He could do it because of *who He is.*

It is because of *who He is* that He did not need to go on paying for our sins throughout eternity as we would have to do. As the Eternal Son and Word of God He had no sin-debt of His own to pay, nor was He bound by time as we are.

It is because of *who He is* that He was able to *"taste death for everyone"* (Hebrews 2:9) in a finite amount of time.

Just as the Lord God did not need any particular quantity of time to create our complex world (though He chose to do it in *six days*), neither did He need any certain amount of time on the cross to redeem mankind (though He chose to do it in *six hours*).

With God, time is as nothing.

"From everlasting to everlasting, You are God! ... For a thousand years in Your sight are like yesterday when it is past, and like a watch [a few hours of guard duty] *in the night."* (Psalm 90:1,4)

"IT IS FINISHED!"

"After this, Jesus, knowing that all things were now accomplished, that the Scripture might be fulfilled, said, 'I thirst!' Now a vessel full of sour wine was sitting there; and they filled a sponge with sour wine, put it on hyssop, and put it to His mouth. So when Jesus had received the sour wine, He said, 'It is finished!' And bowing His head, He gave up His spirit." (John 19:28-30)

Just before Jesus died, He made an announcement:

"It is finished!"

This statement is translated from a single Greek word, *"Tetelestai."* This was a common term in the Roman business world. It was used to indicate that a debt had been completely paid. Ancient receipts have been found with *"Tetelestai"* written across them, meaning:

"Paid in full."

The term *Tetelestai* was also used to announce the completion of a task. In reporting back to the one who had sent him on a mission, a servant could say, *"Tetelestai,"* which meant:

"Mission accomplished."

The other Gospel writers all report that *"Jesus cried out **with a loud voice**, and breathed His last."* (Mark 15:37)

It was a shout of triumph!

The prophecies and symbols which pointed to God's sacrificial Lamb had been fulfilled.

Jesus had dealt effectively with the cause of the curse: *sin*. He had paid the required ransom to God to redeem the defiled, defiant, damned descendants of Adam. God's righteous nature and wrath against sin were fully satisfied. His laws had been enforced.
It is finished! Paid in full! Mission accomplished!

*"You were not **redeemed** with corruptible things, like silver or gold ... but **with the precious blood of Christ, as of a lamb without blemish and without spot**. He indeed was foreordained before the foundation of the world, but was manifest in these last times **for you**."* (1 Peter 1:18-20)

Down through the centuries, blood had flowed from millions of blemish-free, sacrificed animals. But now Jesus' own blood had flowed from His sin-free body. The infinitely *"precious blood of Christ"* would not just temporarily *cover* sin; it would forever *remove it* from the record.
This is what God's first covenant had foretold.

*"'Behold, the days are coming,' says the LORD, 'when I will make a **new covenant**. ... I will forgive their iniquity, and **their sin I will remember no more**.'"* (Jeremiah 31:31,34)

The New Testament Scriptures then explain: *"In that He says, '**A new covenant**,' He has made the first **obsolete**."* (Hebrews 8:13) No more sin offerings would be needed. Animal sacrifices on an altar had been abolished by the Messiah's death on a cross.
Just as the LORD God performed *the first* blood sacrifice (on the day Adam and Eve sinned), so He has provided *the final* acceptable blood sacrifice.
As Abraham prophesied, God has provided *"**for Himself** the Lamb for the sacrifice."* (Genesis 22:8) While God did spare Abraham's son, He *"did not spare **His own Son**, but delivered Him up **for us all**."* (Romans 8:32)
Jesus' shed blood *satisfied **the law of sin and death*** and *fulfilled **the law of the sacrifice**.*
It's no wonder He shouted, ***"It is finished!"***

THE TORN VEIL
So what happened after Jesus shouted, *"It is finished!"*?

"And Jesus cried out with a loud voice, and breathed His last. **Then the veil of the temple was torn in two from top to bottom.** *"* (Mark 15:37-38)

Ancient historians describe the temple veil as being as thick as the palm of a hand and so heavy that it needed 300 men to maneuver it.[220]

What caused this massive curtain to be ripped in two?

Back in chapter 21, we learned that God had commanded His people to hang this special curtain in the tabernacle and later in the temple. The veil shut man out from "the Holiest Place"—that inner sanctuary where God had once placed the blinding light of His Presence. This veil, embroidered with colors of blue, purple and red, symbolized God's own Son who would come from heaven to earth. It also served to remind sinners of their separation from their holy Creator. Only those that met God's standard of perfect righteousness would be granted entrance into God's eternal dwelling place.

Once a year—on the Day of Atonement—the specially anointed high priest would be permitted to go past the veil and enter the Holiest Place. The only way to enter into God's presence without being annihilated was for the high priest to take a bowl of the blood of a sacrificed goat (symbolizing Christ's shed blood). The priest also had to be clothed in a pure linen tunic (symbolizing Christ's righteousness). Once inside the Holiest Place, the high priest would sprinkle the blood seven times (symbolizing completeness) on the Mercy Seat of the Ark of the Covenant. The Ark contained God's Law which condemned all sinners to death. But God showed His mercy to sinners by allowing an innocent animal to die in their stead.

For fifteen centuries, the veil testified to God's absolute holiness and that apart from the shed blood of Christ there could be no permanent atonement for sin. Only *God's sinless, Chosen One,* whom the veil symbolized, could pay sin's price. That is why, when the time was right, God sent His own Son to live a life of perfect obedience to God's laws, and then to willingly pay with His own blood the full penalty for the law-breaking descendants of Adam.

So who tore the veil in two from top to bottom? God did. This act was the Father's *"Amen!"* to the Son's, *"It is finished!"* [221]

God was satisfied.

NO MORE SIN-SACRIFICES

By Jesus' sacrifice on the cross, full atonement (forgiveness of sin and reconciliation to God) had been provided. The Perfect Substitute had willingly shed His blood for the sin of the world.

No longer would God's people be burdened with yearly sacrifices for sin.

No longer would God require temple rituals or high priests.

The once-for-all Sacrifice had been made. The Reality behind the shadows and symbols had spoken: *"It is finished!"*

To all who believe, God Himself says:

> *"'Their sins and their lawless deeds I will remember no more.' Now where there is remission of these, there is **no longer an offering for sin**. Therefore, brethren, **having boldness to enter the Holiest by the blood of Jesus**, by a new and living way which He consecrated for us, **through the veil, that is, His flesh**, and having a High Priest over the house of God, **let us draw near with a true heart in full assurance of faith**."* (Hebrews 10:17-22)

DEAD

The moment Jesus died, not only was the temple veil torn in two, but the earth quaked and the terrified crowd scattered.

> *"So when the centurion and those with him, who were guarding Jesus, saw the earthquake and the things that had happened, they feared greatly, saying, 'Truly this was the Son of God!'"* (Matthew 27:54)

Later, to assure that Jesus was truly dead, a Roman soldier drove a spear into Jesus' side. Blood and water flowed out, providing medical proof that He was dead. The soldier's action also fulfilled more prophecies.[222]

BURIED

> *"Now when evening had come, there came a rich man from Arimathea, named Joseph, who himself had also become a disciple of Jesus. This man went to Pilate and asked for the body of Jesus. Then Pilate commanded the body to be given to him. When Joseph had taken the body, he wrapped it in a clean linen cloth, and laid it in his new tomb which he had hewn out of the rock; and he rolled a large stone against the door of the tomb, and departed."*
> (Matthew 27:57-60)

The prophet Isaiah had predicted that the Messiah's grave would be *"with the rich at His death."* (Isaiah 53:9) God's plan was being fulfilled in every detail. Even so, Jesus' disciples still did not understand that plan. They had truly believed that Jesus was the Messiah who would establish His kingdom on earth, but when they saw Him die, their hopes died with Him. Their miracle-working Master and dearest Friend had been executed and buried.

It was over, or so they thought.

Strangely enough, although Jesus' disciples had forgotten His promise to come back to life on the third day, the religious leaders who plotted Jesus' execution had not.

> *"The chief priests and Pharisees gathered together to Pilate, saying, '**Sir, we remember, while He was still alive, how that deceiver said, 'After three days I will rise.'** Therefore command that the tomb be made secure until the third day, lest His disciples come by night and steal Him away, and say to the people, 'He has risen from the dead.' So the last deception will be worse than the first.'*
> *Pilate said to them, 'You have a guard; go your way, make it as secure as you know how.'*

So they went and made the tomb secure, sealing the stone and setting the guard." (Matthew 27.62-66)

The stone door to the cold tomb holding Jesus' corpse was sealed shut. Well-armed Roman soldiers stationed themselves around the burial site. It seemed that this was the way the story of Jesus of Nazareth would end.

Then came Sunday morning.

DEATH DEFEATED

The Scripture says of Adam, *"and he **died"*** (Genesis 5:5) and that's where his earthly story ends.

It was no different with Adam's descendants. The fifth chapter of Genesis records their epitaph.

"And he died.
...and he died.
...and he died.
...and he died.
...and he died."

Such is the history of sin-infected men and women. They lived, died, and were buried; generation after generation, century after century.

But the Messiah's story doesn't end in a tomb.

THE EMPTY TOMB

"Now after the Sabbath, as the first day of the week began to dawn, Mary Magdalene and the other Mary came to see the tomb. And behold, there was a great earthquake; for an angel of the Lord descended from heaven, and came and rolled back the stone from the door, and sat on it. His countenance was like lightning, and his clothing as white as snow. And the guards shook for fear of him, and became like dead men.

But the angel answered and said to the women, 'Do not be afraid, for I know that you seek Jesus who was crucified. **He is not here; for He is risen, as He said. Come, see the place where the Lord lay.** *And go quickly and tell His disciples that He is risen from the dead,* and indeed He is going before you into Galilee; there you will see Him. Behold, I have told you.'

*So they went out quickly from the tomb with fear and great joy, and ran to bring His disciples word. And as they went to tell His disciples, behold, Jesus met them, saying, '***Rejoice!***'*

*So they came and held Him by the feet and worshiped Him. Then Jesus said to them, '***Do not be afraid.*** Go and tell My brethren to go to Galilee, and there they will see Me.'"*
(Matthew 28:1-10)

Death could not hold the Messiah. Since He had no sin of His own, God raised Him from the dead. Not only had Jesus paid the penalty for the sin of the world, but He had triumphed over that penalty. He had conquered death itself!

Satan and his demons must have shuddered.

The religious leaders were frantic.

"Now while they [the women who had just seen their risen Lord] *were going, behold, some of the guard came into the city and reported to the chief priests all the things that had happened.*

When they had assembled with the elders and consulted together, they gave a large sum of money to the soldiers, saying, 'Tell them, 'His disciples came at night and stole Him away while we slept.' And if this comes to the governor's ears, we will appease him and make you secure.'

So they took the money and did as they were instructed; and this saying is commonly reported among the Jews until this day." (Matthew 28:11-15)

Jesus' enemies knew the tomb was empty. They were desperate to cover up the truth. They did not want people to know that the Man they had killed had come back to life!

DEATH DEFEATED

In the Garden of Eden, God had warned Adam that if he disobeyed his Creator's one rule, he would *"surely die!"* Satan had countered, *"You will **not** surely die!"* and proceeded to lead Adam and the entire human race down a path of death and destruction. For thousands of years death held men, women, and children in its relentless grip. Then the Son of God challenged death, defeated it, and threw open the door to eternal life.

"For as in Adam all die, even so in Christ all shall be made alive." (1 Corinthians 15:22)

Just yesterday an elderly neighbor lady told me, "The one thing I fear in life is death." How glad I was to be able to tell her of the Eternal One who passed through death and came out alive, triumphing over that dreaded enemy.

"Since the children have flesh and blood, [Jesus] too shared in their humanity so that by his death he might destroy him who holds the power of death—that is, the devil—and free those who all their lives were held in slavery by their fear of death." (Hebrews 2:14-15 NIV)

Suppose Jesus had only died for our sin, but had not risen from the dead? Death would have still been something to fear.

By conquering death, the Lord Jesus demonstrated that He is greater than Satan's most powerful weapon and man's most feared enemy. Because Jesus overcame death, those who trust in Him have nothing to fear in this life or the next.

God's message is straightforward. If you trust in His Son who suffered on the cross, went down into death, and came out alive on the third day as your Substitute, He will release you from death's stranglehold and give you His eternal life.

That is God's Good News for a world held hostage by sin.

*"Christ **died** for our sins according to the Scriptures... He was **buried**, and... He **rose again** the third day **according to the Scriptures**."* (1 Corinthians 15:1-4)

To all who believe, Christ Jesus says:

"Because I live, you will live also. ...Do not be afraid; I am the First and the Last. I am He who lives, and was dead, and behold, I am alive forevermore. Amen. And I have the keys of Hades [place of departed spirits] *and of Death."* (John 14:19; Revelation 1:17-18)

SATAN DEFEATED

When Jesus entered death's realm and exited three days later, in terms of warfare, He *took the high ground*—an advantage He will never relinquish. Satan is a defeated foe. Though he and his demons continue to fight desperately, they cannot win.

Do you see how God fulfilled the prophecy He announced in the Garden of Eden on the day Adam and Eve sinned? As He promised, *the Seed of a woman* (Jesus) was wounded by *the Serpent* (Satan), but those very wounds sealed Satan's doom.

"For this purpose the Son of God was manifested, that He might destroy the works of the devil." (1 John 3:8)

Through His death, burial, and resurrection, Jesus triumphed over the curse of sin which stated:

*"... to **dust** you shall return."* (Genesis 3:19)

For thousands of years, Satan sneered as death's putrefying process turned Adam's deceased descendants back into dust. But now here was One whose body did **not** return to dust!

Why did *His* body not decay in the grave?

Death had no power over Him because He was the Sinless One. A thousand years earlier the prophet David had announced:

*"You will **not**...let your Holy One see **decay**."* (Psalm 16:10 NIV)

The Holy One has conquered Satan and death—for us.

THE EVIDENCE

The evidences for Jesus' resurrection from the dead are numerous and convincing.[223]

The tomb was empty.

The corpse was nowhere to be found.

The women were the first to witness the empty tomb, hear the angel's announcement, see Jesus alive, touch Him, and speak with Him. If the Gospel records had been made-up, do you think the four men who wrote them would have given the women credit for being first in everything?!

Jesus' documented post-resurrection appearances were many. For decades to follow, hundreds of credible witnesses would testify to having walked and talked with the risen Messiah.

Jesus' disciples had seen Him suffer and die. They were heartbroken. Their hopes had been dashed since they had the mistaken idea that the Messiah could never die. They had returned to their homes disheartened and afraid.

Then something happened. They saw Jesus alive.

Suddenly they remembered how Jesus had told them He would be crucified and rise again the third day.[224] At last they understood the words of the prophets.

These former cowards became Christ's bold witnesses. Not long after Jesus rose from the dead, Peter, who had been confused and fearful, was in the hostile streets of Jerusalem fearlessly declaring to those who had plotted Jesus' crucifixion:

> *"You disowned the Holy and Righteous One...* **You killed the author of life, but God raised him from the dead.** *We are witnesses of this. ...Now, brothers, I know that you acted in ignorance, as did your leaders.* **But this is how God fulfilled what he had foretold through all the prophets,** *saying that his Christ would suffer. Repent, then, and turn to God, so that your sins may be wiped out."* (Acts 3:14-19 NIV)

For Jesus' disciples, no hardship would be too great to endure for the One who had given them eternal life.

Christ's disciples (also called *Christians*[225]) were ridiculed, imprisoned, flogged, and many were executed because of their bold witness for the Lord Jesus. Peter himself was persecuted and, according to secular history, eventually crucified—upside down. Yet Peter, along with the other disciples, joyfully accepted such persecution since they *knew* that their Savior and Lord had conquered death and hell.[226] They *knew* that God had given them forgiveness, righteousness, and eternal life. Death no longer scared them since they *knew* that the instant their physical body died their eternal soul and spirit would *"be present with the Lord"* in heaven. (2 Corinthians 5:8)

Nothing could frighten them now. They had a message for the world—a message that meant more to them than life itself!

Here is how one of Christ's followers concluded his message to a skeptical, mocking crowd in the ancient city of Athens:

> *"God is now declaring to men that* **all everywhere** *should* **repent,** *because He has fixed a day in which* **He will judge the world in righteousness through a Man whom He has appointed, having furnished proof to all men by raising Him from the dead."** (Acts 17:30-31 NAS)

His conclusion was plain and simple: *Repent!* Stop thinking you can save yourself from God's certain judgment! Instead, rely completely on the Savior who shed His blood for your sins and rose from the dead.

POSITIVE PROOF

How can you and I be sure that Jesus is the Savior and Judge of the world? We just read the answer. God has *"furnished* **proof** *to all men* **by raising Him from the dead.** *"*

What more evidence is needed that Jesus is the one and only Savior? Why would we trust our eternal destiny to anyone else?

Tragically, people around the world venerate *dead men* who contradicted God's story and message while they were alive. Why would anyone choose to place their trust in some man who was unable to conquer death and who contradicted God's Word—when Jesus overcame death and fulfilled the words of the prophets?

Just as fulfilled prophecy is God's way of providing indisputable proof that the Bible is the Word of God, so Jesus' resurrection on the third day is God's indisputable proof that He alone can save us from eternal death and give us eternal life.

THE SAVIOR FOR ALL PEOPLE

The Scripture is clear: the message about Jesus' death and resurrection is for *"all everywhere."* This must be emphasized, because some will try to tell you that Jesus came only for the Jews. Nothing could be farther from the truth.[227]

While it is true that the Messiah's earthly ministry focused on the Jews, His purpose in coming to that nation was to provide salvation for the whole world. Seven hundred years earlier, the prophet Isaiah had written out God's promise to His Son: *"I will also give You as a light to the Gentiles, that You should be My salvation to the ends of the earth. "* (Isaiah 49:6)

Christ came into the world knowing that the Jewish leaders would refuse to receive Him as their King. He also knew that it would be through that very rejection that He would pay sin's penalty and offer salvation to the world.

*"He was in the world, and the world was made through Him, and the world did not know Him. He came to His own, and His own did not receive Him. But **as many** as received Him, to them He gave the right to become children of God, to those who believe in His name."* (John 1:10-12)

Jesus Christ is the Savior for all people, but only those who believe in His name—that is, in who He is and what He did to save sinners—will be granted *"the right to become children of God."*

My friend, God loves you and considers you worth the life of His Son. Nevertheless, He will not force you to believe.

He leaves that choice with you.

*"For God so loved the world that he gave his one and only Son, that **whoever believes in him** shall not perish but have eternal life."* (John 3:16 NIV)

NO MORE CONFUSION

On the same day Jesus rose from the dead, He walked and talked with a couple confused disciples who had not yet understood why it was necessary for the Messiah to shed His blood and come back to life. Jesus said to them:

"'O foolish ones, and slow of heart to believe in all that the prophets have spoken! Ought not the Christ to have suffered these things and to enter into His glory?'

*And beginning at **Moses** [Genesis] and **all the Prophets**, He expounded to them in all the Scriptures the things concerning **Himself.**"* (Luke 24:25-27)

At last, their confusion was cleared up. How could they have been so blind? The Messiah had not come to put down temporal political enemies; He had come to gain victory over the more ruthless spiritual enemies—Satan, sin, death, and hell!

Later that day, Jesus appeared to His disciples in the upper room where they lodged in Jerusalem. He showed them His nail-pierced hands and feet, ate with them, and then told them:

264 PART II: THE JOURNEY

> *"'These are the words which I spoke to you while I was still with you, that **all things must be fulfilled which were written in the Law of Moses and the Prophets and the Psalms concerning Me.**' And He opened their understanding, that they might comprehend the Scriptures. Then He said to them, 'Thus it is written, and thus it was necessary for the Christ to suffer and to rise from the dead the third day, and that repentance and remission of sins should be preached in His name to all nations, beginning at Jerusalem. And you are witnesses of these things.'"*
> (Luke 24:44-48)

Jesus told His disciples that they were to be *"witnesses of these things"* to the nations. Their message was clear: The Lord from heaven has paid sin's penalty and triumphed over death for every person ever born. Wherever there is repentance (a change of mind) combined with faith (heart-level trust) in Christ and His redemptive work, God grants full pardon and true peace.

AN INVITATION TO REST

Think back to the seventh day of creation.

What did the Lord do on that day? He rested.

Why did He rest? He rested because His work was *"finished.* *...God ended His work which He had done, and He rested on the seventh day from all **His work which He had done.**"* (Genesis 2:1-2)

Nothing needed to be added to God's work of creation. *It was finished.* Likewise, nothing needs to be added to God's work of redemption. *"It is finished!"*

Just as God rested and rejoiced in His work of creation, so He invites you and me to rest and rejoice in His finished work of salvation. *"For he who has **entered His rest** has himself also **ceased from his works as God did from His.**"* (Hebrews 4:10)

While ten thousand religions around the world cry out, "Nothing is finished. Do this! Do that! Try harder!" Jesus says, *"Come to Me, all you who labor and are heavy laden, and **I will give you rest.**"* (Matthew 11:28)

Are you resting and rejoicing in what God has done for you?

FORTY DAYS WITH THE LORD

The Lord Jesus spent time with His disciples over a forty day period after He had risen from the dead. He taught them many things about the kingdom of God. They gazed on Him and touched His resurrected body—a permanent, glorified body unfettered by time and space—the same type of body all true believers will one day receive.

The disciples walked, talked, and ate with the Lord Jesus. He reminded them that He would soon leave them, but that the Father would send down the Holy Spirit to live inside them. His Spirit would guide them and strengthen them in their witness to the nations of the world. Then one day He—Jesus—would return to earth to judge the world with perfect righteousness.

On the fortieth day after Jesus' resurrection, He met with His disciples on the Mount of Olives on the east side of Jerusalem. It was time for Him to return to His *"Father's house."* (John 14:2)

ASCENDED

*"And being assembled together with them, He commanded them not to depart from Jerusalem, but to wait for the Promise of the Father, 'which,' He said, 'you have heard from Me; for John truly baptized with water, but you shall be baptized with **the Holy Spirit** not many days from now... You shall receive power when **the Holy Spirit** has come upon you; and **you shall be witnesses to Me** in Jerusalem, and in all Judea and Samaria, and **to the end of the earth.'***

*Now when He had spoken these things, **while they watched, He was taken up**, and a cloud received Him out of their sight.*

*And while they looked steadfastly toward heaven as He went up, behold, two men stood by them in white apparel, who also said, 'Men of Galilee, why do you stand gazing up into heaven? **This same Jesus, who was taken up from you into heaven, will so come in like manner as you saw Him go into heaven.'"** (Acts 1:4-11)

HEAVEN'S VICTORY CELEBRATION

Thus, just as the prophets foretold, the Son of God *"ascended on high."*[228] The One who, some thirty-three years earlier, had willingly exchanged the adoration of heaven's angels for the mockery of men was coming home! But now there was something different about Him. He who had created man in His own image now bore the image of man.

The Scriptures do not reveal many details about the Son of God's return to heaven. Yet this we do know: it was glorious!

We can envision the innumerable host of angels and redeemed descendants of Adam holding their breath as the Lord is about to enter heaven's gates. They knew Him well as *the Son of God and Lord of glory,* but now they would meet Him for the first time as *the Son of Man and Lamb of God.*

All of heaven is silent.

Suddenly the silence is broken by a majestic chorus of trumpets and an angel's booming proclamation: *"Lift up your heads, O you gates! And be lifted up, you everlasting doors! And the King of glory shall come in!"* (Psalm 24:7)

The gates open wide, and to the thunderous applause of heaven, in walks the Champion, God's own Son, the Word, the Lamb, the battle-scarred Son of Man—*Jesus!* Through the adoring throng He walks, making His way up to the Father's throne. Turning, He looks out over the innumerable multitude of Adam's redeemed race and sits down.[229]

Mission accomplished.

The host of the redeemed bow before Him and declare, as if with one voice:

*"**Worthy is the Lamb who was slain!**"* (Revelation 5:12)

What a celebration it must have been! What a celebration it is. It's the celebration that will never end.

26

RELIGIOUS AND FAR FROM GOD

Perhaps you've heard the adage: "Hindsight is always 20/20." The designation "20/20" is the North American optometrist's standard for *clear vision.* If your eyesight is 20/20, you do not need glasses.

Hindsight has to do with looking back on what has already happened. Hindsight allows us to see the course of action that we or someone else should have taken, but only after it is too late. Such hindsight is not very helpful.

However, when it comes to understanding the story and message revealed by God over many centuries, hindsight is tremendously helpful. It allows us to overcome major obstacles; to discern truth from error. That is why Jesus told His disciples:

> *"**Blessed are your eyes for they see**, and your ears for they hear; for assuredly, I say to you that **many prophets and righteous men desired to see what you see**, and did not see it, and to hear what you hear, and did not hear it."*
> (Matthew 13:16-17)

As those living after the Messiah's first coming to earth, we are blessed to be able to look back into history, study the completed Scriptures, and see clearly God's perfect plan.

With this thought in mind, and considering all we have witnessed in our journey through the Scriptures, let us return once more to *the Book of Beginnings.*

SEEING CAIN AND ABEL WITH HINDSIGHT

The fourth chapter of Genesis is clear: both Cain and Abel were born with a sin-problem. As they grew into manhood, each attempted to worship God, but only one was accepted.

> *"The LORD respected Abel and his offering, but He did not respect Cain and his offering."* (Genesis 4:4)

With Biblical hindsight, having now heard the story of Jesus the Savior of sinners, it is easy to understand why, thousands of years earlier, *"The LORD **respected** Abel and his offering, but He did **not respect** Cain and his offering."*

Abel's slain lamb pointed forward to Jesus, the Lamb of God, who would shed His blood for sinners. Cain's vegetables did not point to Jesus.

While Abel looked ahead to what would take place, today we look back to what Jesus has accomplished for us by His death and resurrection.

> *"The blood of Jesus Christ...**cleanses** us from all sin."*
> (1 John 1:7)

SAVING FAITH

God forgave Abel the same way He forgives sinners today. Whenever a sinner admits his or her unrighteousness and trusts in the LORD and His salvation, that person is forgiven and credited with God's gift of righteousness. So it has been with all the prophets and believers of every age.

For example, as we already discovered, Abraham *"**believed** in the LORD, and He accounted* [credited] *it to him for **righteousness**."* (Genesis 15:6) To say Abraham *"believed in the LORD,"* means Abraham had *confidence* that what God said was true. Abraham *trusted* God's Word. His *faith* was in God alone.

Like the prophet Abraham, King David also believed God's promises. With a joyful heart, David wrote, *"Blessed is he whose transgressions are forgiven, whose sins are covered.* **Blessed is the man whose sin the LORD does not count against him.***"* (Psalm 32:1-2 NIV) David also exclaimed, *"Surely goodness and mercy shall follow me all the days of my life; and **I will dwell in the house of the LORD forever.***"* (Psalm 23:6)

As those who lived *before* Jesus came, the sin-debt of people like Abel, Abraham and David was *covered* because they placed their faith in the LORD God and His plan. Then when Christ died, their sin-debt was forever *canceled* from the record books.

Today, we live *after* the time of Christ. The good news of God is that if you believe in what the Lord Jesus did for you through His substitutionary death and victorious resurrection, God will erase your sin-debt from His record books, credit your account with the righteousness of Christ, and guarantee you a place *"in the house of the LORD forever."*

All this and much, much more is yours if you believe.

To believe in the Lord Jesus is to place your total faith in Him and in what He has done for you. To better understand the meaning of faith, imagine yourself walking into a room with many chairs. Some are obviously broken. Others are feeble and about to break. Some look pretty good, but upon closer inspection you notice that they too have weak points and cannot be trusted. Just when you think there is not a sturdy chair in the room, your eye falls on one that is clearly solid and well-constructed. You walk over to it and sit down. You put your faith in it. You rest on it. You know it will hold you and not let you down.

Jesus Christ will never disappoint those who rest on Him and His finished work.

DEADLY FAITH

Our faith is only as good as the object in which it is placed. Everyone has faith, but not all have the same object of faith.

Abel placed his faith in God and His way of forgiveness and righteousness.

Cain placed his faith in his own ideas and self-efforts.

Cain and all who refuse God's diagnosis and remedy for their sin-problem can be compared to a snake-charmer I saw on television. The man was bitten by a huge cobra, but refused the anti-venom injection that could have saved his life. He thought he was strong enough to withstand the serpent's venom.

This man had faith; strong faith; *worthless* faith. He had placed his faith in himself instead of the doctor's remedy.

His choice cost him his life.

The Scriptures are clear. To place our faith in our own efforts, instead of in God's salvation, is to go *"the way of Cain"* and face *"the blackness of darkness forever."* (Jude 1:11,13) Cain's idea—that a person can earn his or her way into God's favor by self-effort— has always been in opposition to God's plan of redemption.

Yet to this day most people cling to *"the way of Cain."*

MAN'S SCALE

One day some religious Jews asked Jesus, *"'What shall **we do**, that **we may work** the works of God?' Jesus answered and said to them, 'This is the work of God, that you **believe** in Him whom He sent.'"* (John 6:28-29) These inquirers wanted to *"work."* Jesus told them to *"believe in Him."*

The confusion expressed by these Jews is widespread.

My sister and her husband live in the highlands of Papua New Guinea. They and their coworkers help isolated tribal people in practical ways and teach them about the one true God and His message of eternal life. Here is a note from one of their colleagues who tells of a conversation he had with one of the men who has been listening to "God's Talk" (as Papuans call the Bible):

> "After hearing the teaching on Jesus as *'the Bread of Life,'* [the man] said, 'It's just too easy, I have worked all my life to try and earn my way to heaven and to be clean in God's eyes, and here you are telling us that all we have to do is believe in Jesus?'
>
> I told him to listen again to what Jesus said, *'I am the Bread of Life.'* (John 6:35) Then I had him reread John 6:29: *'This is the work of God, that you **believe in Him** whom*

He sent.' He also read John 3:16: *'Whoever **believes in Him** shall not perish but have eternal life.'* I asked him if God needed our help, as if God wasn't strong enough to save us.

He laughed, 'Of course not! God doesn't need our help.'

'So then, according to God's Word, does God need your works to help get you to heaven?'

The man shook his head and left deep in thought."

Despite the clarity of God's message, people around the world—from isolated tribal folk to cultured members of synagogues, churches, and mosques—cling to the concept that on the Day of Judgment, God is going to place their good deeds and their bad deeds on a huge weigh scale. They imagine that if they come out with 51% or more on the good-deeds-side of the scale, they will be welcomed into Paradise, but if the scales reveal 51% or more on the bad-deeds-side, they will be sent to hell.

Such a good-works-outweighing-bad-works system is never used in man's earthly courtrooms. Neither will it be used in God's heavenly courtroom.

Think it through. Do you really want God's judgment of you and your eternal destiny to be based on your own goodness and commitment?

Thankfully, this "scales theory" is **not** found in God's Book.

GOD'S STANDARD

God requires perfection.

Only those who receive God's gift of righteousness can dwell with Him. If even a speck of sin is found on your record on Judgment Day, you will not enter Paradise. God demands perfect righteousness.

Sin is as disgusting to God as a decaying pig carcass in our house would be to us. Would spraying perfume on the decaying carcass remove the defilement and stench? Neither can any amount of religious rituals remove our defilement and make us acceptable to God.

A single sin is as intolerable to God as a drop of poison in our tea would be to us. Would adding more water to the poisoned tea remove its lethal quality? Neither can any amount of good works purify us and save us from eternal judgment.

When it comes to getting rid of our sin-debt or making ourselves right before God, we are *helpless*. But thank the Lord we are not *hopeless*. He has provided all we need to live forever in His pure and perfect presence.

FAITH AND WORKS

To all who believe in Jesus Christ who fully paid sin's penalty, God says: *"For by grace* [undeserved kindness] *you have been saved through faith* [trusting in what Christ has done for you], *and that not of yourselves; it is the gift of God, not of works, lest anyone should boast."* (Ephesians 2:8-9)

There will be no bragging in heaven.

Salvation is *"by grace."* Salvation is *"the gift of God."* It is an undeserved gift to be gratefully received, not a medal to be earned, *"lest anyone should boast."* Yet, tragically, most religious people remain confused on this issue, like this correspondent in the Middle East who wrote:

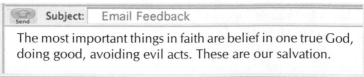

Send   **Subject:** Email Feedback

The most important things in faith are belief in one true God, doing good, avoiding evil acts. These are our salvation.

If salvation from eternal judgment and the right to dwell with God depended on our own efforts, how could we ever know that we had done enough good or sufficiently avoided evil to merit a place in Paradise? Never could we be assured of salvation.

Nearly three millennia ago, the prophet Jonah declared: *"Salvation comes from the LORD."* (Jonah 2:9 NIV)

Praise God for that!

*"For by grace you have been saved through faith, and that **not of yourselves**; it is **the gift of God, not of works**, lest anyone should boast."* (Ephesians 2:8-9)

God's Word is clear: To trust in ourselves and our works to save us from sin's penalty is to reject God's gift of salvation.

So where do performing good works and avoiding sin fit in? The next verse tells us:

*"For we are **His workmanship**, created in Christ Jesus **for good works**, which God prepared beforehand that we should walk in them."* (Ephesians 2:10)

The distinction is clear: We are *not* saved *by* good works. We are saved *for* good works.

*"Our great God and Savior Jesus Christ... gave Himself for us, that He might redeem us **from every lawless deed** and purify for Himself His own special people, **zealous for good works**."* (Titus 2:14)

The prologue of this book began with a village elder's comments to my friend, "For the good works you've done, you deserve to go to paradise..."

The Word of God exposes the error of this man's thinking.

No one "deserves to go to paradise" based on their own "good works." However, those who have received God's great gift of eternal life will *want* to avoid evil and do good for the glory of God and the blessing of others.

THE FRUIT IS NOT THE ROOT

Good works have never been a *requirement for salvation*, but they should always be a *result of salvation*. For example, Jesus taught His disciples:

> *"A new commandment I give to you, that you love one another; as I have loved you, that you also love one another. By this all will know that you are My disciples, if you have love for one another."* (John 13:34-35)

Is loving and caring for people like Jesus loved and cared for them a *precondition* for salvation? No. If it were, none of us could enter Paradise since Jesus is the only One who ever loved others perfectly and constantly.

Should loving and caring for people be a growing *result* in the lives of true believers? Absolutely. *"By this **all will know** that you are My disciples, **if** you have love for one another."*

God's people *show* their faith by the way they live.[230]

It is critical to distinguish *the root* of salvation from *the fruit* of salvation. Believers in Christ should express their thankfulness to the Lord for His gift of salvation (the root) by leading holy, loving, selfless, and disciplined lives (the fruit).

God's people don't do good works to earn His favor; they do good works because He has granted them undeserved favor.

FALSE RELIGION

Cain is the founder of the first "do-it-yourself" religion. Instead of approaching God on the basis of the blood of a sacrificial lamb, he came with his own ideas and efforts. Thus, Cain's prayers were offensive and disgusting to God.

> *"One who turns away his ear from hearing the law, **even his prayer is an abomination**."* (Proverbs 28:9)

God's law required the shed blood of a lamb or other suitable sacrifice to cover sin. Since Cain did not come to God as required, *"even his prayer [was] an abomination* [a detestable act, defilement]. " Cain had religion, but it was false religion. His offering did not point to the promised Savior and His death on the cross. Consequently:

> *"The LORD respected Abel and his offering, but He did not respect Cain and his offering. And Cain was very angry, and his countenance fell.*
> *So the LORD said to Cain, 'Why are you angry? And why has your countenance fallen? If you do well, will you not be accepted?'"* (Genesis 4:4-7)

The LORD mercifully spoke with Cain, giving him time to repent—to turn from his unrighteous works and submit to God's righteous plan.

Cain only got angry. He was not about to trade his beautiful religion of self-effort for the ghastly blood of a lamb. In the name of God, he would do things his own way!

And just where did that way lead him?

HOSTILE RELIGION

> *"Now Cain talked with Abel his brother; and it came to pass, when they were in the field, that **Cain rose up against Abel his brother and killed him**."* (Genesis 4:8)

Cain, who was too proud to kill a lamb as a sin offering, was not too proud to kill his own brother.

Cain set the stage for future religious and political systems that would ridicule, persecute, and even execute those who refuse to submit to the dictates of their laws and traditions.

Like Cain, many religious people around the world today use aggression and murder to defend their religion. By their actions, they are announcing to the world how insecure they are in their faith and how little confidence they have in their God to work things out.

A man living in the United States, with whom I have had extensive e-mail correspondence, wrote:

> **Subject:** Email Feedback
>
> The last man who blasphemed the Holy Prophet to my face swallowed both his front teeth about three seconds later. I took great pleasure in the fact that the next time he spoke blasphemy it would be with a lisp.
> Pagans are to convert or die. Period.

This man's words and actions stand in stark contrast to the Lord Jesus who said, *"But I tell you who hear me:* **Love your enemies**, *do good to those who hate you, bless those who curse you, pray for those who mistreat you."* (Luke 6:27-28 NIV) And on the cross, Jesus prayed for those who crucified Him, *"Father, forgive them, for they do not know what they do!"* (Luke 23:34)[231]

UNREPENTANT CAIN

Getting back to Cain's story, after he killed his brother, God gave Cain a chance to repent of his wrong thinking and evil ways.

> *"Then the LORD said to Cain, 'Where is Abel your brother?'*
> *He said, 'I do not know. Am I my brother's keeper?'*
> *And He said, 'What have you done? The voice of your brother's blood cries out to Me from the ground! So now you are cursed from the earth, which has opened its mouth to receive your brother's blood from your hand.'"*
> (Genesis 4:9-11)[232]

Cain refused to admit his sin and humbly approach God with the blood of a lamb. Instead, *"Cain went out from the presence of the LORD."* (Genesis 4:16)

Cain never repented. Instead of submitting to God's way, he continued to follow his own ideas. Cain founded a thriving civilization, but it was a society devoid of true submission to the Creator God.[233] Like Cain, his descendants rushed down a self-destructive path of self-centered living.

The fourth chapter of Genesis also records the story of Lamech, a sixth-generation descendant of Cain. Like his ancestor, Lamech was a man of conceit, lust, revenge, and murder. His sons developed many of the sciences and arts. They had great knowledge about many things, but did not know God.

Not only had people turned away from *God's way of salvation*; they had turned away from *God's way of living*.

UNREPENTANT MANKIND

Just nine generations after Cain, the LORD would give this evaluation of the human race:

*"The wickedness of man was great in the earth, and... every intent of the thoughts of his heart was **only evil continually**."* (Genesis 6:5)

By the time of Noah the prophet, Noah and his family were the only people on earth who still trusted their Creator. Man's obstinate refusal to heed God's word brought on the universal flood. In His grace, God provided a way of escape, but only eight people availed themselves of it. Noah and his wife, and their sons Shem, Ham, and Japheth, along with their wives, were the only ones who believed God's message (Genesis 6–8).

*"**By faith** Noah, when warned about things not yet seen, in holy fear built an ark to save his family. **By his faith** he condemned the world and became heir of the righteousness that comes **by faith**."* (Hebrews 11:7 NIV)

While many scientists today mock the Biblical record of the universal flood,[234] *none deny* that much of today's dry land was once covered with water and that millions of marine fossils have been unearthed in the world's great deserts and mountain ranges. Neither can any deny the presence of the rainbow following a rainstorm, though they may scoff at its significance as a sign of God's promise to never again destroy the entire world with a flood.

REBELLIOUS AND CONFUSED

Even when blessed with a fresh start following the judgment of the flood, within a few generations, people would soon rebel against their Creator-Owner and follow their own ideas. For example, God had told mankind to spread out and *"fill the earth."* (Genesis 1:28; 9:1) So what did people determine to do? They chose the exact opposite!

> *"Come, let us build **ourselves** a city, and **a tower whose top is in the heavens**; let us make **a name for ourselves**, **lest we be scattered** abroad over the face of the whole earth."* (Genesis 11:4)

Notice the self-centeredness and rebellion of their plans. Instead of following God's good and perfect will for them, they made plans to follow their own wisdom and magnify their own name. Perhaps they thought that by building *"a tower whose top is in the heavens"* they would be safe in case of another flood. They were like many religious people today who hope to escape God's judgment by their own hard work.

God put a stop to man's plan to live together in one place. The LORD knew that such a plan would have led to the rapid corruption and ruin of the human race. Keeping in mind that up to this period in history *"the whole earth had one language and one speech"* (Genesis 11:1), let's see what God did.

> *"The LORD said, 'Indeed the people are one and they all have one language, and this is what they begin to do; now nothing that they propose to do will be withheld from them. **Come, let Us go down and there confuse their language, that they may not understand one another's speech.**'*
> *So the LORD **scattered them** abroad from there over the face of all the earth, and they ceased building the city. Therefore its name is called **Babel**, because there the LORD confused the language of all the earth; and from*

there the LORD scattered them abroad over the face of all the earth. " (Genesis 11:6-9)

Unable to communicate with one another, the people left their tower unfinished and spread out around the world, just as God had intended for them to do in the first place. *"Therefore its name is called Babel."* *Babel* means *"confusion."*

Rejection of God's blueprint always leads to confusion.

THE MISTAKEN MAJORITY

One lesson to be learned from the people of Noah's day and from those who tried to build the tower of Babel is this:

The majority was wrong.

Though sinners took comfort in the fact that millions of others shared their worldview, God's judgment came upon them nonetheless. To this day, many people think their concept of God and His message must be true since so many others believe the same thing.

A man living in Britain e-mailed this note:

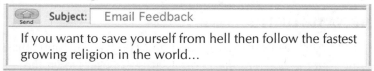

Subject: Email Feedback

If you want to save yourself from hell then follow the fastest growing religion in the world...

If rapid growth or sheer numbers could prove truth, then the descendants of Cain, the people of Noah's day, and the inhabitants of Babel were right too. But they were wrong—dead wrong.

> *"Enter through the narrow gate. For **wide** is the gate and **broad** is the road that leads to destruction, and **many** enter through it. But **small** is the gate and **narrow** the road that leads to life, and only a **few** find it."* (Matthew 7:13-14 NIV)

GOD'S UNSTOPPABLE PLAN

Returning to the narrative about the first family, we learn what happened after Cain killed Abel.

*"Adam knew his wife again, and she bore a son and named him **Seth**, 'For **God has appointed another seed for me instead of Abel**, whom Cain killed.' And as for Seth, to him also a son was born; and he named him Enosh. Then men began to **call on the name of the LORD**."*
(Genesis 4:25-26)

God's desire and design to have a people who trusted in Him would not be thwarted.

The name *Seth* means *"appointed in the place of."* Eve understood that God had appointed *"another seed"* for her in the place of Abel, whom Cain killed. It would be through Seth's line that the promised *Seed of a woman* would be born.

Mary, the virgin maiden who became the mother of Jesus, was a descendant of Seth. She was also a descendant of Abraham and David, just as God had promised. No matter how hard Satan tried to spoil God's agenda, the plan ordained by the LORD God *"before the foundation of the world"* kept rolling forward.

Nothing and no one could stop it.

THE NAME OF THE LORD

Like Abel, Seth trusted in God and His way of forgiveness, calling *"on the name of the LORD."* (Genesis 4:26) Down through the ages, in a world populated with those who, like the people of Babel, try *to make for themselves a name*, there have always been those who, like Abel and Seth, have believed in and called on *the name of **the LORD***.

Some of my friends tell me that God has one hundred names, but they only know ninety-nine of them. Could the missing name from their list be the one that means *"the LORD saves"*?

Which name is that?

Yes, it is ***Jesus***.

Not to trust in that name—in Who He is and what He has done—is to *not* be submitted to God.

Let's listen to the apostle Paul's prayer for his religious and rebellious Jewish countrymen:

"Brethren, my heart's desire and prayer to God for Israel is that they may be saved. For I bear them witness that they have a zeal for God, but not according to knowledge. For they being ignorant of God's righteousness, and seeking to establish their own righteousness, have not submitted to the righteousness of God. For Christ is the end of the law for righteousness to everyone who believes... If you confess with your mouth the Lord Jesus and believe in your heart that God has raised Him from the dead, you will be saved. ... For the Scripture says, 'Whoever believes on Him will not be put to shame.' For there is no distinction between Jew and Greek, for the same Lord over all is rich to all who call upon Him. For 'whoever calls on the name of the LORD shall be saved.'"
(Romans 10:1-4,9,11-13 [Joel 2:32])

WORTHLESS OR WORTHY?

Suppose I were to write out to you a bank check (or cheque) for a million dollars. The check would look wonderful, but it would be worthless. Why?

I don't have that amount of money in my bank account!

Now, what if the richest man on earth were to write out a check to you for a million dollars?

No problem. It would be worth the full amount.

The same bank that rejects the check presented in my name will honor the check bearing the name of the wealthy man.

Our world is filled with people who are attempting to approach God through many names, but, in the sight of the holy God who sent His Son to pay man's sin-debt, they are worthless, sin-tainted names.

Just as the bank will not honor a $1,000,000 check in my name, so God will not grant forgiveness and life through any name but the name of *Jesus*.

*"Nor is there salvation in any other, for there is **no other name** under heaven given among men by which we must be saved."* (Acts 4:12)

Would you like to have your sin-debt erased from God's record book and be credited with the wealth of His righteousness? Do you want to triumph over the curse of sin and enjoy a close relationship with your Creator for time and eternity?

Then only one name will do.

*"Whoever calls on **the name of the LORD** shall be saved."*
(Joel 2:32)

*"Believe on **the Lord Jesus Christ**, and you will be saved, you and your household."* (Acts 16:31)

Do you believe in your heart that the Lord Jesus Christ suffered, died, and rose again to cancel your sin-penalty? Then *"**you will be saved**."*

ONLY TWO RELIGIONS

We began this journey with the observation that our world today has more than *ten thousand* religious systems.

Actually, there are only *two*.

- There is the system of *human achievement* that tells you to **save yourself**.

- There is the system of *divine accomplishment* that says **you need a Savior**.

As long as you are trying to save yourself, any religion or name will do; but once you recognize your need for a Savior, only one name will do. That name is **Jesus**.

*"**To Him** all the prophets witness that, **through His name**, whoever believes **in Him** will receive remission of sins."*
(Acts 10:43)

PART III
JOURNEY'S END

REVERSING
THE CURSE

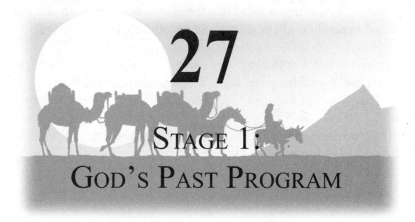

27

STAGE 1:
GOD'S PAST PROGRAM

*"**Today** you will be with Me in Paradise!"*
—The Lord Jesus (Luke 23:43)

A few minutes ago, my laptop computer's battery was almost dead, but now it is being infused with new life. How has its dying condition been reversed?

I plugged it into an electrical outlet.

Whether in a laptop, cell-phone, or flashlight, batteries are constantly dying—losing their charge—until such time as they are recharged by a superior power source.

Adam's descendants are somewhat like dying batteries. We began dying the day we were conceived, with no way to reverse the curse brought on by sin.

As we enter the last part of our journey, I'd like to tell you the story of a wandering Frenchman whose future seemed as hopeless as a dying battery.

LE MISÉRABLE

I met the 26-year old Bruno in March of 1987.

Many years earlier, this young man had begun to ponder the meaning of life. He felt empty on the inside—an emptiness that neither his Roman Catholic upbringing nor worldly pleasures had filled.

As a boy, Bruno noticed that those who taught him about God failed to practice what they preached. As a rebellious teenager, he observed a world filled with injustice. By age 18, Bruno's singular purpose in life was to hang out with his friends on weekends, get drunk and forget his misery. His despair was intensified when his girlfriend was killed in an automobile accident. He became angry with God.

Bruno decided to travel to India. Perhaps he would find the meaning of life among its many religions. After a grueling voyage by land, Bruno arrived in one of India's crowded cities where he was confronted with intense religious fervor and indescribable human misery. In Bruno's own words, "I saw people who, despite their religion and faith, were more miserable than I."

After spending nearly a year in India, Bruno concluded that if he was ever to discover ultimate truth, God alone must reveal it to him. Thus, he addressed this simple prayer to his Creator, "If you exist, reveal yourself to me!"

One day, while walking the streets of Calcutta, Bruno noticed a shop with a sign: *BIBLE HOUSE*. On an impulse, he stepped inside and asked the clerk, "Do you have a Bible in French?" They had one copy.

He bought it and began to read.

Many things surprised him. For instance, he was struck by the first and second of the Ten Commandments in which God says, *"You shall have **no other gods** before Me. You shall not make for yourself a carved image... you shall **not bow down to them** nor serve them."* (Exodus 20:3-5) Yet what Bruno witnessed around him were temples of idols with people bowing before them. And as he thought about the religion in which he had been brought up, he realized that the religious people he knew were also guilty of breaking God's commandments as they bowed and prayed before statues of Mary and the saints.

Bruno was also impressed by this verse: *"This Book of the Law shall not depart from your mouth, but you shall meditate in it day and night, that you may observe to do according to all that is written in it. **For then you will make your way prosperous, and then you will have good success.**"* (Joshua 1:8)

Convinced that the truth he sought could be found only in the Bible, Bruno left India and returned to France. However, instead of continuing to read his Bible, he set it on a shelf and went back to working and partying—a way of life that left him with a bitter taste and an empty heart.

Four years went by.

One day, as Bruno thought on his meaningless existence, he remembered a Bible verse in which God promises: *"You will seek Me and find Me, when you search for Me with all your heart."* (Jeremiah 29:13) Bruno prayed, "OK God, I will search for you with all my heart to find out whether or not your promise is true."

To separate himself from the influences of home, Bruno decided to take another journey, this time to Africa. As he traveled by land, he read his Bible and prayed, "God, lead me to *your* truth and keep me from falsehood." After crossing the Sahara he came into northern Senegal. He spent his first night in the same town where my family and I lived.

The next morning, Bruno went for a walk in town. As in Calcutta, a sign over a door caught his attention. This one said:

ECOUTEZ! CAR L'ETERNEL DIEU A PARLÉ!

(*Listen! for the LORD God has spoken!*)

Bruno entered.

It was my office. Looking up from my work, I saw a bushy-bearded man holding a small, blue, well-worn book—the Bible he had purchased in India. I can still hear his first question:

"What are you, Catholic or Protestant?"

"I'm just a Christian—a follower of Christ," I replied. Bruno was surprised and pleased by this response, since, in reading through the Bible, he had observed that it never mentions *Catholics* or *Protestants*, but it does speak about *Christians*—believers in Christ. Later, Bruno told me that if I had answered either "I'm Catholic" or "I'm Protestant," he would have turned on his heels and walked out. He was weary of religion. He wanted reality.

Over the next several days, Bruno peppered me with questions. I pointed him to God's answers in the Bible. On the eve of his departure (he planned to travel to South Africa), I challenged him, "Reread your Bible and look for what God has done for you."

Six weeks later, my wife and I received a letter from Bruno in which he explained that he was renting a room in a nearby fishing village. He had just finished rereading the entire Bible, comparing the Old and New Testaments.

He had seen Christ in all the Scriptures.

In Bruno's own words, "One night, as I was outside all alone, Jesus' promise came to my heart with power, *'Come to Me, all you who labor and are heavy laden, and I will give you rest.'* (Matthew 11:28) In reviewing my life with all its failures, bitterness and regrets—a great conflict raged in my heart. I knew that if I followed Christ, I would no longer be free to follow my lusts and desires. At last I gave in. God opened my eyes. I believed that Christ shed His blood on the cross and rose again *for me*. Peace flooded my soul. I began to cry and couldn't stop. The heavy burden of my sin was gone!" Bruno went on to say, "En somme, je suis né de nouveau!" ("To sum it up, I've been born again!")

Bruno found what he had been searching for: a cleansed heart and conscience, a relationship with His Creator, and eternal life. He now understood why he was on earth and where he was going.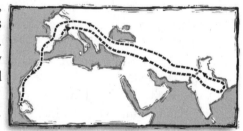

His search was over.

The Bible says:

"If anyone is in Christ, he is a new creation; old things have passed away; behold, all things have become new." (2 Corinthians 5:17)

Immediately Bruno's life began to change in small and big ways. For example, although he had smoked cigarettes since he was eleven years old, the Lord delivered him from this habit. His self-absorbed, drunken and immoral lifestyle became a shameful memory of the past. The Scriptures now made sense to him and prayer became as natural as breathing.

Instead of traveling on, Bruno spent the next six months in Senegal to study the Scriptures, spend time with believers in Christ, and tell others what God had done for him.

Bruno had become a new creation.

Though nearly two decades have passed since I first met Bruno, we still keep in touch. Today the "new Bruno" lives in France where he and his wife are walking with God and raising their four children in the knowledge and blessing of the Lord.

Does this mean that Bruno's life is free from heartache, struggle and pain? No, both he and his family face a variety of trials and temptations, but they are not alone.

The Lord Himself is with them.

GOD'S THREE-STAGE PROGRAM

Perhaps someone is thinking: "Wait a minute. If Jesus has defeated Satan, sin, and death for us—then why do people, including believers in Christ, continue to struggle in so many ways? Why is our world filled with evil and strife? Where is the promised deliverance and perfection?"

The answer is found in the fact that God's age-old plan to intervene in human history includes three stages:

Stage I: God would deliver His people from
            the *PENALTY of sin.*
Stage II: God would deliver His people from
            the *POWER of sin.*
Stage III: God will deliver His people from
            the *PRESENCE of sin.* [235]

The following quotation from the New Testament summarizes God's three-stage program—past, present, and future:

*God has "**delivered us** from so great a death* [Stage I] *and **does deliver us*** [Stage II]*; in whom we trust that **He will still deliver us*** [Stage III]. " (2 Corinthians 1:10)

The remainder of our travels through the Scriptures will focus on this three-stage program by which God will forever undo the effects of Satan, sin, and death. The final leg of our journey will be extra spectacular as it gives us a glimpse into Paradise itself.

REVERSING THE CURSE: STAGE ONE

When Adam and Eve listened to Satan they forfeited their friendship with their Creator-Owner and brought upon themselves and all their descendants the curse of sin. The original, perfect world was suddenly changed into a place where people wanted to hide from God and go their own way. Life became characterized by grief and pain, disease and deformity, poverty and hunger, sadness and strife, old age and death.

Sin brought a curse. But at the appointed time, just as God had promised, the Eternal Son of God came from heaven to earth as *the Seed of a woman* to rescue Adam's descendants from Satan, sin, and death.

> *"**God**, who at various times and in various ways spoke in time past to the fathers by the prophets, **has in these last days spoken to us by His Son**, whom He has appointed heir of all things, through whom also He made the worlds; who being the brightness of His glory and the express image of His person, and upholding all things by the word of His power, **when He had by Himself purged our sins, sat down at the right hand of the Majesty on high**."* (Hebrews 1:1-3)

The Lord Jesus was uncontaminated by sin.

He displayed complete authority over every element of the sin-cursed creation. With a word from His mouth or the touch of His hand, He caused evil spirits to flee, blind eyes to see, lepers to be cleansed, and the dead to be raised. He walked on water, calmed storms, and multiplied bread for the hungry. He forgave sin and brought peace to hurting hearts.

And then He did what He came to do.

He suffered, died, and rose again to glorify His Father, fulfill Scripture, and redeem all who believe in Him.

> *"**Christ has redeemed us from the curse of the law, having become a curse for us** (for it is written, 'Cursed is everyone who hangs on a tree') that the blessing of*

Abraham might come upon the Gentiles in Christ Jesus, that we might receive the promise of the Spirit through faith." (Galatians 3:13-14 [Deuteronomy 21:23])

AMAZING GRACE

Jesus, who kept God's laws perfectly, came to redeem lawbreakers *"from the curse of the law* [which demands perfect obedience], *having become a curse for us!"* Jesus willingly took the punishment we deserve in order to deliver us from everlasting punishment.

Even while the Lord was suffering on the cross, He demonstrated His purpose to reverse sin's curse.

Jesus was crucified between two criminals who had been sentenced to death for treason, theft, and murder. Let us listen again to the conversation that took place between the Lord and these two sinners. At first, both men mocked Jesus, but as the hours wore on, one of them repented.

> *"One of the criminals who hung there hurled insults at him: 'Aren't you the Christ? Save yourself and us!'*
>
> *But the other criminal rebuked him. 'Don't you fear God,' he said, 'since you are under the same sentence? We are punished justly, for we are getting what our deeds deserve. But this man has done nothing wrong.' Then he said, 'Jesus, remember me when you come into your kingdom.'*
>
> *Jesus answered him, 'I tell you the truth, today you will be with me in paradise.'"* (Luke 23:39-43 NIV)

These two lawbreakers were about to die and enter hell. Then, in those final hours, one of them recognized his sin before God and placed his trust in the sinless Savior who was nailed to the middle cross.

Jesus gave him a promise:

"Today you will be with Me in Paradise!"

Instead of spending eternity in the place prepared for the devil and his fallen angels, this forgiven lawbreaker would spend it in the presence of His Creator-Redeemer.

What a switch!

Based on his trust in the Lamb of God who was, at that very moment, shedding His blood to pay sin's penalty, God erased this sinner's sins from the record books, credited him with Jesus' righteousness, and inscribed his name in *the Lamb's Book of Life*—the Book that contains the names of all who have, by faith, received God's gift of pardon, righteousness, and eternal life.

For this helpless sinner, sin's curse was forever reversed.

CAN KILLERS BE FORGIVEN?

This e-mail came from an inquirer:

> **Send** **Subject:** Email Feedback
>
> I would like to know how you explain the term "justice" in light of the statement that **"Jesus (peace be upon him) died in our place for our sins."** Does this mean I will not be held accountable for all the wrong doings I commit during my lifetime? **The killer**, who escapes being brought to justice in this world will be let free hereafter only because Jesus has paid for his sins... I feel hard to subscribe to this view... May we all be led to the right path!

Is Jesus' death on the cross in the place of sinners consistent with "justice"? Can even a "killer" be forgiven by God? Let's address the last question first with a few testimonies from "killers" who have been forgiven and transformed.

CANNIBALS

In his book *Lords of the Earth*, Bible translator and anthropologist, Don Richardson, tells of the Yali people—the fierce, mountain-dwelling cannibals of Irian Jaya, Indonesia. For centuries it had been their practice to torture, kill and, yes, *eat* the enemy people of neighboring villages. Revenge and fear were a "normal" way of life.

Then the Gospel was brought to them.

The Yali and neighboring tribes heard God's good news about forgiveness of sin and new life in Christ. Many believed. Their way of thinking and living was transformed. As born-again children of God, they now had a new standard of "normal." Those who had previously hated and feared each other became brothers. To facilitate friendship with their former enemies, they made "better quality footpaths linking Yali villages."[236]

Today these former killers show compassion to those who try to harm them, since God's Spirit has changed their hearts and taught them: *"Be kind to one another, tenderhearted, forgiving one another, just as God in Christ forgave you."* (Ephesians 4:32)

A DESPERATE GIRL

Emma was brought up in a strict Muslim home in Singapore. Due to her parents' divorce and dysfunctional family life, at age 16 she made the decision to kill someone—herself.

Emma determined to jump from the balcony of their ten-story apartment. Just prior to carrying out her plan, she cried out in anger and desperation to the God she did not know, "If you really exist, somehow tell me!"

As she made her way down a short set of stairs that led out to the balcony, on the steps lay a Bible! She picked it up and hurried back to her room. The Bible fell open to these words:

"The LORD is my shepherd; I shall not want. He makes me to lie down in green pastures; He leads me beside the still waters. He restores my soul; He leads me in the paths of righteousness for His name's sake.
Yea, though I walk through the valley of the shadow of death, I will fear no evil; for You are with me; Your rod and Your staff, they comfort me. You prepare a table before me in the presence of my enemies; You anoint my head with oil; my cup runs over. Surely goodness and mercy shall follow me all the days of my life; and I will dwell in the house of the LORD Forever." (Psalm 23)

As Emma read this Psalm, she was overwhelmed by God's reality AND LOVE. Not long afterwards, she placed her trust in the Lord Jesus who said, *"I am the good shepherd. The good shepherd gives His life for the sheep."* (John 10:11)

She became one of His *"sheep."*

Emma no longer wants to kill herself. She is a joyful wife and mother of five. Emma's passion in life is to help others find what she has found in Christ—THE ABUNDANT LOVE OF GOD.

When I sent this story to Emma to check it for accuracy, she e-mailed it back to me, adding the words in caps about *the love of God.* In the midst of potentially overwhelming pressures and challenges faced by women around the world, Emma finds her daily strength and joy in the Lord's amazing love and care.

A VIOLENT MAN

Finally, consider *Saul of Tarsus*, a religious zealot who killed people in the name of God.

Saul was born during the time of Christ in Tarsus, Asia Minor (modern-day Turkey). Saul did not believe that Jesus was the Messiah and Son of God. Shortly after Jesus returned to Heaven, Saul was commissioned by the Jewish high court to arrest, try, and put to death all followers of Jesus. He believed that he was serving God by imprisoning, flogging, and executing Jews who had believed in Jesus.[237] Here is what happened one day as Saul and his men were carrying out another mission to arrest a group of Jewish Christians.

> *"As he journeyed he came near Damascus, and suddenly a light shone around him from heaven. Then he fell to the ground, and heard a voice saying to him, 'Saul, Saul, why are you persecuting **Me**?'*
>
> *And he said, 'Who are You, **Lord**?'*
>
> *Then the Lord said, 'I am **Jesus**, whom you are persecuting. It is hard for you to kick against the goads.'*
>
> *So he, trembling and astonished, said, 'Lord, what do You want me to do?'"* (Acts 9:3-6)

Saul's view of Jesus did an about face. As a student of the Old Testament Scriptures, he suddenly understood that Jesus was the Messiah of whom all the prophets had written.

The great antagonist became the great protagonist.[238]

Saul (meaning *"great one"*), who later changed his name to *Paul* (*"small one"*), testified:

> *"Even though I was once a blasphemer and a persecutor and a violent man, I was shown mercy because I acted in ignorance and unbelief. The grace of our Lord was poured out on me abundantly, along with the faith and love that are in Christ Jesus. Here is a trustworthy saying that deserves full acceptance: Christ Jesus came into the world to save sinners—of whom I am the worst."*
> (1 Timothy 1:13-15 NIV)

CHRIST'S SPECIALTY

Can even "killers" be forgiven and transformed by God?

That is what has happened to the cannibals of Irian, Emma of Singapore, and Saul of Tarsus. That is what happened to the repentant murderer on the cross next to Jesus. That is what is happening every day to sinners around the world—inside and outside of prisons—when they believe God's message.

Redeeming and changing the hearts of the worst and "best" of sinners is Christ's specialty. That is what God's mercy and grace are all about.

Of course, sin has its consequences.

The criminal on the cross still suffered for his crimes. In his lifetime, he never experienced the peace and joy that comes from knowing the Lord, living for Him, and helping others to know Him too. Nevertheless, *the way* by which a sinner is forgiven and made righteous before God is always the same: by recognizing his or her sinful condition and by trusting in God's provision of salvation.

To not believe in the Lord Jesus is to perish along with the unrepentant criminal crucified on the other side of Jesus.

MERCY AND JUSTICE TOGETHER

The e-mail writer a few pages ago also asked: *"How [do] you explain the term 'justice' in light of the statement that 'Jesus died in our place for our sins'"*? Ahmed raised the same question earlier:

Send **Subject:** Email Feedback

Isn't God great enough to be able to tell people what he wants and delete their sins without having to sacrifice his dear son and torturing him???!

As we have seen repeatedly, it is *because* God is great—in justice and faithfulness—that He cannot *"delete"* people's sins unless those sins have been adequately judged and punished!

Remember the illustration in chapter 13 about the judge who granted mercy without upholding justice. His actions aroused the indignation and contempt of the entire court.

God is not like that whimsical judge. Not a speck of dust can be found on His character or reputation. He never grants mercy at the expense of justice. That is why, out of His great love, He sent His Son from heaven to earth to be nailed to a cross and there to display God's mercy and truth in perfect combination.

*"**Mercy and truth have met together**; Righteousness and peace have kissed. Truth shall spring out of the earth, and righteousness shall look down from heaven."* (Psalm 85:10-11)

Because Jesus endured the wrath of God for us, God can *"look down from heaven"* and offer us His gifts of pardon, perfection, and eternal life. By taking our place, the Lord Jesus demonstrated God's *justice, mercy,* and *grace.* As we already observed:

Justice is receiving what we deserve.
Mercy is not receiving what we deserve.
Grace is receiving what we don't deserve.

All who trust in Christ receive *what no one deserves*: cleansing from sin, Christ's own righteousness, a place in God's family, and eternal life. All who reject or ignore Christ will get *what all deserve*: eternal punishment.

Seven centuries before Christ came, the prophet Micah wrote: *"They will strike the judge."* (Micah 5:1) Think of it! The Judge of all the earth took on human flesh in order to be killed by the ungrateful sinners He came to rescue!

Justice, mercy and grace don't get any better than that.

"When we were still without strength, in due time Christ died for the ungodly. Scarcely for a righteous man will one die; yet perhaps for a good man someone would even dare to die. But God demonstrates His own love toward us, in that while we were still sinners, Christ died for us."

(Romans 5:6-8)

JUST AND THE JUSTIFIER

In the first stage of His plan, God opened a way of pardon for sinners without lowering His own perfect standards. He is both *"just and the Justifier of the one who has faith in Jesus."* (Romans 3:26)

God is *Just* because He has sufficiently punished sin.

God is *the Justifier* of all who trust in the Savior He sent.

The moment I stop relying on my own efforts and transfer my trust to Christ and His death and resurrection for me, the Righteous Judge will stamp across the record book of all my offenses:

JUSTIFIED!

To be *justified* is to be *declared righteous* by a judicial act of God. He clears my record and declares me right.

How can He do that?

He can do it because, on the cross, He paid my sin-penalty.

When Adam sinned, God declared the entire human race as *unrighteous*. But since Jesus died and rose again, God declares all who believe in Him as *righteous*.

"For as by one man's disobedience many were made sinners, so also by one Man's obedience many will be made righteous." (Romans 5:19)

Even as Adam's sin produced defilement and death, so Christ's death and resurrection provides cleansing and life.

"As in Adam all die, even so in Christ all shall be made alive." (1 Corinthians 15:22)

As the Righteous Judge looks down from heaven, does He see you *in Adam* and his filthy unrighteousness? Or does God see you *in Christ* and His pure righteousness?

Heaven's courtroom knows no third option.

MAN'S DOUBLE TROUBLE

As the third chapter of Genesis revealed, when Adam and Eve disobeyed their Creator, they brought on themselves the double dilemma of *sin and shame*.

Their **sin** drove them into hiding.

Their **shame** incited them to cover their nakedness.

God *in His justice* rejected their self-made coverings of fig leaves, but God *in His mercy* clothed them in the skins of sacrificed animals. The animal blood symbolized what was necessary to remove their *sin*, and the animal skins symbolized what was necessary to cover their *shame*.

We share our ancestor's sin and shame. Before God, we are defiled sinners and spiritually naked. We are shamefully unfit to dwell in His presence. We need **His pardon** and **His perfection**.

Our *double trouble* can be summarized in two questions:

1. How can we be **cleansed** from the sin that separates us from our Creator?

2. How can we be **clothed** in perfection so we can live with Him forever?

GOD'S DOUBLE CURE

Only God has the remedy for man's sinfulness and lack of righteousness. When Jesus, God's sinless Son, shed His blood on the cross, *He took **our punishment**,* and, as the One who conquered death, *He offers us **His righteousness**.*

*"God will credit righteousness [to all] who believe in him who raised Jesus our Lord from the dead. He was delivered over to **death for our sins** and was raised to **life for our justification**."* (Romans 4:24-25 NIV)

*"If anyone is in Christ, he is a new creation; old things have passed away; behold, all things have become new.... God...has reconciled us to Himself through Jesus Christ... For He made Him who knew no sin to be **sin for us** [a sin offering], that we might become **the righteousness of God in Him**."* (2 Corinthians 5:17-18,21)

The moment you *abandon your trust* in yourself and your religion, and *place your hope* in Christ and the perfect blood He shed for you:

1) He will *cleanse you* from sin's defilement, and
2) He will *cover you* with His perfect righteousness.

God has no other cure for your sin and shame.

GOD'S EXCHANGE PROGRAM

By His death and resurrection, the Lord Jesus Christ took *our sin* and gives us *His righteousness*. This is God's great exchange program: *My sin for His righteousness.*

Why would anyone refuse such an amazing offer?

The tragic reality is that most choose to refuse God's provision. Nonetheless, His offer stands: All who *receive* God's gift of salvation are declared righteous. All who *refuse* it will pay for their own sins, not in some imaginary, temporary purgatory, but in the everlasting hell prepared for the devil and his demons.

Many religious people insist, "Each person must pay for his or her own sins." There is a sense in which all who reject God's gift of forgiveness and righteousness will do just that. However, their sin-debt will never be paid off, since it is a perpetual debt. Furthermore, while lost sinners will go on eternally paying for their sins in the lake of fire, they will never be able to gain the required righteousness to live in heaven. Only God can give helpless sinners the forgiveness *and* the righteousness they need to live with Him.

Seven hundred years before the Savior came, the prophet Isaiah wrote about God's great exchange program:

> *"We are all like **an unclean thing**,*
> *And all **our righteousnesses are like filthy rags**.*
> *All we like sheep have gone astray;*
> *We have turned, every one, to his own way*
> ***And the LORD has laid on Him the iniquity of us all.***
> *My soul shall be joyful in my God;*
> ***For He has clothed me with the garments of salvation,***
> ***He has covered me with the robe of righteousness."***
> (Isaiah 64:6; 53:6; 61:10)

Are you still *an unclean thing* before God? Or have you been **cleansed** *by the blood of Christ*?

Are you clothed in the *filthy rags of self-righteousness*? Or are you **clothed** *in the pure robe of Christ's righteousness*?

It all comes down to one question.

*"Who has **believed** our report?"* (Isaiah 53:1)

Have you believed God's report? Have you abandoned all other options for His truth?

"THAT YOU MAY KNOW"

God's Word says: *"These things I have written **to you who believe** in the name of the Son of God, **that you may know** that you have eternal life."* (1 John 5:13)

Years ago, I spoke with a very religious lady about God's gift of eternal life. Though she called herself a Christian, she had never placed her trust in God's provision of salvation in Christ.

When I told her, "I know I will go to heaven when I die," she replied with some indignation, "Oh, you think you are *so good* that you will go straight to heaven, do you?"

"No," I replied, "it's not because I'm 'so good.' It's because God is so good. He is the One who has told us that we can *'know that [we] have eternal life'* if we believe in Him and what He has done for us."

*"For the wages of sin is **death**, but the gift of God is eternal **life** in Christ Jesus our Lord."* (Romans 6:23)

HOW ALI CAME TO *KNOW*

In the first chapter of this book, I mentioned Ali, who was rejected by his family for believing God's message.

Like Bruno, Ali was 26 years old when I first met him. However, unlike the pleasure-seeking Bruno, Ali sincerely practiced his religion—reciting his daily prayers in the specified way, observing the month-long annual fast, and trying to treat other people well. Yet in his heart he felt a gnawing lack of peace.

Ali would lie awake in his bed at night thinking, "I've performed my religious duties—why am I so fearful of eternity? Oh God, is there no way for me to *know* where I will go after I die?"

Ali put this question to his father and local religious leaders, "How can I be sure God will let me into Paradise?" Everyone parroted the same answer: "You can't know. No one can know their fate. Only God knows."

Their answer did not satisfy Ali.

At home and school, Ali had been taught from the Qur'an that Jesus, the son of Mary, was a righteous prophet who was born of a virgin. He also learned that Jesus was a mighty miracle-worker who bore the titles *Messiah, Word of God* and *Soul of God.* "Maybe the Prophet Jesus can provide me with the answer I seek," he thought.

Ali decided to find a book about Jesus. Some weeks later, our paths crossed. I gave him a Bible which he began to study with intense interest. Here, in his own words, is what Ali discovered after searching the Scriptures for nearly a year:

"I learned that all the prophets pointed to Jesus. I read where Jesus Himself said: *"I am the way and the truth and the life. No one comes to the Father except through me. ...I tell you the truth, whoever hears my word and believes him who sent me **has eternal life and will not be condemned;** he has crossed over from death to life."* (John 14:6; 5:24 NIV)

These and other verses helped me understand and accept Jesus for who He is: the One and only Savior who shed His blood and rose from the dead to provide a sure salvation. I placed my faith in Him and in the fact that He suffered and died for my sins, in my place.

The moment I believed, I felt an inner peace I had never known before. What a change! I no longer worry about my eternal destiny because I know the Lord has paid the full penalty for all my sins which condemned me. I now *know* that I will go to heaven—not because I am good, but because of God's grace provided in Jesus Christ. Now I *want* to please God in all things—not to earn my salvation, but because God has saved me and changed my heart."

For Ali, sin's curse had been reversed. Today he, his wife, and their sons not only know where they will go after they die, they know why they are on earth: to know, love, and serve their Creator-Redeemer and to lead others to know Him too.

DEATH: THE BELIEVER'S SERVANT

At His first coming to earth, the Messiah fulfilled the first part of God's three-stage plan to reverse sin's curse. Through His life, death, burial, and resurrection, Jesus broke through the seemingly impenetrable wall of sin and death. The thief on the cross, the cannibals, Emma, Saul, Ali, Bruno, and all who accept God's message as true, are the beneficiaries.

For believers in Christ, the cruel tyrant, Death, has been reassigned to the post of a humble servant whose job is to open heaven's door at God's command. As the Scripture says: *"Precious in the sight of the LORD is the **death** of His saints."*[239] (Psalm 116:15)

Who would have ever dreamed the word *"precious"* could describe *"death"*? Thank God it does—for all who believe.

"O Death, where is your sting? O Hades, where is your victory?...Thanks be to God, who gives us the victory through our Lord Jesus Christ!" (1 Corinthians 15:55,57)

The past curse of sin has been reversed.

28

STAGE 2:
GOD'S PRESENT PROGRAM

*"I will put My law **in their minds**,*
*And write it **on their hearts**."*
—The LORD (Jeremiah 31:33)

While not many people give much thought to sin's *deadly curse*, most live in bondage to what might be called life's *daily curses.*

The majority of the world's population lives in fear of misfortune, sickness, and death. Many worry about not having enough money to buy food or to pay off their debts. Others fear bad luck, black magic, or the evil eye, being careful not to speak out loud of their happiness lest some malevolent spirit hear and bring misfortune on the object of their happiness. To ward off evil spirits and calamity, some fasten amulets or charms on themselves and their children, as well as in their houses. Many drink potions or recite formulas for protection.[240]

Thankfully, those who know and trust their Creator-Redeemer have no need for such precautions since He is infinitely greater than all forces of evil, whether imagined or real. There is nothing for a believer to fear since the Lord Jesus has authority over every power including death itself.

Jesus came not only to reverse the curse of sin as it affects *our eternal destiny* by paying for sin. He also came to reverse the curse of sin as it affects *our daily lives.*

REVERSING THE CURSE: STAGE TWO

The Scripture says, *"You are of God, little children, and have overcome them* [the forces of evil], *because **He who is in you is greater*** *than he who is in the world."* (1 John 4:4)

Who is this *"HE who is in"* the believer?

The night before His crucifixion, Jesus told His disciples:

> *"I will pray the Father, and He will give you **another Helper**, that He may abide with you **forever—the Spirit of truth**, whom the world cannot receive, because it neither sees Him nor knows Him; but you know Him, for **He dwells with you** and **will be in you**.*
>
> *I will not leave you orphans; **I will come to you**.*
>
> *These things I have spoken to you while being present with you. But **the Helper, the Holy Spirit**, whom the Father will send **in My name**, He will teach you all things, and bring to your remembrance all things that I said to you.*
>
> *Peace I leave with you, My peace I give to you; not as the world gives do I give to you. **Let not your heart be troubled, neither let it be afraid**."* (John 14:16-18,25-27)

ANOTHER HELPER

Jesus promised His disciples that, after He returned to heaven, the Father would send them *"**another Helper**... the Holy Spirit."*

The Greek word translated *helper* in English is *parakletos*, meaning *helper, comforter, counselor,* or *advocate*. In Scripture, *Parakletos* is used both for *the Son of God* and for *the Holy Spirit of God*.[241] Just as the Son came to save sinners from sin's *penalty*, so the Spirit came to save believers from sin's *power*.

The Holy Spirit has always been with God, even as *the Son* has always been with God. That is why He is identified in the opening declaration of God's Book as *"the Spirit of God."* (Genesis 1:2)

To suggest, as so many do,[242] that the *"Helper, the Holy Spirit"* was the angel Gabriel or a prophet who would come later not only contradicts the Scriptures of the prophets, but it goes directly against what Jesus said and did.

Jesus told His disciples that, after He died on a cross and came back to life, He would ascend to heaven so the Holy Spirit could descend and take up residence in the hearts of all who believe God's message. The Son would go up and the Spirit would come down. Jesus told His disciples: *"I tell you the truth. It is to your advantage that I go away; for if I do not go away, **the Helper** will not come to you; but **if I depart, I will send Him to you.**"* (John 16:7)

Up to this point in history, the Holy Spirit had been at times *with* believers to empower, guide, and bless them. However, it was only after Jesus had dealt with the world's sin-problem that the Holy Spirit could come to live permanently *inside* believers.

The Lord Jesus was announcing a very special event. *"The Spirit of truth... dwells with you and **will be in you.**"* (John 14:17)

THE HOLY SPIRIT'S COMING

After Jesus rose from the dead, the Scripture records:

> *"And being assembled together with [His disciples], He commanded them not to depart from Jerusalem, but to **wait for the Promise of the Father**, which, He said, you have heard from Me; for John truly baptized with water, but you shall be baptized with **the Holy Spirit** not many days from now. ...**You shall receive power when the Holy Spirit has come upon you; and you shall be witnesses to Me in Jerusalem, and in all Judea and Samaria, and to the end of the earth.**"* (Acts 1:4-5,8)

That is what happened on the Day of Pentecost, fifty days after Jesus arose and ten days after He ascended to heaven.[243]

> *"When the Day of Pentecost had fully come, [Jesus' disciples] were all with one accord in one place. And suddenly there came a sound from heaven, as of a rushing mighty wind, and it filled the whole house where they were sitting. Then there appeared to them divided tongues, as of fire, and one sat upon each of them. **And they were all filled with the Holy Spirit....**"* (Acts 2:1-4)

The New Testament records the entire dramatic event in Acts chapter 2. By the power of the Holy Spirit, Jesus' disciples began to proclaim God's good news in the various languages of the many foreigners who had gathered in Jerusalem from Asia, Arabia, and other areas of the world.

The same day the Holy Spirit descended, three thousand people believed God's message and received the gift of eternal life. The number of believers grew rapidly.

The book of Acts records the history of the first believers in Christ and tells how the good news of the risen Messiah spread throughout the Roman Empire—not by the power of the sword, but by the power of God's love and Holy Spirit.

CALLED-OUT ONES

God's main program on earth at this present time is *"to take out of [the nations] a people for His name."* (Acts 15:14)

The coming of the Holy Spirit on the Day of Pentecost gave birth to a special family of believers called *the church*. The original Greek word for *church* is *ekklesia*, meaning simply: "assembly" or "called-out ones." Today the word "church" is riddled with erroneous concepts and innumerable denominations. Many who call themselves Christians openly dishonor the name of Christ by the way they live. They may have *religion*, but they do not have a genuine *relationship* with God. They have never been cleansed from their sins through faith in Jesus' blood.

The good news is that God invites all people everywhere to trust in His Son, become His special new creation, and be adopted into the family of believers that will spend eternity with Him.

All those who believed God's promises *before Jesus came* (in Old Testament times) are a part of God's family, but only those who have believed *since Jesus came* are a part of the living organism known as *"the church."* The church is also called *"the body of Christ"* and *"the bride."*[244] To all who trust in the Lord Jesus Christ, the Scripture says:

*"You are... **His own special people**, that you may proclaim the praises of Him who called you out of darkness into*

*His marvelous light; who once were not a people but are now **the people of God**....* " (1 Peter 2:9-10)

The first and second chapters of the Bible reveal how, in the beginning, God made humans *His own special creation.* The third chapter records how Adam sinned and separated himself and the entire human race from God. However, the Scriptures that follow explain what God has done so that unclean sinners can once again become *"His own special people."*

Are you a part of God's *"special people"*? If so, then you have already entered into the second stage of God's program to reverse the curse.

SAVED AND SEALED

The first thing the Holy Spirit does in the life of a sinner who receives God's gift of salvation is to give him or her *new life.* All who transfer their trust from themselves and their efforts to Jesus Christ and His work of redemption, will be reborn spiritually by the Holy Spirit.

Jesus said,

*"Flesh gives birth to flesh, but the Spirit gives birth to spirit. You should not be surprised at my saying, '**You must be born again.**'...For God so loved the world that he gave his one and only Son, that **whoever believes in him shall not perish but have eternal life.**"* (John 3:6-7,16 NIV)

What a wonderful thing it is to be *"born again!"* For a sinner to be reborn spiritually is the work of the living God in all His complex oneness. The new birth is possible because *the Father* sent His Son, *the Son* shed His blood for sin, and *the Holy Spirit* infuses the believer with new life.

The Holy Spirit not only gives us eternal life; He seals us forever, marks us as God's own possession, and takes up permanent residence inside of us. He also guarantees our safe arrival into the Father's house when it comes our turn to leave this world.

*"In Him you also trusted, after you heard the word of truth, the gospel of your salvation; in whom also, **having believed, you were sealed with the Holy Spirit of promise, who is the guarantee of our inheritance.**"* (Ephesians 1:13-14)

Nothing can cause a true believer to lose his or her eternal salvation. *"The Holy Spirit...is the **guarantee**."*

FREED TO SIN AGAIN?

From time to time, I hear people say cynically, "OK, so all I have to do to be guaranteed a place in Paradise is believe that Jesus died for my sins and then I can go on sinning as I please, isn't that right?"

Using this same logic, if someone rescues you after you were hopelessly lost in a wasteland, would you tell your rescuer, "Thanks! Now I'm free to get lost again!'"?

Or if a creditor forgives you a great debt, would you intentionally want to do the things that offend him?

Or if you just put on clean and neatly pressed clothes, would you think, "Good! Now I can go lie down in the dirt!'"?

Such a mindset is unthinkable.

Why then do the children of Adam think that way when it comes to sin and its consequences?

The answer is sadly obvious. Sin has a powerful grip on our minds and hearts, even to the point of convincing us that sin is good and desirable. Of course, such an outlook is nothing new. Adam and Eve also viewed sin—the prospect of taking the forbidden fruit—as *"**desirable** to make one wise."* (Genesis 3:6)

What needs to be understood is that the moment a sinner believes God's message, he or she is *no longer lost* in the wilderness of sin. That burdensome debt has been *paid in full*. The believer is now *clothed* in the pure righteousness of Christ.

The *Holy* Spirit installs in a newborn child of God the *holy* conviction that sin is a bad thing, not a good thing. He empowers God's people to live lives that reflect His *holy* character and conduct. As members of the heavenly family, God's newborn children will want to live lives that maintain the family honor.

While believers can ignore the Holy Spirit and dishonor the Lord by the way they live, all true believers in Christ have this heavenly Guest living inside them. That is why the Scriptures exhort all who have trusted in Christ:

> *"**Do not grieve** the Holy Spirit of God, by whom **you were sealed** for the day of redemption."* (Ephesians 4:30)

Believers in the Lord Jesus can never lose the salvation they have received by faith, but they can *"grieve the Holy Spirit of God"* by living like unbelievers. While the Lord's people are still *in* the world, they are no longer *"of the world, just as [He is] not of the world."* (John 17:16)

Just as the Lord Jesus hates the ungodly practices of this world, so should His disciples.

> *"What shall we say then? Shall we continue in sin that grace may abound?* **Certainly not!** *How shall we who died to sin live any longer in it?"* (Romans 6:1-2)

> *"**Put to death, therefore, whatever belongs to your earthly nature**: sexual immorality, impurity, lust, evil desires and greed, which is idolatry. Because of these, the wrath of God is coming. You used to walk in these ways, in the life you once lived. But now you must rid yourselves of all such things as these: anger, rage, malice, slander, and filthy language from your lips. Do not lie to each other, since you have **taken off your old self** with its practices and have **put on the new self**, which is being renewed in knowledge **in the image of its Creator**."* (Colossians 3:5-10 NIV)

GOD'S LIFE IN THE BELIEVER

Even as *the Son of God* came to deliver believing sinners from *sin's penalty*, so *the Spirit of God* has come to deliver believers from *sin's daily power*.

Here is how it works.

The moment a person places his or her trust in Christ, God's Spirit establishes His kingdom inside that person by coming to live in their spirit, their inner control center. He gives the believer a new nature that *wants* to please the Lord. This does not mean the person's selfish, sinful nature is removed. The old nature will only be eradicated once the believer is in Paradise. In this world, believers cannot reach a state of sinless perfection. However, they should be deeply grieved whenever they displease the Lord.[245]

In the life of every true believer there is an ongoing battle between the old nature (inherited from Adam) and the new nature (implanted by the Holy Spirit). The indwelling Spirit of Christ gives the believer a heart-felt desire to please God. He teaches His people that although sin can provide *"passing pleasures"* (Hebrews 11:25), *"the end of those things is **death**. But now having been **set free from sin**... you have your **fruit to holiness**."* (Romans 6:21-22) The Holy Spirit produces major changes inside the believer.

> *"The fruit of the Spirit is:*
>   *love, joy, peace,*
>   *patience, kindness, goodness,*
>   *faithfulness, gentleness and self-control.*
>   *Against such things there is no law."* (Galatians 5:22 NIV)

Religions of self-effort do not produce spiritual fruit. While religious laws may modify a person's *outward* behavior to some extent, only the Holy Spirit can change a person's *inward* nature.

God wants to administer His rule in your life. Instead of giving you a list of rules to follow, He lives His life in you and through you for the blessing of others and the glory of His name.

LISTS OR LOVE?

The story is told of a man whose wife died. The widower hired a lady to clean his house and do his laundry three days a week. The man posted on the refrigerator a list of duties he wanted the housecleaner to accomplish each time she came. And, yes, he paid her for her work.

Over time, the man fell in love with this lady and asked her to be his wife. She accepted. After they married, the man removed the task-list posted on the refrigerator. He also stopped paying her an official salary. Why? Because the "housecleaning lady" had become his beloved wife! Now she gladly cleaned the house, did the laundry, and fulfilled a host of other tasks that were never even on *the list.* Why? Because she *loved* her husband and *wanted* to please and serve him. The rules on the refrigerator were now written in her heart.

That is what God does for those who belong to Him.

> *"I will put My law **in their minds**, and **write it on their hearts**; and I will be their God, and they shall be My people."* (Jeremiah 31:33)

Like the list on the refrigerator, man's **religion** presents you with a list of duties to fulfill, promising that you will hopefully get "paid" on Judgment Day, "if God wills it."

In glorious contrast, the Lord offers you a **relationship** with Himself. Not only has He taken your punishment and offered you eternal life, but He wants to come and live inside of you by His Holy Spirit if you will accept His proposal.

Instead of imposing on you a long list of duties you can never fulfill, God promises to give you the *desire* to please Him and to serve Him *from a heart of love.* A relationship of love provides a better motivation for good works than a religion of lists and laws. That's because:

> *"...**love** is the fulfillment of the law."* (Romans 13:10)

Religion may *promise* you a new life and a place in Paradise, but only the Holy Spirit can *provide* it. He is the only One who can fill you with God's love, joy, peace, and eternal security.

> *"Now hope does not disappoint, because **the love of God has been poured out in our hearts by the Holy Spirit** who was given to us."* (Romans 5:5)

JOYFUL OBEDIENCE

Of course, the fact that believers serve the Lord and people from a heart overflowing with God's love, does not mean they have no commands to obey. For example, just before Jesus returned to heaven, He told His disciples:

> *"All authority has been given to Me in heaven and on earth. Go therefore and make disciples of **all the nations**, baptizing them in the name of the **Father** and of the **Son** and of the **Holy Spirit**, teaching them to **observe all things** that I have commanded you; and lo, I am with you always, even to the end of the age."* (Matthew 28:18-20)

Jesus commanded His followers to proclaim the good news of salvation to *"all nations."* After a person receives God's gift of salvation, he or she should then be taught *"to observe all things"* that Jesus has commanded. For example, Jesus taught His disciples to love their enemies and be joyful servants to all. The passion of Christ's followers should be that the one true God might be known, trusted, and praised throughout the world.

Jesus also told His disciples to baptize new believers *"in the name of the Father and of the Son and of the Holy Spirit."* Notice it is *"in the **name** of"* (singular), not "in the names of" (plural). Only those who see themselves as helpless sinners and believe the good news about Jesus' life, death, and resurrection will enter into an eternal relationship with the one true God who is Father, Son, and Holy Spirit.

Those who believe God's message are to show their faith by being baptized in a river or any other body of water.

WHY BAPTISM?

Does a believer need to be ceremoniously put under the water to be cleansed from sin? No, the believer has already been cleansed and declared righteous by God because of what Christ did by His death and resurrection. Water baptism is an outward symbol of an inward reality. Once we have believed God's message, we should be baptized in obedience to our Savior and new Master, but it is not such baptism that makes us fit for heaven.[246]

So where does water baptism fit in? It symbolizes in a visual way a believer's identification with the Lord Jesus in His death, burial, and resurrection. Water baptism is a way for believers to declare their faith in God's rescue plan. The water represents death. As a person is put under the water, he is showing: "Jesus died for my sins and was buried." And as the person rises out of the water, he is showing: "Jesus overcame death for me. Because of His death, burial, and resurrection on my behalf, I have been cleansed from sin, declared righteous, and given eternal life."

Make no mistake about it. A sinner's acceptance before God is found only in the perfect righteousness and finished work of Jesus Christ. As a forgiven sinner, I know that I will live forever with the Lord, not because I am good, but because I am *"found in Him, not having my own righteousness, which is from the law, but that which is through faith in Christ, the righteousness which is from God by faith."* (Philippians 3:9)

Religions of men teach you to look to yourself and your own efforts. The Gospel of God teaches you to look to Christ and His impeccable righteousness.

NO JUDGMENT FOR BELIEVERS?

The fact that Christ has done everything necessary to save sinners from eternal condemnation raises another question in many minds. One e-mail correspondent asked:

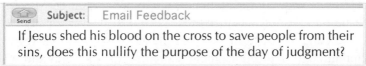

Subject: Email Feedback

If Jesus shed his blood on the cross to save people from their sins, does this nullify the purpose of the day of judgment?

No, Jesus' death on the cross for our sins does not nullify the fact that believers must give account of themselves to God. The Scripture says: *"It is time for judgment to begin with the family of God; and if it begins with us, what will the outcome be for those who do not obey the gospel of God?"* (1 Peter 4:17 NIV)

TWO JUDGMENT DAYS

The Scriptures describe two distinctly different future Days of Judgment. First, there will be *the resurrection and judgment of the righteous* and lastly, *the resurrection and judgment of the unrighteous.*[247]

Judgment of the Righteous: You *want* to be a part of this Day of Judgment. At this *Judgment Seat of Christ* there will be no question whether those present will be sent to heaven or hell. They will already be in heaven based on the fact that they received God's gift of righteousness while they lived on earth. However, based on God's estimation of the motives and value of their work as believers, they will be rewarded or suffer loss. A believer who lived according to God's will, humbly served others, trusted God in trials, loved and spread His Word, and waited expectantly for the Lord's return, will be rewarded, while a self-centered believer *"will suffer loss; he himself will be saved, but only as one escaping through the flames."* (See 1 Corinthians 3:11-15) The Bible mentions five different *"crowns"* believers can receive, which they will gratefully cast at the Lord's feet in worship.[248] *"We shall **all** stand before the judgment seat of Christ. ...**Each of us** shall give account of himself to God."* (Romans 14:10,12)

Judgment of the Unrighteous: You do *not* want to be a part of this fearful *Great White Throne Judgment*, as it is called. This terrible event will be for all who died in their sins without trusting in God's provision of salvation while they were on earth. There will be no question whether they will go to heaven or hell. All will be condemned to the lake of fire, though each will receive different degrees of punishment according to what they did with the truth they had. *"They were judged, **each one according to his works**. Then Death and Hades were cast into the lake of fire. This is the second death. And anyone not found written in the Book of Life was cast into the lake of fire."* (See Revelation 20:11-15)

The good news is that no one reading these words need perish, since the Lord Jesus offers to all freedom from sin's penalty.

CHILDREN OF GOD

As already noted, the moment you place your trust in the Lord Jesus Christ and what He did for you, you will become a member of God's family.

God will no longer seem far away.

He will become your *Father*.

> *"As many as received Him, to them He gave the right to become **children of God**, to those who believe in His name, who were **born...of God**."* (John 1:12) *"Because **you are sons, God has sent forth the Spirit of His Son into your hearts**, crying out, 'Abba, [Papa] **Father!'"***
> (Galatians 4:6)

The world is filled with religions that depict a far-away, ritual-demanding God who does not offer people a personal relationship with Himself. Contrastingly, the God who sent His Son to earth has revealed Himself as a heavenly Father who loves sinners. For all who receive His Son Jesus Christ, He promises to cleanse them, clothe them in the perfection of Christ, and send His Holy Spirit into their hearts.

In her book, *I Dared to Call Him Father*, Bilquis Sheikh of Pakistan tells of her search to discover the message of the one true God. After many months of comparing the Bible with the book of her religious upbringing, she tells of an experience she had while crying out to God to show her the truth:

> "I picked up both books and lifted them, one in each hand. 'Which, Father?' I said. 'Which one is Your book?' Then a remarkable thing happened. Nothing like it had ever occurred in my life quite this way. For I heard a voice inside my being, a voice that spoke to me as clearly as if I were repeating words in my inner mind. They were fresh, full of kindness, yet at the same time full of authority.
> **'In which book do you meet me as Father?'**
> I found myself answering: 'In the Bible.' That's all it took...."[249]

As with this Pakistani woman, God is my Father too. The day I believed God's message, I was born again spiritually. Nothing can cause me to lose my position as a member of God's family. Jesus said, *"My sheep hear My voice, and I know them, and they follow Me. And I give them **eternal life**, and **they shall never perish**; neither shall anyone snatch them out of My hand."* (John 10:27-28)

RELATIONSHIP & FELLOWSHIP

So what happens when I sin? Does that cause me to be once again separated from God?

If a son disobeys his earthly father, does he cease to be a part of the family? No. A son's disobedience does not cause him to be un-born. His physical tie to his parents cannot be undone. So it is with your spiritual tie to God. Nothing can cause you to lose your position as a born-again child of God. All who believe have *"been born again, not of corruptible seed but incorruptible, through the word of God which lives and abides **forever**."* (1 Peter 1:23) God is your heavenly Father. The righteousness of Christ in which you have been clothed will never be taken away. The Holy Spirit will never leave you.

You are eternally safe.

"I am persuaded that neither death nor life...shall be able to separate us from the love of God which is in Christ Jesus our Lord." (Romans 8:38-39)

No action on my part can reverse the *eternal **relationship*** God has established within me. However, sin will affect my *daily **fellowship*** with God.

POSITION & CONDITION

Suppose a father tells his son to go work in the garden, but instead the boy runs off to play football with his friends. The child's *position* as a son of his father would be unaffected, but the *condition* of the son's fellowship with his father would surely be affected! When the son gets home he will be questioned; there will be some firm words and some appropriate disciplinary action. The son must confess his disobedience so he can once again *enjoy a close relationship* with his father.

It is the same way with those who belong to God. He disciplines His children when they sin.

*"My son, do not despise the chastening of the LORD, nor detest His correction; for whom the LORD loves He corrects, **just as a father** the son in whom he delights."* (Proverbs 3:11-12)

Concerning our daily fellowship with God, the Bible says:

*"If we say that we have **fellowship** with Him, and walk in darkness, we lie and do not practice the truth....If we say that we have no sin, we deceive ourselves, and the truth is not in us. **If we confess our sins, He is faithful and just to forgive us our sins** and to cleanse us from all unrighteousness."* (1 John 1:6,8-9)

The indwelling Holy Spirit wants to teach all of God's children to abhor every form of sin, no matter how "small." He wants to make us sensitive to sins in our lives that others may not even label as sin.

For example, if I speak in an unkind manner to my wife, or if I have an unloving attitude towards someone who wronged me, or say something that is less than completely true, the Holy Spirit convicts me of my sin. The remedy is to *"confess [my] sins"* to the Lord and ask forgiveness from any I have offended. Once I have done this, I can once again enjoy close, sweet *fellowship* with my Lord.

Do you see the difference?

In Christ, *my **position*** before God is one of perfection, but in my daily life, *my **condition*** is less than perfect.

His work of salvation *for me* is forever finished, but His work *in me* will continue until I meet Him in Paradise.

REDEEMED FOR A PURPOSE

The Holy Spirit of Christ wants to transform the way God's people think, speak and act. He says:

"Be holy, for I am holy." (1 Peter 1:16)

He also tells His people: *"Do not be foolish, but understand what the Lord's will is. Do not get drunk on wine, which leads to debauchery. Instead, be filled with* [yielded to; controlled by] *the Spirit."* (Ephesians 5:17-18 NIV)

The Holy Spirit doesn't suppress our personalities; rather He frees us to live, on a daily basis, the righteous and victorious lives God intends for us to live. God has saved us for a purpose. We are called to exalt Him in all we think, say, and do.

*"Do you not know that your body is **the temple of the Holy Spirit who is in you**, whom you have from God, and **you are not your own**? For you were **bought at a price;** therefore **glorify God in your body and in your spirit**, which are God's."* (1 Corinthians 6:19-20)

What a life-changing truth this should be for those of us who have believed the gospel! The personal presence of God is living in us! It is as we submit to Him that our lives will glorify His name and bring blessing to others.

Much more could be said about the Holy Spirit's work in the lives of His people.

He comforts, strengthens, guides, enlightens, and instructs.

He helps believers to understand the Scriptures.[250]

He enables them to pray in a way that connects with God.[251]

He gives His people special gifts and abilities so they can help and build up others.[252]

He empowers Christ's followers to work and witness for Him no matter how great the opposition. Jesus told His disciples:

"Behold, I send you out as sheep in the midst of wolves. Therefore be wise as serpents and harmless as doves. But

*beware of men, for they will deliver you up to councils and scourge you...But when they deliver you up, do not worry about how or what you should speak. For it will be given to you in that hour what you should speak; **for it is not you who speak, but the Spirit of your Father who speaks in you.** "* (Matthew 10:16-20)

CONFORMED TO HIS IMAGE

In short, the Holy Spirit makes it possible for the people of God to fulfill God's original purpose for humankind which is to reflect the image of the one true God and to enjoy intimate fellowship with Him forever.

*"The Spirit also helps in our weaknesses. ...And we know that all things work together for good to those who love God, to those who are the called according to His purpose. For whom He foreknew, He also predestined **to be conformed to the image of His Son**, that He might be the firstborn among many brethren."* (Romans 8:26,28-29)

God is using each event and trial in the lives of His people to conform them back into *"the image of His Son."*

The first chapter of God's Book declares that the first man and woman were created *"in the image and likeness of God."* Man's choice to sin against His Creator radically marred that image. However, when the time was right, God sent His perfect, glorious Son into the world.

Jesus' righteous life, death, and resurrection were stage one of God's program to undo the damage caused by sin. But, as we have seen in this chapter, there's more, much more, to His plan.

The moment helpless sinners like you and me believe God's good news of salvation, He gives us His Holy Spirit who begins the process of *conforming us back into His image and likeness*, in our thoughts, motives, words, and deeds. This is stage two of God's program to reverse sin's curse.

God wants His children to reflect *the character and conduct of Christ.* That is what the term *"Christian"* is intended to imply.

Nevertheless, the Holy Spirit's work of *conforming us to the image of Christ* is an ongoing process that will only be completed once we see Him face to face.[253]

> *"How great is the love the Father has lavished on us, that we should be called children of God! And that is what we are! The reason the world does not know us is that it did not know him.*
>
> *Dear friends, now we are children of God, and what we will be has not yet been made known. But we know that when He appears, we shall be like him, for we shall see him as he is."* (1 John 3:1-2 NIV)

Due to the Son of God's work of redemption *for* all who believe in Him, and the Spirit of God's work of transformation *in* all who yield to Him, the power of Satan is being rendered ineffective and God's righteous kingdom of love, joy, and peace is being restored.

With purpose-filled lives and eager anticipation we await the final stage of God's program when He will forever put away Satan, sin, and death.

Jesus is coming back.

29

STAGE 3:

GOD'S FUTURE PROGRAM

*"The God of peace **will crush Satan**
under your feet **shortly**."*
(Romans 16:20)

This promise to believers flows from that mysterious, initial prophecy God announced the day sin corrupted the human race: *the Seed of a woman would crush the head of the Serpent.*

The Creator-Owner of the universe would perform all that He promised. But He would do it according to His own agenda and timetable.

REVERSING THE CURSE: STAGE THREE

At His first coming, the promised Messiah defeated Satan by paying sin's penalty in full. For the believer, hell is no longer a prospect and heaven is sure. As a result, Satan's favorite weapon, death, has lost its sting. *Sin's penalty* has been reversed.

After the Lord Jesus returned to heaven, He sent down His Holy Spirit, *"the Helper,"* to empower His people to overcome the influence of Satan and sin in their daily lives, molding them back into His own image. *Sin's power* is being reversed.

However, it is only when Jesus returns to earth that He will fully crush Satan and deliver His people from *sin's presence.*

THINGS TO COME

Just as God's prophets predicted the Messiah's first coming, so they also predict His second coming.[254] And just as His first visit happened exactly as foretold, so will His return.

The day is approaching when this announcement will resonate from heaven:

"The kingdoms of this world have become the kingdoms of our Lord and of His Christ, and He shall reign forever and ever!" (Revelation 11:15)

When Jesus returns to earth, the sons of Adam will not crown Him with thorns and nail Him to a cross. Nor will they pronounce His name in vain or say that He is no more than a prophet.

Such discourteous treatment of the King will no longer be an option.

The Scripture is clear. When Jesus comes again, *"every knee shall bow."* (Isaiah 45:23) But before that happens, a chain of other prophecies must be fulfilled.

JOY IN HEAVEN

One of the events that must take place before the nations of the world bow the knee to their Creator-Owner is that Jesus will descend into earth's atmosphere to take His redeemed people up to heaven.

"The Lord Himself will descend from heaven with a shout, with the voice of an archangel, and with the trumpet of God. And the dead in Christ will rise first. Then we who are alive and remain shall be caught up together with them in the clouds to meet the Lord in the air. And thus we shall always be with the Lord." (1 Thessalonians 4:16-17)

This secret, stunning event could take place at any moment. When it does, the dead bodies of believers whose souls live in heaven, along with believers still living on earth, will be *"caught up together...to meet the Lord in the air."*[255] Believers in Christ will be instantly transformed into the likeness of Christ. They will receive new bodies fit for eternity, unfettered by time and space.

Some time after being *"caught up together,"* individual believers will receive rewards for the things they selflessly did on earth for the glory of God and for the blessing of others.[256] Next, the people of God, forevermore *"holy and without blemish,"* will be officially presented to their eternal *"Bridegroom,"*[257] the Champion who gave His life to save them from eternal judgment.

> *"'Let us be glad and rejoice and give Him glory, for the marriage of the Lamb has come, and His wife has made herself ready' And to her it was granted to be arrayed in fine linen, clean and bright, for the fine linen is the righteous acts of the saints. Then he said to me, 'Write: 'Blessed are those who are called to the marriage supper of the Lamb!'"* (Revelation 19:7-9)

The relationships to be enjoyed in eternity will be infinitely superior to anything we have ever known on earth.

TRIBULATION ON EARTH

Meanwhile down on earth, the Scripture describes a time of *"great tribulation"*[258] as God pours out His wrath on an obstinate world and prepares the way for His Son's second coming. This period is also referred to as *"the time of Jacob's trouble,"* (Jeremiah 30:7) since it is designed to bring the nation of Israel to repentance.

During this time, an impressive, powerful world ruler referred to in Scripture as *"the Anti-Christ"* and *"the Beast"* (1 John 2:18; Revelation 13) will ascend to power. Multitudes will blindly follow him and his wonder-working false prophet. Every person on earth will be required *"to receive a mark on their right hand or on their foreheads, and that no one may buy or sell except one who has the mark or the name of the beast."* (Revelation 13:16)

Those who refuse to submit will be beheaded. This false messiah will promise peace and prosperity, but instead he will lead people down a path of deception, destruction, and death.

ARMAGEDDON

In the Bible, many of God's prophets have written about the final World War that will be in progress when the Lord Jesus descends from heaven to earth. This dramatic conflict will be fought on the plains of Esdraelon, a vast area that stretches from the Jordan River to the Mediterranean Sea. The Scripture also refers to this ancient and future battleground as *Armageddon*, meaning, "Mountain of slaughter."

> *"Spirits of demons, performing signs, [will] go out to the kings of the earth...to gather them to **the battle of that great day of God Almighty**. 'Behold, I am coming as a thief. Blessed is he who watches, and keeps his garments, lest he walk naked and they see his shame.' And they gathered them together to the place called in Hebrew, **Armageddon**."* (Revelation 16:14-16)

The prophet Zechariah also wrote a dramatic description of the events that will accompany the Messiah's return.

> *"**Behold, the day of the LORD is coming**... For I will gather all the nations to battle against Jerusalem; the city shall be taken, the houses rifled, and the women ravished. Half of the city shall go into captivity, but the remnant of the people shall not be cut off from the city."* (Zechariah 14:1-2)

"All the nations" will surround Jerusalem. It will be a holocaust of epic proportions.

THE RETURN OF MESSIAH

When all hope is lost and the surviving inhabitants of the city have nowhere to look for help but up, they will call out to LORD for deliverance. Then the One whose name means *"the LORD saves"* will descend from heaven. And to their shock and surprise, their Deliverer will be none other than *Jesus*, whom they crucified! But this time, in a spirit of deep repentance and anguish of soul, they will receive their King.

> *"I will pour on...the inhabitants of Jerusalem the Spirit of grace and supplication; then **they will look on Me whom they pierced**. Yes, they will mourn for Him as one mourns for his only son, and grieve for Him as one grieves for a firstborn."* (Zechariah 12:10)

At last the spiritually blind eyes of the Jewish nation will be opened and they will know and believe that Jesus was and is the one and only Messiah.[259]

What takes place next will be the most efficient demonstration of warfare in world history as Jesus, *the Word*, simply speaks and the enemy dissolves.

> *"**Then the LORD will go forth and fight** against those nations, as He fights in the day of battle. And in that day His feet will stand on the Mount of Olives, which faces Jerusalem on the east. And the Mount of Olives shall be split in two, from east to west, making a very large valley....*
>
> *This shall be the plague with which the LORD will strike all the people who fought against Jerusalem: Their flesh shall **dissolve** while they stand on their feet, their eyes shall **dissolve** in their sockets, and their tongues shall **dissolve** in their mouths.*
>
> *It shall come to pass in that day that there will be no light; the lights will diminish. It shall be one day which is known to the LORD—neither day nor night. But at evening time it shall happen that it will be light.*
>
> *And the LORD shall be King over all the earth. In that day it shall be—'The LORD is one,' And His name one."* (Zechariah 14:2-4,12,7,9)

At last the one true God will be rightly praised and honored.

DOMINION RECLAIMED

Several decades before Zechariah wrote the prophecy we just read, God gave a parallel vision to the prophet Daniel:

> *"I was watching in the night visions, and behold, One like* ***the Son of Man, coming with the clouds of heaven!*** *He came to the Ancient of Days, and they brought Him near before Him. Then to Him was given* ***dominion*** *and glory and a kingdom, that all peoples, nations, and languages should serve Him. His* ***dominion*** *is an everlasting* ***dominion****, which shall not pass away, and His kingdom the one which shall not be destroyed."* (Daniel 7:13-14)

The word *dominion* is repeated three times.

When God first created man and woman, He gave them *"dominion...over every living thing that moves on the earth."* (Genesis 1:26,28) When Adam rebelled against his Creator, he surrendered that dominion to Satan. But the reign, authority, and control over this planet which Adam, *"the first man,"* relinquished, Jesus, *"the Second Man,"*[260] will reclaim.

God gave Jesus' disciple, John, a complementary vision in perfect harmony with the prophecies of Zechariah and Daniel:

> *"I saw heaven opened, and behold, a white horse. And He who sat on him was called Faithful and True, and in righteousness He judges and makes war. His eyes were like a flame of fire, and on His head were many crowns. He had a name written that no one knew except Himself. He was clothed with a robe dipped in blood, and* ***His name is called The Word of God****. And the armies in heaven, clothed in fine linen, white and clean, followed Him on white horses. Now out of His mouth goes a sharp sword, that with it He should strike the nations. And He Himself will rule them with a rod of iron. He Himself treads the winepress of the fierceness and wrath of Almighty God. And He has on His robe and on His thigh a name written:* ***KING OF KINGS AND LORD OF LORDS****."* (Revelation 19:11-16)

When *the King of kings* returns, He will be accompanied by *"the armies in heaven, clothed in fine linen,"* consisting of heaven's myriad of angels and Adam's redeemed offspring.[261] The gracious displays of power and glory Jesus demonstrated at His first coming will pale in comparison to the unbridled power and awe-inspiring glory He will display at His second coming.

HEAVEN'S RULE IN HEARTS

Tell me, if you are walking alone through a forest, which would you rather encounter—a lion or a lamb?

When the Messiah came to earth the first time, He came as *"the Lamb"* to save sinners, but when He returns, He will come as *"the Lion"* to judge sinners. [262]

At Jesus' first visit to earth, He preached, *"Repent, for the kingdom of heaven is at hand."* (Matthew 4:17) But instead of repenting of their wrong ideas and receiving their King, the Jews and Gentiles joined forces to crucify their King. Thus, they unwittingly fulfilled God's age-old plan that the Messiah should shed His blood to pay off the sin-debt of the world.

The good news is that whenever sinners place their trust in the Lord Jesus and what He did for them, God will set up His rule in their hearts and make them His subjects forever.

Do you know that every true believer in Christ is already a registered citizen of heaven?

"For our citizenship is in heaven, from which we also eagerly wait for the Savior, the Lord Jesus Christ, who will transform our lowly body that it may be conformed to His glorious body...." (Philippians 3:20-21)

HEAVEN'S RULE ON EARTH

When Jesus returns to earth He will set up His kingdom in Jerusalem from where He will rule over the earth for a thousand years. At last, His kingdom will come and His will shall *"be done on earth as it is in heaven."* (Matthew 6:10) Evil will no longer be tolerated in any nation, for *"He Himself will rule them with a rod of iron."* (Revelation 19:15)

Many people do not believe that God's Son will return physically to earth. Nonetheless the Scriptures speak clearly on this point. Just as the Son of God took on a physical body at His first coming and then ascended back to heaven in His resurrected, physical, and limitless body, so He shall return *physically*. That is what the angels told Jesus' disciples the day He returned to heaven:

> *"**This same Jesus,** who was taken up from you into heaven, **will so come in like manner** as you saw Him go into heaven.'"* (Acts 1:11)

SATAN BOUND

God's Book has much to say about the millennial reign of Jesus Christ. We can only summarize the main events.

One of the first things to take place after Jesus returns to earth has to do with Satan, that old "serpent" who first led the human race down the path of self-destruction.

> *"Then I saw an angel coming down from heaven, having the key to the bottomless pit and a great chain in his hand. **He laid hold of the dragon, that serpent of old, who is the Devil and Satan, and bound him for a thousand years;** and he cast him into the bottomless pit, and shut him up, and set a seal on him, **so that he should deceive the nations no more till the thousand years were finished**. But after these things he must be released for a little while."* (Revelation 20:1-3)

Satan will be bound and quarantined for the entire thousand-year period. With the Evil One locked away and the Righteous One Himself reigning, at last there will be *"peace on earth and goodwill toward men."* (Luke 2:14)

God's righteous government, for which the world yearns, will become a reality.

> *"The God of heaven will set up a kingdom which shall never be destroyed...and **it shall stand forever**."* (Daniel 2:44)

TRUE SUBMISSION

Nearly three thousand years ago, King Solomon[263] wrote about the Messiah's future reign when every nation and person on earth will bow in submission to Him. Many today claim to be submitted to the one true God, but in that day, all people will be.

*"**In His days** the righteous shall flourish, and abundance of peace, until the moon is no more.*

*   **He shall have dominion** also from sea to sea, and from the River to the ends of the earth. Those who dwell in the wilderness will bow before Him, and His enemies will lick the dust. The kings of Tarshish* [European nations] *and of the isles* [nations from distant continents] *will bring presents; The kings of Sheba and Seba* [Africa and Arabia] *will offer gifts. **Yes, all kings shall fall down before Him.***

*   **All nations shall serve Him. For He will deliver the needy when he cries,** the poor also, and him who has no helper. He will spare the poor and needy, and will save the souls of the needy. He will redeem their life from oppression and violence; and **precious shall be their blood in His sight. And He shall live;** and the gold of Sheba will be given to Him; prayer also will be made for Him continually, and daily He shall be praised.*

*   **There will be an abundance of grain in the earth,** on the top of the mountains; its fruit shall wave like Lebanon; and those of the city shall flourish like grass of the earth. **His name shall endure forever;** His name shall continue as long as the sun. **And men shall be blessed in Him; All nations shall call Him blessed.** Blessed be the LORD God, the God of Israel, Who **only** does wondrous things! And blessed be His glorious name forever!*

*   **And let the whole earth be filled with His glory.** Amen and Amen."* (Psalm 72:7-19)

This Psalm provides clear insight into Christ's future kingdom in which *"He shall have **dominion**... to the ends of the earth."*

PERFECT GOVERNMENT

"He will spare the poor and needy." The Messiah's reign will be in total contrast to the corrupt, turbulent world of today. For the first time since the Fall, there will be liberty and justice for all. The life of every infant, child, woman, and man will be respected as infinitely valuable. *"He will redeem their life from oppression and violence; and **precious** shall be their blood in His sight."*

The news media recurrently reports of political and religious leaders who appeal for peace and negotiate for arms reduction. However, due their limited authority and power, these leaders are unable to produce the peace they claim to seek. But when the One to whom the wind and the waves submit returns, the earth will finally enjoy true justice and *"an abundance of **peace**."*

Over the centuries, all kings and rulers of this world have lived *and **died**.* But of Jesus, the King of kings, the Scripture declares: *"And He shall **live**."* The earth will flourish in a millennium of unparalleled peace and prosperity under the administration of the Son of Man who triumphed over sin and death.

> *"Yes, all kings shall bow before **Him**. ...and men shall be blessed in **Him**; All nations shall call **Him** blessed."*
> (Psalm 72:11,17)

The Lord Himself will provide this weary world with the only righteous government it will ever know. Only the redeemed children of Adam, eternal possessors of glorified bodies and holy natures, will reign with Him.

His kingdom will be free from corruption.

> *"Blessed and holy is he who has part in the first resurrection. Over such the second death has no power, but they shall be priests of God and of Christ, and **shall reign with Him a thousand years**."* (Revelation 20:6)

While all forms of government have failed—monarchal, totalitarian, democratic, religious—His shall not fail.

It will be as perfect as He is.

PRINCE OF PEACE

Earlier, we reflected on several prophecies about Christ's first coming. For example, the prophet Micah foretold that the Messiah would be born in Bethlehem. But did you notice that Micah's prophecy also predicted that the Messiah will one day rule over the whole earth?

> *"But you, Bethlehem Ephrathah, though you are little among the thousands of Judah, yet out of you shall come forth to Me the One to be Ruler in Israel, whose goings forth are from of old, from everlasting. ... He shall be great to the ends of the earth. And this One shall be peace."* (Micah 5:2,4-5)

Isaiah, a contemporary of Micah, also prophesied about the male child who was to be born and the eternal Son who was to be given. Isaiah's prophecy also pointed ahead to the Son's worldwide government.

> *"For unto us a Child is born, unto us a Son is given; and the government will be upon His shoulder. And His name will be called Wonderful, Counselor, Mighty God, Everlasting Father, Prince of Peace. Of the increase of His government and peace there will be no end, upon the throne of David and over His kingdom, to order it and establish it with judgment and justice from that time forward, even forever."* (Isaiah 9:6-7)

At last, the entire world will address the Son of God by His rightful titles. *"His name will be called:*
> *Wonderful,*
> *Counselor,*
> *Mighty God,*
> *Everlasting Father,*
> *Prince of Peace."*

The nations will enjoy justice and peace *"from that time forward, even forever."*

God's desire to be with man will be reality. Forever.

"Many nations shall be joined to the LORD in that day, and they shall become My people. And I will dwell in your midst." (Zechariah 2:11)

The good news for today is that all who have the Spirit of Christ dwelling in their hearts can enjoy God's presence and peace *right now.*

NO MORE IGNORANCE

When the Lord first came and lived on earth among humans, most people failed to recognize who He was. To this day, most refuse to recognize Jesus as their King. Nevertheless, a golden age is coming when every soul on earth will acknowledge Him to be the One He claimed to be.

"'And it shall come to pass that from one New Moon to another, and from one Sabbath to another, all flesh shall come to worship before Me,' says the LORD." (Isaiah 66:23)

No longer will thousands of religions, denominations, and sects fill the earth. Nor will anyone dare deny the historical reality that Jesus, the Son of God, died on a cross and rose from the dead. Though not all will trust in Him, all will know the truth about Him and His message.

"For the earth will be filled with the knowledge of the glory of the LORD, as the waters cover the sea." (Habakkuk 2:14)

NO MORE WAR

With the Lord ruling over the earth, strife between North and South, East and West will be a thing of the past. Conflict between Israel and surrounding nations will cease. The horrific sufferings of the African continent will be forever over. That goes for the other continents too. Civil war and oppression will be ended. True peace, prosperity, and purpose will permeate the earth.

"Many people shall come and say, 'Come, and let us go up to the mountain of the LORD, to the house of the God of Jacob; He will teach us His ways, and we shall walk in His paths.'

He shall judge between the nations, and rebuke many people; they shall beat their swords into plowshares, and their spears into pruning hooks; nation shall not lift up sword against nation, neither shall they learn war anymore." (Isaiah 2:3-4)

Peace and unity will be universal as people know and worship the one true God.

The confusion of Babel will be reversed. Once again, the world will speak one language:

"Then I will restore to the peoples a pure language that they all may call on the name of the LORD, to serve Him with one accord." (Zephaniah 3:9)

CURSE LIFTED

To add to the prosperity of this thousand-year period, the Lord will lift the curse that came upon the earth because of sin.

When Jesus first lived on earth, He demonstrated His power to reverse the curse. He cast out demons, reversed deformities, cured diseases, raised the dead, fed the multitudes, and demonstrated perfect control over nature. By such acts He provided irrefutable evidence that He was the promised Messiah and King.

What Jesus provided in sample form at His first coming, He will provide universally at His second coming.

He will bind Satan and his demons. He will eradicate deformity, disease, and death from natural causes. The ground will no longer produce weeds and thorns. Farmers will harvest abundant crops as never before. "Poverty" and "hunger" will become archaic terms.

Every nation will experience this golden age of world history.

The kingdom of heaven rejected by earth's citizens at Jesus' first coming will be established globally at His second coming.

"The eyes of the blind shall be opened, and the ears of the deaf shall be unstopped. Then the lame shall leap like a deer, and the tongue of the dumb sing. For waters shall burst forth in the wilderness, and streams in the desert... 'The wolf and the lamb shall feed together, the lion shall eat straw like the ox, **and dust shall be the serpent's food.** They shall not hurt nor destroy in all My holy mountain,' says the LORD."* (Isaiah 35:5-6; 65:25)

Even the animal kingdom will coexist in peace, reverting to the vegetarian design and Edenic conditions before sin entered.

Nonetheless, the root of sin will still be found in the hearts of those born during Christ's thousand-year reign. As in every age, the descendants of Adam will need to receive God's gift of forgiveness by simply trusting in His provision of salvation.

Did you notice what the last verse we read foretells about the serpent? *"Dust shall be the serpent's food."* During the millennium, snakes will continue to crawl on their bellies. Their slithering on the ground will serve as a reminder that there remains yet one more dramatic event in the third and final stage of God's plan to forever reverse the curse.

EVIL'S FINAL FLING

Earlier, we learned that the *"serpent of old, who is the Devil and Satan"* will be bound and held in a bottomless pit during the millennial reign of Christ, *"so that he should deceive the nations no more till the thousand years were finished. **But after these things he must be released for a little while.**"* (Revelation 20:2-3)

Why would God release Satan again? Why not just keep him locked up?

The Lord, in His infinite wisdom, will allow man's sinful, depraved heart to be exposed one final time before evil is forever put away. As humanity transitions from time to eternity, this truth will become patently clear: Adam's descendants are helpless to rise above their fallen nature. Only the LORD God can make sinners righteous and transform their wayward hearts.

> *"The heart is deceitful above all things, and desperately wicked; Who can know it? I, the LORD, search the heart, I test the mind, even to give every man according to his ways, according to the fruit of his doings."* (Jeremiah 17:9-10)

Just how *"desperately wicked"* is the heart of man? Even after a thousand years of living in a perfect environment, under a perfect government with a perfect King, the moment Satan is released, a great horde of those born on earth during the millennium will believe Satan's lies and side with him! They will join forces with God's adversary and rebel against their Creator, just as their ancestors did in Eden.

It will be evil's final fling.

SATAN'S LAST STAND

> *"Now when the thousand years have expired, Satan will be released from his prison and will go out to deceive the nations which are in the four corners of the earth... to gather them together to battle, whose number is as the sand of the sea. They went up on the breadth of the earth and surrounded the camp of the saints and the beloved city. **And fire came down from God out of heaven and devoured them.**"* (Revelation 20:7-9)

The Lord will allow Satan's legion of rebellious humans to surround Jerusalem, but as soon as they are assembled, fire will descend from heaven and consume them. Satan and all who sided with him will have reached the end of the road.

THE SERPENT CRUSHED

What takes place next is the most solemn event in history:

> *"**The devil, who deceived them, was cast into the lake of fire and brimstone** where the beast and the false prophet are. And they will be tormented day and night forever and ever.*

*Then I saw a great white throne and Him who sat on
it, from whose face the earth and the heaven fled away.*
And there was found no place for them. And I saw the
dead, small and great, standing before God, and books
were opened. And another book was opened, which is
the Book of Life. And the dead were judged according to
their works, by the things which were written in the books.
The sea gave up the dead who were in it, and Death and
Hades delivered up the dead who were in them. And they
were judged, each one according to his works.
*Then Death and Hades were cast into the lake of
fire.* **This is the second death. And anyone not found
written in the Book of Life was cast into the lake of fire."**

(Revelation 20:10-15)

The conflict of the ages will be forever over.

Following the Great White Throne Judgment, the curse of sin
will be history. But the lessons gleaned from God's judgment of
evil will never be forgotten. All creation will have witnessed the
repulsiveness of sin and the righteousness of God.

At last, the head of *the serpent* will be crushed.

Satan and all who followed him will be forever encapsulated
in *"the everlasting fire prepared for the devil and his angels."*
(Matthew 25:41) From that everlasting prison the condemned
will never escape. Nor will they be able to blame God for their
punishment, for even when blessed with a thousand years on a
perfect earth with a perfect King, they still opted to rebel against
their Creator-Owner.

Man will be without excuse.

The reputation and message of the one true God will be forever
vindicated.

All who have their names written in *the Book of Life* will
be eternally with the Lord, *"but the cowardly, unbelieving,
abominable, murderers, sexually immoral, sorcerers, idolaters,
and all liars shall have their part in the lake which burns with fire
and brimstone, which is the second death."* (Revelation 21:8)[264]

Never again will evil raise its ugly head. All creation will be
forevermore in submission to the one true God.

WITH HIM!

What happens next is almost too wonderful to imagine.

> *"I heard a loud voice from heaven saying, 'Behold, the*
> *tabernacle of God is with men, and He will dwell with*
> *them, and they shall be His people. God Himself will be*
> *with them and be their God. And God will wipe away*
> *every tear from their eyes; there shall be no more death,*
> *nor sorrow, nor crying. There shall be no more pain, for*
> *the former things have passed away.' Then He who sat*
> *on the throne said, 'Behold, I make all things new.'"*
> (Revelation 21:3-5)

Just as the first two chapters of the Old Testament describe God's original creation, so the last two chapters of the New Testament describe His new creation. With Satan, sin, and death banished, all will once again be in perfect harmony with the Creator's holy nature. Never again will humans or angels fall prey to sin. The needed lessons will have been learned and *"God Himself will be with them and be their God."*

God's program embraces much more than merely removing the effects of Adam's sin. It includes making *"all things new."* The Lord's people will enjoy glorious heavenly bodies fit for His dazzling presence. Throughout eternity, redeemed souls from every nation and era will take part in His awesome and timeless plans. As believers, it will be our joy to be forever with Him and it will be His joy that we are there.

The *"God with us"* theme will be a full-time reality.

LIKE HIM!

Sweet fellowship between the Redeemer and His people will never cease. What Adam lost in the earthly paradise will be restored and surpassed in the heavenly Paradise. When God was about to create the first man and woman, He said,

> *"Let Us make man in Our image, according to Our*
> *likeness."* (Genesis 1:26)

Everything will turn out just the way He planned it.

Heaven will be filled with men and women who bear *His image and likeness* in their character and conduct. Sin will no longer even be a possibility. God's people will be sealed in righteousness. The prophet David foresaw this when he wrote: *"As for me, I will see Your face in righteousness; I shall be satisfied when I awake in Your likeness."* (Psalm 17:15)

Ransomed men, women, and children will be forever secure as God's new creation, *"conformed to the image of His Son."* (Romans 8:29)

> *"It has not yet been revealed what we shall be, but we know that when He is revealed, we shall be like Him, for we shall see Him as He is."* (1 John 3:2)

FOR HIM!

From the beginning, the Creator's purpose was to establish His kingdom among mankind in such a way that we might know and appreciate His glory, purity, love, justice, mercy, and grace.

All through the long war with Satan, it was always God's plan to *"visit...the Gentiles to take out of them a people for His name."* (Acts 15:14) The Lord will have what He came to earth to win: a redeemed people in His own image who, from thankful and adoring hearts, will love, enjoy and praise Him forever.

The third and final stage of God's plan to reverse the curse could begin at any moment.

Are you ready?

Does the thought of Jesus' return fill you with joy or terror?

The Bible gives us many more insights into the end times which we don't have time to view on this journey through the Scriptures. For now, it is enough to know that our trustworthy Creator will make good on a little prophecy buried in the last chapter of His Book:

> *"There shall be no more curse!"* (Revelation 22:3)

30

A PREVIEW OF PARADISE

Much of the world's population holds a *yin-yang* view of evil. Yin means "shady" and yang means "sunny." Perhaps you've seen the yin-yang symbol—a circle with a unique blend of black and white. While this ancient Chinese philosophy contains truth, it blurs the distinction between good and evil, right and wrong, life and death. It views good and evil as a natural and never-ending feature of man's existence.

As we have seen, the Bible provides a different analysis of good and evil. It does not support the idea that suffering and sadness have always been and will always be an integral part of our universe. The Scriptures are clear. A day is coming when Evil, Pain and Death will take their final bow and vanish from the stage of history.

This graph depicts God's unalterable program:

← ETERNITY   [T I M E]   ETERNITY →
PERFECTLY GOOD   **[Good / Evil]**   **PERFECTLY GOOD**

The current mix of evil and good is bracketed. It will not be around forever.[265]

The first two and the final two chapters of God's Book portray a sin-free world, a world in which God is rightly loved and exalted. It is between those first and last chapters that we see God

339

working out His plan to deal with sin and its curse, and to redeem for Himself a people who know Him, love Him, and *want* to spend eternity with Him.

Like any good story, God's history of redemption has a beginning, middle, and end.

BEGINNING: Genesis 1 & 2:
A perfect world—before evil entered.
MIDDLE: Genesis 3 to Revelation 20:
A corrupted world—God's intervention.
END: Revelation 21 & 22:
A perfect world—after evil is eradicated.

THE BOOK OF ENDINGS

Just as the first book of the Bible is the *book of beginnings*, so the last book of the Bible is the *book of endings*.

Genesis	Revelation
◊ Beginning of all things	√ Consummation of all things
◊ Creation of heaven & earth	√ Creation of new heaven & earth
◊ God creates the sun for earth	√ God is the Light of heaven
◊ Satan's first temptation of man	√ Satan's final temptation of man
◊ God's first judgments	√ God's final judgments
◊ Entrance of sin & death	√ Abolishment of sin & death
◊ "First Adam" loses dominion	√ "Last Adam" restores dominion
◊ God promises to crush Satan	√ Satan cast into the Lake of Fire
◊ First lamb sacrificed	√ God's Lamb glorified
◊ Man shut out of earthly paradise	√ Man in heavenly Paradise
◊ Man cut off from the Tree of Life	√ Man eating from the Tree of Life
◊ Mankind separated from God	√ Rescued mankind forever with God

The list could go on and on, but you get the idea.

THE REVELATION

As we complete our journey together, we want to reflect on the "end" of God's story, which is really the inauguration of a whole new beginning.

The Bible's closing book begins with these words:

*"**The Revelation** of Jesus Christ, which God gave Him to show His servants—things which must shortly take place. And He sent and signified it by His angel to His servant John, who bore witness to the word of God, and to the testimony of Jesus Christ, to all things that he saw. Blessed is he who reads and those who hear the words of this prophecy, and keep those things which are written in it; for the time is near... **To Him who loved us and washed us from our sins in His own blood... to Him be glory and dominion forever and ever. Amen. Behold, He is coming with clouds, and every eye will see Him, even they who pierced Him.** And all the tribes of the earth will mourn because of Him. Even so, Amen. 'I am the Alpha and the Omega* [first and final letters of Greek alphabet], *the Beginning and the End,' says the Lord, who is and who was and who is to come, the Almighty.'"* (Revelation 1:1-3, 5-8)[266]

God gave these words *"to His servant John."* John was one of the twelve disciples who accompanied Jesus during His earthly ministry.[267] Six decades after Jesus returned to heaven, His Holy Spirit inspired John to write this final book of God's library.

Revelation means "unveiling." This fascinating book unveils events no human could conceive. It outlines how the Lord will vindicate His name and restore the dominion that man lost through sin. This book also gives us a preview of Paradise.

THE THRONE

A select few of God's prophets and apostles were given a glimpse of God's dwelling place, but none more clearly than John the apostle. John wrote:

*"After this I looked, and there before me was **a door standing open in heaven**. And the voice I had first heard speaking to me like a trumpet said, 'Come up here, and I will show you what must take place after this.' At once I was in the Spirit, and there before me was **a throne in heaven with someone sitting on it**. And **the one who sat***

there had the appearance of jasper and carnelian [two precious stones[268]]. *A rainbow, resembling an emerald, encircled the throne."* (Revelation 4:1-3 NIV)

John struggled to describe heaven's throne room. It was unspeakably glorious. Soaring around the throne of God were angelic beings that declared incessantly: *"Holy, holy, holy, Lord God Almighty, Who was and is and is to come!"* (Revelation 4:8) John could only report that what he saw slightly resembled things he had seen on earth, but everything was infinitely more beautiful and spectacular. He gazed on a place of sparkling light and supernatural colors. He heard deep thundering sounds and myriads of joyful, praise-filled voices, but what captivated John most was *the One* seated on the throne.[269]

THE THRILL

The religions of the world portray Paradise in many ways.

Some descriptions are positively boring. Perhaps you've seen the cartoons: people sitting around on clouds, dutifully plucking harps. That is not how the Bible describes God's majestic abode.

Others describe paradise as a male-centered garden of non-stop sensuality. That concept is also wrong. When the Lord was on earth, He taught that in Paradise His redeemed people *"neither marry nor are given in marriage, but are like angels of God in heaven."* (Matthew 22:30)

Heaven is a God-centered realm where the joy, wonder, and thrill of being in the presence of infinite wisdom and love will never fade. Heaven is a place where relationships are on a higher plane than anything known on earth. God designed earthly marriage to give us a faint idea of the glorious relationship that will exist between the Lord and His redeemed people throughout eternity. Even the best earthly marriages fall short of illustrating the intense joy and holy companionship that people united to Christ will enjoy with Him. The Scripture calls this *"a great mystery"* (Ephesians 5:32) and goes on to say, *"Blessed are those who are called to the* **marriage supper of the Lamb!**" (Revelation 19:9)

Paradise is all about being with HIM.

The angels that were created untold millennia ago are more awed today by God's presence than ever. So it will be for the redeemed children of Adam. We will need all eternity to take in the splendor, wisdom, and perfection of the Lord our God!

> *"How precious also are Your thoughts to me, O God! How great is the sum of them! If I should count them, they would be more in number than the sand; when I awake, I am still **with You.**"* (Psalm 139:17-18)

The thrill and joy of being with the Lord will never grow old. The question is not whether we will ever get bored, but rather, will we ever be able to take our eyes off Him?

> *"**In Your presence is fullness of joy**; at Your right hand are pleasures forevermore."* (Psalm 16:11)

THE THRONG

The apostle John not only got a glimpse of the Lord on the throne—he also saw the throng of the redeemed.

> *"After these things I looked, and behold, a great multitude which no one could number, **of all nations, tribes, peoples, and tongues**, standing before the throne and before the Lamb, clothed with white robes… and crying out with a loud voice, saying, 'Salvation belongs to our God who sits on the throne, and to the Lamb!'"* (Revelation 7:9-10)

Do you remember how God promised to offer His *blessings to all nations and peoples on earth* through the Savior born in the family line of Abraham, Isaac and Jacob?[270] God allowed John to look into the future and witness the fulfillment of His promise.

Every people group on earth, every nation, and every language will be represented around God's throne. With grateful and joyful voice, this innumerable throng of redeemed sinners will forever praise and worship *the Lamb* who shed His blood to deliver them from eternal death and give them eternal life.

"They sang a new song, saying: 'You are worthy... for You were slain, and have redeemed us to God by Your blood out of every tribe and tongue and people and nation, and have made us kings and priests to our God; And we shall reign on the earth.'

Then I looked, and I heard the voice of many angels around the throne, the living creatures, and the elders; and the number of them was ten thousand times ten thousand, and thousands of thousands, saying with a loud voice: 'Worthy is the Lamb who was slain to receive power and riches and wisdom, and strength and honor and glory and blessing!'" (Revelation 5:9-12)

MY REDEEMER!

Four thousand years ago, the prophet Job exulted:

"I know that my Redeemer lives, and He shall stand at last on the earth; and after my skin is destroyed, this I know, that in my flesh I shall see God, whom I shall see for myself, and my eyes shall behold, and not another. How my heart yearns within me!" (Job 19:25-27)

Does your heart *yearn*, like Job's, to *"see God"*? Do you know Him as *your* Redeemer?

All true believers share Job's sure hope. My friend, I cannot speak for you, but I know that *I* shall see *my* Redeemer face to face! I am going to walk and talk with *"the Son of God, who loved me and gave Himself for me!"* (Galatians 2:20)

Yes, I look forward to wonderful times of fellowship with the people of God from every era, along with family and friends who are already with the Lord, and with all my heart, I hope *you* will be among them too. But, above all, I want to see *Jesus*!

He took my hell for me.

Without question, one of the most amazing truths my mind can attempt to contemplate is this:

HE wants *me* to spend eternity with *HIM!*

On the night that Jesus was arrested to be condemned and crucified, He prayed:

> ***"Father, I desire that they also whom You gave Me may be with Me where I am,*** *that they may behold My glory which You have given Me; for You loved Me before the foundation of the world."* (John 17:24)

This is the heart of God's message. He designed humans to be *with Him*, but He won't force you to accept His offer.
He leaves the choice with you.

> *"To him who overcomes, I will give the right to eat from the tree of life, which is in the paradise of God. ...Who is it that overcomes the world? Only he who believes that Jesus is the Son of God."* (Revelation 2:7; 1 John 5:5 NIV)

THE PERFECT HOME

The last two chapters of the Bible record John's glimpse of the eternal home-base where believers from every era will live together with their Creator-Redeemer and participate in all that He has prepared for His people.

> *"Now I saw **a new heaven** and **a new earth**, for the first heaven and the first earth had passed away. Also there was no more sea. Then I, John, saw the holy city, New Jerusalem, coming down out of heaven from God."* (Revelation 21:1-2)

This glorious city will come *"down out of heaven from God"* to unite with our recreated planet. The new earth will have *"no more sea."* There will be no more separating continents.

> *"And God will **wipe away every tear** from their eyes; there shall be **no more death, nor sorrow, nor crying.** There shall be **no more pain,** for the former things have passed away."* (Revelation 21:4)

All will be perfect. The celestial city will be glorious beyond imagination. John had difficulty describing it.

> *"The city is laid out as a square; its length is as great as its breadth. And he measured the city with the reed: twelve thousand furlongs* [2200 kilometers]. *Its length, breadth, and height are equal... The construction of its wall was of jasper; and the city was pure gold, like clear glass. The foundations of the wall of the city were adorned with all kinds of precious stones... The twelve gates were twelve pearls: each individual gate was of one pearl. And the street of the city was pure gold, like transparent glass. But I saw no temple in it, for the Lord God Almighty and the Lamb are its temple. The city had no need of the sun or of the moon to shine in it, for the glory of God illuminated it. The Lamb is its light. And the nations of those who are saved shall walk in its light... But there shall by no means enter it anything that defiles, or causes an abomination or a lie, but only those who are written in the Lamb's Book of Life."* (Revelation 21:16-24,27)

This colossal city will be glorious in every detail; even its streets are of *"pure gold, like transparent glass."* Every component is designed to reflect the glory of the Lord.

The city has no temple or sun, since the Lord Himself is the city's worship center and Light Source. *"The Lamb is its light."*

Heaven will be illuminated by the same One who, on the first day of creation, said, *'Let there be light."* The Light of that city will be the same dazzling splendor that dwelt in the Holiest Place of the Tabernacle, the Temple, and in Jesus Himself who said, *"I am the light of the world."* (John 8:12)

This heavenly city will have the form of a perfect cube—as did the Holiest Place in the Tabernacle which symbolized Heaven. The length and width of the city are 2200 kilometers (1500 miles) in each direction. The same is true of its height. Apparently, the city will tower right up through the new earth's stratosphere and out into space.

This glorious home will have ample room for every person who was ever born. However, not all people will be there, *"but only those who are written in the Lamb's Book of Life."* Only those who, while on earth, placed their trust in the one true God and His Salvation will be there.

The final chapter describes the garden found within the city.

*"He showed me a pure river of water of life, clear as crystal, proceeding from the throne of God and of the Lamb. In the middle of its street, and on either side of the river, was **the tree of life**... and there shall be no more curse, but the throne of God and of **the Lamb** shall be in it, and His servants shall serve Him. They shall see **His face**, and His name shall be on their foreheads. ...And they shall **reign** forever and ever."* (Revelation 22:1-5)

THE PERFECT STORY

God's story has come full circle.

*"In the middle of its street, and on either side of the river, was **the tree of life**."*

What began in a lovely garden ends in a magnificent city with an exquisite garden. In contrast to Eden, the heavenly Paradise will not include *the tree of the knowledge of good and evil*, but it will feature *the tree of life* from which Adam and Eve were cut off when they sinned. Perfect holiness and everlasting life will be the only option in the heavenly city.

The time of testing and living by faith will be history.

*"The throne of **God** and of **the Lamb** shall be in it, and His servants shall serve Him. They shall **see His face**... And they shall **reign forever and ever**."*

Never in eternity will God's people forget the great price paid by *"God and...the Lamb"* to redeem their helpless souls from judgment and qualify them to live forever with Him.

Sweet, unbreakable fellowship between the Lord and His people will be a constant feature. That God should be with us and that we should be with Him will be even more wonderful than anything Adam and Eve could have known had they never sinned.

Why will it be *even more* wonderful?

The answer is found in the word **redemption**.

*"He has **rescued us from** the dominion of darkness and **brought us into** the kingdom of the Son he loves, in whom we have **redemption**, the forgiveness of sins."*
(Colossians 1:13-14 NIV)

What could be more wonderful than being **rescued from** *the worst possible fate* as condemned law-breakers in the dark dungeon of sin and death, and then being **brought into** *the best possible state* as favored citizens in God's kingdom of light and love?

That is what our Creator-Redeemer has done for all who trust Him alone for salvation. Out of His great love, with His infinitely-valuable blood, He has redeemed helpless sinners from hell and qualified them for heaven.

It is the Perfect Story—the Story of Redemption to be reviewed and appreciated throughout eternity.

*"After these things I looked, and behold, **a great multitude which no one could number, of all nations, tribes, peoples, and tongues**, standing before the throne and before the Lamb, clothed with white robes, with palm branches in their hands, and crying out with a loud voice, saying, 'Salvation belongs to our God who sits on the throne, and to the Lamb!'"* (Revelation 7:9-10)

*"And they sang a new song, saying: '**You are worthy... for You were slain, and have redeemed us to God by Your blood** out of every tribe and tongue and people and nation...Blessing and honor and glory and power be to Him who sits on the throne, and to the Lamb, **forever and ever!**'"* (Revelation 5:9.13)

HAPPILY EVER AFTER

Around the globe, people of every age love stories of romance and rescue—stories with happy endings.[271]

Whether an ancient legend dramatized by a village storyteller to a group huddled around a flickering fire under the night sky, or a fairy tale read by a parent to a child at bedtime, the story shares a similar plot. It goes something like this:

A young maiden in distress, enslaved by some evil character, is delivered from her hopeless predicament by some combination of supernatural intervention and a brave warrior or handsome prince. Having rescued his beloved, the hero takes her to be his bride, to live with him in his magnificent home.

And how does the tale end?

And they lived happily ever after.

Why do people tell such stories?

They tell them because God has built into the human soul a desire to be delivered from evil, to be loved, and to live happily ever after. That is why children and adults alike love such tales.

But God's story is no imaginary tale.

A figment of the imagination is not rooted in history, nor is it confirmed by archaeology. An invented story is not written by dozens of people over fifteen centuries, nor is it heralded by hundreds of detailed prophecies. A make-believe hero could not speak with the heavenly wisdom of Jesus, nor would he tell those he has come to rescue, *"Behold, we are going up to Jerusalem, and all things that are written by the prophets concerning the Son of Man will be accomplished. For He will be...mocked and insulted and spit upon. They will scourge Him and kill Him. And the third day He will rise again."* (Luke 18:31-33) Fiction cannot provide hell-bound sinners with a cleansed conscience and assurance of eternal life. Fantasy cannot give us a personal relationship with our Creator and transform our sinful and selfish hearts into those with a passion to glorify God and serve others.

Only God's story can do this.

It's the real thing.

To sum it up: The story and message of the one true God is about His eternal Son who became a man, lived a perfect life, shed His perfect blood, and rose from the dead to rescue helpless sinners from Satan, sin, death, and hell, so that He might share, with all who believe, the endless delights of His wisdom and love in the glory of His Father's home.

That is God's good news for a world in distress.

It is because of what He has done for us that we can live *happily ever after.*

*"I know that whatever God does, it shall be **forever**."*
(Ecclesiastes 3:14)

INVITATION AND WARNING

God's Book concludes with these words:

*"**I, Jesus**, have sent My angel to testify to you these things... I am the Alpha and the Omega, the Beginning and the End, the First and the Last."* (Revelation 22:16,13)

*"**And the Spirit and the bride** [rescued sinners] **say, 'Come!'** And let him who hears say, 'Come!' And let him who thirsts come. **Whoever desires, let him take the water of life freely.** For I testify to everyone who hears the words of the prophecy of this book: **If anyone adds** to these things, God will add to him the plagues that are written in this book; and **if anyone takes away** from the words of the book of this prophecy, God shall take away his part from the Book of Life, from the holy city, and from the things which are written in this book. He who testifies to these things says, '**Surely I am coming quickly**.' 'Amen. **Even so, come, Lord Jesus!**' The grace of our Lord Jesus Christ be with you all. **Amen**."* (Revelation 22:17-21)

Thus, with a final *"Amen"* (which means, "It is trustworthy and true"), the Author who exists outside of time concludes His story and message.

GOD AND MAN TOGETHER

Do you remember Adam's response when the LORD came into the garden calling out, *"Where are you?"*
Adam had shamefully replied:

"I heard Your voice in the garden, and I was afraid."
(Genesis 3:10)

The man and the woman attempted to hide from their Creator-Owner because they had sinned.
But now, at the end of history, how do believing men, women, and children react to their Creator-Redeemer's promise to come back to take them to live forever with Him?
They joyfully respond:

"Amen. Even so, come, Lord Jesus!" (Revelation 22:20)

What brought about such transformation? Why do some of Adam's descendants no longer want to hide from their Lord? Why instead are they passionate about the prospect of seeing Him face to face?
The answer is found in the one true God's message:

"God...has saved us and called us to a holy life—
not because of anything we have done
but because of his own purpose and grace.
This grace was given us in Christ Jesus
before the beginning of time,
but it has now been revealed
through the appearing of our Savior,
Christ Jesus, who has destroyed death
and has brought life and immortality to light
through the gospel." (2 Timothy 1:9-10 NIV)

ONE RULE

Just as God made His one rule clear to Adam in the earthly garden of paradise, so He has made His one rule clear to Adam's descendants regarding the heavenly city of Paradise:

> *"There shall by **no means** enter it anything that defiles, or causes an abomination or a lie, but **only** those who are written in the Lamb's Book of Life."* (Revelation 21:27)

Is *your* name written in the Lamb's Book of Life? If it is, then here is a personal word from Him to *you*:

> *"Let not **your** heart be troubled;*
> ***You** believe in God, believe also in Me.*
> *In My Father's house are many mansions;*
> *If it were not so, I would have told **you**.*
> *I go to prepare a place for **you**.*
> *And if I go and prepare a place for **you**,*
> *I will come again and receive **you** to Myself;*
> *that where I am, there **you** may be also....*
>
> ***I am the way, the truth, and the life.***
> *No one comes to the Father except through Me."*
> — Jesus (John 14:1-3,6)

EPILOGUE

Writing this book has been an exhilarating journey for me. I have been blessed beyond description in musing on my Creator-Redeemer and His matchless message. His presence and direction over the past year have been evident as I have awakened before dawn most mornings, my mind spinning with the next thought to be written.

THANK YOU

Though I have refrained from including a long list of names, let there be no doubt: this book would not be what it is apart from the patient support of my wonderful wife Carol and the invaluable input of gifted friends and family. The cover and drawings are the work of my brother Dave. From my heart I thank you all.

"God is not unjust to forget your work and labor of love which you have shown toward His name." (Hebrews 6:10)

I am also grateful to the countless Muslim inquirers whose e-mails motivated me to write.

Above all, I want to thank *you* for joining me on this brief journey. I say *brief* because it could have been much longer. The Scriptures we have read along the way comprise less than 4% of the total verses in the Bible. So even though we have come to the end of our journey, we've really just begun.

THE CONTINUING JOURNEY

While the one true God has made His message plain for all who want to understand it, He Himself is complex, profound, and infinite. Neither man nor angel will ever comprehend everything there is to know about Him. The apostle John expressed this reality in the final verse of the Gospel record:

"There are also many other things that Jesus did, which if they were written one by one, I suppose that even the world itself could not contain the books that would be written." (John 21:25)

I can relate. Perhaps the most difficult aspect of writing ONE GOD ONE MESSAGE was selecting which Scriptures to include and which to leave out. Truly, the Word of God is glorious and inexhaustible. It is delicious and satisfying to the soul. As our friend in Lebanon discovered, "I realize that it's not enough to say, 'I've read the Bible.' It's a book that needs to be *perpetually read*." (From chapter 7)

Now that you have completed this journey, you may want to go back through ONE GOD ONE MESSAGE and look up in a Bible the many verses cited, reading the section in which each quotation is found. Better yet, read through your Creator's entire library as you breathe this prayer to Him:

"Open my eyes, that I may see wondrous things from Your law." (Psalm 119:18)

If you feel the need for further documentation or clarification, be sure to look over the endnotes. And do not hesitate to write to me with your comments or questions. I will be happy to hear from you, even if those e-mails compel me to write another book!

With this 3,500 year-old blessing I bid you farewell:

"The LORD bless you and keep you;
The LORD make His face shine upon you,
*   and be gracious to you;*
The LORD lift up His countenance upon you,
*   and give you peace."* (Numbers 6:24-26)

Paul D. Bramsen

www.twor.com
TWOR@iname.com

END NOTES

"Teach me what I do not see."
(Job 34:32)

PROLOGUE

[1] Sahel: the semiarid transition zone that separates Africa's Sahara from its tropical rainforests. This band of sand and scrub-brush stretches from Senegal to Egypt.

[2] While *monotheists* believe in one God—*polytheists* believe in many gods and goddesses, *pantheists* view everything as part of god, *secular humanists* exalt man instead of God, and *atheists* say there is no God.

CHAPTER 1: BUY THE TRUTH

[3] In ONE GOD ONE MESSAGE, this phrase, along with more than 1,000 other quotes from the Scriptures of the prophets, comes from the Bible. Sometimes only a portion of a verse is quoted, as is the case here. Proverbs chapter 23, verse 23, in its entirety reads: *"Buy the truth, and do not sell it, also wisdom and instruction and understanding."*

[4] Barrett, David B., George T. Kurian and Todd M. Johnson. *World Christian Encyclopedia: A Comparative Survey of Churches and Religions in the Modern World.* London: Oxford University Press, 2001. [5] "Today, Scriptures are available in no less than 2,403 languages, with the complete Bible having been translated into at least 426 languages, and the New Testament into some 1,115. In addition, parts of the Bible have been made available in a further 862 languages." United Bible Societies, 2007. (www.biblesociety.org) Also: www.wycliffe.org/About/Statistics.aspx

[6] Foxe, John (edited by G.A. Williamson). *Foxe's Book of Martyrs.* Toronto: Little, Brown & Company, 1965.

[7] It is incorrect to speak of any country as a "Christian nation" since Jesus Christ said, *"My kingdom is not of this world. If My kingdom were of this world, My servants would fight, so that I should not be delivered to the Jews; but now My kingdom is not from here."* (John 18:36)

[8] Wurmbrand, Richard. *Tortured for Christ – 30th Anniversary Edition.* Bartlesville, OK: Living Sacrifice Book Co., 1998.

[9] *The Way of Righteousness* radio series has been or is being translated into more than 70 languages for broadcast worldwide. To read these 100 programs online visit: www.twor.com or www.injil.org/TWOR

[10] The full Qur'anic verse says: *"And in their footsteps We sent Jesus the son of Mary, confirming the Law that had come before him: We sent him the Gospel: Therein was guidance and light, and confirmation of the Law that had come before him: A guidance and an admonition to those who fear Allah."* (Sura 5:46) Unless otherwise indicated, the English version of the Qur'an used in ONE GOD ONE MESSAGE was translated by Abdullah Yusuf Ali. *The Qur'an Translation.* New York: Tahrike Tarsile Qur'an, Inc., 2003. **Note**: The Qur'an is divided into chapters called *suras*. Verse numbers vary depending on the Qur'anic translation. When looking for a verse, it may be necessary to search surrounding verses.

[11] Who is the "We"? In the Qur'an, Allah often refers to himself in first person plural. In the Bible, the LORD also sometimes refers to Himself in the plural. **Note**: Arabic speakers use the word "Allah" in two ways: 1) "Allah" is the generic term for "God" used by Arabic Christians, other non-Muslims, and Muslims. When used this way it is *not* God's proper name. Among Arabic speakers, no one group owns the generic term *Allah.* 2) Muslims use "Allah" as God's primary proper name. More about this in chapter 9.

[12] E-mail excerpts in ONE GOD ONE MESSAGE are presented anonymously to protect the identity of those who wrote them.

[13] "p.b.u.h." stands for: "peace be upon him," often added by Muslims after writing or speaking the name of a prophet. The Arabic formula Muslims use after Muhammad's name is: *Salla Allahu Alaihi Wa Sallam* (s.a.w.), which means: "the prayers of Allah be upon him and peace." They base this practice on this Qur'anic verse: *"Lo! Allah and His angels pray upon the prophet. Oh ye who believe, pray on him and salute him with peace."* (Sura 33:56) The use of this formula is inconsistent with the Bible which says: *"It is appointed for men to die once, but after this the judgment."* (Hebrews 9:27) Once a person has died, his or her eternal destiny is fixed. No amount of praying can change where or how he or she will spend eternity (Revelation 22:11).

[14] [*sic*] is Latin for "thus" and "so." It is used in brackets following a printed quotation to show that the original has been quoted accurately even though it contains an apparent error. **Note**: Except for condensing and correcting spelling and grammar (to make them more easily understood), e-mail quotes used in ONE GOD ONE MESSAGE are presented as they were received. For example, this particular e-mail from "Ahmed" had virtually no capital letters. This has been corrected.

[15] *The Meaning of the Glorious Koran: An Explanatory Translation by Mohammed Marmaduke Pickthall.* New York: Meridian, 1997.

[16] For example, the Qur'an says in sura (chapter) 40, verses 70-72: *"Those who reject the Book **and the revelation with which We sent Our apostles:** but soon shall they know, —when the yoke shall be round their necks, and the chains; they shall be dragged along—in the boiling fetid fluid; then in the Fire shall they be burned...."* Also: *"In their footsteps We sent Jesus the son of Mary, confirming **the Law that had come before him:** We sent him **the Gospel:** Therein was guidance and light, and confirmation of the Law that had come before him: **A guidance and an admonition** to those who fear Allah."* (Sura 5:49) *"O ye who believe! Believe in Allah and His Apostle, and the scripture which He hath sent to His Apostle **and the scripture which He sent to those before him.** Any who denieth Allah, His Angels, **His Books, His Apostles,** and the Day of Judgment, hath gone far, far astray. ...We have sent thee inspiration, as We sent it to Noah and the Messengers after him: We sent inspiration to Abraham, Ismail, Isaac, Jacob and the Tribes, to Jesus, Job, Jonah, Aaron, and Solomon, and to David We gave **the Psalms."** (Sura 4:136,163) For more such Qur'anic statements, see first page of chapter 3 and accompanying footnotes.

[17] Proverbs 23:23. Instead of "buying" the truth, many people "sell" it because they fear what family or friends might think of them if they are caught studying the Bible, even though it is the world's best seller and the holy Book the Qur'an commands Muslims to believe.

CHAPTER 2: OVERCOMING THE OBSTACLES

[18] Doyle, Sir Arthur Conan. *Treasury of World Masterpieces: The Celebrated Cases of Sherlock Holmes.* R.R. Donnelley and Sons Company, 1981, p. 17. (First published in Great Britain in 1891.)

[19] Romans 14:1-15:7; Matthew 7:1-5

[20] Doyle, p. 16

[21] Numbers 12

[22] 2 Kings 5

[23] Jonah 4

[24] See these books in the Bible: Daniel, Ezra and Esther

[25] John 4

[26] "The Greatest Journey," *National Geographic Magazine,* Mar. 2006, p. 62.

[27] Psalm 90:1-12; Mark 8:36; 2 Corinthians 4:16-18; Romans 8:18; James 4:13-15

[28] In human history, God has permitted and/or sent a variety of catastrophic events upon the earth. In Noah's generation, after a hundred years of patience and warning, God sent a worldwide flood in which

all but eight souls were exterminated (Genesis 6-8). While many view that flood as a myth, both the geological and fossil record affirm it. In Abraham's day, all but three souls perished in the fire that fell on Sodom and Gomorrah. During and after the time of Moses, God ordered the Israelites to destroy the Canaanite nations (Joshua 1–10). These battles were carried out under specific commands from God and often included miraculous interventions from heaven, such as Jericho's wall falling' outward (confirmed by archaeology) after the Israelites had marched around the city seven consecutive days. God waited hundreds of years before judging these nations, giving them time to repent and turn from their idolatry, immorality and human sacrifice (Genesis 15:16; Exodus 12:40), yet they ignored the witness of godly men like Abraham, Joseph, and Moses. Only a few Canaanites repented and believed in the one true God who had sent ten supernatural plagues on Egypt and opened a path in the Red Sea. When God used His ancient people to carry out His judgments, He remained fair and impartial. For example, the Torah records that God first punished the Israelites (due to their idolatry 'and adultery) with a plague in which 24,000 Israelites died (Numbers 25-31). Only after God had judged Israel did He send them to execute His judgment on the surrounding corrupt and evil nations. It is false to assume these nations were innocent. The Scripture tells us that they were so grossly corrupt that *"the land vomited out its inhabitants."* (Leviticus 18:25 NIV) God's goodness and patience are great, but His wrath is also great and His judgment is sure.

[29] One reason God does not instantly judge evil is to give sinners time to repent and accept His provision of salvation: *"Do not forget this one thing, dear friends: With the Lord a day is like a thousand years, and a thousand years are like a day. The Lord is not slow in keeping his promise, as some understand slowness.* ***He is patient with you, not wanting anyone to perish, but everyone to come to repentance.*** *"* (2 Peter 3:8-9 NIV)

[30] Chapters 8, 12, and 28–29 of ONE GOD ONE MESSAGE provide answers to these three supposed contradictions.

[31] Matthew 7:1-20; Compare Romans 14 and 1 Corinthians 6.

[32] Several websites continue to post a long list of *"101 Clear Contradictions in the Bible,"* even though, for many years now, another article has been posted called: *"101 Cleared-up 'Contradictions' in the Bible."* www.debate.org.uk/topics/apolog/contrads.htm

[33] Two rules for correctly interpreting any verse in the Bible:
   1) Read the surrounding context.
   2) Compare Scripture with Scripture.

To illustrate, in the book of Deuteronomy, Moses spoke this prophecy to the children of Israel: *"The LORD your God will raise up for you a Prophet like me from your midst, from your brethren. Him you shall hear...."* (Deuteronomy 18:15) What did Moses mean when he said to the Israelites that God would raise up a Prophet *"from your midst, from your brethren"*? Some say Moses was talking about the Ishmaelites, others say the Israelites. The surrounding context provides the correct answer (e.g., Deuteronomy 17:15,20; 18:2,5, etc.). Who was this special *"Prophet"* God promised to *"raise up"*? While many try to make this prophecy fit the founder of their particular religion, the correct interpretation is clearly stated later on in the Scriptures. See John 5:43-47, John 6:14 and Acts 3:22-26 to find the answer.

[34] BC = Before Christ / AD = *Anno Domini,* meaning, *"In the year of our Lord."* Many today now use BCE (Before Common Era) and CE (Common Era) which removes "Christ" from the abbreviation, even though the dividing point in history is still the birth of Christ.

[35] If you have ever borrowed money from a bank, then you signed a kind of testament—a legal document. The bank's part in the covenant was to give you the promised sum; your part was to pay back the loan over a specified period of time. To fail to respect your part of the contract would result in unpleasant consequences. Similarly, the Bible spells out the covenants our Creator provides for mankind—promises that make it possible for people like you and me to enjoy His eternal blessings. God making *"a covenant"* with people is unique to the Scriptures of the Bible.

[36] We will consider this divine hallmark of Scripture in chapter 5. One powerful example of God announcing history before it happens is found in the book of Daniel chapters 7 to 12. Daniel describes the history of world empires from 400 BC to the time of Christ, and goes on to describe events yet to take place in the last days. Daniel wrote it all down between 600 and 530 BC.

CHAPTER 3: CORRUPTED OR PRESERVED?

[37] Additional examples of Qur'anic references which declare to Muslims that the Biblical Scriptures are inspired by God: Sura 2:87-91, 101,136,285; 3:3-4; 4:47,54,136,163; 5:43-48,68; 6:92; 10:94; 20:133; 21:105; 28:43; 29:46; 32:23; 40:53-54,70-72; 45:16; 46:12; 57:27, etc.

[38] Down through the centuries, the Old Testament Scriptures have been jealously guarded by the Jewish religious community. Would they have allowed anyone to tamper with their Holy Scriptures, books for which many were willing to die? There is no other known case in history where

one religious community (Christians) has based its faith on a book (Old Testament) that is revered and protected by another religious community (orthodox Jews). Would not this fact alone have made it practically impossible for anyone to alter the Old Testament Scriptures?

[39] *The Holy Qur'an*. Translated by M.H. Shakir. Tahrike Tarsile Qur'an, Inc., Electronic version, 1993.

[40] Metzger, Bruce M. and Michael D. Coogan. *The Oxford Companion to the Bible*. NY: Oxford University Press, 1993, p. 754.

[41] See footnote number 37.

[42] We have no verifiable Qur'anic or Islamic documents before AD 750 (more than 100 years after Muhammad's death). http://debate.org.uk/topics/history/bib-qur/qurmanu.htm

[43] Metzger and Coogan, p. 683.

[44] Here is an example of the kind of apparent variants which can be found in ancient manuscripts. In the Old Testament book of Second Kings, we read: *"Jehoiachin was **eighteen** years old when he became king."* (2 Kings 24:8) Meanwhile, the book of Second Chronicles states: *"Jehoiachin was **eight** years old when he became king."* (2 Chronicles 36:9) How can such differences be explained? Some scholars suggest that it was at the age of 8 that young Jehoiachin's father took him into *partnership* in the government, and that he began to *reign* at 18 following the death of his father, which is possible. However, a more likely explanation is that this numerical variation is simply the result of an early-century scribe penning "8" instead of "18." If this were the case, that wrong number would be transcribed into all the manuscripts which "descended" from that scribe's copy. Whatever the case, such variations do not affect or alter God's message to us in any way. In most cases, the sheer volume of ancient Bible manuscripts allows scholars to determine the correct rendering by comparing the various texts.

[45] The Hadith records: *"Uthman then ordered Zaid bin Thabit, 'Abdullah bin Az-Zubair, Sa'id bin Al-'As and 'Abdur Rahman bin Hari-bin Hisham **to rewrite the manuscripts in perfect copies**... They did so, and when they had written many copies, 'Uthman returned the original manuscripts to Hafsa. 'Uthman sent to every Muslim province one copy of what they had copied, and **ordered that all the other Qur'anic materials whether written in fragmentary manuscripts or whole copies, be burnt.***" (Hadith, Sahih Bukhari, VI, No. 510) (The *Hadith* ["Sayings"] are ancient writings by Muhammad's wives and acquaintances. Muslims base many beliefs and practices on the Hadith.)

[46] Even before the discovery of the Dead Sea Scrolls—to verify that the Scriptures had remained unchanged—one only needed to compare the

present day Old Testament with the Septuagint (Greek translation of the Old Testament completed around 270 BC). The Septuagint substantiates the claim that the Old Testament Scriptures are uncorrupted and preserved.

[47] Abegg, Martin Jr., Peter Flint and Eugene Ulrich. *The Dead Sea Scrolls Bible*. San Francisco: Harper, 1999, page xvi.

[48] McDowell, Josh. *A Ready Defense*. Nashville: Thomas Nelson Publishers, 1993, pp. 42-48. www.debate.org.uk/topics/history/bib-qur/bibmanu.htm

[49] The New Testament Scriptures are translated from a few primary Greek texts (Majority Text, Textus Receptus, Alexandrian Text). The NKJV translates the New Testament from the Majority Text, while the NIV translates from the Alexandrian Text. Where "significant" variations occur between Greek New Testament texts, most Bible translations include a note in the margin indicating those variations. The lengthiest passages in question are Mark 16:9-20 and John 7:53–8:11, each 12 verses in length. While these passages are absent in a few of the oldest surviving manuscripts (Alexandrian Text), they are found in the hundreds of others (Majority Text). Keep in mind that *older* does not necessarily mean *more accurate*, since the various texts descended from different ancient copies. It is most likely that a distracted copyist omitted these selections by accident. Whatever the case, all truths taught in these omitted passages are also taught elsewhere in Scripture. God's message remains unaffected. Is it wise to reject God's message because a few ancient copies are missing a few sections—sections which in no way change God's message?

[50] In recent times, books have been published and movies produced which are calculated to cast doubt on the Bible. Some Bible critics point to contradictory, "alternative gospels." All such "gospels" were written long after the time of Messiah and lack historical corroboration.

[51] This statement is also found in Matthew 11:15; 13:43; Mark 4:9,43; 7:16; Luke 8:8; 14:35; Revelation 2:7,11,29; 3:6,13,22;13:9.

CHAPTER 4: SCIENCE AND THE BIBLE

[52] Solomon, Eldra Pearl, PhD and Linda R. Berg, PhD. *The World of Biology*. London: Saunders College Publishing, 1995, p. 24.

[53] Bucaille, Maurice. *La Bible, le Coran et la science*. Paris: Seghers, 1976, p. 35. In response to Dr. Bucaille's book, Dr. William Campell has written *The Qur'an and the Bible in Light of History and Science*. Second Edition; Middle East Resources, 2002. Dr. Campell's carefully-researched rebuttal can also be read online in six languages. http://answering-islam.org/Campbell

⁵⁴ Biological evolution suggests that the population of life forms such as algae and apes can—when spread over millions of generations—change into populations of plants and people. According to evolution, man, monkeys, and minnows share a common ancestry. The truth is that neither random evolution nor purposeful creation can be proven by modern science. Both require faith.

⁵⁵ http://www.gma.org/space1/nav_map.html

⁵⁶ Additional verses that affirm the hydrologic cycle: Psalm 135:7; Jeremiah 10:13; Ecclesiastes 1:7; Isaiah 55:10

⁵⁷ www.artsci.wustl.edu/~landc/html/cann ; *Newsweek Magazine*: "a trail of DNA...led [scientists] to a single woman from whom we all descended." *Newsweek,* January 11, 1988, pp. 46-52.

⁵⁸ *Time Magazine*: "...there was an ancestral 'Adam' whose genetic material on the chromosome is common to every man now on earth." *Time,* December 4, 1995, p. 29. **Note**: Scientists claim that our common male ancestor does not date back as far as our common female ancestor. Their claim lines up with the Bible, which shows that we all descend from Noah. But our common mother is Eve, since Noah had three sons and *three daughters-in-law* from which all people come.)

⁵⁹ www.mtn.org/quack/devices/phlebo.htm

⁶⁰ www.bible.ca/tracks/matthew-fontaine-maury-pathfinder-of-sea-ps8. htm **Note**: Maury discovered that the paths of the seas are so fixed that the navigator can literally "blaze his way" across the ocean. (Rozwadowski, Helen M. *Fathoming the Ocean.* Cambridge, MA: The Belknap Press of Harvard University Press, 2005, p. 40); When David wrote of *"the paths of the seas"*, the only seas known to him and his people were the Mediterranean, the Sea of Galilee, the Dead Sea and the Red Sea. These bodies of water did not have *"paths"* or significant observable currents.

⁶¹ *World Book Encyclopedia* 1986; Stars.

⁶² "On a clear dark night, a few thousand stars are visible to the naked eye. With binoculars and powerful telescopes, we can see so many stars that we could never hope to count them. Even though each individual star is unique, all stars share much in common." (Cornell University Astronomy website: http://curious.astro.cornell.edu/stars.php) The Bible also states that the number of stars cannot be counted. (Genesis 15:5; 22:17).

⁶³ Ramsay, Walter M. *The Bearing of Recent Discovery on the Trustworthiness of the New Testament.* Grand Rapids, MI: Baker Book House, 1953, p. 222.

⁶⁴ Josephus, Flavius. *Josephus: The Essential Works.* (Paul L. Maier, editor) Grand Rapids, MI: Kregel Publications, 1988. pp. 268,277. The book includes photos of the Pilate-inscription stone and Herod's theater.

⁶⁵ Bruce, F.F. *Archaeological Confirmation of the New Testament.* (*Revelation and the Bible.* Edited by Carol Henry) Grand Rapids, MI: Baker Book House, 1969.

⁶⁶ Josephus, Flavius. *Antiquities* 18: 2, 2; 4, 3

⁶⁷ Photo and details on Caiaphas' burial box: http://www.kchanson.com/ANCDOCS/westsem/caiaphas.html

⁶⁸ Glueck, Nelson. *Rivers in the Desert.* NY: Farrar, Strauss & Cudahy, 1959, p. 136. Glueck specialized in Middle East digs.

⁶⁹ Mormonism is a religion followed by millions of people worldwide. Unlike the Bible, the book Mormons call sacred is not confirmed by archaeology. The Smithsonian Institution in Washington, DC concluded: "Smithsonian archaeologists see no direct connection between the archaeology of the New World and the subject matter of [the Book of Mormon]." (Martin, Walter. *The Kingdom of the Cults.* Minneapolis, MN: Bethany House Publishers, 1997, pp. 200-202.) See also footnote 91 on the same subject in chapter 6. For a comparative view of archaeology as it relates to the Bible and Qur'an, see: http://debate.org.uk/topics/history/bib-qur/contents.htm

⁷⁰ Free, Joseph P. and Howard F. Vos. *Archaeology and Bible History.* Grand Rapids, MI: Zondervan, 1992, p. 294.

⁷¹ Both Muslims and Mormons claim that one of the greatest proofs that their holy books are from God can be seen in the literary style in which they are written. *A Muslim website* states: "The Great Challenge…of the Holy Quran: …Ever since the Quran was revealed, fourteen centuries ago, no one has been able to produce a single chapter like the chapters of the Quran in their beauty, eloquence, splendor..." (www.islam-guide.com/frm-chl-2.htm). *A Mormon website* makes a similar claim: "Book of Mormon Challenge: …You must write your record using a number of ancient Hebrew poetry and writing styles which will not be rediscovered and announced to the English speaking world until years after you publish your record..." (www.greatlakesrestorationbranches.org/newpage34.htm).

⁷² Psalm 119, the longest chapter in the Bible, provides an example of the amazing kinds of literary construction found in the Scriptures. Psalm 119 is an alphabet acrostic, composed of 22 sections with 8 verses each. All 8 verses of each section begin with the same letter of the Hebrew alphabet. In section 1, each verse begins with *Aleph* (first letter of the Hebrew alphabet). Section 2, all eight verses begin with *Beth* (second letter of alphabet), and so on it goes through the entire Hebrew alphabet. Try to duplicate that! No, don't. Instead, read Psalm 119 and immerse yourself in the power of its words.

CHAPTER 5: GOD'S SIGNATURE
73 Wallenfels, Ronald and Jack M. Sasson. *The Ancient Near East.*
Volume IV. NY: Charles Scribner's Sons, 2000; also see: Carl Roebuck.
The World of Ancient Times. NY: Charles Scribner's Sons, 1966, p. 355.
74 "Alexander the Great reduced the city after a siege of nine months
(332 BC), though he did not completely destroy it. From this blow Tyre
never fully recovered..." (Avery, Catherine B. and Jotham Johnson. *The
New Century Classical Handbook.* NY: Appleton-Century-Crofts, Inc.,
1962, p. 1130.)
75 Matthews, Samuel W. "The Phoenicians Sea Lords of Antiquity,"
Washington, DC: *National Geographic,* August 1974, p. 165. Also:
L.L. Orlin. Tyre. *Grolier Multimedia Encyclopedia.* Retrieved
September 7, 2006 from Grolier Online http://gme.grolier.com/cgi-bin/
article?assetid=0297240-0
76 Genesis 26:3; 28:15 **Note:** The land God promised to give to the nation
to come from Abraham, Isaac and Jacob was strategically placed *"in the
midst of the nations."* (Ezekiel 5:5) See also Acts 1:8; 2:5.
77 Josephus, Flavius, *The Complete Works of Josephus.* (William
Whiston) Grand Rapids, MI: Kregel Publications, 1967, pp. 566-568,
580-583, 588-589.
78 For example, at the outset of World War II, multitudes of Jews in
Hitler's Germany did not want to be recognized as Jews. They spoke
German, paid German taxes, and had fought for Germany in World
War I. Yet the Nazis insisted, "No, you are Jews!" Within a few years 6
million Jews were exterminated in the death camps.
79 Isaiah 44:18; Jeremiah 5:21; John 5:39-47; 2 Corinthians 3:12-16;
Romans 9-11. **Note:** About 2600 years ago, God revealed to Ezekiel that
Israel's rebirth would happen in three distinct stages. He compared Israel
to a valley littered with *dry bones,* which would *come together* as a body
and ultimately have *life breathed into them* (Ezekiel 37:1-14).
80 Compare Genesis 37-50 with the Gospels. Recommended reading:
Joseph Makes Me Think of Jesus, by William MacDonald. Grand Rapids,
MI: Gospel Folio Press.

CHAPTER 6: CONSISTENT WITNESS
81 *"What may be known about God is plain to them, because God has
made it plain to them. For since the creation of the world God's invisible
qualities—his eternal power and divine nature—have been clearly
seen, being understood from what has been made, so that men are
without excuse."* (Romans 1:18-20 NIV) Even people who do not have
the Scriptures, *"show the work of the law written in their hearts, their*

conscience also bearing witness, and between themselves their thoughts accusing or else excusing them... " (Romans 2:15). Yet, instead of seeking for more truth, most people pursue falsehood.

[82] By computing the ages recorded in the genealogies recorded in the Bible, we learn that Adam didn't die until Noah's father (9th generation after Adam) was more than 50 years old (Genesis 5).

[83] *"Then the magicians said to Pharaoh, 'This is the finger of God.'"* (Exodus 8:19) See also Exodus 12:30-33. For full story: Exodus 5-14.

[84] While Moses wrote the first section of Scripture, it is likely that the book of Job was written before the Torah (around the time of Abraham), making it one of the oldest pieces of finished literature in existence. If this date is correct, then the Bible was written over about 2,000 years.

[85] DeHaan, Dennis. *Our Daily Bread*, May 6, 2006. Grand Rapids, MI: RBC Ministries.

[86] Some ask, "Why would God allow false prophets to proclaim their deceptive messages?" Moses answered that question in the Torah, explaining, *"If there arises among you a prophet or a dreamer of dreams, and he gives you a sign or a wonder, and the sign or the wonder comes to pass, of which he spoke to you, saying, 'Let us go after other gods'—which you have not known—'and let us serve them,' you shall not listen to the words of that prophet or that dreamer of dreams, for LORD your God is testing you to know whether you love the LORD your God with all your heart and with all your soul."* (Deuteronomy 13:1-3)

[87] 1 Kings 18; 1 Kings 19:18; Romans 11:14

[88] Smith, James E. *What the Bible Teaches about the Promised Messiah.* Nashville, TN: Thomas Nelson Publishers, 1993, pp. 470-474; Also: Phillips, John. *Exploring the World of the Jew.* Neptune, NJ: Loizeaux Brothers, 1993, pp. 80-81.

[89] Taylor, John. "Jones Captivated San Francisco's Liberal Elite," *San Francisco Chronicle*, November 12, 1998.

[90] Smith, Joseph. *Pearl of Great Price.* Joseph Smith—History; 1:15-16.

[91] Unlike the Bible which is confirmed by history and archaeology, the book of Mormon is not. Thomas Stuart Ferguson is the professor who founded the Department of Archaeology at Mormonism's own Brigham Young University for the sole purpose of discovering confirming evidence for their "holy book." After 25 years of dedicated research, the department found nothing to confirm the flora, fauna, topography, geography, peoples, coins, or settlements described in the Book of Mormon. Ferguson concluded that the geography of the Book of Mormon is "fictional." (Martin, Walter. *The Kingdom of the Cults.* Minneapolis, MN: Bethany House Publishers, 1997, pp. 200-202)

CHAPTER 7: THE FOUNDATION
[92] The Bible contains 66 individual books—39 in the Old Testament and 27 in the New Testament. Later in history, the Roman Catholic Church (which, like many Protestant churches, elevates their church traditions above the Word of God) decided to include 11 additional books between the Old and New Testaments. These books, known as the *Apocrypha* (or *Deutercanonical* books), were written primarily in the era between the Old and New Testaments. While they contain interesting historical and legendary material, Hebrew believers never accepted them as inspired Scripture. Many of the Dead Sea Scrolls discovered in 1947 are commentaries. However, they comment only on the 39 Old Testament books and not on the Apocrypha. When the Messiah was on earth, He frequently quoted from the Old Testament, but never from the Apocryphal books. The Apocrypha is never quoted in the New Testament. The 39 books contained in the Old Testament were written by prophets to whom God spoke directly and to whom He confirmed His word, *"bearing witness both with signs and wonders, with various miracles, and gifts of the Holy Spirit."* (Hebrews 2:4) As for the New Testament, believers who lived in the time following Christ's visit to earth accepted the apostles' authority and New Testament Scriptures as equal to the Old Testament prophets and Scriptures. This could not be said of the Apocrypha.
[93] Read Luke 24:13-27-48; John 5:39-47. For a variety of resources that present God's message chronologically, visit www.goodseed.com.

CHAPTER 8: WHAT GOD IS LIKE
[94] Cosmologists' attempt to figure out the history of the universe is based on a "combined observational and theoretical effort." (Loeb, Abraham. "The Dark Ages of the Universe," *Scientific American*, November 2006) While their knowledge is based on *observation and theory*, the knowledge of those who believe the Bible is based on *observation and revelation*—revelation that bears the divine signature, as observed in chapters 5 and 6 of ONE GOD ONE MESSAGE. God has revealed His truth in such a way that we can *know* it is true.
[95] The book of Job 38:6-7 indicates that the angels were observing and rejoicing when God created the earth. Job is a poetic book, thus angels are described as *"morning stars"* and *"sons of God."* These two expressions do not indicate different beings. This double description is an example of parallelism, a characteristic of Hebrew poetry. See also Job 1:6; 2:1.
[96] More than half of the Bible's 66 books clearly refer to angels. Here are some samples: Genesis 3:25; 16:7-11; 18:1-19:1; 1 Kings 19:5-7; Psalm 103:20-21; 104:4; Daniel 6:22; Hebrews 1:4-7,14; 12:22; Matthew 1:20;

2:13,19-20; 22:30; 26:53; Luke 1 & 2; 2 Thessalonians 1:7, Revelation 5:11; 18:1; 22:6-16, etc. (Revelation uses the word "angel/s" 70+ times).
[97] Deuteronomy 10:14; 2 Corinthians 12:2,4; John 14:2; Psalm 33:13; 115:3; 1 Kings 8:39
[98] Vine, W.E., M.A. *An Expository Dictionary of New Testament Words.* Westwood, NJ: Fleming H. Revel Company; 1966, p. 229.
[99] God's six days of creation, and seventh day of rest, established for mankind a divinely appointed time cycle which is observed around the world to this day. Unlike days, months and years, *the week* is unrelated to astronomy. It is ordained by God.
[100] Proponents of the "big bang" hypothesis theorize that light preexisted the sun and earth by 9,000,000,000 years! (Loeb, Abraham. "The Dark Ages of the Universe," *Scientific American*; November 2006, p. 49.)
[101] Next time you take a drink of water, you might want to tell your Creator, "Thank You!" Besides the fact that H_2O (water) quenches our thirst and keeps us alive, it is truly amazing. Water is the only liquid that expands when frozen, thus becoming less dense and floating. If water behaved like other matter and condensed when frozen, it would sink to the bottom of the seas, lakes and rivers. Much of it would not melt and eventually our fresh water would be locked up, frozen at the bottom. Good thing our Creator thought of this!
[102] The moon's dark side was first seen by three humans on December 24, 1968 when the Apollo 8 spacecraft orbited the moon. Interestingly, on that same day, the astronauts read Genesis chapter 1, which was televised to earth from outer space. (Reynolds, David West. *Apollo: The Epic Journey to the Moon.* NY: Harcourt, Inc., 2002, pp. 110-111)

CHAPTER 9: NONE LIKE HIM
[103] Additional examples in the Bible where God refers to Himself as *"We"* and *"Us"*: Genesis 3:22; 11:7; Isaiah 6:8 (Note: In the Qur'an, "Allah" constantly speaks in the plural form. The Qur'anic verses quoted in chapter 3 of ONE GOD ONE MESSAGE demonstrate this.)
[104] Genesis 1:1-3 While the opening section of Genesis does not explain God's existence as a tri-unity, the way it is worded is in perfect harmony with explanations later revealed in the Bible. The Scriptures make it clear that all three Persons of the Godhead were involved in creation.
[105] When David became King over Israel, the Scripture narrates: *"The children of Benjamin gathered together behind Abner and became a unit [echad], and took their stand on top of a hill."* (2 Samuel 2:25) The same word used to declare: *"the LORD is one"* is used to describe a unity in which there is plurality.

[106] Other examples of Old Testament verses that affirm God's complex oneness: Genesis 17:1-3; 18:1-33 God appeared to Abraham in bodily form. These were face-to-face encounters and not a dream or vision. Genesis 35:9-15; Exodus 3:1-6; 6:2-3; 24:9-11; 33:10-11. Compare Exodus 33:11 with 33:20. Moses spoke face-to-face with One of the Persons in the Godhead (the Son), but he was not allowed to see the face of the other Person in the Godhead (the Father). Complex? Yes. God is God. See John 1:1-18. Here are more Old Testament verses that cannot be rightly understood apart from the concept of God's plural oneness. Psalm 2; Psalm 110:1 (compare Matthew 22:41-46); Proverbs 30:4; Isaiah 6:1-3 (compare John 12:41); Isaiah 26:3-4; Isaiah 40:3-11; Isaiah 43:10-11 (Isaiah 7:14; 9:6-7); Isaiah 48:16; Isaiah 63:1-14; Isaiah 49:1-7; Jeremiah 23:5-6; Daniel 7:13-14; Hosea 12:3-5; Micah 5:2; Malachi 3:1-2, etc.

[107] Luke 15:11-32; Read also the First Epistle of John.

[108] Read Psalm 2 in which the prophet David refers to the Messiah as *God's Son.* Consider too some of the Son's other names and titles. He is called: *"the door,"* (John 10) but that does not mean He is a door of wood or metal. He is also called: *"the Bread of Life,"* (John 6) but that does not mean He is a loaf of bread. Nor does *"Son of God"* imply that God took a wife and had a son. Read John chapters 1, 3 and 5.

[109] Senegal's national newspaper, *Le Soleil*, mercredi 14 mars 1984: "Bienfaiteur sincère, il considérait ses 2.000 employés **comme ses enfants** et partageait leur problèmes, leur soucis et leur joie. Le 'Vieux' comme l'appelaient familièrement et tendrement son personnel, était **un grand fils du Sénégal.**"

[110] Like God Himself, the Holy Spirit will not be forced into our preconceived mold. One of God's prophets, who was given a glimpse of Heaven, beheld the Holy Spirit as *"seven lamps of fire...burning before the throne, which are the seven Spirits of God."* (Revelation 4:5) Another prophet described Him as the One who imparts seven qualities that come from God alone: *"The Spirit of the LORD...the Spirit of wisdom and understanding, the Spirit of counsel and might, the Spirit of knowledge and of the fear of the LORD."* (Isaiah 11:2)

[111] When on earth, the Son of God promised His disciples, *"The Holy Spirit, whom the Father will send in My name, He will teach you all things, and bring to your remembrance all things that I said to you."* (John 14:26) These words display the absolute unity that has always existed between the Father, Son, and Holy Spirit. Like the Father and the Son, the Holy Spirit is a Personal Being (*"He..."*). For more about the Holy Spirit, see chapters 16, 22, and 28. Also read *the Epistles* and *the Acts* in the Bible, paying close attention to the role of the Holy Spirit.

[112] The Gospel records the Son speaking to the Father of *"the glory which I had with You before the world was."* We also hear the Son saying: *"Father...You loved Me before the foundation of the world."* (John 17:5,24) See also Micah 5:2; Isaiah 9:6. As for the Holy Spirit, one of His titles is *"the eternal Spirit."* (Hebrews 9:14)

[113] Exodus 20:22; Hebrews 12:25; Luke 3:22; 5:24; John 1:1-18; 3:16-19; 17:22; Acts 5:3; 7:51: Galatians 4:6; etc.

[114] In the Arabic language, the term *Allah*, in its original meaning, is the Arabic equivalent of the English term *God*. Whether in an Old Testament verse like Genesis 1:1: *"In the beginning God created..."*, or a New Testament verse like John 1:1: *"In the beginning was the Word, and the Word was with God, and the Word was God."*, the generic word for *God* in Arabic is *Allah*, meaning *the Supreme Being*. It is important to understand that the Supreme Being has personal names by which He wants to be known. "Allah" is not God's proper, personal name, although many believe it to be so. Neither is "God" His proper, personal name, though some may think it so.

CHAPTER 10: A SPECIAL CREATION

[115] Guinness, Alma E. *ABC's of The Human Body*. Corporate Author: The Reader's Digest Association, 1987, p. 22.

[116] Gates, Bill. *The Road Ahead*. NY: Penguin Group, 1995, p. 188.

[117] In illustrating a greater spiritual truth, the Bible describes the harmonious system of the human body in these terms: *"the whole body, joined and knit together by what every joint supplies, according to the effective working by which every part does its share, causes growth of the body...."* (Ephesians 4:16)

[118] These thoughts are adapted from John Phillips' outstanding commentary on Genesis (Phillips, John. *Exploring Genesis*. Chicago: Moody Press, 1980). **Note**: The Scripture distinguishes between spirit, soul, and body. See 1 Thessalonians 5:23; Hebrews 4:12-13; John 4:24.

[119] The notion that Eden was located in the region of Iraq is based on the geographical information of Genesis 2:13-14. **Note**: Some refer to the Garden of Eden as *the garden of paradise*, though the Scripture does not. The earthly Eden must not be confused with the heavenly Paradise.

[120] Henry, Matthew. *Matthew Henry's Commentary*. Grand Rapids, MI: Zondervan, 1960, p. 7.

[121] Adam (*Adamah*) is the Hebrew word for *man*, literally meaning "red earth" because he was taken from the ground. Eve (*chavvah*) means "life"— *"because she was the mother of all living."* (Genesis 3:19-20)

CHAPTER 11: EVIL'S ENTRANCE

[122] *"How you are fallen from heaven, O **Lucifer**, son of the morning! How you are cut down to the ground, You who weakened the nations!"* (Isaiah 14:12) In this verse, the name "Lucifer," meaning "light bearer," does not appear in the Hebrew text. It is a Latin translation of the Hebrew word *helel*, meaning "shining one." Isaiah 14 and Ezekiel 28 provide us with an example of the law of double interpretation. On the surface, these passages refer to earthly kings. Isaiah refers to the *"king of Babylon,"* and Ezekiel writes of the *"prince of Tyre."* Yet both passages make statements that cannot apply to mere men. When studied in light of other Scriptures (Luke 10:18; Job 1:6-12; Revelation 12:10; 1 Peter 5:8; etc.), it becomes clear that these passages are commentaries on the fall of Satan—the influence and instigator behind these wicked kings.

[123] Revelation 12:4

[124] Matthew 10:28; 23:33; Mark 10:43-45

[125] Revelation 20:10-15

CHAPTER 12: THE LAW OF SIN AND DEATH

[126] A common question: What happens to babies and little children that die? Will they be judged for their inbred sin nature (Psalm 51:5; 58:3)? The Righteous Judge will do right (Genesis 18:25). He does not condemn a person for that which he or she is incapable of understanding. He holds people accountable for what they know and *could have known* had they made an effort to seek God's truth (Romans 2:11-15; Psalm 34:10; Isaiah 55:6). A human becomes accountable before God once he or she is mature enough to make moral choices (Deuteronomy 1:39; Isaiah 7:16; 2 Samuel 12:23; Matthew 18:10; 2 Timothy 3:14-17). Only God knows at what age an individual becomes accountable for his or her sins and choices. Whatever the case, God's message to each of us is: *"Behold, **now** is the accepted time; behold, **now** is the day of salvation."* (2 Corinthians 6:2)

[127] Revelation 20:14-15; 2:11; 21:8; Matthew 25:46

CHAPTER 13: MERCY AND JUSTICE

This chapter has no endnotes.

CHAPTER 14: THE CURSE

[128] "Pythons and boa constrictors…have nub-like legs beneath their skins and tiny, half-inch claws that protrude out above the nubs but nestle close to their bellies near the anus. Actually, even the nubs are not legs but rather a remnant of upper-leg (thigh or femur) bones. The males still use the spurs—but only during courtship and fighting—not to walk.

No other snakes have legs." www.wonderquest.com/snake-legs.htm (includes photos). Some interpret this biological fact as support for their evolutionary hypothesis. The point is: the anatomy of these snakes is in harmony with what the Scripture recorded thousands of years ago.

[129] Also: Revelation 20:2; Luke 10:18 and 2 Corinthians 11:3,14: *"As the serpent deceived Eve by his craftiness,"* so *"Satan himself transforms himself into an angel of light."*

[130] Exodus 29:7; 1 Samuel 10:1; 2 Kings 9:6; Psalm 45:7

[131] Chapter 18 presents three reasons why God encoded His rescue plan. One of the delights of studying the Scriptures chronologically is to discover the unfolding drama of God's plan to deliver sinners from Satan, sin and death. God, in His wisdom, revealed His plan progressively, *"line upon line, here a little, there a little."* (Isaiah 28:10)

[132] In a comic strip entitled, "You Call That Intelligent?" *Time Magazine* belittles the concept of an Intelligent Designer (God): "Couldn't aging have been handled with more flair and dignity? For instance: What if old people instead of getting wrinkly and decrepit, just sort of poetically faded away?" (Handy, Bruce and Glynis Sweeny. *Time*, July 4, 2005, p. 90) Also, the book *The Improbability of God*, in a chapter entitled *Neither Intelligent nor Designed*, states: "Is it any more than an overweening human ego that proposes Intelligent Design for such a poorly designed creature?" (Bruce and Frances Martin in *The Improbability of God* by Michael Martin and Ricki Monnier. Amherst, NY: Prometheus Books, 2006, p. 220)

CHAPTER 15: DOUBLE TROUBLE

[133] ABC News, May 20, 2006;
http://abclocal.go.com/ktrk/story?section=nation_world&id=4189656

[134] Ceremonial washings were a part of Old Testament law (see Leviticus). They were intended to teach sinners their spiritual uncleanness before God. Since He has provided full cleansing and righteousness through the Messiah, such rituals are no longer required by God. Read Acts 10 and Colossians 2. To this day, many religions emphasize outward rituals of cleansing. This e-mail came to me from a Muslim in London: "All non-Muslims including Christians are dirty…Muslims are so clean and near to Allah because they wash…."

[135] After God announced the commandments orally (Exodus 20), He called Moses up into the mountain and gave him two stone tablets on which the commandments were etched (Exodus 24:12; 31:18). *"The tablets were the work of God, and the writing was the writing of God engraved on the tablets."* (Exodus 32:16)

[136] See Luke 18:9-14; Ephesians 2:8-9.

[137] The Messiah is the only One who kept all of God's laws and could say, *"I delight to do Your will, O My God, Your law is within my heart."* (Psalm 40:8) The Law points us to Him. *"The Law was our tutor to bring us to Christ, that we might be justified by faith."* (Galatians 3:24) God's solution for man's sin is powerfully outlined in Romans 3:20-27.

CHAPTER 16: THE SEED OF A WOMAN

[138] *"For as in Adam all die, even so in Christ all shall be made alive."* (1 Corinthians 15:22); read also Romans chapter 5; Galatians 4:4-5.

[139] Neo-birth Pregnancy Care Center   www.neobirth.org.za/development. html

[140] *"Bethlehem Ephrathah"* was an older name for Bethlehem, the town south of Jerusalem (Genesis 35:16-19; 48:7). King David was born in Bethlehem (1 Samuel 16:1,18-19; 17:12), as was his Greater Descendant (Matthew 2:1-6; Luke 2:1-12). Jews who lived in Jesus' day were confused since He grew up in Nazareth, Galilee (John 7:42).

[141] For Biblical references, see the list of prophecies in chapter 5.

[142] For more on the meaning of "Messiah" see chapter 14, under subheading: THE TWO "SEEDS."

[143] Genesis 1:2; The Holy Spirit of God is not to be confused with Gabriel. The angel Gabriel was a created being. The Holy Spirit is the uncreated, ever-active Spirit of God Himself. See chapters 9 and 28.

[144] After Jesus was born, Mary lived with her husband Joseph as any normal couple would, and together they had sons and daughters (Matthew 13:55-56; Luke 8:19; John 7:3-10).

[145] The prophets foretold that the Messiah would be conceived of a virgin: Isaiah 7:14; He would be a descendent of the family line of Abraham, Isaac, Jacob and Judah: Genesis 17:18-21; 26:3-4; 28:13-14; 49:8-10; He would be of the royal line of King David: 2 Samuel 7:16; He would be born in Bethlehem: Micah. 5:2.

[146] Matthew 2. King Herod was jealous at the thought of another "king" being born and attempted to destroy Jesus by ordering the execution of all male children in and around Bethlehem, from two years old and under. Satan was behind it all. His goal was to destroy *the Seed of the woman* who had invaded "his territory!" However, God preempted Satan's attempts to kill Jesus by warning Joseph and directing him to take Mary and the young child to Egypt for refuge. These events had also been foretold by the prophets (Matthew chapter 2; Micah 5:2; Hosea 11:1; Jeremiah 31:15). After King Herod died, Joseph, Mary, and Jesus returned to Nazareth where the boy Jesus grew into manhood.

CHAPTER 17: WHO CAN THIS BE?

[147] Adapted from Jayyusi, Salma Khadra. *Tales of Juha*. Interlink Books. Northampton, MA, 2007, p. 19.

[148] Here are some of the ancient, non-Biblical historical writers who made reference to Jesus of Nazareth: Tacitus, Roman historian (AD 55-120) [*Tacitus* 15:44]; Josephus, Jewish historian (AD 37-101) [*Antiquities* 18:3]; the Talmud, rabbinical commentary on the Torah [*The Babylonian Talmud*. Sanhedrin, 43a]; a Greek named Lucian [*The Death of Pereguire*, p. 11-13 in *The Works of Samasota*, translated by H.W. Fowler and F.G. Fowler, 4 volumes. Oxford: Claredon Press, 1949; Suetonius (AD 117-138), the chief secretary to Emperor Hadrian [*Claudias*, 25]. **Note**: J. Oswald Sanders wrote: "To contend that the Christ of the Bible is the offspring of mere human imagination and had no historical reality, would make the gospels as great a miracle in the realm of literature as the living Christ in the realm of history. Ernest Renan remarked that it would take a Jesus to invent a Jesus. J.J. Rousseau contended that it is more inconceivable that a number of persons should agree to write such a history, than that one should form the subject of it." (Sanders, J. Oswald. *The Incomparable Christ*. Moody Press. Chicago, 1971, p. 57.)

[149] Matthew 13:55-56. Jesus grew up in Nazareth (Matthew 2:22-23; Luke 2:51-52), working as a carpenter alongside His legal father, Joseph. Mark 6:3. Jesus' lowliness offended those who wanted a conquering hero, not a humble Servant.

[150] *"Now Jesus Himself began His ministry at about thirty years of age, being (as was supposed) the son of Joseph...."* (Luke 3:23)

[151] Jesus frequently referred to Himself as *"the Son of Man,"* a Messianic title meaning, "Son of Mankind/Humanity" (Greek: *Anthropos*). What a title! Whether we like it or not, we are all "sons (kin) of mankind." But in the case of the exalted Son of God, He **chose** to be become *the Son of Man* and identify Himself with the human race! Thus, this title emphasizes Jesus' divinity as much as it does His humanity, since it points to God's personal intervention in humanity. Read Daniel 7:13-14; Matthew 8:20; Luke 5:24; 22:69-70; John 5:27; 13:31; Revelation 1:13-18; 14:14.

[152] For example, this Old Testament verse Jesus quoted (in Luke 4:4) is from the Torah of Moses: Deuteronomy 8:3.

[153] Because of man's sin, Satan had indeed become *"the ruler of this world"* and *"the prince of the power of the air, the spirit who now works in the sons of disobedience."* (John 12:31; Ephesians 2:2) The Son of God had come to restore man's lost dominion because of sin, but He did not do it Satan's way. He did it God's way.

[154] Psalm 110 and Psalm 2; Matthew 21:41-46

[155] Qur'an 19:19; Contrast: 48:2; 47:19
[156] Qur'an: 19:19; 3:45-51; 5:110-112; 19:19
[157] Qur'an: 4:171
[158] The ultimate sin in Islam is *"shirk"* (Arabic for *association*). *Shirk* is the sin of regarding anything or anyone as equal to God.
[159] Notice the titles ascribed to the promised Messiah:
Wonderful = A title used for God alone. It means *"Out of the ordinary."*
Counselor = The Messiah would be the *Personification of Wisdom.*
Mighty God = *God Himself* would take on a human body.
Everlasting Father = He would be the *Possessor of Eternity.*
Prince of Peace = He would provide for sinners *peace with God, inner peace,* and ultimately, *universal peace.*
[160] The prophet David foretold that the LORD would come to earth in Person: *"Behold, I come; in the scroll of the book it is written of Me."* (Psalm 40:7) Malachi prophesied that God would send a forerunner to prepare people for the arrival of *"the LORD."* (Malachi 3:1)
[161] Is it below God's majesty to come down to our level? Imagine that you and your friend talking about two highly respected spiritual leaders—we'll call one Omar and the other Aaron. Your friend says, "Aaron plays with toy cars, but Omar does not." As one who has great respect for Aaron, you respond, "Never! Far be it from Aaron that he should play with toy cars!" Initially such a reaction sounds reasonable and right. Then the story unfolds that both Omar and Aaron have young sons who love for their fathers to get down on the floor and join them in playing with their toys. Now what if we learned that Aaron was happy to spend time with his sons in this way, while Omar refused to do so because he thought it below his dignity to do so? Who would be the better father, man and leader: Omar or Aaron? Similarly, when people say, "It is below the majesty of the Almighty that He should appear on earth as a man," their intentions may be good, but instead of magnifying God's majesty, they are marring it.
[162] John 13 tells of Jesus washing His disciples' feet—the job of a servant! To read the Gospels is to meet the ultimate Servant: the Lord Himself!
[163] Matthew 14; Mark 6; John 6
[164] If Jesus had wanted only to say that He existed before Abraham, He would have said, "Before Abraham was, I was," instead of *"Before Abraham was, I am."* See chapter 9 about YHWH (Exodus 3:14).
[165] The word used for "worship" regarding those who worshiped Jesus is the same word for those who worship God. (Compare Matthew 8:2 with Revelation 7:11. In both cases, "worshiped" is the Greek word *proskneo* meaning "to prostrate oneself in adoration, worship.")

[166] If you still cling to the unsubstantiated notion that the Scriptures of the Bible have been tampered with, reread chapter 3 entitled: "Corrupted or Preserved?"

[167] Lewis. C.S. *Mere Christianity*. NY: Macmillan-Collier, 1960, pp. 55-56.

[168] For a review on God's complex oneness, reread chapter 9.

[169] Many stumble over another aspect of this story of Jesus and the rich young ruler. The man came running to Jesus and asked, *"Good Teacher, what **good thing** shall I do that I may inherit **eternal life?**"* (Matthew 19:16; Mark 10:17; Luke 10:25) To the crowd, the young man's question seemed good, but not to the Lord. Jesus knew that this religious man had not yet grasped the foundational truths about God's infinite holiness and man's utter sinfulness. This self-righteous man imagined that he could earn his way into paradise; that he could somehow be good enough. He was like a child holding out a grimy fistful of copper coins to the world's wealthiest man and asking him, "How many shall I give you that I may inherit your estate?" How did Jesus answer the man? He directed him back to the Torah and the Ten Commandments to show him that he could never, in his own strength, satisfy God's standard of perfect righteousness. There is *no "eternal life"* for those who think they can merit it by doing some *"good thing."*

[170] Jesus also said: *"Let not your heart be troubled; you believe in **God**, believe also in **Me**. ... I am the way, the truth, and the life. No one comes to the Father except through Me. ... He who has seen Me has seen the Father; so how can you say, 'Show us the Father'? Do you not believe that I am in the Father, and the Father in Me? ...Believe Me that I am in the Father and the Father in Me, or else believe Me for the sake of the works themselves."* (John 14:1,6,9,11)

[171] Isaiah 53:1; John 12:28; Luke 1:51; See also: Isaiah 40:10-11; 51:5; 52:10; 59:16; 63:5; Jeremiah 32:17.

[172] While God empowered two prophets (Elijah and Elisha) to raise a dead person back to life, no prophet ever claimed to be *the Source* of Life. Jesus alone could say, *"I am the resurrection and the life."*

[173] Before the Messiah came to earth, He was in heaven. He was there when Lucifer was cast out. Thus, Jesus said to His disciples: *"I saw Satan fall like lightning from heaven."* (Luke 10:18)

CHAPTER 18: GOD'S ETERNAL PLAN

[174] Hebrews 11:6; Jeremiah 29:13; Isaiah 29:11; Matthew 11:25; 13:13-14; Luke 8:4-15; John 6. Many of God's truths are revealed with a certain intentional indefiniteness—so that only those who search for His truth will find it. God will not force people to listen, understand and believe.

Those who are *willing* will discover His truth. Those who are *willfully blind* will not.

[175] Did you notice how many prophecies were written in the past tense even though they were written hundreds of years before the event? God's plans cannot be thwarted. When the Creator says something will happen, it is as good as done. That is why the Messiah is also called *"the Lamb slain from the foundation of the world."* (Revelation 13:8)

[176] Psalm 2. Elsewhere in Scripture, the Messiah (at His second coming) is likened to a massive Rock from heaven that will crush all who refuse to submit to God's plan of redemption (Daniel 2:34-35 and Matthew 21:42-44).

[177] For more words of Peter, read Acts chapters 2 to 5; Acts 10; 1 Peter 1:10-12; 2:21-25; 3:18; etc. Also consider these words written by the apostle Paul: *"The message of the cross is foolishness to those who are perishing, but to us who are being saved it is the power of God. ... the weakness of God is stronger than men ...God has chosen the weak things of the world to put to shame the things which are mighty."* (1 Corinthians 1:18,25,27)

CHAPTER 19: THE LAW OF THE SACRIFICE

[178] How did Abel know to do all this? God had told him. Hebrews 11:4 tells us that he brought the sacrifice *"by faith"*—faith in what God had commanded and promised. Later, the Scriptures would set forth God's detailed laws concerning the substitutionary sacrifice, just as Abel had obediently presented long beforehand. For example, Genesis 4 tells us that Abel brought *"the firstborn"* (compare Exodus 13:12-13). Abel brought a lamb *"of his flock"* (see Leviticus 5:6). Abel offered *"of their fat"* (see Leviticus 3:16). It is not stated that Abel offered his lamb on an altar, but it is likely he did so—as the believers who came after him would do. Genesis 8:20; 12:7; 13:4,18; 22:8-9; Exodus 20:24-26; etc.

[179] Daniel 6; Esther 3:8-15; 8:7-17

[180] Strong, James. *The Exhaustive Concordance of the Bible.* NY: Abingdon-Cokesbury Press, 1948, p. 57. Compare Genesis 6:14 (*"cover"*) with Leviticus 5:18 (*"atonement"*). The same Hebrew word *Kâphar* (atonement) is used in these verses.

[181] Leviticus 5:7

[182] More than 50 times the Scriptures declare that the sacrifice had to be *"without blemish."* For example, *"If his offering is of the flocks—of the sheep or of the goats—as a burnt sacrifice, he shall bring a male without blemish."* (Leviticus 1:10)

CHAPTER 20: A MOMENTOUS SACRIFICE

[183] *Eid al-Adha* is the most significant Islamic holiday of the year. It points back to the event when God provided a ram for Abraham to sacrifice in place of his son. According to widespread Muslim belief it was Ishmael, not Isaac—though the Qur'an itself never states that it was Ishmael, and the Bible makes it clear that it was Isaac. The sacrifice of Eid is carried out by Muslims worldwide. It is also performed as a final ritual in the pilgrimage (*Hajj*) to Mecca. Pilgrims complete the Hajj by shedding the blood of an animal (usually a sheep or a cow) after the morning Eid prayer. Most Muslims believe these rituals provide them with a kind of "new birth" and that if they perform it correctly their sins are washed away. However, Muslims also acknowledge that these rituals cannot provide assurance of salvation since they immediately begin to accumulate more sins after the Hajj and sacrifice of Eid. (For the Biblical perspective, read Hebrews chapter 10 and John chapter 3.)

[184] At first, Abraham's name was Abram, though due to space constraints, I have not explained that part of the story in One God One Message. See Genesis 17. For Abraham's full story, read Genesis 11 to 25; also read Romans 4, Galatians 4, and Hebrews 11.

[185] Deuteronomy 7:6-7; 14:12

[186] Here are a few examples in which God used the nation of Israel to bless non-Jewish people: Joseph saved the lives of millions of Egyptians (Genesis 37–50). Naomi, a daughter of Abraham, was a blessing to two Moabite women, Orpah and Ruth (Ruth). The prophet Elijah was a blessing to a Sidonian widow (1 Kings 17; Luke 4:26). Jonah, though reluctantly, delivered a message of salvation to the Ninivites (Jonah). King Solomon was a blessing to Queen Sheba of Arabia (1 Kings 10; Luke 11:31). Daniel blessed the Babylonians (Daniel 1–6). Esther and Mordecai brought blessing to the Persian Empire (Esther)...

[187] Genesis 12:2-3; 22:16-18; Hebrews 6:13-18; John 4:22; Acts 1–10, etc.

[188] *"By faith Abraham, when he was tested, offered up Isaac, and he who had received the promises offered up his only begotten son, of whom it was said, 'In Isaac your seed shall be called, concluding that God was able to raise him up, even from the dead, from which he also received him in a figurative sense."* (Hebrews 11:17-19)

CHAPTER 21: MORE SHED BLOOD

[189] I started counting the "sacrifice stories" in the Old Testament, but stopped counting after reaching the 200th story! The four words: *"blood," "sacrifice," "offering"* and *"altar"* are found more than 1400 times in the Bible (NKJV).

[190] Genesis 15:13-14 *"Then He said to Abram: 'Know certainly that your descendants will be strangers in a land that is not theirs, and will serve them, and they will afflict them* **four hundred years.** *And also the nation whom they serve I will judge;* **afterward they shall come out with great possessions.'"* The fulfillment of God's promise is recorded in Exodus 1:1-12; 12:35-41. Our Sovereign God's plans always happen.

[191] Exodus 5-11

[192] Some time earlier, from within the burning bush on Mount Sinai, God had promised Moses: *"I will certainly be with you. And this shall be a sign to you that I have sent you: when you have brought the people out of Egypt, you shall serve God on this mountain."* (Exodus 3:12)

[193] Exodus 13-17; *"He opened the rock, and water gushed out; it ran in the dry places like a river."* (Psalm 105:41)

[194] Exodus 28:9-19; Later, when the Messiah was on earth, He said, *"I am* **the door.** *If anyone enters by Me, he will be* **saved.***"* (John 10:9) Every element in the tabernacle pointed to His Person and work.

[195] *"And he shall* **lay his hand** *on the head of his offering, and* **kill it** *at the door of the tabernacle of meeting; and Aaron's sons, the priests, shall* **sprinkle the blood all around on the altar**... *and Aaron's sons shall* **burn it** *on the altar."* (Leviticus 3:2,5)

[196] The Tabernacle presented a kind of picture of the Savior who would come from heaven to earth. To those who really know that Savior, *"He is altogether lovely"* (Song of Solomon 5:16)—like the inside of the tabernacle. To those who don't know Him, *"there is no beauty that we should desire Him."* (Isaiah 53:2-3)—like the outside of the tabernacle.

[197] *Adam* (*Adamah*) is the Hebrew word for "man" and literally means "red earth," because God formed Adam's body from the earth's soil.

[198] Numbers 3:23-39

[199] Leviticus 16; Today Jews call the Day of Atonement *Yom Kippur*, but the Day is devoid of its original meaning since they have no temple, no priesthood, and no sacrificial lamb. Ironically, the symbol of Judaism today is a wall (the Western Wall—a retaining wall built by Herod the Great to enlarge the Temple Mount area). Jews stand before it daily and pray for the Messiah—who has already come—to come! As foretold by the prophets, the Jewish nation is spiritually blind (Isaiah 6:10; 53:1; Jeremiah 5:21; Ezekiel 12:2; 2 Corinthians 3:12-4:6). One day their eyes will be opened to know that Jesus (*Yeshua*) is the One who fulfilled the symbolisms of the temple, priesthood, and sacrifices (Hebrews 8–10; Ephesians 2). The wall of spiritual blindness will come down (Ephesians 2:14; Romans 9-11). See chapter 5 in this book, under subtitle: PROPHECIES ABOUT A PEOPLE and footnotes.

[200] 2 Chronicles 3:1 compare with Genesis 22:2. This is also the location where Muslims built the Dome of the Rock mosque in the 7th century.
[201] 2 Chronicles 7:5

CHAPTER 22: THE LAMB
[202] One of the LORD's titles in Scripture is *Immanuel,* meaning literally, *"With us (is) God."* (Isaiah 7:14; Matthew 1:23)
[203] 2 Corinthians 5:1-4; 1 Corin. 6:19; 2 Peter 1:13-14; Ephesians 2:21
[204] Isaiah 40:3-9; Malachi 3:1; Luke 1; John 1
[205] Throughout the Bible, whenever a man was chosen by God to be a priest or king, an authorized person such as a prophet would anoint him with oil to show that he was selected by God for a specific task. God anointed His Son with the Holy Spirit Himself. In Scripture oil is often used to symbolize the Holy Spirit. **Note:** Just as all three Persons of the Godhead were involved in the work of *creation*, so the Father, the Son, and the Holy Spirit were also involved in the work of *redemption.*
[206] *"The righteous will live **by his faith.**"* (Habakkuk 2:4) While the sacrifice Jesus came to offer would be sufficient to *"take away the sin of the world,"* it would only benefit those who believed that Jesus' sacrifice was for them. This truth can be illustrated by our "Way of Righteousness" radio programs in Senegal (www.twor.com; www.lesprophetes.com). On many broadcasts, listeners are offered a free copy of the Scriptures. All who write and ask for it receive it free of charge. Is this offer valid for *all* the millions of people who tune in? *Yes.* Do *all* listeners write to us to request their free copy of the Scriptures? *No.* Most do not take advantage of the offer. Similarly, through the all-sufficient sacrifice of His Son, God has provided forgiveness and eternal life for all. However, only a small percentage of Adam's offspring accept God's offer. See Luke 14:15-24.

CHAPTER 23: FULFILLING SCRIPTURE
[207] Isaiah 53; Psalm 22. See also Daniel 9:24-27, which outlines God's plan of the ages. Part of this total plan was: *"Messiah shall be cut off, but not for Himself."* (Daniel 9:26)
[208] Matthew, chapters 21 to 25
[209] Betrayed: See Psalm 41:9; Zechariah 11:12-13 and Matthew 26:14-16; 27:3-10.
[210] As the Jews were celebrating their yearly Passover feast, Jesus would become the final and perfect Passover Lamb, delivering believers from God's wrath against sin. *"For indeed **Christ, our Passover,** was sacrificed for us."* (1 Corinthians 5:7)
[211] The Gospel of John, chapters 13 to 17.

²¹² What Jesus said to those who came to arrest Him was simply, *"I AM."* The phrase *"I am He"* is the way the English translators have rendered it, but the word *"He"* is not found in the Greek text. Jesus was declaring who He is: the Eternal Self-Existent *"I AM"* who came down from heaven. That is why when Jesus said, *"I AM,"* the religious leaders and soldiers were thrown backwards.

²¹³ *"I was watching in the night visions, and behold, **One like the Son of Man, coming with the clouds of heaven!**"* (Daniel 7:13) **Note:** The tearing of one's clothes was a customary way of showing extreme grief or anger. Interestingly, the law God gave to Moses stated, *"He who is the high priest among his brethren... shall not...tear his clothes."* (Leviticus 21:10) By this act (Matthew 27:65; Mark 14:63), Caiaphas disqualified himself as high priest. The new eternal High Priest was Jesus Himself who had come to earth to offer up His own body as the sacrifice. He is the Only One who can truly reconcile sinful man to a holy God (Hebrews 2:17; 3:1; 4:14-16; 7:26; 8:1; 9:11,25; 10:21-23).

²¹⁴ John 18:38; 19:4,6; John 19:15; Luke 23:21

CHAPTER 24: PAID IN FULL

²¹⁵ If you have not yet grasped chapters 8–9 and 16–17 of ONE GOD ONE MESSAGE, you may find this statement blasphemous. I have heard some sarcastically say, "So while 'God' was in the virgin's womb and on the cross, who was taking care of the universe?" This question reveals a defective view of the Scriptures and of the God who gave them. *"Jesus answered and said to them, 'You are mistaken, not knowing the Scriptures nor the power of God.'"* (Matthew 22:29) Since God has always existed as a complex tri-unity, being on earth and in heaven at the same time poses no problem. If the sun can be in outer space at the same time its sunlight and heat are with us on earth, why cannot the Creator of that sun be in heaven and on earth at the same time?

²¹⁶ *Calvary* (*kranion*) is the Greek name for the Hebrew *Golgotha*, meaning *the place of a skull* (Matthew 27:33; Mark 15:22; John 19:17). This hill where Jesus was crucified, located outside old Jerusalem and rounded like a bare skull, is a part of the same mountain ridge where Abraham offered up the ram in place of His son.

²¹⁷ The historian Josephus reported that before the fall of Jerusalem in AD 70, the Roman soldiers "caught every day five hundred Jews; nay, some days they caught more...the soldiers, out of the wrath and hatred they bore the Jews, nailed those they caught, one after one way, and another after another, to the crosses, by way of jest; when their multitude was so great, that room was wanting for the crosses, and crosses wanting for the bodies."

Josephus also wrote the victims "were first whipped, and then tormented with all sorts of tortures...." (Josephus, *Antiquities* 11:1, p. 563)
[218] The Jews calculated time beginning at 6:00 in the morning. *"Now it was the third hour* (6:00 + 3 hours = 9:00), *and they crucified Him... Now when the sixth hour* (12:00) *had come, there was darkness over the whole land until the ninth hour* (15:00)." (Mark 15:25,33)
[219] Genesis 8:20; 22:2-8; Exodus 29:18. The phrase *"burnt offering"* is found 169 times in the Old Testament. Jesus became the final burnt offering for sin. Mark 12:33; Hebrews 10:6-14. **Note**: To further understand why God turned away from the Lord Jesus as He hung on the cross, read Isaiah 53 and Psalm 22. In the same Psalm where David predicted that the Messiah would say: *"My God, My God, why have You forsaken Me?"* (Psalm 22:1), David tells us why God turned away from His Son. *"You are holy!"* (Psalms 22:4) God turned away from Jesus because He is perfectly holy and *"cannot look on wickedness."* (Habakkuk 1:13). During those hours of darkness, the sinless Son of Man was suffering in the place of the wicked as God lashed out against Him as though He were the sinner. Jesus, the holy Lamb of God, became the Sin-Bearer (without becoming a sinner). The song-writer expressed it well: "'Tis mystery all! The Immortal dies! Who can explore His strange design?" ("Amazing Love", Charles Wesley, 1707–1788)
[220] Edersheim, Alfred. *The Life and Times of Jesus the Messiah.* 1883, p. 614.
[221] Read Hebrews 9–10. **Note**: As stated in chapter 22 of ONE GOD ONE MESSAGE, the glory of God which once dwelt in the Holiest Place of the tabernacle and temple was no longer behind the veil. It was now *in Jesus.*
[222] John 19:31-37

CHAPTER 25: DEATH DEFEATED
[223] Matthew 28; Mark 16; Luke 24; John 20-21; 1 Corinthians 15. **Note**: Many who set out to disprove Jesus' resurrection have ended up writing books proclaiming the overwhelming evidence that Jesus did indeed rise from the dead. For example: Morrison, Frank. *Who moved the Stone?* Grand Rapids, MI: Zondervan, 1987; McDowell, Josh. *Evidence that Demands a Verdict.* Nashville, TN: Thomas Nelson, Inc., 1993; Strobel, Lee. *The Case for Christ.* Grand Rapids, MI: Zondervan, 1998.
[224] Not only had Jesus said that He would *"be raised **the third day**,"* (Matthew 16:21) but He also said, *"As Jonah was three days and three nights in the belly of the great fish, so will the Son of Man be **three days and three nights** in the heart of the earth."* (Matthew 12:40). Many understandably argue that if Jesus was put in the tomb on Friday night

and was in the tomb only until Sunday morning, that is not three full days. However, the period during which Jesus was to lie in the grave is expressed in round numbers, according to the Jewish way of speaking, which was to regard any part of a day, however small, as a full day (e.g., Matthew 27:63-64; Genesis 42:17-18; 1 Samuel 30:12-13; Esther 4:16-5:1). Here is another point: The Scripture does not state that Jesus was crucified on Friday. While many are quick to shout, "Contradiction!" there are good explanations to resolve all such apparent contradictions in the Bible.

[225] Acts 11:26; 26:22-28; 1 Peter 4:16

[226] Acts 5:41 *"...rejoicing that they were counted worthy to suffer shame for His name."* Peter imprisoned and beaten: Acts 5; see also Acts 12. Jesus predicted Peter's death as a martyr (John 21:18-19).

[227] Some quote what Jesus told a Gentile woman, *"I was not sent except to the lost sheep of the house of Israel,"* (Matthew 15:24), but they don't tell you that Jesus proceeded to heal her daughter! (For more examples of Jesus' ministry and compassion to non-Jews, see Matthew 12:41-42; 21:33-43; Luke 9:51-55; 10:30-34; 17:11-19; John 4; 1 John 2:1-2; Luke 24:45-48.)

[228] Psalm 68:18; 110:1; Psalm 24

[229] Jesus *"sat down at the right hand of the Majesty on high"* because *"He had by Himself purged our sins."* (Hebrews 1:3) *"Every priest stands ministering daily and offering repeatedly the same sacrifices, which can never take away sins. But this Man, after He had offered one sacrifice for sins forever, sat down at the right hand of God...."* (Hebrews 10:11-12) See also Hebrews 8:1; 12:2; Revelation 3:21.

CHAPTER 26: RELIGIOUS AND FAR FROM GOD

[230] James 2:18; Matthew 5:13-16; Hebrews 11

[231] While God grants governments the right to defend their people, and assigns them the responsibility to use the *"sword"* as *"God's minister, an avenger to execute wrath on him who practices evil"* (See Romans 13:1-4; Genesis 9:6), the use of violence to spread God's truth is in absolute opposition to the example and teaching of Jesus, who said, *"You have heard that it was said, 'You shall love your neighbor and hate your enemy.' But I say to you, love your enemies, bless those who curse you, do good to those who hate you, and pray for those who spitefully use you and persecute you, that you may be sons of your Father in heaven; for He makes His sun rise on the evil and on the good, and sends rain on the just and on the unjust. For if you love those who love you, what reward have you? Do not even the tax collectors do the same? And if you greet your brethren only, what do you do more than others?"* (Matthew 5:43-47)

Contrastively, the Qur'an says: *"Fight those who believe not in Allah nor the Last Day, nor hold that forbidden which hath been forbidden by Allah and His Apostle, nor acknowledge the Religion of Truth, even if they are of the People of the Book, until they pay the Jizya* [a special tax for non-Muslims] *with willing submission, and feel themselves subdued."* (Qur'an, sura 9:29)

[232] *"This is the message you heard from the beginning: We should love one another. Do not be like Cain, who belonged to the evil one and murdered his brother. And why did he murder him? Because his own actions were evil and his brother's were righteous."* (1 John 3:11-12 NIV) Two driving forces that inspired Cain to kill Abel were the devil and envy (Compare Matthew 27:18).

[233] How to meet the skeptic's classic challenge: "Where did Cain get his wife?" Genesis 5 provides the answer. Adam and Eve had other *"sons and daughters."* (Genesis 5:4) Evidently, Cain married one of his sisters— which would not yet have produced any harmful effects genetically. Later, God would forbid such intermarriage. And what happened to Abel after he was killed? Abel's body returned to dust, but his soul and spirit went to Paradise, since God had forgiven him of his sins and declared him righteous on the basis of his faith. Hebrews 11:4

[234] Moses and other prophets describe the universal flood and geological upheavals of Noah's day: Genesis 7 & 8; Psalm 104:6-8; Job 22:16; Matthew 24:37-39; 2 Peter 2:5-6.

CHAPTER 27: STAGE 1: GOD'S PAST PROGRAM

[235] In one way or another, every section of the Bible relates to one of three themes:

I. What God has done

II. What God is doing

III. What God will yet do

In theological terms, these three themes of Scripture are classified as:

1) *Justification* = When you believe the Gospel, God declares you perfectly righteous in your **position**. (Romans 3 to 5)

2) *Sanctification* = As a believer, God is at work in your life to help you to live righteously in your **practice**. (Romans 6–8 and 12–15)

3) *Glorification* = In heaven, you will be **perfectly righteous** in both your position and practice. (Revelation 21 & 22)

[236] Richardson, Don. *Lords of the Earth.* Oxnard, CA: Regal Books; 1977, pp. 354. (For another classic cannibal-conversion story by Don Richardson read: *Peace Child.* Oxnard, CA: Regal Books, 1975.)

[237] Acts 26:9-11; 7:58-60; 8:1-3; 9:1-2

238 Acts 9:1-31; see also Acts, chapters 11; 13-14; 16-28 (In Acts, chapters 22 and 26, Paul tells his conversion story). Also: Galatians 1:13,23; Philippians 3:6; Corinthians 15:9; etc.

239 A "saint" in Biblical terms is one who is *set apart* for God; one who has been *declared holy* by God through faith in His way of forgiveness and righteousness. The man-made tradition of "canonizing" certain deceased people and thereby making them "saints" is completely contrary to what the Bible teaches (see Deuteronomy 33:2-3; Psalm 30:4; Proverbs 2:8; Daniel 7:21-27; Matthew 27:52; Acts 26:10; Ephesians 1:1, 2:19, etc.).

CHAPTER 28: STAGE 2: GOD'S PRESENT PROGRAM

240 What most do not realize is that they are siding with the enemy when they use such methods for protection. Deuteronomy 18:10-14; Isaiah 47:13; Acts 19:19; Galatians 5:20

241 1 John 2:1; John 14–16

242 In chapter 1, we quoted an e-mail from Ahmed in which he wrote: "...there are predictions in your Bible, the original one, and in the Old Testament as well to the coming of Muhammad (pbuh), even now... not to mention the stuff that was corrupted...."

243 Pentecost means *fiftieth*. It was an Old Testament celebration in which the Israelites thanked God for His blessings (Leviticus 23:16). From the beginning, God planned to send down the ultimate blessing on this day: His Holy Spirit.

244 1 Corinthians 12:27; Ephesians 4:21; 5:25-32; Revelation 19:7-9; 22:17; John 5:29

245 1 John 1:8-10; 2:1-2; Romans 6-8

246 The moment you repent of your wrong thinking and believe in the Lord Jesus Christ who died for your sins and rose again, you are *"baptized into Christ"* (Romans 6:3), not with water (that comes later), but by the Holy Spirit (Romans 6:1-5; Acts 1:5; 1 Corinthians 12:13). *"Baptized into"* means "united with, identified with." When you believe, you become a part of God's own family made up of all who *"have been united together"* with His sinless Son (Romans 6:5). Your new, eternal position is *"in Christ."*

247 Acts 24:15; Luke 14:14; John 5:28-29; Daniel 12:2; Revelation 20:6, 11-15; Revelation 22:12

248 2 Corinthians 5:10. The Scripture speaks of no less than five different crowns (trophies/awards) believers will receive: 1 Corinthians 9:25-27; 1 Peter 5:4; James 1:12; 1 Thessalonians 2:19-20; 2 Timothy 4:8. These crowns will not be for our own glory, but for His. Revelation 4:10. The Lord will not forget any good work that His redeemed people have done in His name and for His glory (Matthew 10:41-42; Hebrews 6:10).

²⁴⁹ Sheikh, Bilquis. *I Dared to Call Him Father.* New York: Fleming H. Revell Company, 1978; p. 53.

²⁵⁰ 1 John 2:27; John 4:14; 14:26; 16:13; Jeremiah 31:33-34; Ephesians 4:21

²⁵¹ There is a critical difference between mechanically reciting a prayer and truly connecting with God and receiving God's answers to our prayers. Romans 8:26-27; Ephesians 8:18; 1 John 5:14-15; John 14:13-14; 15:7; Philippians 4:6-9

²⁵² Romans 12; 1 Corinthians 12; Ephesians 4

²⁵³ 2 Corinthians 3:18; Philippians 1:6; 3:20-21

CHAPTER 29: STAGE 3: GOD'S FUTURE PROGRAM

²⁵⁴ A few pages from now we will read several verses from the Old Testament in which the prophets foretell the Messiah's second coming to earth and describe the events that will accompany His return. Some of the passages we will consider are Zechariah, chapter 14; Daniel 7:13-14; Psalm 72, and Isaiah 9:6-7.

²⁵⁵ 1 Thessalonians 4:13-18; 1 Corinthians 15:51-58

²⁵⁶ See chapter 28, subtitle: TWO JUDGMENT DAYS.

²⁵⁷ Read Ephesians 5:27 and surrounding verses. This great theme is touched on in chapter 10 of ONE GOD ONE MESSAGE. The Scriptures consistently picture the Lord as the *"Bridegroom"* and His people as His *"Bride."* Marriage—in its ideal form—was designed to give us a faint idea of the close, spiritual relationship that the Lord God plans to enjoy with His people throughout eternity (Isaiah 54:5; 62:5; Psalm 45; Song of Solomon; Hosea 2:16,19,20; Matthew 9:15; 25:1-13; John 3:29; 2 Corinthians 11:2-3; Ephesians 5:22-33; Revelation 21:2,9; 22:17).

²⁵⁸ Matthew 24:21; Revelation 7:14; The most complete description of the Tribulation is found in Revelation, chapters 6 to 19.

²⁵⁹ Romans 11:26-27. **Note**: This event is prefigured in the story of Joseph in Genesis 37-45. Amazing parallels!

²⁶⁰ 1 Corinthians 15:45-47; Romans 5:12-21. Terms such as *"First Adam"* and *"Last Adam"* are also mentioned in chapter 16 of ONE GOD ONE MESSAGE. Just as Adam's sin caused all men to die, so Jesus' righteousness and shed blood restores eternal life for all who believe.

²⁶¹ 2 Thessalonians 1:7-10; Revelation 19:6-14; Jude 14; Zechariah 14:5

²⁶² Isaiah 53:7; John 1:29; Revelation 5:5; 2 Thessalonians 1:5-10; John 3:17-18; 12:47; Daniel 9:24-27; Compare Isaiah 53 with Zechariah 14. Also consider the contrasts between *"suffering"* and *"glory"* in these passages: Luke 24:25-26; 1 Peter 1:10-12; Hebrews 2:9; Philippians 2:5-11; Psalm 22; etc.

[263] Psalm 72 is titled: *"A Psalm of Solomon."* It seems that Solomon wrote this Psalm, although it concludes with this statement: *"The prayers of David the son of Jesse are ended."* (Psalms 72:20) This verse signals the end of the second of the five-book division found in the Psalms. David was the primary writer of the second section of the Psalms.

[264] Who will be forever condemned? *"The **cowardly** [and the] **unbelieving**,"* that is, those who never believed God's message because they were afraid of what their family and friends might say or do. When Jesus was on earth, He warned His listeners plainly, *"Do not fear those who kill the body but cannot kill the soul. But rather fear Him who is able to destroy both soul and body in hell. ... Do not think that I came to bring peace on earth. I did not come to bring peace but a sword. For I have come to 'set a man against his father, a daughter against her mother, and a daughter-in-law against her mother-in-law'; and 'a man's enemies will be those of his own household.' He who loves father or mother more than Me is not worthy of Me. And he who loves son or daughter more than Me is not worthy of Me."* (Matthew 10:28,34-37)

CHAPTER 30: A PREVIEW OF PARADISE

[265] Matthew 13:24-30. This parable of Jesus declares that the mix of good and evil will only be around for a limited time.

[266] The remainder of the first chapter of Revelation provides an awe-inspiring description of the Lord Jesus—a stunningly different portrayal of Him than seen in most books, movies, and religions.

[267] Mark 3:14-19; John 19:26-27; John penned the following books of the Bible: *the Gospel of John; 1 John; 2 John; 3 John* and *The Revelation.*

[268] The Jasper stone comes in many colors. The Carnelian stone is generally of a clear red translucent color. Its color is deepened and enhanced when exposed to light.

[269] Look who is on the throne. Compare Isaiah 6 (the vision presented in chapter 15 of ONE GOD ONE MESSAGE) with John 12:36-41.

[270] Genesis 12:2-3; Matthew 1. (For more on God's promises to Abraham, review chapter 20 in ONE GOD ONE MESSAGE.)

[271] For example, the classic fairy tale of Cinderella, first told in China, also comes in versions for Europe, America, Persia, Iraq, Egypt, Korea, India, etc. Each country has its version, but the themes are similar. A longing for redemption and eternal life is embedded in the hearts of people worldwide. Solomon wrote: *"[God] has made everything beautiful in its time. He has also set eternity in the hearts of men; yet they cannot fathom what God has done **from beginning to end**."* (Ecclesiastes 3:11 NIV)

ADDITIONAL RESOURCES

Each of the following books have their own unique style. Like ONE GOD ONE MESSAGE, each provides a clear and chronological presentation of the story and message of the one true God.

BY THIS NAME by John R. Cross
www.goodseed.com

This captivating, well-illustrated arrangement of God's story and message clearly shows how all that the prophets wrote fits together like pieces to a puzzle. Although especially designed to lead polytheists from confusion to clarity, BY THIS NAME is for anyone who knows little or nothing about the Bible.

FIRM FOUNDATIONS by Trevor McIlwain
www.ntm.com

Designed for those who want to teach the Scriptures to others, FIRM FOUNDATIONS' fifty chronological studies, first taught to tribal people in the Philippines, have been used with great success in making God's message clear to people of vastly different educational and cultural backgrounds.

THE WAY OF RIGHTEOUSNESS by P.D. Bramsen
www.twor.com

This through-the-Bible series consists of one hundred 15-minute radio programs first written in the Wolof language for the Muslims of Senegal, West Africa. THE WAY OF RIGHTEOUSNESS has been or is being translated into more than 70 languages for radio broadcast around the world.